The Economics of Resource Allocation in Health Care

The question of how to allocate scarce medical resources has become an important public policy issue in recent decades. Cost-utility analysis is the most commonly used method for determining the allocation of these resources, but this book counters the argument that overcoming its inherent imbalances is simply a question of implementing methodological changes.

The Economics of Resource Allocation in Health Care represents the first comprehensive analysis of equity weighting in health care resource allocation that offers a fundamental critique of its basic framework. It offers a critique of health economics, putting the discourse on economic evaluation into its broader socio-political context. Such an approach broadens the debate on fairness in health economics and ties it in with deeper-rooted problems in moral philosophy. Ultimately, this interdisciplinary study calls for the adoption of a fundamentally different paradigm to address the distribution of scarce medical resources.

This book will be of interest to policy makers, health care professionals, and post-graduate students looking to broaden their understanding of the economics of the health care system.

Andrea Klonschinski is a lecturer at the Department of Philosophy at the University of Regensburg, Germany.

Routledge advances in social economics

Edited by John B. Davis,
Marquette University

This series presents new advances and developments in social economics thinking on a variety of subjects that concern the link between social values and economics. Need, justice and equity, gender, cooperation, work poverty, the environment, class, institutions, public policy and methodology are some of the most important themes. Among the orientations of the authors are social economist, institutionalist, humanist, solidarist, cooperatist, radical and Marxist, feminist, post-Keynesian, behaviouralist, and environmentalist. The series offers new contributions from today's most foremost thinkers on the social character of the economy.

Publishes in conjunction with the Association of Social Economics.

For a complete list of titles in this series, please visit www.routledge.com.

Previous books published in the series include:

1 **Social Economics**
Premises, findings and policies
Edited by Edward J. O'Boyle

2 **The Environmental Consequences of Growth**
Steady-state economics as an alternative to ecological decline
Douglas Booth

3 **The Human Firm**
A socio-economic analysis of its behaviour and potential in a new economic age
John Tomer

4 **Economics for the Common Good**
Two centuries of economic thought in the humanist tradition
Mark A. Lutz

5 **Working Time**
International Trends, Theory and Policy Perspectives
Edited by Lonnie Golden and Deborah M. Figart

6 **The Social Economics of Health Care**
Edited by John Davis

7 **Reclaiming Evolution**
A Marxist institutionalist dialogue on social change
William M. Dugger and Howard J. Sherman

8 **The Theory of the Individual in Economics**
Identity and value
John Davis

9 Boundaries of Clan and Color
Transnational comparisons of inter-group disparity
Edited by William Darity Jnr. and Ashwini Deshpande

10 Living Wage Movements
Global perspectives
Edited by Deborah M. Figart

11 Ethics and the Market
Insights from social economics
Edited by Betsy Jane Clary, Wilfred Dolfsma and Deborah M. Figart

12 Political Economy of Consumer Behaviour
Contesting Consumption
Bruce Pietrykowski

13 Socio-Economic Mobility and Low-Status Minorities
Slow roads to progress
Jacob Meerman

14 Global Social Economy
Development, work and policy
Edited by John B. Davis

15 The Economics of Social Responsibility
The world of social enterprises
Edited by Carlo Borzaga and Leonardo Becchetti

16 Elements of an Evolutionary Theory of Welfare
Assessing welfare when preferences change
Martin Binder

17 Poverty in the Inner City
Overcoming financial exclusion
Paul Mosley and Pamela Lenton

18 The Capability Approach
Development practice and public policy in the Asia-Pacific region
Edited by Francesca Panzironi and Katharine Gelber

19 Poverty and Social Exclusion
New methods of analysis
Edited by Gianni Betti and Achille Lemmi

20 Social Capital and Economics
Social values, power and social identity
Edited by Asimina Christoforou and John B. Davis

21 The Economics of Values-Based Organizations
An introduction
Luigino Bruni and Alessandra Smerilli

22 The Economics of Resource Allocation in Health Care
Cost-utility, social value, and fairness
Andrea Klonschinski

The Economics of Resource Allocation in Health Care

Cost-utility, social value, and fairness

Andrea Klonschinski

Routledge
Taylor & Francis Group
LONDON AND NEW YORK

First published 2016
by Routledge
2 Park Square, Milton Park, Abingdon, Oxon OX14 4RN

and by Routledge
711 Third Avenue, New York, NY 10017

Routledge is an imprint of the Taylor & Francis Group, an informa business

British Library Cataloguing in Publication Data
A catalogue record for this book is available from the British Library

Library of Congress Cataloging in Publication Data

Names: Klonschinski, Andrea.
Title: The economics of resource allocation in health care: cost-utility, social value, and fairness / Andrea Klonschinski.
Description: Abingdon, Oxon; New York, NY: Routledge, 2016. | Includes bibliographical references and index.
Subjects: LCSH: Medical care—Cost effectiveness. | Resource allocation. | Social medicine.
Classification: LCC RA410.5 .K565 2016 | DDC 362.1068/1—dc23LC record available at http://lccn.loc.gov/2015040533

ISBN: 978-1-138-18416-9 (hbk)
ISBN: 978-1-315-64537-7 (ebk)

Typeset in Times New Roman
by Book Now Ltd, London

Contents

List of illustrations ix
Acknowledgments xi
List of abbreviations xiii

1 Introduction **1**

2 The utility concept in economics: from pleasure maximization to rational choice **7**

2.1 Introduction: the merits of a historical account 7
2.2 The Jevonian revolution: the mechanics of utility and self-interest 9
2.3 The ordinal revolution 23
2.4 The formalist revolution and rational choice theory 39
2.5 Preference and utility in modern economics 46

3 On the rise, rationale, and authority of economic evaluation **60**

3.1 Introduction 60
3.2 The market ideal and the evolution of health economics 61
3.3 The raison d'être of economic evaluations: mimicking markets 70

4 The empirical failure of CUA and the approach of equity weighting **88**

4.1 Introduction 88
4.2 Cost-utility analysis and its fairness issue 88
4.3 Equity weighting: basic idea, normative claim, and state of the art 99
4.4 Economic evaluation as applied consequentialism 105

5 Values, weights, and trade-offs: the conception of choice in economics **117**

5.1 Introduction 117
5.2 Choices in economics and the role of metaphors 117
5.3 Social preferences and social value maximization 121
5.4 Equity weights and representational consequentialism 131
5.5 On the equity-efficiency trade-off, or whose benefit is it anyway? 141

6 Inconsistencies in the determination and measurement of social values **151**

6.1 Introduction 151
6.2 Preference anomalies in empirical studies 152
6.3 Disability discrimination and the equal value of life approach 173

7 On the normative status of empirically elicited prioritization preferences **186**

7.1 Introduction 186
7.2 Two alleged dead-ends of the normative-theoretical discourse 187
7.3 The role of empirical data within applied ethics 191
7.4 On ethical expertise 194
7.5 Respecting individual autonomy 197

8 Conclusion **203**

Bibliography 204
Index 230

Illustrations

Figures

2.1 Indifference curves 30
4.1 Standard gamble 90
4.2 Scale of probabilities 90
5.1 HrSWF and health possibility frontier 128
6.1 Multiplicative transitivity in person trade-offs 153

Tables

4.1 Upper-end compression of the QALY scale 100
6.1 Embedding effect in the valuation of consumption goods 156
6.2 Questionnaires on colon cancer screening test 162
6.3 Johannesson's equity weights 176
6.4 Williams' equity weights 176

Acknowledgments

This study is a revised version of my dissertation at the Department of Philosophy at the University of Regensburg (Germany). I was referred to the issue of equity weighting by my advisor Weyma Lübbe, who gave me the opportunity to work in cooperation with her on the subject in the realm of the interdisciplinary research group "Setting Priorities in Medicine: a theoretical and empirical analysis within the context of the German statutory health insurance," funded by the German Research Foundation (DFG). The study very much profited from discussions within this group. I also want to thank all the colleagues and friends who supported me in the course of writing the thesis, either academically, in terms of helpful advice on the manuscript and stimulating discussions, or personally.

Abbreviations

ADA	Americans with Disabilities Act
AS	Analog scale
CBA	Cost-benefit analysis
CEA	Cost-effectiveness analysis
CUA	Cost-utility analysis
CV	Contingent valuation
CVA	Cost-value analysis
CVM	Contingent valuation method
DALY	Disability-adjusted life year
DCE	Discrete choice experiment
DMA	Decision-maker approach
EQALY	Equity-weighted quality-adjusted life year
EVL	Equal value of life approach
GDP	Gross domestic product
HrQOL	Health-related quality of life
HrSWF	Health-related social welfare function
KH criterion	Kaldor–Hicks criterion
MRS	Marginal rate of substitution
NHS	National Health Service
NICE	National Institute for Health and Clinical Excellence
OHSC	Oregon Health Service Commission
PPBS	Planning–programming–budgeting system
PTO	Person trade-off
QALE	Quality-adjusted life expectancy
QALY	Quality-adjusted life year
QWB	Quality of well-being scale
RAND	Research and Development (a US military think tank)
RPT	Revealed preference theory
RS	Rating scale
SB	Senate Bill
SG	Standard gamble
SWF	Social welfare function
TPE	Jevons (1911/2006) *The Theory of Political Economy*

TTO	Time trade-off
VNM	John von Neumann and Oscar Morgenstern
VNM (1953)	von Neumann/Morgenstern (1953) *Theory of Games and Economic Behavior*
WHO	World Health Organization
WTA	Willingness to accept
WTP	Willingness to pay

1 Introduction

The impression that economic thinking constitutes *the* paradigm of the modern world is widely shared – "We live in the age of the economist" (Harpham/Scotch 1988: 216). Considering any kind of choices in terms of costs and benefits not only characterizes theories in the social sciences, but also permeates the vernacular and shapes our quotidian perception of social reality. The economization of all spheres of life continues to expand and the discourse on public policy already is to a large extent dominated by concerns for efficiency. Thereby, the ubiquitous application of economic evaluation and cost-benefit analysis as its prime manifestation can be regarded as both a symptom and a result of this "economic worldview." Although this development is sometimes reckoned with some unease, it is by no means obvious what exactly should be wrong about applying economic techniques to issues of public policy. After all, if economics is regarded as the discipline studying the "rational," "efficient" use of scarce resources, economists are certainly the experts to turn to when it comes to allocating resources under conditions of scarcity in the public realm, an example *par excellence* being the resource allocation in health care.

Given the scarcity of medical resources, postulating that every monetary unit should be spent so as to maximize the induced benefit appears reasonable. Initially, health economists sought to accomplish this goal by means of cost-utility analysis (CUA), a form of health economic evaluation which defines the benefit at stake in terms of health-related quality of life (HrQOL), measured by the quality-adjusted life year (QALY).[1] An attempt to allocate medical resources strictly on the basis of CUA and subsequent socio-empirical studies in the 1990s revealed, however, that maximizing QALYs leads to resource allocations that are seriously at odds with people's fairness intuitions.[2] For anyone familiar with utilitarianism and its critics, this did not come as a surprise. Just like utilitarianism, CUA only focuses on the *sum* of QALYs generated over and above all persons concerned and disregards their distribution. Interestingly, within health economics, the rejection of QALY maximization was not interpreted as a rejection of CUA as such.[3] Instead, it was argued that the problem was entirely methodological in character, and so was its solution. By focusing on individual health as the unit of benefit, CUA had simply maximized the wrong measure. Since people apparently care about the distribution of QALYs on different persons as well, the correct maximand needs to incorporate their respective *social preferences*.[4] Henceforth, researchers have empirically investigated the public's social preferences as to how they want health care to be distributed in order to discover the different factors influencing the perceived fairness of a distribution – for instance, the patient's age or the severity of illness. By quantifying the relative importance of these factors and incorporating them into CUA via attaching *equity weights* to QALYs, the correct *social value* of a resource allocation could be tackled. This social value, thus the idea, combines concerns for efficiency in terms of the sum of QALYs and equity in terms of their distribution at once,[5] so that its maximization mirrors the socially desired equity-efficiency trade-off in medical resource allocation.[6]

The weighting approach basically presents an attempt to solve CUA's fairness issue by modifying its maximand within the value-maximizing framework of CUA. Although the extent to which such a corporation is feasible is discussed in the literature,[7] the underlying interpretation of CUA's fairness issue is broadly shared, even among fierce critics of mainstream health economics and ethicists.[8] It is generally assumed that efficiency is not the only aim of health care resource allocation, but needs to be supplemented by concerns for fairness, and the task of allocating scarce resources is regarded as pursuing the socially desired equity-efficiency trade-off – indeed, "equity-efficiency trade-offs prevail in virtually all areas of social policy," the philosopher Schmidt (1994: 45) states. This study challenges this interpretation. The basic thread of the criticism it provides goes back to Lübbe (2005, 2009b, 2009c, 2009d, 2010a, 2010b, 2010c, 2011, 2013, 2015), who has pointed out that this value-oriented framework is by no means normatively innocuous – in fact, it is inappropriate to consider health care resource allocation in a satisfying manner. Lübbe argues that CUA's fairness issue actually does not stem from a mistaken conception of the maximand, but results from the value-maximizing framework of CUA as such. Insofar as both the weighting approaches and the trade-off notion stick to this paradigm, they rely on strong and ultimately unjustified premises as to the choice behavior of the respondents in empirical studies, the nature of equity judgments, and the accurate relationship between equity and efficiency. CUA's equity problem thus does not call for piecemeal corrections but rather for a fundamentally different paradigm.

Building on and elaborating Lübbe's claims,[9] the present study offers a comprehensive critical examination of the weighting approaches' normative-ethical framework. Providing a thorough conceptual analysis of the health economic debate and connecting this applied field with fundamental issues in moral philosophy and economics, it explicates the normative assumptions underlying the weighting approaches. In doing so, it demonstrates that the problems these accounts are facing are by no means methodological in nature but rather point toward intricate and still unresolved problems in both disciplines. For one thing, the debate on CUA's potential to incorporate concerns for fairness resembles the debate on the scope and limits of consequentialism in moral philosophy. This is important for health economists to be aware of because, as mentioned above and as will become clearer in the following, the value-maximizing paradigm and its implications are not sufficiently reflected in the literature. The considerations are also of interest for philosophers as they illustrate the practical relevance of current fundamental debates. For another, the study reveals that the concepts and methods used and implicit assumptions made in the realm of economic evaluation ultimately stem from its consumer choice framework, which is inextricably connected with the utility concept and the very idea of value maximization. This connection is elaborated by embedding the tools and concepts of health economic evaluations into the history of the utility concept in economics. Thereby, the historical consciousness of health economics is fostered, the lack of which has been explicitly criticized in the literature. Finally, this study seeks to serve a mediating function as it makes the health economic discourse approachable to a broader audience, thereby enabling policy makers to grasp (health) economic reasoning and its pitfalls.

The study proceeds as follows. Examining the literature on equity weights and social value shows that it is replete with implicit assumptions on people's equity judgments and with conceptual ambiguities, especially regarding the concepts of value and utility. As both phenomena are deeply rooted in economics, Chapter 2 offers an analysis of the historical development of the utility concept from its first introduction to economics at the end of the nineteenth century to its formalization in the middle of the twentieth century. Yet, while the concepts became more and more formal, the terminology from early consumer choice theory and the associated connotations remained the same; economists still speak of utility as something substantial that can actually be maximized. This leads to serious conceptual vagueness in modern economics in general and in health economics in particular.

Chapter 3 pigeonholes health economic evaluations into another development of recent decades: the rise of the market ideal and cost-benefit analysis (CBA) as its epitome in both public policy and economic theory. It is against this background that the establishment of health economics as a subdiscipline of economics and the current authority and influence of (health) economic evaluations needs to be considered. The chapter also provides for the welfare economic basis of economic evaluation. It illustrates that within economics, the market advanced to the ideal allocation mechanism with the statement of the two fundamental theorems. Henceforth, interventions in the market have been regarded as legitimate only when the market fails, and this is where economic evaluations enter the scene, their rationale being to mimic the market, i.e., to guarantee an efficient resource allocation. However, when it comes to health care, this aim seems beside the point: as it turns out, some costs and benefits are habitually excluded from actual CBAs in health care, an observation indicating a fundamental problem of seeking efficiency in the realm of health care.

Chapter 4 introduces CUA, outlines the happenings in Oregon around 1990 that put the issue of distributive justice irrevocably on the agenda, and elaborates the basic idea, the normative claim, and the current implementations of equity weighting. Characterizing economic evaluation as a form of applied consequentialism, the chapter offers the conceptual prerequisites for the subsequent considerations. In addition, it illustrates that the development from CUA to equity weighting resembles the development from classic utilitarianism to modern consequentialism. In the latter case, it was also argued that the problems of utilitarianism could be ameliorated by changing its axiology while sticking to the maximizing formula. Implicitly, however, both modern consequentialist theories and the weighting approach still rely on certain assumptions of classical utilitarianism.

This claim is elaborated in Chapters 5 and 6, which present the central analysis and critique of the weighting approach. Chapter 5 carves out that the interpretation of CUA's failure and the weighting approach are based on the economic conception of choices as trade-offs, revealing the relative value of the alternatives at stake. Thereby, the consumer choice framework is implicitly and illegitimately transferred to the interpretation of prioritization judgments. To buttress this claim, the pivotal concepts of health economic fairness discourse are characterized as metaphors, which highlight certain aspects of their subject and suppress others. As it turns out, the metaphors used are inappropriate insofar as they restrict the perspective on the subject far too much (not all choices are value maximizing choices), lead to the usage of meaningless concepts (social value, good for society, etc.), imply high demands on the individuals' distributive judgments and the functioning of equity considerations (stable equity weights, atomism of reasons and values), and suggest a mistaken relationship between equity and efficiency (trade-off).

Chapter 6 reinforces the claim that the weighting approaches make unjustified assumptions on people's equity judgments by considering preference anomalies arising in empirical studies. It is argued that the apparent inconsistencies – such as scope insensitivity of the stated willingness to pay – indicate the inappropriateness of the value-oriented framework presumed by the surveys, according to which the respondents' task in a stated preference study is to indicate how much a particular item or alternative is worth to them. The hypothesis that the respondents do not share the value-maximizing framework is buttressed by analyzing so-called protest responses, data on the respondents' actual reasons behind their choices stemming from qualitative studies, and CUA's problem of disability discrimination. Up to now, attempts to solve the latter by axiological modifications have not been successful, but ran into theoretical inconsistencies. The chapter argues that this failure stems from the fundamental opposition of economic evaluation's value orientation on the one hand, and the attempt to take non-consequentialist concerns for equal treatment and non-discrimination into account on the other hand. All in all, there is much evidence that the respondents' answers do not meet the requirements outlined in Chapter 5 so that equity weights are probably only artefacts of the value-maximizing paradigm presumed by the surveys.

Chapter 7 challenges the weighting approaches from another angle and examines the normative-ethical relevance of empirically elicited prioritization preferences. For this purpose, the different rationales in favor of public participation on the level of the theoretical-normative prioritization discourse put forward in the literature are considered and rejected. They can be divided into two categories: one thread maintains that the elicitation of public preferences somehow improves prioritization decisions, while the other rests on the claim that individual autonomy in a democratic system requires public participation. In a nutshell, however, the first group of arguments does not sufficiently differentiate between empirical ethics and empirically informed ethics and neglects the expertise of professional ethicists, while the latter is based on a category error. Hence, even if the attempt to solve CUA's fairness issue by attaching equity weights to QALYs was theoretically sound, it would have to be rejected for other normative reasons anyway.

To sum it up, the study shows that the weighting approaches rely on more controversial assumptions than the literature generally acknowledges. These premises remain largely unreflected since they are deeply embedded in the consumer choice framework of economic analysis and are carried by metaphors. Yet, if the respondents' choice behavior does not align with the basically consequentialist assumptions presumed by the theoretical weighting approach and the empirical surveys, the derived weights lack any informative value beyond the concrete study. The attempt to solve CUA's fairness issue by modifying its maximand is thus not promising. In fact, the problem is rooted in the value-maximizing framework of economic evaluation as such.

Before concluding this introduction, it is important to emphasize what is and what is not within the scope of this study. To make it clear right from the start, the critical analysis of the weighting approaches provided here is neither accompanied by a positive suggestion of an alternative algorithm for resource allocation, nor is it supplemented with an elaborate account of the demands of justice in health care. As to the first aspect, critics might argue that "destroying" a method without simultaneously coming up with a better one is worthless. However, as Chapter 7 elaborates, I take it that the tasks of philosophers working in applied fields primarily consist in critically monitoring the discourse, carefully analyzing the proposed arguments, investigating their consistency, disclosing implicit premises, and questioning fundamental premises and arguments the researchers themselves take for granted. When it comes to health care, a supervision of the economic discourse is even more important because health economics has been gaining more and more influence on public policy and thus exerts an existentially important impact on people's lives. Therefore, carving out CUA's ethically unacceptable implications and the impossibility of removing them by means of equity weights is of immediate pragmatic relevance. Using an inherently unjust measure is by no means better than having no quantitative measure at all, so that defending CUA as "the best method we currently have" is unwarranted and the critical stance of this study is perfectly legitimate and worthwhile.

A similar argument can be made regarding the second point, the lack of a well-articulated theory of fairness at the base of this study. As should have become clear already, the study's general stance is decidedly non-consequentialist and the importance of treating everyone as an equal and to avoid unfair discrimination in health care resource allocation is stressed. Still, elaborating what exactly "equal treatment" or "unfair discrimination" requires in concrete allocation scenarios is clearly beyond the scope of this study. To this extent, the study has programmatic value since it offers the conceptual basis for further research on a comprehensive theory of fairness in health care and – concomitantly, because these endeavors cannot be separated – on alternatives to orthodox health economics.

Notes

1 Note that what is called CUA in this study is sometimes dubbed cost-effectiveness analysis (CEA) in the literature.
2 The terms equity and fairness are commonly used synonymously in the health economic literature. See Williams/Cookson (2000: 1865, 2006: 2).
3 The generalizing references to "health economics" and "*the* health economists" are certainly not meant to suggest that all health economists form a homogeneous group and can be assigned one theoretical stance. For the sake of readability, however, the phrase *the* health economists is used in the following to denote the considerable group of health economists who in fact do interpret CUA's fairness issue in the described manner and try to solve it accordingly. The term is also supposed to embrace researchers from other disciplines, such as psychology, sociology, and medicine, who engage in the project of social value measurement. This seems warranted for, although they are not economists by profession, the quoted scholars are applying economic concepts and methods nonetheless.
4 These preferences go under different headings in the literature and are also labelled "societal preferences" (Menzel *et al.* 1999: 14), "equity preferences" (Olsen 2000), "rationing preferences" (Ubel 2001; Ubel *et al.* 1996b), "social resource allocation preferences" (Drummond *et al.* 2009), "allocation preferences" (Ubel 1999), "prioritization preferences" (Dolan *et al.* 2008), "distributional preferences" (Nord *et al.* 1999), "distributive" or "public values" (Ubel *et al.* 2000c).
5 The term social value is usually taken to refer to the overall value of a resource allocation, which takes both equity and efficiency into account (see Nord *et al.* 1999: 25). By contrast, social *values* refer to the individual concerns for equity regarded as important by the respondents, i.e. to the relative value of the equity relevant factors captured in equity weights. See Dolan/Green (1998), Menzel (1999), Walker/Siegel (2002), Powers/Faden (2006: 185), and Williams *et al.* (2012: 22). Other labels for social values include "societal" values (Nord *et al.* 1999: 25; Ubel *et al.* 2000b), "community values" (McKie/Richardson 2005a: 1), "social benefits" (Ubel 1999: 869), and "moral value" (Bognar/Hirose 2014: 71).
6 Although this aspect will be tackled more thoroughly in Chapter 5, it should be noted that the equity-efficiency trade-off concept is misleading. In particular, it conceals that efficiency itself is an inherently normative concept.
7 See Section 4.3.
8 See for instance Mooney (2009: 62, 211), Daniels (2008: 293f.), and Cohen/Ubel (2001: 95).
9 While Lübbe (2005, 2009c, 2010a, 2010b, 2013) tackled the weighting approaches in shorter, mostly German papers, the fundamental argument is worked out by Lübbe (2015). As mentioned in the acknowledgments, the basic idea for this study stems from Lübbe, but we have been working on the issue together recently. See Klonschinski/Lübbe (2011), Klonschinski (2013, 2014).

2 The utility concept in economics

From pleasure maximization to rational choice

2.1 Introduction: the merits of a historical account

As outlined in the first chapter, crucial tasks of applied ethics consist of checking arguments for consistency, revealing implicit premises, and clarifying concepts. At the center of the health economic attempts to solve CUA's fairness issue are the notions of social preference, social value, and equity weights. And yet, notwithstanding their crucial significance, these terms remain peculiarly nebulous. To give some examples, Dolan and Tsuchiya (2006: 382) maintain that the term social value expresses "the relative importance of QALYs to society." In a similar vein, Tsuchiya (1999: 267) states that she uses the term "in a loose sense: value to others and not necessarily to the individual," whereas Donaldson *et al.* (2011b: 4) refer to the task of "valuing QALYs in others."[1] Dolan *et al.* (2008: 8) focus on "equally good states of affairs from a societal point of view" and Schwappach (2002: 211) defines social value as describing "a measure of societal desirability." Similarly, when it comes to social preferences, Dolan and Tsuchiya (2009: 213) maintain that their elicitation "requires respondents to identify points that they consider to be equally good for society, rather than points they consider to be equally good for them personally, or for any particular party." Finally, Menzel (1999: 250) states that social preferences express the individual's "preferences about what constitutes their society's well-being." In empirical preference elicitation studies, in turn, the respondents are confronted with questions such as the following:

A. Which do you think would bring the most benefit?

   ____ ten people cured of appendicitis
   ____ [twenty] people cured of knee damage
   ____ Indifferent

B. How many people would have to be cured of knee damage to equal the benefit brought by curing ten people of appendicitis?

(Ubel *et al.* 1996b: 111)

And yet, which kind of benefit do the researchers have in mind here? What does it mean to say that something is good for society or socially desirable? Is the value in others and the value to others the same? And, crucially, what exactly is maximized when the social value of a resource allocation, incorporating equity and efficiency, is at its maximum?[2]

Such conceptual ambiguities, which are endemic in the discipline of economics more generally as well, are deeply rooted in the history of economics, as this chapter demonstrates. Based on the assumption that "the evaluation of ideas cannot be separated from their past usage" (Mandler 1999: 13), it provides a historical account of the development of the utility concept from its inception to economics in the course of the so-called marginal revolution at the end of the nineteenth century to modern rational choice theory. Yet, the chapter neither claims to present the history of economic evaluation in general or CUA in particular, nor does it seek to provide a comprehensive account of *the* history of utility theory or economics in recent decades.[3] As to the first restriction, there can be no doubt that health economic evaluations stem from the contributions of many various disciplines (see Garber *et al.* 1996: 25f.).[4] That being said, since the present focus is on the economic concepts applied and, especially, the underlying value-maximizing framework of economic evaluations, the considerations embed CUA in the history of economics. Regarding the second qualification, the chapter homes in on three important watersheds in the history of economic thought – the marginal revolution in the late nineteenth century, the ordinal revolution in the 1930s, and the formalization of economics after World War II – and illustrates these turning points using the example of distinguished economists. Thereby, the considerations in this chapter are always oriented toward the applied issue of this study and ultimately seek to provide a deeper understanding of the premises underlying CUA and the problems it currently encounters. That is, although the present chapter does not directly deal with health economics, it plays a crucial systematic role for the whole study. More specifically, the historical account serves the following five important purposes.

First, the chapter demonstrates that right from the start the utility concept and the notion of utility maximization were closely connected with consumer choice theory. William S. Jevons introduced the hedonic utility concept into economics because he sought to explain the self-interested behavior of consumers. Although economists tried to purge utility from all psychological and, especially, hedonic content eventually, even the modern, allegedly merely formal utility notion still carries connotations of demand theory. That is to say, economists still speak of utility as if it was something substantial, something "good" for the individual that the latter seeks to maximize.[5] As the quotes above indicate and as Chapter 5 and 6 of this study elaborate, such equivocations constitute a pervasive problem in health economics as well. Second, the attempt to purge utility theory of all psychological content cannot succeed as long as the theory is supposed to explain individual behavior. The concepts of indifference and choice cannot be understood without reference to inner procedures and terms such as sacrifice or benefit even require a hedonic reading. This finding has important implications for the interpretation of social preferences and social values in Chapter 5. Third, the examination of the utility concept's history reveals that the simple dichotomy between hedonic utility on the one hand and modern, formal utility on the other, amounts to a glaring over-simplification of the matter. In fact, the utility notion was characterized by considerable vagueness right from the start. It is, for instance, not even clear whether Pareto actually endorsed an ordinal utility concept and the concrete aim of Hicks and Allen also remains somewhat unclear. Considered against this background, it does not come as a surprise that nowadays, the literature on utility is replete with conceptual ambiguities. Fourth, it needs to be stressed that although the developments in the history of the utility concept presented may not provide any new information for historically sensitive economists and for scholars working at the intersection of philosophy and economics, they cannot be regarded as common knowledge within the target audience of the study, which includes medical ethicists, philosophers, health care professionals, and policy makers.[6] In this respect, the study serves an important mediating function as it provides the conceptual basis both for a thorough understanding of CUA's problems and for the criticism presented in the subsequent study. Fifth, the applied and relatively young discipline of health economics still has to be regarded as a rather ahistorical endeavor (see Cohen 1997; Forget 2004; McMaster 2007). This, however, significantly restricts the discipline's potential to analyze and solve its current problems:

> Without a historical consciousness, practitioners are held captive by the historical path that they and their teachers actually trod. The perspective that they can bring to their work, and the nature of the critique that they can imagine, is constrained by the debates of which they are aware. A historical perspective [...] opens up all kinds of new possibilities for theoretical innovation.
>
> (Forget 2004: 617f.)[7]

This lack of a historical consciousness was explicitly criticized in the literature, so that the present chapter provides an important contribution to research.

2.2 The Jevonian revolution: the mechanics of utility and self-interest

2.2.1 The marginal revolution and the unity of science

Although it can be argued that utilitarian thinking has permeated classical political economy since the very beginning (see Schabas 2003b: 181), the utility concept did not come to the fore in economics until the end of the nineteenth century in the course of the marginal revolution (see Mandler 1999: 68).[8] This term denotes the independent, but allegedly simultaneous, introduction of the differential calculus to economics and the discovery of the principle of diminishing marginal utility by William Stanley Jevons in England and Léon Walras in France.[9] The marginal revolution can be regarded as "the most important watershed in the history of economics" (Schabas 2003a: 236) and heralded the neoclassical era of economics.

Jevons (1835–1882), "the founder of English neoclassicism" (Mandler 1999: 74) and especially his *Theory of Political Economy* (Jevons 1911/2006, subsequently cited as *TPE*), first published in 1871, have influenced modern economics to a major extent: "there is no particle of economic science, theoretical or empirical, to which Jevons did not make important contributions that are considered revolutionary today. Jevons is the father of modern economics, indeed" (Maas 2005: 1).[10] Before investigating Jevons' use of the utility concept in more detail, this introductory section considers his broader conception of the methodological framework of economics. As will become clear, these considerations are a necessary prerequisite for grasping Jevons' notion of utility and utility maximization.

What was so revolutionary about the marginalist school in general and about Jevons' approach to economics in particular, then? Despite the fact that some authors question the appropriateness of labelling the marginalists' work *revolutionary* (see Blaug 1997: 291; Morgan 2003: 279; Backhouse 2008a), two aspects are generally considered a novelty: first, a strong orientation toward the scientific ideal of physics and, second, the comparatively extensive use of mathematics (see Mirowski 1989: 194f.). Considering the ideal of physics first, it is certainly true that the natural sciences had served as an ideal for political economy before. And yet, the prestige and importance physics enjoyed at the end of the nineteenth century was unprecedented and the influence it exerted on other disciplines had nowhere been as extensive as in marginal economics and, especially, in the *TPE* (see Colvin 1985: 11; Mirowski 1989: 35, 195, 198, 201).[11] It deserves emphasis that Jevons' ample appeals to the ideal of physics and his extensive use of mechanical metaphors are not just a matter of style but actually indicate a crucial change in methodology as is symbolized by the fact that *TPE* was the first publication substituting *political economy* as the name of the discipline for *economics* (see *TPE:* xiv). This change of concepts not only illustrates the turn away from the decidedly political character of former economic science but also puts the discipline of economics on a par with mathemat*ics* and phys*ics* (*TPE:* xiv–xv).

The formal congruity hints to Jevons' deeper conviction of a fundamental unity of the sciences: just as the physical world was governed by mechanical laws, so was the social and moral sphere (see Colvin 1985: 11; Schabas 1990: 80; Maas 2005: 235). Therefore, the economists' task was to discover the "underlying mechanics" (Colvin 1985: 11), or, as it were, "the natural laws of Economics" (*TPE:* 11). The existence of such laws had already been taken for granted by classical political economists, of course, but they had considered economic phenomena part of physical nature (see Schabas 2007: 2, 102ff.). At Jevons' time, John Stuart Mill, the leading figure in political economy, strictly distinguished between the social and the natural sciences which, he argued, deal with "categorically different phenomena" and therefore required the application of different methods (Maas 2005: 177; see Mill 1871a: 129ff.).[12] While the natural sciences allowed for observation and experimentation, the social sciences rested on the method of introspection (see Maas 2005: 42). Hence, the tools and methods of economics "were thought to exclude experiments and mathematics" (Maas 2005: 270).

Jevons, by contrast, denied any categorical difference between the phenomena of the mind and those of the outer world and regarded physics and economics as being susceptible to the same method of inquiry. His account of the human mind and the corresponding approach to economics needs to be considered against the background of a changing worldview in Victorian Britain as to the relationship between mind and matter.

In the nineteenth century, Britain saw an intense debate on the relationship between physical stimuli and mental phenomena (see Cohen 1997: 151; Forget 2004: 630; Maas 2005: 162; Bruni/Sugden 2007: 151; Hands 2010: 641ff.). Current developments in physiology gave rise to the view of man as "some sort of machine," and, concomitantly, to a physiological account of psychology which became known as psychophysiology (Maas 2005: 164). According to psychophysiology, some correlation between mental forces and nerve forces exists so that "bodily states could be used as indices for mental states, just as the thermometer was used to indicate temperature" (Maas 2005: 167). Hence, it was supposed that mental phenomena could be measured by their bodily manifestation. This relationship was investigated empirically, especially in the realm of psychophysics, the German pendant to psychophysiology.[13] The development of psychophysics heralded nothing less than a paradigm change regarding the conception of mind and matter, as Maas (2005: 12) points out:

> Halfway through the century, the categorical distinction between the phenomena of the mind and matter vanished under the developments within psychophysiology. This enabled economists such as Jevons to transgress the boundaries traditionally set to the tools of investigation with regard to the mind and to explore how the tools of the natural sciences might be used to disclose the laws of mind.

The assumed parallelism between mental and physiological phenomena allowed for the application of the same method to both areas. As Maas (2005: 23) puts it: "In Jevons' approach to science, a material mechanism served to unlock the secrets of the world: the material and the mental."

It is against this background that Jevons' conception of economics as a task of "tracing out the mechanics of self-interest and utility" needs to be understood (*TPE:* xvii f.). Crucially, Jevons took the individual as the point of origin and applied the tools of the natural sciences to the investigation of the mind (see Maas 2005: 12).[14] The proper method to do so, he firmly believed, was mathematics. In his view, economics is inherently mathematical because it deals with quantities and the functional relationships between these quantities (see *TPE:* xxi, 3f.). Because these relations are complicated, common language is not precise enough to grasp the sophisticated connections in question. They call for the use of mathematics, instead:

> It is clear that Economics, if it is to be a science at all, must be a mathematical science. There exists much prejudice against attempts to introduce the

> methods and language of mathematics into any branch of the moral sciences. Many persons seem to think that the physical sciences form the proper sphere of mathematical method, and that the moral sciences demand some other method, – I know not what. My theory of economics, however, is purely mathematical in character.
>
> (*TPE:* 3)

This quote alludes to the opposition that the application of mathematics to economic issues was confronted with. And indeed, although former economists had already used some mathematics, at the end of the nineteenth century the discipline of economics was still very much characterized by a verbal tradition (see Morgan 2003: 277).[15] The *TPE* thus neatly exemplifies marginalism's "most discontinuous aspect," i.e., its mathematical character (Mirowski 1989: 195).

2.2.2 The subjective theory of value and the calculus of pleasure and pain

Having sketched two important changes in the conceptual and methodological framework of economics, this section turns to the marginal revolution's theoretical cornerstone, the subjective theory of value. It constitutes a major departure from classical economic theory, which regarded commodity prices as being basically determined by the costs of production in general and of labor in particular. Classical economists did not consider demand in any systematic fashion, but merely assumed that it existed (see Robbins 1934: 91f.; Cooter/Rappoport 1984: 510; Clark 1995: 39; Mandler 1999: 68ff.).[16] The lack of any theory explaining "fully the relationships between utility, demand and market price was not a matter of concern to most of them" (Black 2008), though, as they were primarily interested in the natural price of commodities. While this value was something intrinsic to a particular good, the marginalists located a good's value "in the eye of the purchaser" (Amadae 2003: 224).[17] That is to say, they put the individual valuations inherent in the process of exchange into the center of attention and, in doing so, shifted the analytic focus to demand as "the driving force behind economic activity" (Endres 1999: 601).[18]

Accordingly, Jevons rejects the labor theory of value as "directly opposed to facts" (*TPE:* 163) and turns the relationship between consumption and production upside down: "We labour to produce with the sole object of consuming, and the kinds and amounts of goods produced must be determined with regard to what we want to consume" (*TPE:* 39).[19] In order to systematically explain prices in terms of demand, to be sure, some assumptions concerning the behavior of the consumer were necessary (see Mandler 1999: 73f.). For this reason, Jevons refers to the concept of utility:

> Repeated reflection and inquiry have led me to the somewhat novel opinion, [*sic*] that value depends entirely upon utility. Prevailing opinions make labour rather than utility the origin of value; and there are even those who assert that

> labour is the cause of value. I show, on the contrary, that we have only to trace out carefully the *natural laws of the variation of utility,* as depending upon the quantity of commodity in our possession, in order to arrive at a satisfactory theory of exchange, of which the ordinary laws of supply and demand are a necessary consequence.
>
> (*TPE:* 1f.)[20]

Utility, or rather, marginal utility is held to be the crucial determining factor of demand behavior and, therefore, exchange value.[21]

This shift of focus gives rise to the inherently individualistic stance of neoclassical economics. Making the "mechanics of utility and self-interest" (*TPE:* 21) the foundational explanatory factors for economic phenomena, marginalism conceived of economics as "mind-driven through and through" (Schabas 2003a: 237; see Schabas 2007: 134ff.). In this vein, the *TPE* "presumes to investigate the condition of a mind, and bases upon this investigation the whole of Economics" (*TPE:* 15). Jevons claims that the crucial laws of the variation of utility are "entirely based on a calculus of pleasure and pain" (*TPE:* 23). Thereby, the notions of pleasure and pain may not be defined too narrowly but need to be considered as embracing "all forces which drive us to action" (ibid.). This conception meshes neatly with Jevons' endorsement of psychophysics. Following Alexander Bain, who is one of the first contributors to the emerging discipline of psychology and who especially studied the connection between feelings and movements, Jevons is convinced that the greater of two pleasures sways the resulting action so that "we cannot make a choice, or manifest the will in any way, without indicating thereby an excess of pleasure in one direction" (*TPE:* 13).[22] He regards the human mind as a "balance which makes its own comparisons, and is the final judge of quantities of feeling" (*TPE:* 12). In doing so, Jevons does not conceive of pleasure and pain as motives or factors exerting a certain influence on choices, but rather as physical forces driving the will (see Maas 2005: 273). With a view to later developments in economics and the applied context of the present study, it deserves emphasis that at the end of the nineteenth century, the emerging disciplines of economics and psychology were closely connected and the latter was in fact regarded as providing the former with a scientific basis. Using the words of Schabas (2007: 137), "economics was firmly rooted in psychology, which was something to relish, not fear. It would bring greater rigor and objectivity to the subject and provide the proper ontological foundation for the newly developed mathematical theory."[23]

Jevons believes that the diverse pleasures of which people are capable are of different kinds and can be brought into a hierarchical order. While physical pleasures and pains stemming from "bodily wants and susceptibilities" constitute the lowest stage of feelings, people are also capable of "mental and moral feelings of several degrees" and have "higher motives" or "higher duties" such as caring for the "safety of a nation" (*TPE:* 25). Due to his mechanistic conception of the human mind, Jevons treats feelings, motives, and duties as categorically equivalent: basically, they are all forces leading to certain actions. The different forces are not of equal strength, though, but a higher motive may trump the lower ones (see *TPE:* 25). The discipline of economics only needs to be concerned with "the lowest rank of feelings" because it is primarily the "ordinary wants" which lead people to buying and selling, borrowing and lending, working and relaxing (*TPE:* 11). Economics rests upon "the laws of human *enjoyment*" (*TPE:* 39), it is about "pushpin, not poetry," as it were (Schabas 2003a: 239). In view of the subsequent developments in utility theory, it deserves to be highlighted that Jevons thereby restricted his analysis to standard economic consumption goods and took care to exclude ethical issues from utility theory (see Mandler 2001: 376). In the economic sphere, Jevons assumes, it is "the inevitable tendency of human nature to choose that course which offers the greatest possible advantage at the moment" (*TPE:* 59). On the market, the individual acts "from a pure regard to his own requirements or private interests" (*TPE:* 86) so that, within this realm, hedonism presents the appropriate psychology (see *TPE:* 27). These behavioral assumptions still present the core of the modern microeconomic model of economic agents.

Understanding the underlying mechanistic conception of the human mind is also crucial to grasp Jevons' considerations as to the measurability of pleasure. The latter is indeed essential for *TPE* given that the scientific analysis of economics is to constitute a "Calculus of Pleasure and Pain" (*TPE:* vi). To begin with, for Jevons, it goes without saying that "pleasure, pain, labour, utility, value [...] etc. are all notions admitting of quantity" (*TPE:* 9f.). The question remains, however, whether units of pleasure and pain are conceivable at all and how their quantities can be measured exactly. Entirely in the spirit of psychophysics, Jevons argues that pleasures can be gauged indirectly by way of measuring their quantitative effects (*TPE:* 11). Just as forces could be measured by the motions they induce, the strength of the underlying feelings could be read off the prices of the commodities, as Jevons illustrates using a mechanical analog again:

> We can no more know or measure gravity in its own nature than we can measure a feeling; but just as we measure gravity by its effects in the motion of a pendulum, so we may estimate the equality or inequality of feelings by the decision of the human mind. The will is our pendulum, and its oscillations are minutely registered in the price lists of the markets. I know not when we shall have a perfect system of statistics, but the want of it is the only insuperable obstacle in the way of making Economics an exact science.
>
> (*TPE:* 11f.)

Apparently, Jevons believes that feelings could be measured indirectly provided that, first, the required empirical data were available, and, second, the method of statistics was improved (see Howey 1989: 48f.). It should be noted that at the time of Jevons' writings, statistics basically amounted to "fact-gathering" (Maas 2005: 233) and was neither an acknowledged part of political economy nor of mathematics (see Schabas 1990: 33). According to the then dominant conviction, statistical data revealed "nothing but the particularities of history" (Maas 2005: 220).[24] By contrast, Jevons emphasized the pivotal role empirical data plays for economics as a "strict science" and persistently sought to integrate statistics into economic theory. That being said, Jevons points out that there is no need to determine units of pleasure and measure their exact amount anyway. Instead, the "theory turns upon those critical points where pleasures are nearly, if not quite, equal" (*TPE:* 13). According to the conception of the human mind as a balance, a certain action indicates an excess of pleasure on one of its sides (see ibid.). Consequently, in the area of demand, an individual who stops purchasing expresses that the balance is in equilibrium, so that "he would derive equal pleasure from the possession of a small quantity more as he would from the money price of it" (ibid.).[25] This conception of consumer behavior will be referred to again in Chapter 5 when the economic notion of value-oriented choices is considered. At this point, we turn to Jevons' interpretation and modification of Bentham's felicific calculus.

Jevons very much endorses the moral philosopher Jeremy Bentham, because he had clearly realized "the quantitative character of the subject" and adopted a "thoroughly mathematical" account to moral science (*TPE:* 10).[26] The mathematical character of Bentham's analysis is especially embodied in the so-called felicific calculus, an algorithm showing "how pleasure and pain can be estimated as magnitudes" (*TPE:* 28). In the version originally put forward by Bentham (1823: 29ff.), the calculus works as follows. To begin with, he differentiates four factors influencing the value of a pleasure or a pain experienced by an individual: intensity, duration, certainty and uncertainty, propinquity and remoteness. If the tendency of an act to bring about pleasure or pain is considered, the two factors of fecundity (the chance any pain or pleasure "has of being followed by sensations of the same kind") and purity ("the chance it has of not being followed by sensations of the opposite kind") have to be accounted for as well (Bentham 1823: 30). In order to assess an act affecting the whole community, one first needs to consider its effect on each individual person. In a second step, the number of the persons affected becomes relevant, a factor called extent:

> Take an account of the number of persons whose interests appear to be concerned; and repeat the above process with regard to each. Sum up the numbers expressive of the degrees of good tendency, which the act has, with respect to each individual, in regard to whom the tendency of it is good upon the whole: do this again with respect to each individual, in regard to whom the tendency of it is bad upon the whole: Take the balance; which, if on the side of pleasure, will give the general good tendency of the act, with respect to the total number or community of individuals concerned; if on the side of pain, the general evil tendency, with respect to the whole community.
>
> (Bentham 1823: 31)

It seems highly dubious whether this calculus is indeed feasible, though. Obviously, it relies on the premises that it is possible to assign concrete numbers to the amount of pleasures and pains experienced and to render the sensations of different persons comparable with each other. These assumptions seem quite severe, to say the least, and the idea of the felicific calculus has indeed been sharply criticized in the literature. And yet, some authors query whether Bentham himself indeed wanted the calculus to be understood literally at all. These arguments draw a more differentiated picture of Bentham's utilitarianism and, furthermore, illustrate why Jevons had to modify the calculus and Bentham's account of pleasure in an important way. In order to answer the question of whether the calculus is to be taken literally it is helpful to consider whether the feasibility of the calculus is buttressed by Bentham's other considerations on pleasure and measurability.

To begin with, he explicitly declares that intensity is "not susceptible of precise expression: it not being susceptible of measurement" (Bentham quoted in Warke 2000b: 181). Furthermore, in the chapter following the delineation of the calculus, Bentham (1823: 33) considers several sorts of pleasures and pains subsumed under the heading "interesting perceptions." These can be either simple or complex and while the latter can be dissolved into the former, simple perceptions cannot be resolved into more basic perceptions. Interestingly, Bentham (1823: 33–42) lists fourteen of such simple pleasures and twelve simple pains. Among them are, for instance, the pleasures of amity, pleasures of benevolence, and pleasures of imagination.[27] This enumeration illustrates that Bentham defines pleasure very broadly, as the term obviously not only denotes sensual pleasures but also "those of the heart and the mind" (Viner 1949: 366).[28] He thus might not have been the "thorough-going hedonist" he is generally described as (Griffin 1986: 38). More interesting in the present context, though, is the definition of simple sensations as those which cannot be dissected any further. As the different simple pleasures and pains fall into mutually exclusive categories, there is no "generic pleasure" by means of which the individual could compare and order the different pleasures and pains unequivocally (see Warke 2000a: 11). In other words, the different pleasures lack a common denominator (see Mitchell 1918: 36; Warke 2000b: 180). Therefore, it seems impossible even for one individual to quantify the qualitatively different pleasures and pains so that the calculus faces a problem at the "most microscopic level" (Warke 2000a: 11; see Mitchell 1918: 35). It can thus be concluded with Warke (2000a: 9) that Bentham did not consider pleasure and pain as precisely quantifiable, but rather as "irreducibly multidimensional."

While the balancing of pleasure and pain is problematic at the individual level already, further complications arise when it comes to interpersonal comparisons. Bentham (1823: 44f.) observes that diverse individuals can experience one and the same stimulus quite differently:

> in the same mind such and such causes of pain or pleasure will produce more pain or pleasure than such or such other causes of pain or pleasure: and this proportion will in different minds be different. [...] One man, for instance, may be most affected by the pleasure of the taste; another by those of the ear.

He continues with listing 32 different "circumstances influencing sensibility," such as bodily imperfection, moral sensibility, pecuniary circumstances, and even the climate (see ibid.). Thus, the evaluation of generated pleasures and pains seems to be a decisively subjective task so that it would be impossible for the legislator to know how a decision will affect the different individuals (see Warke 2000b: 177). The subjectivity of pleasure and pain is acknowledged by Bentham in another, rather surprising respect as well. He concedes in an unpublished manuscript:

> 'Tis in vain to talk of adding quantities which after the addition will continue distinct as they were before, one man's happiness will never be another man's happiness: a gain to one man is no gain to another: you might as well pretend to add 20 apples to 20 pears, which after you have done that could not be forty of any one thing but twenty of each just as there was before. [...] This addibility of the happiness of different subjects, however, when considered rigorously, it may appear ficticious, is a postulatum without the allowance of which all political reasoning is at a stand.
>
> (Bentham quoted in Halévy 1946: 495)

It seems as if Bentham had realized quite well that the overall sum of pleasure is an artificial construct and that the virtual application of the felicific calculus is impossible (see Barry 1965: 45; Mirowski 1989: 206f.; Riley 2008).

These considerations raise the question as to why he presented such an unrealistic device in the first place. The most probable answer is twofold: first, the late seventeenth century marks the beginning of the century of science, especially symbolized by the work of Newton (see Halévy 1946: 5f.). In this situation, Bentham may have aimed at providing a rational, scientific basis for morals and legislation without reference to any metaphysical entities or outdated traditions, i.e., he sought to transform legislation, economics, and ethics into *real* science (see Mitchell 1918: 32). In this respect, he regarded utilitarianism and the calculus "as an instrument of criticism, and thought that by appeal to it they could show that many Victorian moral beliefs were mistaken and irrational" (B. Williams 1972: 108).[29] In the present context, however, a second branch of explanation is much more interesting since it helps to illustrate the difference between Bentham's and Jevons' use of the utility concept. Bentham was a member of the philosophical radicals; that is to say, he did not only aim at fostering the theoretical progress of the sciences of morals and legislation for its own sake, but also intended to construct measures for criticizing and changing social circumstances (see Viner 1949: 361f.). And indeed, the focus on each individual's happiness and the postulate that everyone counts for one and no one for more than one have to be considered revolutionary at a time when power and wealth were concentrated on very few privileged members of society (see Viner 1949: 361).[30] Most likely, the principle of utility was never supposed to "reduce policy making to a simple rule" (Backhouse 2004: 136), but should provide a rational and scientific benchmark for political decisions. In exactly this vein, Bentham (1823: 31) himself argues that while the calculus cannot always be applied when moral judgments or judicial operations are at stake, it always needs to be "kept in view: and as near as the process actually pursued on these occasions approaches to it, so near will such process approach to the character of an exact one." It becomes apparent that the intentions to base morals and legislation on a more scientific fundament and to use this rational science "as the basis for criticizing the institutions of society and advocating policies of reform" were closely connected (Backhouse 2004: 137). All in all, it seems safe to assume that "Bentham never intended to take the [felicific calculus'] formal mathematical aspects seriously" (Mirowski 1989: 206), but rather regarded it as a device for "a mental comparison of the comparative weights of the pros and cons" of certain collective choices (Viner 1949: 367).[31]

In the context of the present study, these findings serve as a background against which Jevons' central modification and different application of the calculus can be carved out. To begin with, adopting the calculus in order to 'estimate' pleasure and pain as "magnitudes" (*TPE:* 28), Jevons reduces Bentham's seven dimensions of feelings to the two dimensions of intensity and duration (see Warke 2000a: 12ff.; Sigot 2002: 265ff.). Fecundity, purity, and extent, Jevons argues, are relevant for the sphere of morals but do not matter for the "more simple and restricted" problems of economics (*TPE:* 29). And although he concedes that the dimensions of certainty/uncertainty and propinquity/remoteness are of eminent importance for economics, he does not treat them as qualitatively different considerations, but incorporates them into the dimensions of intensity and duration instead. Concerning propinquity, he states that the "intensity of present anticipated feeling must [...] be some function of the future actual feeling and the intervening of time, and it must increase as we approach the moment of realisation" (*TPE:* 34). And as to certainty, Jevons suggests that one "should multiply the quantity of feeling attaching to every future event by the fraction denoting its probability" (*TPE:* 36).[32] It becomes apparent that especially by dropping the factor of extent, Jevons dissolves the calculus from its embedding in Bentham's broader socio-political concerns and applies the calculus to one and the same person only. He thus gives the utilitarian calculus the decidedly *individualistic* reading which is characteristic for marginal economics. Beside these changes, Jevons follows Bentham in treating pleasure and pain as one homogeneous sensation differing only in direction, a conception allowing for the mathematic operations of addition and subtraction of quantities of pleasure on one and the same scale (see *TPE:* 32, 64; Warke 2000a: 16). At its zero point, positive pleasure changes over to negative pleasure: "It is obvious that utility passes through inutility before changing into disutility, these notions being related as +, 0 and –," whereby inutility denotes "the absence of utility" (*TPE:* 58).[33] To be sure, the assumption that all pleasures are commensurable is a prerequisite for the notion of well-ordered preferences that are representable by a single utility function (see Davis 2003: 64).

Jevons' reinterpretation of the felicific calculus has important consequences for economics. For one thing, the reduction to two dimensions provides a clear-cut criterion for determining which of two pleasures is of greater quantity – at least if one dimension is held fixed, as Jevons assumes in his examples.[34] For another, Jevons turned the concept of pleasure into "a suitable maximand for determinate choice" (Warke 2000a: 7).[35] This modification is crucial: due to the fact that pleasure provides a criterion according to which different alternatives are to be ranked, well-ordered preferences satisfying the assumptions of completeness and transitivity are guaranteed (see Mandler 1999: 76, 96ff.).[36] It thus seems as if it was in marginal economics rather than in "morals and legislation" that the – modified – felicific calculus became highly influential. In fact, Viner (1949: 368) reports that

> [n]one of Bentham's immediate disciples showed any interest in this aspect of Bentham's thought, and it was not until Jevons drew attention to it and made it the basis of his subjective theory of economic value that it had any influence, for good or bad.

Arguably, the popularity of Bentham's calculus actually owes a lot to Jevons.

2.2.3 Utility maximization

Having considered Jevons' considerations as to the nature and the measurability of pleasure and pain, this section turns to the relationship between these feelings and the utility concept. Again in close resemblance with Bentham (1823: 2), Jevons takes the term utility to designate "the abstract quality whereby an object serves our purposes, and becomes entitled to rank as a commodity" (*TPE:* 38). A commodity, in turn, is "any object, substance, action, or service, which can afford pleasure or ward off pain" (*TPE:* 37f.). Thereby, utility is not inherent in objects, but needs to be regarded as "a circumstance of things arising out of their relation to man's requirements" (*TPE:* 43). Jevons thus emphasizes the decidedly subjective character of utility. Something only possesses utility for individual A if the item in question is actually desired by A:

> Whatever can produce pleasure or ward off pain may possess utility [...]; but we must beware of restricting the meaning of the word by any moral considerations. Anything which an individual is found to desire and to labour for must be assumed to possess for him utility.
>
> (*TPE:* 38)

Hence, the same good may be of different utility for different individuals. Beyond that, Jevons highlights that the amount of utility a unit of a certain commodity has for the individual depends on how much of the respective commodity the individual in question already has consumed (see *TPE:* 44). Even in the case of "the most useful of all substances" (ibid.), water, there comes a point where an additional unit of water does not provide any further pleasure and, hence, cannot be regarded as possessing utility at all.[37] In general, utility cannot be considered as proportional to the amount of a commodity, but "the very same articles vary in utility according as we already possess more or less of the same article" (ibid.).

These considerations already hint toward an intimate connection between utility and pleasure. In further dwelling on the law of the variation of utility, Jevons maintains:

> Utility must be considered as measured by, or even as actually identical with, the addition made to a person's happiness. It is a convenient name for the aggregate of the favourable balance of feeling produced – the sum of the pleasure created and the pain prevented.
>
> (*TPE:* 45)

That is, the concept of utility was first defined as a quality of an object, then became a circumstance of things arising out of the individual's requirements, and is finally regarded as actually identical with happiness. Although this might seem to be an equivocation of the concept at first glance, the reasoning is straightforward when considered within the realm of psychophysics: the utility of an object can only be inferred from the pleasure it generates in the individual; this feeling, in turn, is embodied in the price of the respective commodity. According to Broome (1991b: 1f.), the reference to utility as a characteristic of an object was totally abandoned only after Jevons when utility became equated with pleasure.

Having defined the utility of an object as being tantamount to the pleasure felt by the individual when consuming the respective object, the utility concept can now be used to explain demand behavior. This behavior, Jevons argues, does not depend upon the total utility of a commodity, but rather on its "degree of utility," that is, in modern terminology, on marginal utility (*TPE:* 49). This term denotes the pleasure generated by the consumption of a further unit of a certain good. Thereby, the "final degree of utility," i.e., "the degree of utility of the last addition, or the next possible addition of a very small, or infinitely small, quantity to the existing stock" is of particular interest (*TPE:* 51). In fact "the final degree of utility is that function upon which the Theory of Economics will be found to turn" (*TPE:* 52).[38] It is at this point that the integration of the differential calculus to economics enfolds its power and it is this focus on the final degree of utility which gives the *marginal* revolution its name in the first place. As to the functional relationship between the degree of utility and the quantity of a commodity, Jevons explicitly refers to psychophysics. He praises Richard Jennings for his consideration of the law of utility in *Natural Elements of Political Economy*, treating "the physical groundwork of Economics, showing its dependence on physiological laws" (*TPE:* 55). He postulated that an increase in a physical stimulus does not lead to a proportional increase in sensation, but that the latter diminishes gradually, as Jennings illustrates by means of the following examples:

> We may gaze upon an object until we can no longer discern it, listen until we can no longer hear, smell until the sense of odour is exhausted, taste until the object becomes nauseous, and touch until it becomes painful.
>
> (Quoted in *TPE*: 56)[39]

Based on these psychophysiological observations, Jevons states that the degree of utility varies with the quantity of a commodity "and ultimately decreases as that quantity increases" (*TPE:* 53) – a relationship nowadays known as the principle of diminishing marginal utility (see *TPE:* 52).[40] By embedding it in the context of psychophysics, Jevons treats this economic principle as a special instance of a more general law of psychology (see Bruni/Sugden 2007: 150).

Jevons elucidates this law by considering individual decisions regarding the distribution of a commodity on different potential uses, i.e., the marginal utility theory of consumption (*TPE:* 58ff.). Barley, for instance, could be used for making beer, baking bread, or feeding the cattle (see *TPE:* 59). How does the individual decide on the good's distribution on these different applications, then? As said before, Jevons takes it to be an "inevitable tendency" of individuals to always choose according to their "greatest possible advantage at the moment" in the economic sphere (ibid.). Thus, if a person is satisfied with a certain distribution of the commodity, no alternative distribution could yield more pleasure and the marginal utilities in both uses are identical. As a general result, Jevons concludes "that commodity, if consumed by a perfectly wise being, must be consumed with a maximum production of utility" (*TPE:* 60). This is the nowadays so-called equimarginal principle, lying at the heart of neoclassical economics (see Schabas 1990: 42; Blaug 1997: 280, 577f.; Kliemt 2009: 3). It cannot only be applied to individual consumption decisions but also to market exchange (see *TPE:* 75ff.). Granted the conditions of perfect information, perfect competition, and no transaction costs, the economic agents, each acting "from a pure regard to his own requirements or private interests," engage in market transactions until no further exchange would provide them more pleasure (*TPE:* 86). This is the case when the marginal utilities of both commodities are equal and the respective pleasures of the individuals are at a maximum. In effect, the exchanging parties have reached their "greatest advantage" (*TPE:* 97f.) and "rest in satisfaction and equilibrium, and the degrees of utility have come to their level" (*TPE:* 96).

At this point, two observations need to be highlighted. First, note that Jevons focuses on the quantities of pleasure as estimated by the respective individual (see Schabas 1990: 40). The equalization of utilities applies to different goods consumed by the same individual and it is the individual pleasure that is thereby maximized, not an aggregate of pleasure (see *TPE:* 141). As a general law of exchange, Jevons proposes the following relationship: "The ratio of exchange of any two commodities will be the reciprocal of the ratio of the final degrees of utility of the quantities of commodity available for consumption after the exchange is completed" (*TPE:* 95). If the individual utility functions were known, the laws of demand and supply could be derived from "what seems to me the true theory of value or exchange" (*TPE:* 101). Having thus connected demand theory with a "physiological account of the production of pleasure," Jevons established a behavioral fundament for demand theory (Mandler 1999: 74).[41] Second, by referring to equilibrium and the level of utilities, Jevons reinvokes the metaphor of a balance. He illustrates the deliberation of an individual by means of a diagram showing the utility curves of two different commodities which are superposed and laterally reversed (see *TPE:* 97; Maas 2005: 273f.). The amount of the goods is measured on the horizontal axis and their utility is measured on the vertical axis. According to Jevons, there automatically emerges an equilibrium point at the intersection of the two curves. To quote Maas (2005: 274):

> This balancing model, stemming from mechanics, was taking to represent the individual's balancing of pleasures and pains at the margin. In making this analogy between the balancing of feelings and the balancing of material balance [...] the distinction between the laws of mind and matter that had haunted Victorian discourse evaporated. Human deliberation and choice were depicted mechanically.

Consequently, Jevons sketched an equilibrating market mechanism on the basis of what we today call a preference ordering (see Maas 2005: 277).

In summary, the basic ingredients of Jevons' economics are Bentham's utilitarianism, psychophysiology, and the use of the differential calculus. Jevons strictly rejected the labor theory of value and made the individuals' feelings of pleasures and pains the building blocks of his theory. Psychophysiology's mechanistic conception of the human mind allowed him to apply the methods of the natural sciences and, in particular, mathematics to the investigation of individual decision making as a calculus of pleasure and pain. The application of the calculus, in turn, permitted Jevons to focus on marginal changes in the amounts of utility or, what comes to the same thing in a psychophysiological framework, on the marginal units of pleasure the individual economic agent derives from commodities. These changes are not proportional to the increase in the amount of a commodity but are in fact decreasing. This principle of diminishing marginal utility enabled Jevons to derive the equimarginal principle according to which the individual allocates his resources so as to maximize his own pleasure or, as it were, utility. Methodologically, the economic theory of utility-maximizing behavior can hence be considered the "child of the marriage of utility with the technique of marginal increments and decrements, which itself led directly to the consideration of extremal problems" (Dobb 1973: 172).

As to the adoption of the Benthamite utility concept it deserves emphasis again that while Bentham's *Principles* first and foremost addressed the legislator who should build institutions to the advantage of all, Jevons' individualistic account of utility maximization was totally detached from any societal concerns. Here, the utility concept serves an explanatory function within demand theory. To accomplish that task, it referred to "subjective scales of valuation which were supposed to reside in the consumer's mind" (Endres 1999: 602). Thereby, pleasure or utility are considered as being quantities that provide "agents with a monotonic criterion by which to carry out the ordering of the alternative outcomes they face" (Warke 2000a: 20). Put differently, utility provided for an ordering principle, explaining how subjects generate their preference rankings (see Mandler 2001: 374). The maximization of pleasure, then, was regarded as the subjects' aim and motive for action. Henceforth, utility maximization in economics became more and more associated with the idea of individual rationality (see Cudd 1993: 106) and the problem an economic agent faces became framed as the problem of allocating his resources "in such a way that his well-being is enhanced to the greatest degree possible" (Colvin 1985: 9). The publication of *TPE* can thus be conceived as the hour of birth of the economic man, i.e., of the "discrete, self-contained, self-interested" individual of modern microeconomics (Colvin 1985: 5), aiming at the maximization of pleasure (see Little 1957: 10). Put differently, the *TPE* gave rise to the fundamental principle of modern economics that "economic behaviour is maximising behaviour subject to constraints" (Blaug 1997: 280).[42] On the whole, the marginal revolution profoundly changed the character of economics and, of pivotal concern for the present study, established a firm place for the utility concept and the notion of utility maximization within economic theory. The ordinal revolution of the 1930s, in turn, represents another "dramatic change in the conceptual framework of economics" and "restricted the concept of utility acceptable to economics" (Cooter/Rappoport 1984: 508, 507), as the following section demonstrates.

2.3 The ordinal revolution

2.3.1 The changing framework of economics in the 1930s: Lionel Robbins

A central figure in this second major upheaval in the history of economics in general and in utility theory in particular is Lionel Robbins (1898–1984). His *Essay on the Nature and Significance of Economic Science* was "one of the most cited, if not most read, books on the subject in the period 1932–60, [...] it influenced greatly economists' views about the nature of their discipline" (Corry 2008), and heralded the "overthrow of early neoclassical theory" (Mandler 1999: 7). The *Essay* can be regarded as seminal in at least three respects: first, Robbins stressed the decidedly positivist nature of economic science and postulated the removal of any value-laden assumptions from its realm. In doing so, he triggered a still-ongoing debate on the role of value judgments within economics. Second, and as a corollary of this methodological stance, Robbins (1935: 139) regarded the hedonic, cardinal utility concept of early neoclassicism as being based on "essentially normative" assumptions and argued for restricting economic theory to the analysis of observable, ordinal preference rankings. His considerations significantly contributed to the development of the modern theory of consumer choice theory and foreshowed the emergence of the new welfare economics. Third, Robbins proposed a new definition of economics in terms of scarcity, which abandoned any reference to a particular subject of the discipline and thus paved the way for the prospective expansion of the scope of economics. These closely entangled aspects are all relevant in the present context and will be examined in turn. Since they can only be grasped against the background of the intellectual climate at Robbins' time, though, a short consideration of logical positivism precedes the analysis.

Originally, the term logical positivism referred to the stance of a group of scientists, philosophers, and mathematicians who started meeting in the early

1920s and called themselves the Vienna Circle (see Ayer 1966: 3; Giocoli 2003: 28ff.). During the 1930s, the doctrine of logical positivism spread to England and considerably influenced both Anglo-American philosophy and the social sciences so that, after World War II, it had advanced to the "reigning orthodoxy in philosophy" (Mirowski 2006: 350).[43] Put in a nutshell, logical positivism aimed at developing criteria by means of which science could be distinguished from pseudo-science and metaphysics; i.e., they sought to solve the so-called demarcation problem (see Aslanbeigui 1990: 622). Thereby, the natural sciences were regarded as the epitome of science and served as the ideal for any kind of scientific endeavor (see Hands 2008). Logical positivism thus repudiated the view that there was any inherent difference between the natural and the social sciences (see Ayer 1966: 21). Against the background of this conviction the positivists argued that there were only two kinds of significant propositions: factual, empirical verifiable statements on the one hand and tautological, logically true sentences on the other (see Ayer 1966: 10). Any utterance not fitting into one of these categories was deemed nonsensical. This was especially true for ethical statements which became regarded as mere emotive expressions of feelings (see Ayer 1966: 22). According to emotivism, both "normative positions and simply value-laden ones (value judgments) are treated interchangeably as subjective expressions of attitude used persuasively to affect opinion and belief in a non-cognitive manner" (Davis 1990: 141). Consequently, all statements and concepts with an ethical or subjective "tinge" were deemed metaphysical and, hence, taken to be outside the scope of economic science (see Cooter/Rappoport 1984: 522). Soon, good economics became tantamount to positive economic theory and even though emotivism was soon rejected by philosophers as fundamentally misguided, it proved viable in economics (see Davis 1990: 141f.).

At first glance, this account of economics seems very similar to Jevons', who also aimed at the formulation of scientific laws in economics, advocated the ideal of physics, and believed that the same methods could be applied to the natural and the social sciences. This apparent similarity is only superficial, though, since between 1870 and 1930 the general conviction as to what counts as scientific and as empirical evidence had changed profoundly (see Hands 2010: 644). Whereas in Jevons' time, psychophysics with its "empirically-verified psychological laws" provided economics for a scientific basis (Bruni/Sugden 2007: 149), this foundation soon came under pressure, primarily due to theoretical developments within the discipline of psychology (see Coats 1976: 45f.). Especially the hedonic theory of motivation and "subjective and unscientific notions such as introspection" became discredited by professional psychologists and evidence derived from introspection was no longer regarded as *scientific* (Coats 1976: 48). Instead, psychology saw a trend toward more objectivism and focused increasingly on "the objective and measurable aspects of human behaviour" (ibid.).[44] Economists joined in the critique of hedonism as a theoretical basis for marginal utility analysis so that, by the early twentieth century, "denouncing hedonism had become a ritual exercise" (Mandler 1999: 115).[45] Concurrently, it became a vital issue what exactly the rejection of hedonism implied for economics (see Coats 1976: 47).

These two interrelated threads – the positivist image of science and the rejection of hedonism – lie at the core of Robbins' *Essay*. Referring to Max Weber, Robbins (1935: 91) stresses that if economics was to be a *positive* science, it needs to be *wertfrei*.[46] This means that although economists could investigate the valuations of individuals, they are not allowed to introduce their own evaluations into economic analyses. Economics, Robbins (1935: 147) claims, had to be neutral toward ends. In his view, the early neoclassical economists violated this very requirement for the following two reasons (see Robbins 1935: 136ff.). First, the concept of cardinal utility and the assumption of interpersonal comparability of pleasures are essentially value-laden and, as such, had no place in economic science. Second, while the marginalists claimed that their policy advice rests upon a scientific basis their proposition actually relied on empirically untestable assumptions (see Mandler 1999: 134).

The line of argument Robbins (ibid.) criticizes resembles a case made by Arthur C. Pigou (1877–1959) in *The Economics of Welfare*.[47] Pigou (1932: 5) adopted a decidedly pragmatic attitude as to the purpose of economics. In his view, the interest of the sciences of human society in general and of economics in particular is not the gain of knowledge for its own sake but rather the application of the results for social improvement: "It is not wonder, but rather the social enthusiasm which revolts from the sordidness of mean streets and the joylessness of withered lives, that is the beginning of economic science" (ibid.). Consequently, the goal of economics "is to make more easy practical measures to promote *welfare* – practical measures which statesmen may build upon the work of the economist" (Pigou 1932: 10).[48] Crucially, instead of focusing on the *wealth* of nations, Pigou introduced the term *welfare* (see Little 1957: 78f.). It deserves to be noted that it was only in the course of the marginal revolution that social welfare became a distinct issue in the first place. Before, there was no necessity to investigate the conditions for improving overall well-being, as Harris (1990: 369) points out:

> Most mid- and late-nineteenth-century makers of social policy simply assumed a high degree of coherence between private and public welfare and between social and economic laws. What was deemed rational for the individual was deemed to be rational for the community as a whole.[49]

The individualistic stance of neoclassical economics, however, caused a tension between the well-being of the individual and the common good (see Harris 1990: 397; Schabas 2007: 140).[50]

Accordingly, Pigou critically examined the classical theory of free competition and the question of how to augment societal welfare by means of governmental intervention (see Aslanbeigui 1990: 620). This approach obviously raises the question of what welfare consists of. As to welfare in general, Pigou merely lays down two "more or less dogmatic" presuppositions: the elements of welfare are states of consciousness and they are quantities, i.e., welfare can be regarded as being greater or less (see Pigou 1932: 11). These remarks are sufficient from his vantage point, because Pigou's interest is not with welfare in general. As such a broad focus would render the inquiry "impracticable," the subject of welfare economics has to be limited:

> In doing this we are naturally attracted towards that portion of the field in which the methods of science seem likely to work at best advantage. This they can clearly do when there is present something measurable, on which analytical machinery can get a firm grip. The one obvious instrument of measurement available in social life is money. Hence, the range of our inquiry becomes restricted to that part of social welfare that can be brought directly or indirectly into relation with the measuring-rod of money. This part of welfare may be called economic welfare.
>
> (Ibid.)

In order to assess economic welfare, Pigou (1932: 31) takes the "national dividend," i.e., the nation's aggregate real income as the "objective counterpart of economic welfare." On the basis of the law of the decreasing marginal utility of money, he deduces the following conclusion as the economic welfare:

> In considering this matter we must not forget that the economic welfare enjoyed by anybody in any period of time depends on the income that he consumes rather than on the income that he receives; and that, the richer a man is, the smaller proportion of his total income he is likely to consume, so that, if his total income is, say, twenty times as large as that of a poorer man, his consumed income may be only, say, five times as large. Nevertheless, it is evident that any transference of income from a relatively rich man to a relatively poor man of similar temperament, since it enables more intense wants to be satisfied at the expense of less intense wants, must increase the aggregate sum of satisfaction. The old 'law of diminishing utility' thus leads securely to the proposition: Any cause which increases the absolute share of real income in the hands of the poor, provided that it does not lead to a contraction in the size of the national dividend from any point of view, will, in general, increase economic welfare.
>
> (Pigou 1932: 89)

In effect, neoclassical welfare economics shifted the strictly individual notion of utility toward "an organic and metaphysical" comprehension of welfare (Harris 1990: 397).[51] Note that for Pigou, the conclusion that a redistribution of income from the rich to the poor follows "securely" from the law of decreasing marginal utility. This thread epitomizes the way Pigou (1932: 5) conceives of welfare economics in general, namely as *positive* science, dealing with what is and not with what ought to be.

Robbins (1935: 138f.) regards this welfare economic argument for a more equal distribution of wealth as "specious." In so far as it transfers the principle of diminishing marginal utility from the consideration of one and the same individual within consumer choice theory to society as a whole, the case relies on illegitimate premises:

> The theory of exchange assumes that I can compare the importance to me of bread at 6d. per loaf and 6d. spent on other alternatives presented by the opportunities of the market. [...] But it does not assume that, at any point, it is necessary to compare the satisfaction which I get from the spending of 6d. on bread with the satisfaction which the Baker gets by receiving it. That comparison is of an entirely different nature.
>
> (Ibid.)[52]

Not only does Pigou thereby presuppose the possibility of such interpersonal comparisons, he also assumes without further ado that different individuals derive equal satisfaction from a further unit of income, i.e., he adopts the premise of the identity of marginal utility functions. These assumptions, however, are neither tautological nor can they be tested empirically; there "is no means of testing the magnitude of A's satisfaction as compared with B's," as Robbins (1935: 140) puts it. Thus, interpersonal comparisons of utility are "essentially normative," begging a "great metaphysical question," and, hence, fall "outside the scope of any positive science" (Robbins 1935: 137, 139). To make it worse, Pigou claims that his conclusions derived from these untenable premises could be reached by positive analysis while, in fact, they are based on a value judgment (see Robbins 1938a: 639). In fact, the whole discipline of welfare economics does not meet the requirements for being considered a positive science because its very purpose, the aim of welfare maximization as such, is essentially normative (see Howson 2004: 432; Scarantino 2009: 453).[53]

This is not to say that Robbins sought to reject the possibility of interpersonal comparisons of satisfaction *per se* and neither did he aim at inhibiting economists from giving policy advice. Instead, he argues that if economic methods were to be applied, they indeed would have to be supplemented by normative considerations:

> Once it was recognized how completely neutral were the findings of economic science, it would surely leap to the eye how necessary it was, if these findings were to be applied to human improvement, that they should be supplemented by political philosophy.
>
> (Robbins 1938a: 639)[54]

The crucial point, however, is that economists cannot give normative advice *qua* being economists (see Scarantino 2009: 464). And yet, this reply was not satisfactory to Robbins' critics, as Scarantino (ibid.) points out, since economists had known already that "nobody prevented them from giving advice, but this was not the point. The profession wanted to be reassured about the possibility of transferring the authority of science on to policy advice."[55] Robbins' considerations thus have to be regarded as a postulate for a clear-cut separation between "judgment of fact" and "judgment of value," that is, for a clear delineation of the borders between economics and other, normative disciplines (Robbins 1938b: 345).[56]

While the rejection of interpersonal comparisons of pleasure presents a vital issue for welfare economics, Robbins claims that positive economics can get along without them very well. Since the basic idea of economic analysis is "the idea of relative valuations" (Robbins 1935: 94), all that is required for a complete theory of exchange is the empirically observable ordering of alternatives. To construct a theory of value, it only needs to be assumed that "individuals can arrange their preferences in an order, and in fact do so" (Robbins 1935: 78f.). In stark contrast to Jevons and Pigou, however, Robbins (1935: 138) carves out that economic analysis does not assume any *magnitudes* lying behind these orderings which could be measured and compared interpersonally and neither does the theory make any assumptions as to the reasons or motivations behind the rankings: "*Why* the human animal attaches particular values in this sense to particular things, is a question which we do not discuss" (Robbins 1935: 86).[57] This question could be investigated by psychologists, but as far as economics is concerned, individuals "can be pure egoists, pure altruists, pure ascetics, pure sensualists or – what is much more likely – mixed bundles of all these impulses" (Robbins 1935: 94). Therefore, it would be a "misapprehension" to think that economics is solely concerned with a "low type of conduct," considering men as "egoists or 'pleasure machines'" (Robbins 1935: 25, 94). The "hedonistic trimmings" of Jevons' theory and his followers notwithstanding, Robbins (1935: 85) maintains that the connection between economics and utilitarian psychology is in fact purely arbitrary.[58] This is not to say, however, that economics can get along without any psychological assumptions whatsoever.[59] On the contrary, Robbins (1935: 87f.) emphasizes that economics has to involve psychological elements if it wants to *understand* and *explain* economic phenomena, for it is questionable how one could make sense of "terms such as choice, indifference, preference, and the like" without any reference to inner experience, i.e., psychological processes.[60] Since the theory of demand deals with individual valuations, it cannot get along without introspective data so that Robbins (1935: 89) decidedly rejects "the queer cult" of behaviorism.[61]

Grounding economic analysis on individual preference rankings without making any assumptions on the subjects' reasons or motivations leads to the *Essay's* "most important achievement," its definition of economics (Giocoli 2003: 85). Rejecting the then prevailing materialist definition of economics as the study of the causes of material welfare,[62] Robbins (1935: 16) proposed the now famous definition in terms of scarcity: "Economics is the science which studies human behaviour as a relationship between ends and scarce means which have alternative uses." Accordingly, an economic problem is characterized by the following attributes:

> when time and the means for achieving ends are limited and capable of alternative application, and ends are capable of being distinguished in order of importance, then behaviour necessarily assumes the form of choice. Every act which involves time and scarce means for the achievement of one end involves the relinquishment of their use for the achievement of the other. It has an economic aspect.
>
> (Robbins 1935: 14)

Hence, "the central object of economic inquiry is the disposal of scarce goods" (Robbins 1934: 90).

Although all typical problems of economic theory, such as the "market price, the rate of interest, [and] the value of money" (ibid.) meet the mentioned conditions, the definition has a much broader scope. In fact, even a man on a desert island with abundant resources faces a multitude of economic problems each day in so far as he has to choose between spending his limited time with digging potatoes or talking to his parrot (see Robbins 1935: 10f.). Irrespective of what he does, he misses an alternative; his choice has an opportunity cost (see Robbins 1935: 25). Although there are some exceptions, such as the "choice" to breathe air, human choices usually meet the criteria enumerated (see Robbins 1934: 90, 1935: 14f.). It pays to stress that Robbins' definition of economics is analytical to the extent that it does not focus on a certain object or on a specific activity, but defines an economic problem in terms of a particular aspect of behavior, that is, "the form imposed by the influence of scarcity" (Robbins 1935: 17). In essence, an economic problem is an issue of making choices; thus, at the core of economics is the theory of choice (see Backhouse 2004: 239). Robbins' definition of economics thus paved the way for the conception of choices as trade-offs, which nowadays is deeply ingrained in the discipline and, as will become clear in Chapter 5, is at the bottom of the health economic attempts to solve CUA's fairness issue.

The long-term influence of this definition on the economic discipline cannot be overestimated, although the immediate reactions were largely negative, as Backhouse and Medema (2009a: 815) report: "Robbins' definition of economics was challenged from the start. In the journals it was frequently attacked, and it was hardly ever accepted without qualification."[63] This is especially interesting since Robbins himself did not claim any originality as to this definition and gives several references in a footnote (see Robbins 1935: 16). Also, he suggested that his characterization of economics merely summarized what economists generally agreed upon and how they have treated their subject ever since anyway (see Robbins 1934: 90). Yet, in keeping with Backhouse and Medema (2009a: 805, 810), there had been little trace of the scarcity definition in the leading textbooks before and the nature and methodology of economics was in fact very much contested at the time of the *Essay's* publication (see Coats 1976: 58; Morgan/Rutherford 1998: 6ff.). For several reasons, some of which will be spelled out below, Robbins' definition of economics did not become accepted in the discipline until the 1960s. Nonetheless, the *Essay* instantaneously triggered two developments in economic theory: for one thing, it gave rise to the so-called new welfare economics (see Scarantino 2009: 455). For another, Robbins' work influenced John Hicks' elaboration of ordinal consumer choice theory. While the new welfare economics will be considered in Chapter 3, the following section deals with the creation of modern consumer choice theory.

2.3.2 Modern consumer choice theory: Pareto, Hicks, and Samuelson

John R. Hicks' (1904–1989) contribution to ordinal consumer choice theory firmly relies on the work of Vilfredo Pareto (1848–1923). In 1906, in the *Manual of Political Economy,* he presented a crucial part of the ordinal revolution's conceptual framework so that his work can be considered "as the first important step towards contemporary choice theory" (Davis 2003: 28).[64] His most important contribution to positive economics consists of the demonstration that equilibrium analysis does not call for cardinal utility numbers, but can get along with ordinal preference orderings (see Giocoli 2003: 67f.). Pareto (1927: 113) claims:

> Thanks to the use of mathematics, this entire theory [...] rests on no more than a fact of experience, that is, on the determination of the quantities of goods which constitute combinations between which the individual is indifferent. The theory of economic science thus acquires the rigor of rational mechanics. It deduces its results from experience, without bringing in any metaphysical entity.

The combinations of goods between which an individual is indifferent can be represented geometrically by means of indifference curves (see Figure 2.1).[65]

Pareto adopts this tool from Edgeworth, but while Edgeworth started his analysis with utility functions and derived indifference curves, Pareto (1927: 119) uses the latter as starting point: "I consider the indifference curves as given, and deduce from them all that is necessary for the theory of equilibrium, without resorting to ophelimity." The term ophelimity requires a short clarification. Pareto (1927: 110f.) realized that at the end of the nineteenth century, the economic use of the word utility differed significantly from the notion's meaning in the vernacular. In order to avoid misunderstandings, he proposed a more sophisticated terminology: whereas the term utility should refer to the ordinary sense of

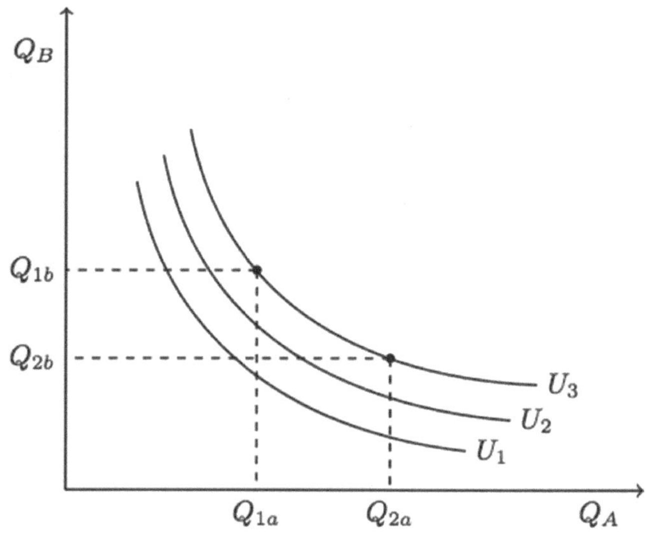

Figure 2.1 Indifference curves.

usefulness, his neologism "ophelimity" was meant to denote the economic meaning of utility.[66] Something is useful in the former sense if it is "conducive to the development and prosperity of the individual, a people, or a human race" (Pareto quoted in Cooter/Rappoport 1984: 515). Ophelimity, by contrast, designates the "capacity to satisfy desire," irrespective of what the desire consists of (ibid.). To give an example, for a sick child bitter medicine has utility but no ophelimity since it is useful but the child does not desire to take it (see ibid.). The difference can hence be described as one between objective needs or utility in the colloquial sense on the one hand and subjective desires on the other (see Cooter/Rappoport 1984: 515f.).

The crucial aspect about Pareto's account is that he takes the individuals' preferences as to the combinations of goods embodied in the indifference curves as primitives of the theory. In doing so, he replaced "the language of preferences for that of utility" (Giocoli 2003: 90). Once indifference curves are given, they can be assigned an index, which, according to Pareto (1927: 119), has to satisfy the following two conditions: first, combinations of goods between which the individual is indifferent must be given the same index and, second, if one combination of goods is preferred to the other, the former must get a higher index. Consequently, given the assumption that an individual prefers combinations with more of both goods to combinations with less of both goods, combinations represented by higher indifference curves must be assigned a higher index: "Thus we have the indices of ophelimity, or of the *pleasure* which an individual *feels* when he *enjoys* a combination which corresponds to a given index" (ibid.).[67] Note that as long as the stated requirements are met, the numbers attached to the curves are wholly arbitrary so that it is not possible to derive one specific utility function from the scale of preferences (see Hicks/Allen 1934: 52; Hicks 1946: 17).

In effect, Pareto established that an ordinal utility concept is sufficient for demand theory. The accentuated, hedonic vocabulary in the former quote suggests, however, that he still considered ophelimity to be a quantity of pleasure, albeit not a cardinally measurable one. At this point, some conceptual clarifications as to the utility concept are required, which provide an essential background for the following analysis. A basic differentiation already invoked at several points of this study is the difference between a cardinal measurement scale and an ordinal measurement scale. While the former allows for the comparison of the differences between the assigned numbers, the latter presents a mere ordering of different items, while the differences between the assigned numbers are arbitrary.[68] This is an issue of measurability. According to Giocoli (2003: 94), measurability means that "it is possible to associate each quantity with a real number, unique up to the choice of the unit of measure." That being said, it is perfectly possible to claim that utility is some kind of quantity, i.e., some "stuff of such a kind that various lumps of it are capable indeed of being set out in an order of magnitude," but that it is not measurable (Robertson 1954: 17). The difference between quantification and measurement is tantamount to the difference between being technically measurable and being actually measurable (see Robertson 1954: 25). Cardinality and ordinality, then, describe the inner capacity of agents to make cardinal or ordinal comparisons of something, but do not say anything about measurability (see Mandler 1999: 111).

The question of what this something consists of is yet another issue. The quantity can be conceived of in hedonic terms so that a cardinally measurable, hedonic utility concept would indicate the intensity of a feeling and allows for "measuring one gain or loss in well-being [in terms of pleasure] relative to another" (Mandler 1999: 82), whereas an ordinal hedonic utility concept only indicates more or less pleasure. Despite their logical independence, psychologically, "cardinalism and hedonism are natural partners," as Mandler (1999: 84) points out. This is because "hedonism provides the most common psychological justification for cardinality; and in order to be plausible, cardinality requires some account of how agents make judgments of preference intensity" (ibid.). But even in the case of ordinal utilities, it is actually hard to come up with a quantity behind the preference rankings *other* than certain sensations. Alternatively, the assumption of the existence of an underlying quantity can be dropped altogether and this is in fact what happens in the course of the formalist revolution. Suffice it to carve out at this point that the aspects of the *quantitative* nature of utility, the underlying *psychology*, and the *measurability* of utilities are logically independent from each other. As will become clear in the following, several combinations of these elements have been proposed throughout the history of economics.

Against the background of these conceptual remarks, two different interpretations of Pareto's contribution can be discerned in the literature, both of which exerted a major influence on the discipline of economics and its utility concept. According to the first, which was already appealed to above, Pareto regarded utility as a quantity of pleasure, albeit a cardinally immeasurable one. Since it considers the demonstration that demand theory can be rebuilt with ordinal instead of cardinal utility functions Pareto's major innovation, this reading can be dubbed the *ordinal interpretation* of Pareto (see Giocoli 2003: 91).[69] And yet, in view of the passage quoted earlier, in which Pareto (1927: 113) claims to base his theory solely on experience without introducing "any metaphysical entity," it seems as if he wanted to purge the theory from any reference to psychological assumptions whatsoever (see Bruni/Sugden 2007: 155). Pursuant to this second *behaviorist reading*, Pareto "actually sought to abandon every reference to utility and embrace in its place a proto-behaviorist approach" (Giocoli 2003: 91). It can thus be argued with Giocoli (ibid.) that Pareto's work laid the foundation for two subsequent major developments in economic theory: while the ordinal interpretation led to ordinal consumer choice theory, the behaviorist reading triggered revealed preference theory (RPT) (see Bruni/Guala 2001: 23ff.). The question of which reading corresponds to Pareto's actual intention is contested in the literature (see Bruni/Guala 2001: 32f.; Giocoli 2003: 67ff.; Bruni/Sugden 2007: 154). That being said, it is not decisive for the present study what Pareto actually meant to say, anyway. More interesting is how he was interpreted and how these interpretations shaped the subsequent development of economic theory. In the following, the utility concepts explicitly endorsed and actually used within both accounts will be investigated. In doing so, it will turn out that although ordinalism and behaviorism seek to eschew psychological assumptions in general and hedonist premises in particular from consumer choice theory, their efforts remain ultimately unsuccessful.

Pareto's ideas became resurrected and popularized by John R. Hicks and Roy G. D. Allen (see Bruni/Guala 2001: 24). As to their interpretation of Pareto, the opening passage of Hicks and Allen's (1934: 52) seminal paper "A Reconsideration of the Theory of Value" hints toward the ordinal interpretation:

> Of all Pareto's contributions, there is probably none that exceeds in importance his demonstration of the *immeasurability of utility*. To most earlier writers [...] utility had been a quantity theoretically measurable; that is to say, a *quantity* which would be *measurable* if we had enough facts. Pareto definitely abandoned this, and replaced the concept of utility by the concept of a scale of preferences.[70]

The authors explicitly aim at completing what Pareto, in their view, has left unfulfilled, that is, the reformulation of demand theory in terms of ordinal utility theory (see Backhouse 2003: 311f.); or more precisely, the investigation "of what adjustments in the statements of the marginal theory of value are made necessary by Pareto's discovery" (Hicks/Allen 1934: 54). And yet, a closer look at the italicized terms in the quoted passage reveals that the aim of the paper is not stated unambiguously because, as illustrated above, the questions of whether utility is *measurable* and of whether it is a *quantity* are two distinct issues. It seems that Hicks and Allen are actually tackling the issue of measurability, presumably taking for granted that a cardinal, psychologically charged utility concept needed to be abandoned anyway (see Giocoli 2003: 92). Accordingly, they continue by specifying their goal as the investigation of which assumptions of demand theory "are affected by the immeasurability of utility" in order to establish "a theory of value in which all concepts that pretend to quantitative exactitude, can all be rigidly and exactly defined" (Hicks/Allen 1934: 55).

In *Value and Capital,* Hicks (1946: 91) tacitly shifts the focus of inquiry and describes his aim as follows: "We have now to undertake a purge, rejecting all concepts which are tainted by quantitative utility." He seeks to revise Marshall's demand theory and base it solely on the assumption of a scale of preference so that given wants no longer have to be understood as "a given intensity of desire" but could be defined in terms of "a given scale of preferences" instead (Hicks 1946: 18). He states that

> we need only suppose that the consumer has a preference for one collection of goods rather than another, not that there is ever any sense in saying that he desires the one collection 5 per cent more than the other, or anything like that.
>
> (Ibid.)

Although in this quote he only rejects a cardinal utility concept, Hicks continues by asserting that a "quantitative concept of utility is not necessary in order to explain market phenomena" (ibid.). For the sake of simplicity, it should hence be dispensed with altogether. Yet, the intention to obliterate any quantitative understanding of utility or preferences is unnecessarily ambitious from the vantage point of an ordinalist. In fact, Hicks seems to reject not only a cardinal utility concept, but the idea that preferences relate to any quantity whatsoever. If this is true, he would adopt a behaviorist reading of Pareto. Mandler (1999: 84) indeed interprets Hicks in this vein as postulating that "consumer theory should not use cardinality or other nonordinal properties as theoretical primitives" since the implied "psychological theorizing going behind preference is an unnecessary excursion outside the domain of economic analysis." Although Hicks did not explicitly express the intention to deliver the theory of demand from any definite psychological assumptions (see Giocoli 2003: 97), the following quote strengthens this hypothesis:

> What I mean by action according to a scale of preference is the following. The ideal consumer [...] chooses that alternative, out of the various alternatives open to him, which he most prefers, or ranks most highly. In one set of market conditions, he makes one choice, in others other choices; but they must always express the same ordering, and must therefore be consistent with one another.
>
> (Hicks 1959: 17)

Here, Hicks focuses on well-behaved, consistent preferences (see Mandler 1999: 84, 105). In doing so, he does not deny the possibility that the preference rankings could rely on hedonism, though. By contrast, Hicks (1946: 18) explicitly points out that although his account of demand theory allows for an interpretation in terms of a quantitative measure of utility and even in terms of utilitarianism, it does not presuppose such a reading:

> Now of course this does not mean that if any one has any other ground for supposing that there exists some suitable quantitative measure of utility, or satisfaction, or desiredness, there is anything in the above argument to set against it. If one is a utilitarian in philosophy, one has a perfect right to be a utilitarian in one's economics. But if one is not (and few people are utilitarians nowadays), one also has the right to an economics free of utilitarian assumptions.

Up to now, it was carved out that it does not become unambiguously clear what exactly Hicks and Allen (1934) and Hicks (1946) want to purge Marshallian demand theory of. The following consideration of the marginal rate of substitution (MRS) reveals that they do not succeed in dismissing any quantitative measures from demand theory anyway. Hicks and Allen (1934: 55) propose the MRS as a substitute for the immeasurable marginal rate of utility and define it as follows:

> The marginal rate of substitution of any good Y for any other good X is defined as the quantity of good Y which would just *compensate* him [the consumer] for the loss of a marginal unit of X. If he got less than this quantity of Y, he would be *worse off* than before the substitution took place; if he got more he would be *better off*.[71]

Graphically, the MRS is represented by the indifference curve's slope. Two assumptions as to the form of the MRS are worth delineating (see Giocoli 2003: 95). For one thing, Hicks and Allen (1934: 55) assume that the MRS is positive in all points, which amounts to the normative assumption that the consumer always prefers more goods to less. This premise of insatiable wants is indeed a central assumption of economic theory and is sometimes even regarded as the defining characteristic of an economic good:

> By definition, a larger collection of goods gives more satisfaction than a smaller collection [...]. This means that if a man *likes* 7 apples *better* than 8 apples then for him an apple cannot be called a good. The abstract concept 'good' can only be applied to things in the real world if it is true that more things *give more satisfaction* than fewer things.
>
> (Little 1957: 16)[72]

Note, however, that this assumption only holds if the goods in question can be stockpiled because if an economic agent knows that he can only consume seven apples until they rot, preferring seven to eight apples would barely imply that he does not consider an apple a good. Second, Hicks and Allen (1934: 57) assume that "the more we substitute *Y* for *X*, the greater will be the marginal rate of substitution of *Y* for *X*." This notion of an increasing MRS replaces the principle of diminishing marginal utility.[73] It is based on the normative premise that individuals prefer mixed bundles of goods to bundles only containing one of the two goods. Reasonable as this postulation might seem at first glance, it can only be justified with reference to the principle of diminishing marginal utility (see Blaug 1997: 330; Quiggin 1999: 592). To quote Giocoli (2003: 96), it arguably

> concealed a lasting faith in the validity of the old utilitarian argument according to which, in order to increase his/her own *satisfaction*, an agent must be more willing to exchange one good for another the more he/she has of the first good relative to the second.[74]

Apparently, these conjectures not only refer to "a non-measurable notion of preference or satisfaction" (Giocoli 2003: 95), but also make substantial demands as to the nature of the individuals' preferences, though. It is particularly striking that even in the very definition of the MRS quoted above, Hicks and Allen are referring to mental states when they regard the individual as being compensated, better-off or worse-off. Yet, it remains entirely unclear how these notions shall be understood without reference to a hedonic quantitative entity such as pleasure or satisfaction at all (see ibid.). The same problem even applies to the concept of indifference. To quote Blaug (1997: 332):

> if we are going to dismiss introspective evidence, the notion of indifference is as objectionable as the concept of preference intensity. No single act of choice on the part of the consumer can prove his indifference between two situations. Unless we are going to give indifference a statistical meaning – the individual does not choose A over B more frequently than he chooses B over A in a large number of observations – we must dismiss the concept of indifference with the same behaviourist argument we used against preference intensity.[75]

It thus seems safe to conclude that the ordinal account of utility, which was "spread among economists" by Hicks and Allen (1934) and Hicks (1946), rejects cardinal measurability but is nevertheless based on a quantitative notion of utility (see Bruni/Guala 2001: 24; Giocoli 2003: 95). The authors are still referring to psychological states and explain consumer behavior by means of associating it with processes in his mind (see Robertson 1954: 19). Such an "introspective ordinalism" (Blaug 1980: 162) still underlies modern microeconomics and, in particular, consumer choice theory. Little (1957: 15), for instance, states with regard to the indifference curve analysis of rational consumer's behavior:

> The assumption that the individual tries to maximize his satisfaction is retained. But 'maximizing satisfaction' no longer means 'achieving the greatest sum total of satisfaction' but rather 'achieving the highest level of satisfaction' Satisfaction is like a hill; one can say that one is higher up, or lower down, or at the same height.

The MRS, then, represents "the rate at which X can be substituted for Y remaining on the same level of satisfaction" (Little 1957: 18). Hicks' consideration of utility and demand theory heralded the beginning of modern consumer choice theory and still provides the latter's backbone in mainstream microeconomic textbooks (see Bruni/Guala 2001; Giocoli 2003: 98; Black 2008; Hands 2010: 636).[76] Henceforth, the consumer has been supposed to be able to rank all available commodity bundles and choose the most preferred outcome (see Mirowski/Hands 2006b). Nevertheless, utility is usually still regarded as a psychological quantity: "Utility is the subjective *satisfaction* of the household" (Boadway/Bruce 1984: 39).[77]

Hicks' and Allen's failure to succeed in purging the theory of utility of all its immeasurable hedonic ingredients was clearly realized by Paul Samuelson, who presented his revealed preference theory (RPT) as an attempt to restrict economic analysis to "operationally meaningful theorems," i.e., to hypotheses "about empirical data which could conceivably be refuted, if only under ideal conditions" (Samuelson 1947: 3, 4).[78] The only viable data on which to erect demand theory were taken to be observable choices of individuals (see Samuelson 1938: 71).[79] In effect, Samuelson aimed at formulating a completely behaviorist account without any reference to psychological assumptions or any other "'suspect' entities"

(Bruni/Guala 2001: 25). RPT can thus be regarded as the most far-reaching attempt to amend economic theory according to the positivist criteria for science and as "the culmination of the neoclassical economists' 45-year-long escape from psychology" (Giocoli 2003: 99).[80]

RPT was chiefly elaborated in two articles. In the paper "A Note on the Pure Theory of Consumer's Behaviour," Samuelson (1938) seeks to derive the results of Hicksian ordinal utility theory without bearing on any nonobservable notions (see Blaug 1980: 167). He argues that the behavior of marginal utilities and indifference relations could no more be observed than the behavior of utility (see Samuelson 1938: 61). In making use of the former concepts, however, modern economic analysis still "shows vestigial traces of the utility concept" (ibid.). To quote Hands (2010: 636): "For Samuelson in 1939, even though ordinal utility theory was a step in the right direction, it was still a *utility* theory." His behaviorist account therefore requires starting "anew in a direct attack upon the problem, dropping off the last vestiges of the utility analysis" (Samuelson 1938: 62). Samuelson showed that the consistency of observable choices is enough to infer almost all implications of demand theory. If an agent's choices are consistent, i.e., satisfy the so-called weak axiom of revealed preferences, "then one can impute to the agent a 'preference' relation R that is complete and transitive and that implies the agent's choice" (Hausman 2012: 26).[81] In effect, he derived the same conclusions as Hicks had without making use of assumptions on individual psychology or mental phenomena. In this respect, as Hands (2010: 640) points out, Samuelson's account presented a "distinct break" with former theories of consumer choice. Indeed, his paper does not even mention the notion "revealed preference theory" because there is nothing to be revealed in the first place (see Giocoli 2003: 104). This point deserves emphasis. Note that within RPT, the preference concept has no meaning of its own, but is *defined* in terms of choices. Consequently, one cannot have preferences over alternatives between which one is not actually facing a choice (see Hausman 2012: 27). This position needs to be thoroughly distinguished from the practice of inferring *underlying* preferences from observed choices since this procedure assumes the existence of preferences independent of overt choices (see Hausman 2012: 24).[82]

And yet, as already indicated earlier, it is highly questionable whether all assumptions on nonobservable phenomena can be expelled from consumer choice theory, for even to speak of "choices" instead of referring to mere "behavior" already implies reference to an inner state (see Hands 2010: 643).[83] Beyond that, the conceptual equation of preference with choice has been convincingly criticized as being implausible (see Hausman/McPherson 2006: 48).[84] In particular, it is inappropriate for what economists are actually up to, because in order "to predict, explain or give advice economists must assign preferences to states of affairs that are not objects of choice" (Hausman 2013: 220). Indeed, in the paper "Consumption Theory in Terms of Revealed Preferences," Samuelson (1948) himself seems to have abandoned the goal of reducing demand theory to observable phenomena (see Blaug 1980: 167; Mirowski 1989: 363ff.; Mirowski/Hands 1998: 285f.; Davis 2003: 30; Giocoli 2003: 103ff.; Hands 2010: 640f.)

Apparently, he now assumes that there in fact *is* – or at least might be – a preference pattern *revealed* by observable choices, as the introductory passage shows:

> By comparing costs of different combinations of goods at different relative price situations, we can infer whether a given batch of goods is preferred to another batch; the individual guinea-pig, by market behaviour, reveals his preference pattern – if there is such a consistent pattern.
>
> (Samuelson 1948: 149)

Recall that the notion of individuals revealing their preference patterns by choices was crucial to Hicks' ordinal utility theory (see Hicks 1959: 16f.; Mongin/D'Aspremont 1999: 386). Since Samuelson now uses RPT to derive indifference maps from observed choices, he tacitly acknowledges ordinal utility theory as the leading paradigm (see Blaug 1980: 167; Mirowski 1989: 364). As a corollary, "the behaviorist idiom disappears, and the (now) standard mentalist language of preference, choice, and ordinal utility theory returns with a vengeance" (Mirowski/Hands 1998: 286). It was demonstrated eventually that the ordinal utility approach to consumer choice theory and RPT are logically and observationally equivalent – a result simultaneously marking "the triumph and the defeat of RPT" (Giocoli 2003: 105).[85] Somewhat paradoxically, "revealed preference theory actually ended up bolstering the scientific credentials of the (ordinal) utility theory that it had originally been designed to replace" (Hands 2010: 643).[86]

Its ultimate failure notwithstanding, the influence Samuelson's RPT exerted on economics cannot be overestimated (see Giocoli 2003: 106). Beside the fact that RPT is still part of standard textbooks on microeconomics (see Black 2008), it especially buttressed the "informal behaviorism" of the economic discipline and still serves to support its scientific image (Mandler 1999: 88).[87] This is because the mere possibility of starting with the actual observation of consumer's choices instead of their preferences "confers a flavor of scientific respectability on the whole argument," as Giocoli (2003: 106) surmises. It seems as if economics is still "under the spell" of the "elegant concept" of revealed preferences (Güth/Kliemt 2013: 3).[88] Moreover, RPT reinforced the economists' focus on consequences since by avoiding any theorizing going beyond mere observation, it gives up the aim of explaining *why* a consumer chooses a certain commodity bundle (see Giocoli 2003: 103, 110). By describing choices in purely formal terms, the individual economic agent was replaced by an abstract "depersonalized 'rational economic agent'" and this "model person" was used to "explore not the reasons for action, but the consequences of acting rationally, as defined by those economics, in a special situation" (Morgan 2003: 299).[89] Note that the abandonment of any explanatory power of demand theory was not an unintended side-effect of RPT, but followed straightforwardly from the positivist methodology endorsed by Samuelson (see Mirowski/Hands 1998: 282). For if a theory is "to be explanatory and informative, it must go beyond redescription of what is to be explained" (Wong 1973: 318). If, on the other hand, the assumptions of a theory may not go beyond those that can be deduced from observable choices, *explanans* and *explanandum* are necessarily equivalent. Within this framework, a theory should thus function as "a tool for the organization of a system of observations" and was not supposed to explain these observations (Giocoli 2003: 103). According to Backhouse (2003: 314), the majority of economists in the 1930s and 1940s did bite the bullet and generally agreed on the fact that "utility functions must be ordinal, describing rather than explaining choice."[90]

All in all, the contributions of Pareto, Robbins, Hicks, and Samuelson changed the nature and scope of economics to a major extent.[91] The rejection of hedonism as a psychological foundation for demand theory and the endorsement of ordinal instead of cardinal utility measures still constitute central theoretical commitments of modern demand theory (see Backhouse 2003: 314; Mirowski/Hands 2006: 2f.). In the course of the ordinal revolution, the economic theory of choice changed to such an extent that its scope became significantly broader, as Hicks and Allen (1934: 54) themselves clearly realized: "By transforming the subjective theory of value into a general logic of choice, they [the methodological implications of the ordinal conception of utility] extend its applicability over wide fields of human conduct."[92] Although their contribution can thus be regarded as marking the "technical turn" in utility theory (Mongin/D'Aspremont 1999: 385),[93] the complete axiomatization of utility theory did not take place until the late 1950s, as the following section illustrates.

2.4 The formalist revolution and rational choice theory

2.4.1 The axiomatization of economics in the 1950s: background

The third "revolution" in utility theory was again accompanied by a profound change in the character of economics. At the beginning of the twentieth century, the scientific ideal of the natural sciences in general and physics in particular became ever more replaced by the ideal of formal mathematics (see Giocoli 2003: 109, 206). From the 1920s on, there was a tremendous rise of the use of formal and mathematical methods in economics and in the 1960s, economics had already turned into a "predominantly mathematical discipline" (Backhouse 2010: 101). To give an example, the number of articles using some type of mathematics increased from zero in 1920 to almost 80 percent in 1960 (see Backhouse 1998a: 92f.).[94] This development certainly does not allow for any one-dimensional explanation. Still, for illustrative reasons, some catalyzing factors influencing the fundamental change of the image of economics will be sketched in the following.

The changing character of economics needs to be considered against the background of World War II and the Cold War. First, economists working for the government during World War II were not only engaged in planning the economy but worked on all kind of issues related to the war effort (see Morgan/Rutherford 1998: 13; Backhouse 2010: 101f.). They were "employed as general problem solvers, working alongside [...] mathematicians, physicists and engineers" (Backhouse 2010: 102). Focusing on problems of resource allocation, this "interdisciplinary environment" contributed to the development and application of mathematical methods (ibid.; see Backhouse 2008b). As mathematical techniques had proven helpful during the war, mathematically oriented research continued to be funded afterwards (see Amadae 2003: 158).[95] A second reason for the formalization of economics and, in fact, of the social sciences more generally, presumably lies in the need for "depoliticizing research by translating contentious social debates into the 'objective' language of mathematics" which arose in the intellectual climate of the McCarthy era (1947–1956) (Amadae 2003: 158).[96] To this respect, Backhouse (2010: 137f.) observes:

> Anti-communist hysteria in the late 1940s and early 1950s led to the charge that communism was being freely used to undermine any ideas that might be linked with planning. Many economists, including Paul Samuelson, were attacked for their views, sometimes in very strong terms. In such an environment, as Samuelson has admitted, it could be invaluable to present one's work as scientific, and the more technical, the better.

A third transmission belt by means of which World War II and the Cold War bolstered the mathematization of economics is education. After World War II, several factors triggered high public investments in education and especially in the discipline of mathematics (see Weintraub 2002: 247f.), which were only in part directly related to the war. First, the "baby boomers" happened to arrive at the universities, which, therefore, needed to enlarge their general capacities. Second, the generation of the parents who had seen the Great Depression now lived in relative prosperity and encouraged their children to seek college degrees. Third, in 1944 the *Servicemen's Readjustments Act* granted financial support for those ex-servicemen who wanted to continue their education and receive a college degree (see Backhouse 2008b). This Act led to an enormous increase of students, especially in economics, and, consequently, a further extension of the university system (see ibid.). Finally, the Sputnik-shock in 1957 exerted a major influence as well: fearing to lag behind the Soviet Union in this respect, the US government invested heavily in education and research in the areas of science and mathematics (see Weintraub 2002: 247f.; Amadae 2003: 158).

To grasp the importance of this increased interest in mathematics for the history of economics it deserves notice that at the beginning of the twentieth century, the discipline of mathematics itself underwent a profound change. This transformation especially emanated from the so-called Bourbaki group. Nikolas Bourbaki was the pseudonym under which, from the 1930s on, a group of French mathematicians set out to write an up-to-date mathematical textbook and came to influence the discipline to a major extent (see Weintraub 2002: 104; Giocoli 2003: 26). In the present context, the Bourbaki group's most important characteristic is its adoption of a decidedly formal attitude and the conception of mathematics as an axiomatic system, i.e., an "autonomous abstract subject, with no need of any input from the real world" (Lax quoted in Weintraub 2002: 102). Whereas the classical approach to axiomatization adhered to the aim of capturing the "true mathematical structure contained in the empirical phenomena," the Bourbaki group abandoned this goal, cut any necessary link between axioms and reality, and emphasized formal features of axiomatic systems – such as consistency and completeness – at the expense of their content (Giocoli 2003: 26, 15f.). The actual application of a mathematical model was not considered as being the mathematician's business (see Giocoli 2003: 16). Therefore, Bourbakism is usually regarded as embodying the most extreme version of mathematical formalism (see Weintraub 2002: 103; Giocoli 2003: 14). Coming back to the expansion of academic education during the Cold War in the US, the students of that generation "were America's first fully Bourbakist generation of mathematics students, thoroughly inculcated with the ideals of Bourbaki mathematics, in love with structure, avoidant of applications" (Weintraub 2002: 252).

As to the influence of Bourbakism on economics, the French mathematician Gerard Debreu (1921–2004), who was trained by a member of the Bourbaki group, and his work at the Cowles Commission are of particular significance (see Vilks 1998: 30; Giocoli 2003: 124).[97] In the light of the economists' inability to forecast the happenings at the stock market, the businessman Alfred Cowles established the Cowles Commission in 1932 in order to foster research on improved economic techniques (see Mirowski/Hands 1998: 274, 276; Backhouse 2010: 102). While, initially, it had been occupied with practical inquiries – such as the study of financial assets, government policy, and the development of econometrics – it went through a phase of reorientation in the 1940s and became ever more engaged with mathematical methods (see Mirowski/Hands 1998: 274ff.; Weintraub 2002: 118). The Commission increasingly gathered "a dazzling array of mathematical talent [...] precisely in order to infuse economics with a double shot of rigor" (Mirowski 1991: 238) and by the late 1940s had become "the main focus for mathematical economics" in the US (Backhouse 2003: 320).[98] After Debreu had joined the Commission in 1950, Bourbakism rapidly advanced to its "house doctrine" (Weintraub 2002: 119) and it became the "stronghold of Bourbakism in US economics" (Giocoli 2003: 373).[99]

With the Commission's move from Chicago to Yale in 1955, Bourbakism spread to the major American economics departments (see Weintraub 2002: 119). Just as mathematics was regarded as an abstract system, disconnected from the real world, so became economics. Crucially, it was no longer the economists' aim to uncover "true descriptions of the economic world," but to construct consistent axiomatic theories instead (see Morgan/Rutherford 1998b: 19).[100] This development is part of what Blaug (2003: 396) calls the "formalist revolution" in economics, which, according to him, was characterized

> by extreme 'formalism' – not just a preference, but an absolute preference for the form of an economic argument over its content – which frequently (but not necessarily) implies reliance on mathematical modeling and whose ultimate objective is [...] the complete axiomatization of economics.[101]

As a consequence, arguments or hypotheses which could not be couched in the mathematical language of general equilibrium theory were neglected and no longer regarded as belonging to the core of economics (see Backhouse 2003: 321).[102] It can be concluded with Weintraub (2002: 255) that by the late 1950s, economics had profoundly "changed its character, its language, [and] its way of representing its own concerns."[103]

2.4.2 The representation theorems and expected utility theory

Coming back to the history of the utility concept, the influence of mathematical formalism on economics is epitomized in Debreu's *Theory of Value* (1959) (see Weintraub/Mirowski 1994: 257; Vilks 1998: 30). The author himself leaves no doubt as to his intellectual credentials and his intentions right from the start:

> The theory of value is treated here with the standards of rigor of the contemporary school of mathematics. [...] Allegiance to rigor dictates the axiomatic form of the analysis where the theory, in the strict sense, is logically entirely disconnected from its interpretations.
>
> (Debreu 1959: x)

While the theory belongs to mathematics proper, its interpretation serves to connect the theory "to economic intuition" (Vilks 1998: 30).[104] This account implies as to demand theory that its primary aim is neither the explanation of behavior, nor the latter's formal description. In fact, it can be said that "behavior" or the "individual" no longer play any role in the formulation of the theory at all; these concepts only enter the equation when it comes to the theory's interpretation. Within the realm of theory, economic agents are reduced to mathematical relations or, more precisely, to a "binary relation which is assumed to satisfy the properties of completeness and transitivity" (Giocoli 2003: 121; see Debreu 1959: 50ff.). Note that Debreu's account goes further than Hicks and Allen's (1934) approach. Although they shifted the focus from a hedonic interpretation of cardinal utility measures to ordinal utility based on preferences, Hicks and Allen still took utility functions as point of origin in their mathematical characterization of ordinal preferences. According to Mandler (1999: 80), this is because utility functions had simply been "too mathematically useful to be sacrificed." Yet, this endeavor not only made the account mathematically "clumsy" and "awkward," but was also problematic for the following reasons:

> In terms of generality, beginning with utility functions reverses the advantages and liabilities of the indifference curve approach. Preferences need not be differentiable, but since a utility function assigns a real number to each consumption bundle, and numbers are transitively ordered, the assumption of transitivity is preordained. More embarrassingly, taking utility functions as primitive [...] ill suits a theory supposedly eschewing utility as a foundational entity.
>
> (Ibid.)

These difficulties were solved by Debreu (1959: 55ff.) who placed all restrictions "directly on binary preference relations" (Mandler 1999: 81) and demonstrated that if preference orderings meet the requirements of completeness, transitivity, reflexivity, and continuity, they can be represented by a class of continuous mathematical utility functions. These functions assign numbers to the alternatives such that preferred options receive higher numbers and indifferent options are given the same number.[105] By means of this ordinal representation theorem, Debreu axiomatized Hicks' ordinal utility theory, enabling economists to develop their preference theories mathematically. Utility "became an attribute of preferences rather than a mathematical or psychological presupposition" (Mandler 1999: 82). Debreu thus finally put the nail into the coffin of the hedonic conception of utility and, in doing so, reduced consumer choice theory to "nothing but an economic application of the logical theory of ordering" (Hicks 1959: 19).[106]

Though Debreu did not use the term rationality in the *Theory of Value* at all, economists henceforth came to define a rational agent as one whose preferences are complete and transitive (see Giocoli 2003: 120). An axiomatic account of human rationality was additionally catalyzed by two authors working in a different context, namely John von Neumann (1903–1957) and Oskar Morgenstern (1902–1977) (cited here as VNM) (see Amadae 2003: 6). Von Neumann – a mathematical physician from Hungary and the "intellectual engine of the couple" (Giocoli 2003: 215) – was very much influenced by the mathematician David Hilbert (see Giocoli 2003: 216; Thompson 2008). Although Hilbert endorsed an axiomatic approach to mathematics, his formalism was of a very different kind than the one advocated by the Bourbaki group. He decidedly viewed axiomatic systems as tools and stressed that any theory needs to contain intuitive conceptions and insights (see Giocoli 2003: 18f.). After immigrating into the US in 1930, von Neumann became heavily engaged in work on military matters during World War II so that by 1955, he had advanced to "one of the most powerful scientific men in the United States (Mirowski 1991: 230).[107] His involvement in work related to the war is noteworthy in the present context because it coincided with the evolvement of the *Theory of Games and Economic Behavior* and is largely responsible for the monograph's success (see Mirowski 1991: 231).

Even though the *Theory of Games* explicitly addressed economists (see VNM 1953: 1), the discipline did not receive the work with immediate enthusiasm.[108] Due to von Neumann's engagement in the war and, concomitantly, his prestige and influence, game theory soon found a home in the context of work related to the Cold War, especially at RAND (see Mirowski 1991: 240). Game theory seemed especially apt for the strategic decisions associated with the war, as Amadae (2003: 7) carves out:

> There was as yet no standard operating procedure for atomic weapons strategy, and over the next several years the new science of decisionmaking provided by game theory proved to be well suited to the unprecedented bipolar nuclear standoff between the Unites [*sic*] States and the Soviet Union. Both von Neumann and the new theoretical approach soon found a home, the Santa Monica-based RAND-Corporation, where game theory was enthusiastically developed during the late 1940s and 1950s.

Hence, it can be said that the rational actor at the center of game and decision theory had a clear counterpart in reality: arguably, it was "a nation-state locked in the icy and treacherous grip of the Cold War" (Amadae 2003: 77). Although at the outset of the *Theory of Games,* VNM (1953: 1) pigeonhole their work into the tradition of economic theory, the previous considerations indicate that their research evolved in a different context and that they had a different intention than the other economists considered in this study so far. Whereas Pareto, Hicks, and Samuelson were chiefly interested in consumer choice theory and regarded utility or preferences as a pivotal concept to investigate consumers' choices, VNM's work developed against the background of strategic, military problems (see Amadae 2003: 77) and focused on strategic interaction (see VNM 1953: 2). The very concept of utility was only treated in the course of a short "digression" of no more than a few pages (Ellsberg 1954: 537).[109]

To model interactions between rational actors, a numerical representation for the respective payoffs was required and this was the original purpose of the axiomatic derivation of expected utility theory (see Giocoli 2003: 380). Because the actors are facing decisions under risk or uncertainty, expected utility theory needs to take probabilities into account so that a cardinal utility concept was necessary (see Cudd 1993: 110).[110] VNM (1953: 17) demonstrate that "under the conditions on which the indifference curve analysis is based very little extra effort is needed to reach a numerical utility." If, in comparison to ordinal preferences, preferences between lotteries, i.e., "functions from uncertain states of affairs to outcomes," satisfy some additional conditions, a cardinal utility function representing these preferences can be constructed (Hausman 2012: 37).[111] This function has the "expected utility form" (Broome 1991b: 5) so that the utilities assigned to lotteries are tantamount to the "the sum of utilities of the payoffs weighted by their probabilities" (Hausman 2012: 38). Just as in the case of ordinal utility theory, a person acting on her rational preferences (as defined by the expected utility theory axioms) maximizes her expected utility by definition. VNM have thus established the cardinal representation theorem (see Cudd 1993: 107ff.).

At first glance, it seems puzzling that VNM come up with a cardinal utility concept again, given all the previous attempts to dispose of it. And yet, it needs to be emphasized that they did not relapse into a cardinal *hedonic* conception, initial interpretations to the contrary notwithstanding (see Giocoli 2003: 379).[112] Both utility functions have in common that they are determined up to a linear transformation; of course, this is the very meaning of cardinality (see Mandler 1999: 111). And yet, this mathematical property does not imply that the utility number mirrors the agent's "intensity of feelings" or, indeed, any quantity at all (ibid.).[113] According to Ellsberg (1954: 530ff.), the difference between the hedonic and the VNM utility concept lies in the latter's behaviorist essence. As shown above, the marginalists considered utility to represent the mental phenomena of pleasure and pain. In order to measure utility, it was thus necessary to reveal the subjects' "internal measurements of satisfaction," be it via introspection or by using measurement techniques of psychophysics (Ellsberg 1954: 534). To measure utility differences, in turn, one would have to elicit *how much* the subject prefers one good to another (see Giocoli 2003: 381). For VNM (1953: 23f.), however, this procedure is not "one which can be interpreted by reproducible observations" so that it needs to be abandoned. To quote Ellsberg (1954: 538), utility "is not 'measurable' in the sense that it is correlated with any significant economic quantity such as quantity of feeling or satisfaction, or intensity, such as intensity of liking or preference." Instead of measuring a quantity called utility, VNM *define* utility in terms of observable choices under risk (see Ellsberg 1954: 537ff.). Thus, the concepts of utility and utility differences have "no particular relationship to strength of preference, preference-difference comparisons, or notions of 'a psychological entity measurable in its own right'" (Fishburn 1989: 135f.).[114] Therefore, utility numbers do not allow for the interpersonal comparison of utility differences (see VNM 1953: 29).[115] In effect, VNM "succeeded in combining an extensive application of the axiomatic method with a strong behaviorist/operationalist penchant. That is, they tied up [....] Debreu's axiomatization of Hicks's ordinal utility theory and Samuelson's revealed preference theory" (Giocoli 2003: 378).[116] This synthesis lead to the modern utility concept, marked the beginning of rational choice theory, and influenced both economics and other disciplines to a great extent (see Schoemaker 1982: 529).

Now that a profound change of the character of economics had taken place, Robbins' scarcity definition of the economic problem became widely accepted.[117] Following Backhouse and Medema (2009b: 487), it is no coincidence that Robbins' definition was accepted in the discipline with a lag in the late 1950s in the course of the increasing axiomatization of economics:

> there are important connections between the rise of axiomatic methods in economics and acceptance of the Robbins definition of economics. [...] If economics was to be dominated by rigorous economic theory based on consumers' utility maximization [...] and cost-minimization – with axiomatic methods at the heart of the modeling process – it was necessary that economics be defined according to the Robbins definition, thereby excluding problems for which this type of economic theory could not provide a solution. Our claim is that in this period the spread of mathematical methods and axiomatization was closely linked to the narrowing of economics implied by the acceptance of the Robbins definition.

Robbins' definition heralded the *narrowing* of the discipline which increasingly relied on axiomatic methods and eschewed all problems not approachable by this account.[118] But while Robbins' definition set the course for narrowing the discipline, it also gave rise to the *broadening* of economics' scope of analysis (see Giocoli 2003: 86; Backhouse 2010: 112). Recall that the definition did not specify the sort of means and ends or the nature of the individual's motives. By focusing on choices under scarcity, his definition of an economic problem encompasses a very wide range of behavior, as Robbins (1935: 17) clearly realized:

> It follows from this, […], that in so far as it presents this aspect, any kind of human behaviour falls within the scope of economic generalisations. We do not say that the production of potatoes is economic activity and the production of philosophy is not. We say rather that, in so far as either kind of activity involves the relinquishment of other desired alternatives, it has an economic aspect. There are no limitations on the subject-matter of Economic Science, save this.

While his contemporaries had regarded the scope of the definition as too wide, the spread of the formal rational choice model altered this assessment (see Backhouse/Medema 2008, 2009a: 813f.).[119] From the acceptance of Robbins' definition, "it was just a short step to defining economics in terms of a method – that of rational choice" (Backhouse/Medema 2008). Accordingly, in the course of the 1960s, the boundaries of the scope of economics increasingly expanded and economic methods became applied to diverse subjects such as law, politics, the family, and, of course, health (see Backhouse/Medema 2009a: 813). This "economic imperialism" reflected "a view of the discipline that was likely far beyond anything Robbins might have imagined in 1932" (ibid.).[120]

2.5 Preference and utility in modern economics

At this point, it is helpful to review the different utility concepts discussed in the present chapter. To begin with, it is worth emphasizing that the utility concept primarily served as an instrument within demand theory, which, following Blaug (1980: 161),

> has a long and complex history […] from the *introspective cardinalism* of Jevons, Menger, Walras, and Marshall to the *introspective ordinalism* of Slutsky, Allen, and Hicks, to the *behaviorist ordinalism* of Samuelson's revealed preference theory, to the *behaviorist cardinalism* of the Neumann-Morgenstern theory of expected theory.

Within the marginalists' account of consumer choices, the notion of utility maximization had a straightforward meaning: individuals were supposed to make their consumption decisions with the aim of maximizing their individual pleasure derived from the goods they purchased. Thereby, hedonism served as the benchmark for choices and the idea of diminishing marginal utility provided an explanation for demand patterns (see Mandler 1999: 104). The notions of utility as something substantial and of the economic agent as seeking higher levels of utility in terms of happiness or satisfaction are still retained in Hicks' ordinalism and, concomitantly, in modern demand theory. Nevertheless, the satisfaction was no longer regarded as being cardinally measurable. The work of Samuelson and, especially, VNM heralded axiomatic utility theory and, thereby, changed the meaning of the term utility substantially.

It pays to stress again that within axiomatic utility theory, the utility numbers only represent preferences, which have lost their psychological interpretation altogether (see Davis 2003: 31).[121] Note that in comparison with the marginalist approach, the logical relation between utility and preference is effectively reversed: within marginal economics, individuals were regarded as preferring one good to another precisely *because* the former afforded them more utility in terms of pleasure or satisfaction, whereas now, the preference ordering precedes the utility function. That is, certain options are assigned certain utility numbers *because* they rank higher in the scale of preferences (Mandler 2001: 380).[122] Thereby, any connection between utility and the commonsense notion of usefulness or the "old technical sense" in which it referred to pleasure or desire have vanished (Mongin/D'Aspremont 1999: 382). Crucially, modern utility theory does not provide for an ordering principle. Instead, it describes an individual's choices in mathematical terms and, given the respective utility function, can predict that the alternative with the highest utility number will be chosen (see Mandler 2001: 382f.). The whole endeavor of early demand theory of trying to explain *why* an agent chooses a particular good is abandoned (see Davis 2003: 31).[123]

This shift from explanation to prediction reinforces the move in economic theory away from the focus on reasons for action toward the consequences of rational action which can be traced at least to Samuelson's RPT.[124] Now, preferences, "whatever they may be," are treated as exogenously given primitives of economic theory (Hausman/McPherson 2006: 46).[125] The processes of preference formation and change are for others to deal with; as far as the economist is concerned, individuals can prefer anything – as long as they do so consistently (see Hausman 2012: 19, 42). In effect, with VNM, utility theory finally merged into the theory of rational choice and utility maximization became analytically equivalent to rational choice. The history of utility theory can thus be interpreted as a continuous emptying of the utility concept, culminating in the ordinal and cardinal representation theorems in the 1940s and 1950s. Nowadays, introspective ordinalism still constitutes the basis of modern consumer choice theory, while the axioms of the VNM utility concept provide for the "mathematical foundations of much modern economic analysis," for instance, social choice, game theory, and decision analysis (Anand 1987: 189). These examples reveal that the theory of individual rational choices can indeed be regarded as the "centerpiece of scientific achievement in the field" of economics (Davis 2003: 1).[126]

Due to the facts that the preference concept is *the* fundamental notion of modern utility theory and that it plays a crucial role in the health economic attempts to solve CUA's fairness issue, it deserves special attention. Subsequently, the focus is on the axioms of ordinal utility theory, which present "the core of positive economic theory" and "constitute a fragmentary theory of rationality" at once (Hausman 2012: 13).[127] These axioms and the actual use made of the preference concept by economists allow for some general conclusions on the nature of individual preferences. Hence, relying on Hausman (2012), this section contributes to the clarification of what can and what cannot be inferred from the respondents' choices in social preference elicitation studies. In doing so, it provides the conceptual background for the Chapters 5 and 6 of the present study. In the following, four requirements on preferences are presented – completeness, transitivity, stability, and choice determination – which, taken together, characterize preferences as the outcome of a complex mental process that takes into account all relevant aspects of the respective choice situation. However, this conceptualization of preferences leads to a pivotal problem for rational choice theory. In a nutshell, neither preferences nor choices as such can actually be observed because the spectator never knows how the individual conceives of the alternatives at stake (see Sagoff 2004: 58ff.).[128] To regard a perceived choice as rational or irrational thus requires for interpretation on part of the observer.

To begin with, as said already, for the construction of an ordinal utility function to be possible, the individual's preference have to be consistent, that is, fulfill the demands of completeness and transitivity. Typically, these axioms are not regarded as positively describing preferences, but as normatively defining which preferences count as rational (see Anand 1987: 189; Broome 1991a: 91). Completeness means that the individual is able to form a weak preference between any two alternatives. That is, given two alternatives x and y, the individual either prefers x to y, prefers y to x or is indifferent between the options.[129] An individual A's preferences satisfy the axiom of transitivity if the following condition holds true: if A prefers x to y and y to z, then A also prefers x to z. The same applies to the relation of indifference: if A is indifferent between x and y and between y and z, A should also be indifferent between x and z. The requirement of transitivity can in fact be regarded as "the most basic ingredient to a theory of rational choice" and, concomitantly, to a theory of demand (Amadae 2003: 239).[130]

The transitivity axiom is closely connected with the assumption of stable preferences for the following reasons. As pointed out above, an account of demand requires a theory "which will tell us something about the ways in which consumers would be likely to react if variations in current prices and incomes were the only causes of changes in consumption" (Hicks 1959: 17). That is, preferences are assumed to be stable while prices and incomes fix the constraints (see Mirowski/Hands 2006b: 1f.; Hausman 2012: 18). By contrast, if preference changes were allowed for, any change in demand pattern could be explained in terms of changing preferences, and demand theory would be pointless. Additionally, without the assumption of stability, the requirement of consistency would lose any normative bite since any arising inconsistency could be interpreted as a preference change.[131] For the derivation of a utility function to be possible, it is not only presumed that the preference between A and B is stable, though. Instead, it is furthermore supposed that they stem from an *underlying stable preference scale* (see Mongin/D'Aspremont 1999: 383), as the following quote from Hicks (1959: 17) illustrates:

> What I mean by action according to a scale of preference is the following. The ideal consumer [...] chooses that alternative, out of the various alternatives open to him, which he most prefers, or ranks most highly. In one set

> of market conditions, he makes one choice, in others other choices; but they must always express the same ordering, and must therefore be consistent with one another.

This is a very important condition and quite severe at that, as will become clear in the analysis of prioritization preferences below.

The quoted passage exposes a further characteristic of the economic preference concept: as the previous considerations of the history of economics already illustrated, the preference concept is intimately connected with choices. To assume that choices "express" preferences implies *vice versa* that preferences, together with beliefs and constraints, determine choices (see Mongin/D'Aspremont 1999: 383). This requirement of "choice determination" has an important implication, for if preference orderings are to determine choices, they need to take into account everything relevant to that choice so that preferences have to be preferences all things considered (Hausman 2012: 15, 17). This claim can be illustrated by contrasting the economic preference concept with the use of the preference notion in the vernacular. In ordinary parlance, the term preference is often considered to denote an egoistic, self-interested desire (see Hausman 2012: 65). It is thus possible that although a person actually prefers *x* to *y,* she chooses *y* out of, say, a sense of duty. In this case, the narrowly conceived preference ranking does not determine the choice and, put the other way round, the chosen alternative does not allow for inferring anything about the agent's preferences. Hence, if preferences are to determine choices, any factor influencing choices must do so via influencing preferences, which "is another way of saying that preferences must be total comparative evaluations" (Hausman 2011: 10).[132]

The need for preferences to reflect total comparative evaluations of alternatives also arises from another consideration: just as preference changes would render the transitivity axiom moot, so would partial orderings. An individual could consistently prefer *x* to *y* and *y* to *z* according to some criterion *a*, and prefer *z* to *x* according to another criterion *b*. One may, to give a concrete example, prefer vanilla to chocolate and chocolate to strawberry when comparing these types of ice creams in terms of taste and at the same time prefer strawberry to vanilla when judged according to the color. The respective choices would not be intransitive from the respective persons' point of view. And yet, if an observer wants to assign the individual a utility function over vanilla, chocolate, and strawberry ice cream, the different types of ice cream have to be ranked according to one global principle, taking all relevant factors (e.g. taste, color, calories, and texture) at once into account. That is to say, if the transitivity axiom is to be meaningfully employable, "the alternatives over which preferences are defined must specify everything that matters to the agent" (Hausman 2012: 18).[133]

Before elaborating the problems of this preference notion, note that preference formation is a cognitively demanding task. A consistent preference ordering does not express a mere desire or a taste, but is the result of a complex evaluation procedure (see Hausman 2012: 117). Therefore, a preference ranking has to be regarded as "a goal that agents strive to construct, not something with which they are naturally endowed" (Mandler 1999: 106). In economics, this aspect is usually underexposed because frequently, the focus is on the monetary benefits of different alternatives (see Mandler 1999: 107). Note that for the early marginalists, the notion of well-behaved preferences did not constitute a problem in the first place because if "all pleasures and pains can be reduced to a single dimension of utility" and if "all desires can be reduced to the desire to maximise utility," it "follows straightforwardly that preferences are complete and transitive" (Sugden 1991: 754). In lack of such a common standard, however, it does not go without saying that the individual is capable of forming a consistent preference ordering.[134]

Beside the cognitive challenge of reaching complete overall comparisons there arises a more fundamental problem with the preference concept. As the ice cream example already indicated, strictly speaking, neither preferences nor choices can be observed. In fact, witnessed behavior only allows for inferring choices and, concomitantly, preferences *given that* the alternatives between which the individual actually chooses are known (see Sagoff 2004: 63f.). To this respect, preferences are inherently subjective as only the individual ultimately knows what she considers the respective opportunity set (see ibid.; Lehtinen 2013: 206). Sagoff (2004: 65f.) illustrates this case using the example of a sudden decline in the demand for fish in Boston in 1966. As it turned out, this collapse most probably resulted from the fact that in the course of the year, the pope had lifted the ban on eating meat on Fridays. The opportunity set the (catholic) individuals chose from thus looked as follows: "1. Eating meat with papal consent. 2. Eating fish with papal consent. 3. Eating meat without papal consent." The crucial point to note is that the particular choice cannot be observed without presuming a commitment to obey the pope, that is, without describing the set of alternatives correctly in the first place (see Sagoff 2004: 73).

This "option specification problem" (Pattanaik 2013: 217) remains relevant even if the alternatives seem well specified beforehand. To take another example from Hausman (2012: 16), one might reasonably prefer to drink beer instead of hot chocolate in summer, but reverse one's preferences in winter. In this case, the alternatives over which the preferences are defined are not {beer} and {hot chocolate}, but {beer in summer}, {hot chocolate in summer}, {beer in winter}, and {hot chocolate in winter}. Obviously, the 'discovery' of preferences is very much "a matter of imputation or interpretation" (Sagoff 2004: 66). Beyond that, both the ice cream and the beer and hot chocolate example point toward another problem: if any definition of the alternatives were allowed for, the consistency axioms would lose their normative force altogether (see Broome 1991a: 100f.). As some factors evidently seem irrelevant for particular choices – the haircut of the waitress, for instance, cannot plausibly be considered as relevant for the choice between ordering beer or hot chocolate – some substantial constraints are required (see Broome 1991a: 102ff.; Hausman 2012: 16f.). This is not the place to discuss this intricate issue in greater detail. Suffice it to emphasize, first, that the formal preference axioms only apply at a very general level and, second, that the identification of choices and preferences requires for specifying the opportunity set in the first place. The latter aspect is closely connected with the fact that observed preferences as such do not tell anything about the underlying motives of the individual. These important results will be taken up again when it comes to the discussion of prioritization preferences in Chapter 5 and 6.

The considerations of the present section characterized the modern utility concept and emphasized the crucial difference between the latter and the hedonic utility notion prevalent in early neoclassical economics. It is of pivotal importance to keep the different utility concepts separate, especially when it comes to the interpretation of economic theory. A skip through the economic literature, however, instantly reveals that the arguments are in fact replete with ambiguities and downright equivocations of the utility concept. The notion of utility as an agreeable mental state, for instance, is invoked whenever individuals are regarded as seeking the maximization of (expected) utility or as "attempting to maximize U(x)" (Rabin 1998: 11). Similarly, Tay (1999: 157) maintains that "economic theory postulates that the consumer will choose an alternative *i* if it yields the highest utility among all alternatives" and Lancaster (1966: 134) argues that the good's characteristics "give utility to the consumer." [135] And yet, as utility numbers only represent preference orderings, modern utility theory does not presuppose that there is anything to "accumulate" or to maximize, no "'stuff' that people seek" or stand to gain whatever (Hausman 2012: 14, 39). *What* people seek and *why* they do so is beyond the scope of modern economic theory. Hence, it can neither be assumed that people act out of pure self-interest, nor that they always prefer what is good for them.[136] When it comes to the preference concept, speaking of the satisfaction or the fulfillment of preferences also carries hedonic connotations in so far as they refer to agreeable feelings. And yet, modern utility theory has dropped any "Experience Requirement" (Griffin 1986: 13). That is to say, to

> satisfy a preference is for a preference to come true. When one knows that one's preferences have been satisfied, one may feel satisfied. But there is only this contingent connection between the satisfaction of a preference and the satisfaction of a person. The satisfaction of a preference [...] has no necessary connection to any feeling of satisfaction.
>
> (Hausman/McPherson 2009: 10)

Given Hands' (2008) observation that hedonist accounts of utility can not only be found in the literature, but are also "still heard in casual conversation and in the classroom," it seems safe to conclude that equivocations of the utility concept are an endemic issue in the economic discipline. Apparently, given its hedonic roots and its meaning in the vernacular, it seems all too easy to slide from utility as an index of preferences into an interpretation of utility in terms of a substantial benefit for the person concerned or as a pleasant mental state (see ibid.).[137]

In conclusion, two results deserve emphasis: for one thing, it turned out that the use of the utility concept was characterized by some ambiguity right from the start. Reviewing the different contributions against the background of the respective authors' intentions, it turns out that the dichotomy between utility as pleasure or a number representing preference rankings falls way too short. In fact, at least four concepts of what utility means have to be distinguished. As these meanings differ from each other to a considerable extent, anyone who uses or discusses utility theory should be sensitized to this history of changing meanings and conceptual vagueness. For another, the chapter delineated that the utility concept was introduced to economics in the context of individual consumer choice theory with the particular purpose to explain consumer choice behavior. It is in this area that notions such as maximizing utility or deriving satisfaction have their origin and in which they make sense. Within modern utility theory, by contrast, such phrases either have to be interpreted metaphorically or make no sense at all. These insights provide the background for the analysis of the attempts to solve CUA's fairness issue by means of equity weighting in Chapters 5 and 6. Before, however, the following chapter pigeonholes health economics in general and the weighting approaches in particular into another development of the last decades, namely the encompassing rise of the market ideal and CBA as its epitome in both public policy and economic theory.

Notes

1 See also Sassi *et al.* (2001: 16).
2 This question is also raised by Lübbe (2015: 29).
3 For reviews of the history of utility theory see Viner (1925), Stigler (1950a), (1950b), Ellsberg (1954), Robertson (1954), Cooter/Rappoport (1984), Broome (1991b), Sugden (1991), Mandler (1999), Cudd (1993), Mongin/D'Aspremont (1999), Giocoli (2003), Davis (2003), Black (2008), Blume/Easley (2008), and Riley (2008).
4 See also Culyer (1981: 8), Forget (2004), and Richardson (2009: 248). For the different strands of work on indicators combining mortality and morbidity see Murray (1994: 436f.).
5 As Broome (1991b: 4) states, "many economists adopt the official definition of 'utility', while at the same time also using the word to stand for a person's good." And Riley (2008) remarks: "Despite the ordinal revolution, some version of utilitarianism continues implicitly to serve as the ethical basis for economic policy judgements". See also Robertson (1954) and Broome (1991a: 65f.).
6 The claim that the shift in the meaning of utility and utility maximization remains underappreciated outside the discipline of economics is also made by Mandler (2001: 373).
7 Likewise, Mandler (1999: 14) states: "The evaluation of assumptions by current practice alone [...] will only confirm the preconceptions of the moment and, in a longer span, perpetuate the churning of inadequate alternatives."
8 See also Quiggin (1999: 591) and Blume/Easley (2008).
9 Although Carl Menger is sometimes also regarded as a pioneer of neoclassical economics, his status is contested in the literature. See Mirowski (1989: 259ff.) and Backhouse (2004: 167ff.). For a comparison of the work of Jevons, Walras, and Menger, see Howey (1989).
10 Hence the chapter title "Jevonian Revolution" (Dobb 1973: 166). See also Colvin (1985: 10f.) and Groenewegen (2003: 259).
11 On the influence of physics on marginalism more generally see Colvin (1985: 7), Harpham/Scotch (1988: 219f.), Clark (1995: 35), and Amadae (2003: 220ff.). An issue still contested in the literature is the question of which branch of physics served

as the blueprint for Jevons' economic thinking. While Schabas (1990: 80ff.), for instance, highlights Jevons' ample use of mechanical metaphors, Mirowski (1989: 217, 35) stresses the influence of thermodynamics and the pivotal role of the energy concept and claims that the early marginalists "boldly copied the reigning physical theories in the 1870s" (Mirowski 1989: 3). For a synthesis of these positions see White (2004) and for an overview of the debate see Maas (2005: 4ff.).

12 See also Maas (2005: 42ff., 155ff.) and Schabas (2007: 125ff.).

13 The publication of Fechner's *Elemente der Psychophysik* in 1860 is generally regarded as the "birth of modern psychology" (Bruni/Sugden 2007: 151).

14 Jevons' ideas were carried to the extreme by Edgeworth (1845–1926) (see Schabas 1990: 123f.), who was much more radical in his endorsement of psychophysics.

15 See also Blaug (1997: 279) and Backhouse (2004: 167f.)

16 For a concrete example see Mill (1871a: 318).

17 See also Colvin (1985: 7) and Schabas (2007: 134ff.).

18 See also Dobb (1973: 168), Mandler (1999: 68f.), Amadae (2003: 224), Morgan (2003: 278), and Backhouse (2008a).

19 Most likely, this change in focus was also influenced by the socio-economic circumstances:

> The economy was moving away from a supply-constrained economy, where all the economic problems centered on producing more goods, to a demand-constrained economy where the economy is limited not by its ability to produce but by its ability to consume.
>
> (Clark 1995: 39)

See also Schabas (2003a: 237).

20 Italics added. Jevons does not disregard the role of labor in the determination of value entirely, though. See *TPE* (165f.).

21 See also Viner (1925: 127), Little (1957: 19), Blaug (1980: 162, 1996: 334), Endres (1999: 600f.), Mandler (1999: 66f., 74, 76), White (2004: 231), and Backhouse (2004: 169, 2008a).

22 Apparently, Jevons refers to the pleasures *expected* to result from the actions in question here. On Bain see Maas (2005: 167).

23 See also Forget (2004: 630) and Bruni/Sugden (2007: 149), who argue that neoclassical economists "did claim that their theory was scientific by virtue of its being grounded in empirically-verified psychological laws."

24 Especially J. S. Mill's methodology of economics "erected a roadblock between economists and [...] elementary statistical procedures" (Peart 1996: 177). The role of statistics in the nineteenth century and the fundamental shifts in worldview required for its acknowledgment as a scientific device are depicted thoroughly by Maas (2005: 217–253). See also Backhouse (2004: 245–248).

25 Note that Jevons' remarks as to the interpersonal comparability of pleasure throughout the *TPE* are not unambiguous. See Samuelson (1947: 205), Stigler (1950a: 318f.), Howey (1989: 52), Dobb (1973: 174), and Schabas (2003a: 238).

26 See also *TPE* (23f., 28ff.).

27 The fourteen pleasures are again presented and extensively illustrated by means of examples in Bentham's *Table of the Springs of Actions*, http://www.ucl.ac.uk/Bentham-project/tools/bentham_online_texts/table/table1/Table3.jpg?hires, November 22, 2012.

28 See also Warke (2000a: 6). That pleasures may have to be understood broadly is also indicated by Bentham's (1823: 2) definition of utility as "that property in any object, whereby it tends to produce benefits, advantage, pleasure, good, or happiness, (all this in the present case comes to the same thing)." Evidently, neither an advantage nor the good for an individual can be equated with pleasure narrowly conceived (see Griffin 1986: 38).

29 See also Mitchell (1918: 32), Halévy (1946: 5f., 27), Viner (1949: 365), Davis (2003: 27), and Schofield (2008). According to Warke (2000a: 8), Bentham embraced the utility concept

> as an alternative he had been seeking to the 'fictions' of natural rights or divine relations on the one hand and social contract theory on the other, for he believed that all such moral criteria were merely artifices for propagating their proponents' own 'sympathies' and 'antipathies'.

30 The slogan "everyone counts for one and no one for more than one" was attributed to Bentham by Mill (1871b: 299). A hint on the original source is given by Warke (2000b: 178). This egalitarian idea is prone to quite inegalitarian consequences, as will be discussed below. As examples for changes provoked by Bentham and his disciples, Viner (1949: 362) lists "prison reform; adult population suffrage, including women suffrage; free trade; [...] general education at public expense; free speech and free press" and "free justice for the poor."

31 Likewise, Robbins (1952: 181) avers:

> There is much talk in the Benthamite literature of a felicific calculus; and the term naturally suggests a most pretentious apparatus of measurement and computation. But, in fact, this is all shop window. [...] The fact is that their [Bentham's and his friends'] use of the felicific calculus lay in quite another direction – in rough judgements about the expediency of particular items of penal law, in general estimates of the suitability of existing institutions or the desirability of other institutions to take their place. It is not necessary for all this that they should have used such a pretentious label [...]. But if we are to form correct views, it is by what they did, rather than by what might be read into their terminology, that they must be judged: and there can be no doubt that their practice was in the sphere of broad appraisals rather than quantitative computations.

32 This reasoning reveals that Jevons regarded the individual as being capable of making cardinal comparisons of pleasure (see Mandler 2001: 378), but it does not tell anything about his stance as to cardinal measurability. See on this conceptual difference Section 2.3.2.

33 Yet, following Schabas (1990: 35), it is doubtable whether such a "neutral feeling" actually exists. If it does not, it would be impossible to view pleasure and pain as positive and negative as the same kind of quantities measured on one and the same scale.

34 Jevons states:

> If in two cases the duration of feeling is the same, that case will produce the greater quantity which is more intense. [...] On the other hand, if the intensity of a feeling were to remain constant, the quantity of feeling would increase with its duration. Two days of the same degree of happiness are to be twice as much desired as one day; two days of suffering are twice as much feared.
>
> (*TPE:* 29f.)

35 See also Schabas (1990: 35) and Warke (2000a: 18). Note that Jevons' representation of the relationship between increments of consumption of a good and the pleasure derived by means of a diagram was revolutionary at his time. He anticipated what is known today as the demand curve. See *TPE* (29–32) and Schabas (1990: 34–36).

36 See also Mandler (2001: 375ff.), Warke (2000a: 17), and Davis (2003: 64).

37 Note that the argument refers to the *direct* consumption of water or other commodities but does not hold when goods can be stored "for subsequent use" (*TPE:* 44).

38 To be sure, Jevons was not the first to discover this idea. Pursuant to Schabas (1990: 33), it was only after 1871 that Jevons found out about the work of Cournot, Dupuit,

Gossen, and Thünen and according to Howey (1989: 74), it took Jevons some time "to recover from the shock that Gossen had worked out the use of utility in much the same way that he and Walras had." See also Amadae (2003: 223). Jevons gives credit to his predecessors in the Preface to the Second Edition of the *TPE* (xxviii).

39 The same relationship with regard to the subjective value of changes in income had already been stated by Bernoulli in 1738. See Stigler (1950b: 373ff.), Schoemaker (1982: 530f.), Blaug (1997: 316ff.), Cohen (1997: 151ff.), and Forget (2004: 630).

40 The application of the calculus to economics and the development of a subjective theory of value allowed for solving some of the problems classical economists had been facing for decades, perhaps most popularly the paradox of value. See *TPE* (78f.), Harpham/Scotch (1988: 221), and Mirowski (1989: 195).

41 The reference to utilitarianism reinforced the authority of Jevons' economics, since the utilitarian doctrine was generally endorsed in England back then. See Mandler (1999: 73).

42 See also Schabas (1998: 261).

43 See also Ayer (1966: 9), Cooter/Rappoport (1984: 521), and Hands (2010: 639).

44 See also Riley (2008) and Hands (2010: 46).

45 See also Coats (1976: 50f.) and Riley (2008).

46 "Value-free." See also Robbins (1934: 100).

47 Robbins does not address Pigou explicitly and indeed had other welfare economists in mind, as Howson (2004: 432) and Backhouse (2009) point out.

48 See also Pigou (1932: 3–5, 10, 845).

49 Similarly, Fetter (1920: 473) states as to classical political economy: "There was no place for the consideration of popular welfare in such a scheme of thought where all industry was ruled by inexorable natural law, and self-aggrandizement by profit-making was held to be the truest public service."

50 Arguably, the development of welfare economics and Pigou's interest in improving the people's economic well-being also needs to be considered against the historical background of the rise of socialism and a great pressure for social reform. See Backhouse (2003: 318f., 2004: 269f.).

51 See also Little (1957: 8) and Hicks (1959: 6).

52 This shift presented itself, as Little (1957: 8) argues, giving emphasis to Bentham's influence on welfare economics:

> The 'maximum happiness principle' invited the application of the differential calculus to the problems of ethical economics, and the development of welfare theory has largely been the result of applying mathematics to the quantitative ethical concepts which lay ready as a result of Bentham's philosophy.

See also Little (1957: 76) and Dobb (1973: 174).

53 It deserves to be mentioned that the eschewal of interpersonal comparisons of utility and the attack on classical welfare economics might also have had political reasons. Since Robbins, Hicks, and Kaldor held a liberal stance as to government intervention, a plea for the redistribution of wealth from the rich to the poor might not have pleased them and one way to avoid such egalitarian conclusions consisted in refuting the premises in the first place. See Dobb (1973: 240f.), Barry (1965: 15), Aslanbeigui (1990: 617f.), and Quiggin (1999: 592).

54 See also Robbins (1938b: 345) and Robbins quoted in Howson (2004: 432f.).

55 The reference to the authority of economic science is especially interesting in the context of this study as will become clear in Chapter 3.

56 See also Howson (2004: 417ff.).

57 Italics added. Robbins (1934: 98) illustrates this claim as follows:

> To explain why this man, in these circumstances, prefers fish to flesh; and that man flesh to fish; why to one love is more important than hunger and to another

> hunger than love – these are questions which, presumably, would be regarded by the psychologist as falling within his province. For the economist it is sufficient to assume that such preferences exist: his task is to examine their implications as regards the disposal of scarce goods.

See also Robbins (1935: 94f.).

58 See also Robbins (1934: 95).

59 See also Mandler (1999: 89) and Hands (2010: 639f.).

60 See also Robbins (1934: 97ff., 1938b: 343).

61 This is also pointed out by Cooter/Rappoport (1984: 523) and Giocoli (2003: 87f.).

62 See therefore Howson (2004: 415), Backhouse/Medema (2009a: 810), and Scarantino (2009: 451). An example is provided by Pigou (1932: 10).

63 See also Scarantino (2009) and Backhouse (2010: 101ff.). Backhouse/Medema (2009a: 805f.) point to the irony of defining economics in terms of scarcity at the very time when

> the world was at the deepest point of the worst depression ever encountered in the capitalist world. [...] In 1932 it may have seemed counter-intuitive (to put it mildly) to argue that economics involved working out the implications of scarcity, at least at the societal level, where the pressing economic problem was a glut of capital and labour.

See also Backhouse (2010: 101).

64 See also Giocoli (2003: 67f.).

65 The indifference curve is a central tool within health economics and will concern us again in Chapter 5.

66 According to Bruni/Guala (2001: 28), the term ophelimity derives from the Greek word for profitable, *ophelimos*.

67 Italics added.

68 See on the interval scale, a version of a cardinal scale, Chapter 4 of this study.

69 To be precise, Giocoli (2003: 91) dubs this account "utilitarian interpretation."

70 Italics added.

71 Italics added.

72 Italics added.

73 Note that in *Value and Capital,* Hicks (1946: 20ff.) changed his terminology and refers to the diminishing instead of the increasing MRS to describe the same phenomenon.

74 Italics added.

75 See also Blaug (1980: 165).

76 For a textbook-example see Mas-Colell *et al.* (1995: 5ff.).

77 Italics added. Further examples are Lancaster (1966: 134), Mas-Colell *et al.* (1995: 5ff.), and Mankiw/Taylor (2014: 108).

78 On RPT see Blaug (1997: 332ff.), Mirowski/Hands (1998: 282ff.), Giocoli (2003: 100), Amadae (2003: 231ff.), Hausman (2011), and (2012: 25ff.).

79 See also Robertson (1954: 19f.), Blaug (1997: 332f.), Mirowski/Hands (1998: 284), Davis (2003: 30), and Hausman (2012: 24).

80 See also Mirowski/Hands (1998: 283), Davis (2003: 30), Backhouse (2010: 106), and Hands (2010: 636).

81 See also Blaug (1980: 166) and Giocoli (2003: 100).

82 See also Mongin/D'Aspremont (1999: 386), Mirowski/Hands (2006b: 3), and Hands (2010: 641).

83 See also Robbins (1934: 98) and Hausman (2012: 29ff.).

84 See also Giocoli (2003: 106ff.) and Kliemt (2009: 68).

85 See also Blaug (1980: 166f.) and Hands (2010: 643).

86 See also Mirowski (1989: 365).

87 See also Griffin (1986: 10).

88 The behaviorist heritage of economics is criticized by Güth/Kliemt (2013: 16): "The pride economists still take in the allegedly solid foundation of their discipline in utility functions that represent choice behavior rather than the motives underlying behavior stands in the way of scientific development."

89 See also Davis (2003: 30f.) and Giocoli (2003: 110).

90 See also Mandler (1999: 66ff.) and (2001: 378f.).

91 Pursuant with Mandler (1999: 7), the "overthrow of early neoclassical theory was unmistakable and decisive. [...] Hicks and Allen met only tepid resistance and, and by the 1940s, the ordinalists had become the establishment."

92 See also Hicks (1959: 19).

93 See also Broome (1991b: 3).

94 See also McCloskey (1998: 139f.).

95 The percentage of military research and development within the whole budget for federal research and development exploded during World War II (from 25 in 1935 to about 90 in 1943) and remained high thereafter. See Mirowski (1991: 229).

96 See also Morgan/Rutherford (1998b: 15f.), Morgan (2003: 296f.), and Backhouse (2008b), who all point out that this alleged connection remains to be investigated more thoroughly.

97 Debreu presents one example for the influence exerted by émigrés from continental Europe, who either came to the US in the course of the Great Depression or due to the threat and eventually the reality Nazism, on the discipline of economics. See Mirowski (1991: 230), Backhouse (1998a: 96), and Backhouse/Medema (2009b: 485f.). See on Debreu's biography more extensively Weintraub/Mirowski (1994: 258) and Weintraub (2002: 115ff.).

98 See also Mirowski/Hands (1998: 276), Davis (2003: 31), and Backhouse (2008b).

99 See also Giocoli (2003: 124).

100 See also, with special consideration of Arrow's contribution, Davis (2003: 90ff.).

101 Blaug (2003: 397) regards Arrow and Debreu's existence proof as a prime example of "formalism run riot", in so far as "what was once an economic problem [...] has been transformed into a mathematical problem, which is solved, not by the standards of the economic profession, but by those of the mathematics profession."

102 Backhouse (2003: 321) puts it as follows:

> For earlier generations, mathematical models, when they were used, instantiated economic theory, whereas for the later one, they became the theory. Perspectives that could not be captured with the mathematical apparatus were no longer regarded as part of the theoretical core.

103 Note that the so-called formalist revolution was indeed composed of various heterogeneous threads, as Weintraub (2002: 72ff.) and Backhouse (2008b) emphasize. For the present concern, a fine-grained differentiation of these threads is not necessary.

104 In the wake of Debreu, this strict separation between theory and interpretation became common under mathematical economists, as Vilks (1998: 30) points out. In this respect, it is illuminating to note that Debreu regarded Bourbakism as "the definite break with physical metaphors, since physics was dependent for its success upon bold conjectures and experimental refutations, but economics had nothing to fall back upon but mathematical rigor" (Weintraub 2002: 122). See also McCloskey (1998: 92).

105 See, for instance, Hargreaves Heap (1992: 6), Mongin/D'Aspremont (1999: 401), Hausman/McPherson (2006: 46), and Hausman (2012: 14).

106 See also Davis (2003: 31), Giocoli (2003: 378), and Hausman/McPherson (2006: 48).

107 He was, for instance, a member of the Manhattan Project. See Mirowski (1991: 231), Amadae (2003: 6f.), and Thompson (2008).

108 See Mirowski (1991: 238f.), Amadae (2003: 7), and Giocoli (2003: 347ff.). Ellsberg (1954: 528) states:

> The most common reaction was dismay. To 'literary' economists who had freshly amputated their intuitive feelings of cardinal utility at the bidding of some other mathematicians, it seemed wanton of von Neumann and Morgenstern so soon to sprinkle salt in their wounds.

109 See VNM (1953: 8):

> The conceptual and practical difficulties of the notion of utility, and particularly the attempts to describe it as a number, are well-known and their treatment is not among the primary objectives of this work. We shall nevertheless be forced to discuss them in some instances.

110 VNM (1953: 19) applied the concept of objective probabilities and interpreted "probability as frequency in the long run." This notion became replaced with the concept of subjective probabilities eventually. See Mandler (1999: 108). The seminal work in this respect is Leonard Savage's *The Foundation of Statistics.* See Schoemaker (1982: 536), Sudgen (1991: 757, 761ff.), and Blume/Easley (2008).

111 See also Hausman/McPherson (2006: 53). On different versions of the axioms see VNM (1953: 26ff.), Schoemaker (1982: 531), Broome (1991a: 90ff.), and Hargreaves Heap (1992: 8ff.).

112 According to Giocoli (2003: 382), Ellsberg's (1954) paper presents a turning point in the VNM reception since it rectified the thorough confusion as to the relationship between the two utility concepts.

113 See also Ellsberg (1954: 538), Schoemaker (1982: 533), and Fishburn (1989: 129).

114 See also Ellsberg (1954: 553f.) and Giocoli (2003: 385).

115 See also Hargreaves Heap (1992: 11) and Hausman/McPherson (2006: 54).

116 To be precise, the quote actually refers to the contributions of VNM and Savage.

117 See Backhouse (2004: 239ff., 2010: 101) and Backhouse/Medema (2008, 2009a, 2009b).

118 Note that the axiomatization of economics and the "elimination of everything human from the analysis" was not what Robbins had had in mind (Giocoli 2003: 86). For one thing, Robbins stressed the crucial role of psychology for the explanation of individual economic choices; for another, he was not particularly fond of using mathematics (see Backhouse/Medema 2009b: 489).

119 It should be noted that the scarcity definition was never universally accepted by all economists, of course. Among its critics were, for instance, Boulding (1969) and Buchanan (1964).

120 On the path from Robbins to economic imperialism see Scarantino (2009: 452).

121 See also Broome (1991b: 5).

122 See also Kliemt (2009: 67) and Güth/Kliemt (2013: 6).

123 See also Mandler (1999: 66ff.) and Backhouse (2003: 321).

124 See also Morgan (2003: 299) and Hausman (2012: 29).

125 See also Davis (2003: 31) and Kliemt (2009: 49).

126 See also Hands (2008) and Kliemt (2009: 21).

127 On the debate of whether the axioms actually constitute reasonable demands on rational preferences see Anand (1987), Broome (1991a: 90ff.), and Hausman/McPherson (2006: 55ff.).

128 See also Lehtinen (2013: 206) and Pattanaik (2013: 217).

129 The completeness axiom is not investigated at this point, but it shows up again when it comes to the analysis of the trade-off metaphor in Chapter 5. Objections to this premise are offered by Broome (1991a: 92f.) and Mandler (1999, 2001).

130 See also Blaug (1997: 339).

131 The pivotal role the assumption of stable preferences plays for economic theory is stressed by Blaug (1997: 338f.):

> Insofar as demand theory is concerned, it is perfectly true that one cannot get along without the assumption of stable tastes. The fundamental principle of utility theory is that consumers act 'as if' they were maximizing utility and this principle can be translated into the 'consistency postulate': if an individual prefers A to B in one situation, s/he will not be found to choose B in preference to A in another situation. It is clear that consistency means stable tastes and that inconsistency can be interpreted as a change in tastes.

132 Hausman's (2012) account of preferences was received positively in the literature. See Lehtinen (2013), Teschl (2013), and Pattanaik (2013). For a critique of the conception of preferences as total comparative evaluations see Pattanaik (2013: 215f.) and for a response Hausman (2013).

133 See also Sugden (1991: 763), Mandler (1999: 66), and Lehtinen (2013: 206, 209).

134 See on the incommensurability of options for instance Broome (1991a: 92).

135 See on Lancaster's theory of demand Chapter 5 of this study.

136 See Broome (1991a: 65, 1991b), Hausman/McPherson (2009), and Hausman (2011: 10f.).

137 Note that some authors explicitly postulate a return to a hedonic utility concept. See with regard to health Dolan/Kahneman (2008) and, for a more general overview, Hands (2008).

3 On the rise, rationale, and authority of economic evaluation

3.1 Introduction

The previous chapter carved out that the formalization of economics and the concomitant adoption of Robbins' definition of economics in terms of choices under scarcity significantly increased the scope of economic theory. This is because the "neoclassical view that economic theory studies the allocation of scarce means with alternative uses [...] did not preclude the study of scarce *non*economic means with alternative *non*economic uses" (Cohen/Ubel 2001: 94).[1] As government actions commonly involve the allocation of scarce resources, the economic "conceptual and analytical tool kit" originally employed "for understanding and explaining how markets allocate resources" can be applied to public policy issues as well (Smith 2006: 729). Using neoclassical methods for analyzing health care, health economics can be regarded as a prime example for economic imperialism (see Culyer 1981: 26f.; Cohen/Ubel 2001: 94f.). It is therefore no coincidence that economic systematic research on health care started in the 1960s and that health economics advanced to a proper economic subdiscipline in the 1980s (see Cohen/Ubel 2001: 94f.; Forget 2004: 623). Beside this reason stemming from developments within economic theory, health economics arguably did not forge ahead earlier for at least two others as well. First, although the implementation of health insurance systems in most developed countries reaches back to the nineteenth century, until the 1950s the possibilities of medical care had been rather limited, providing little incentive for the government to provide and for the citizens to adopt medical insurance (see Harris 1990: 396; Cutler 2007: 387). Therefore, the organization and the funding of health care was neither an issue of public concern, nor of interest for economists. Second, originally, the establishment and the expansion of public health care systems were largely guided by equity considerations: "In most developed countries universal insurance coverage was designed to guarantee equal access to medical care for all. Solidarity in health care dictated no rationing by price", medical care "was perceived as a right, not a good" (Cutler 2007: 385, 387).[2]

The purpose of the present chapter's first section is to tackle the question as to why health care turned into a "good," falling into the realm of economics, in the first place. The issue needs to be considered against the rising influence of the ideal of the market in public policy since the late 1960s (see Backhouse 2005: 355),[3] which came along with a profound change in both the economists' public role and prestige and in public rhetoric. In the present context, these alterations are significant as they paved the way for, first, the rise of health economics to the influential discipline it is today and, second, applying cost-benefit analyses in all parts of public policy. Therefore, CBA, CUA, and the weighting approaches might not have gained their current importance and authority had this shift not taken place. Presumably, this authority also illustrates why health economists keep sticking to economic evaluation techniques in the face of severe fairness issues.[4]

The esteem of the market mechanism and its efficient results was reinforced by concurrent developments in welfare economics, as the chapter's second section shows. For one thing, the two fundamental theorems turned market efficiency into the ideal of welfare economics and the benchmark of public policy. For another, the potential Pareto criterion embedded CBA into the normative framework of welfare economics. These considerations serve the purpose of presenting the normative-theoretical basis of economic evaluation in neoclassical welfare economics to an audience not acquainted with economics. In addition, they highlight the basic rationale of economic evaluation: they are supposed to identify efficient outcomes where an actual market mechanism is lacking. Just as demonstrated in the previous chapter with regard to the utility concept, it turns out that the economic concepts and methods applied in public policy rest on the paradigm of the individual's rational behavior on the market as well. That being said, it is doubtable whether this market-inspired logic of economic evaluation can be transferred to health care resource allocation just like that, as the application of CBA to health illustrates. Note at this point that although the focus of the present study is on CUA and the attempts to solve its fairness issue, considering CBA is merited as it provides a key for understanding the attraction as well as the fundamental problems of (health) economic evaluation (see Powers/Faden 2006: 144). Since it is argued in line with Lübbe (2015) that the objections leveled against CBA basically stem from its value-maximizing framework, they inevitably show up in the discussion of both CUA and the weighting approaches again.

3.2 The market ideal and the evolution of health economics

3.2.1 The rise of the economist, the market ideal, and CBA

Before the free market as allocation device advanced to a normative ideal in the 1960s, the belief in the government's ability to secure the economy's thriving was generally strong. This confidence roots in the experiences during and after the Great Depression and the two world wars. The gravity of the economic downturn in the wake of the stock market crash in 1929 shattered the belief in a well-functioning market mechanism and called for political action (see Morgan/Rutherford 1998b: 11f.; Heilbroner 2000: 277; Amadae 2003: 88; Morgan 2003: 289). Note that until the 1920s, it was generally believed that business cycles constituted a natural trait of the capitalist economic system so that the government was not considered responsible for the economic situation of its citizens anyway and the need for economists' advice in public policy issues was quite limited (see Morgan/Rutherford 1998: 5; Morgan 2003: 288). Now, however, it became more and more accepted even by "the most laissez-faire minded economists" that state intervention was necessary to tackle society's problems, predominantly the devastating unemployment rate (ibid.).[5] In effect, World War I and the Great Depression "created the view that governments were responsible for intervening to maintain the health of the domestic economy, and thus for the economic security of their own people" (Morgan 2003: 289). It was in this "pro-interventionist" (Morgan/Rutherford 1998b: 12) climate that US President Franklin D. Roosevelt (1933–1945) launched his New Deal policy, implying heavy interventions in the US economy on an exceptional scale and setting the economy irrevocably on the government's agenda (see Morgan/Rutherford 1998b: 5). The New Deal was sustained by the basic conviction that the economic policy of laissez-faire was biased toward "monopoly, inequitable distribution of wealth, market failure, and cyclical instability" (Kelley 1997: 2). This belief also gained hold among economists who started to focus on investigating phenomena of market failure (see Backhouse 2005: 357).

The theoretical framework for the required government interventions was provided by John M. Keynes. Within the classical paradigm of economic theory, voluntary unemployment is impossible as the market is supposed to always balance supply and demand at a point of full employment (see Kelley 1997: 2). Therefore, the classical economists were not able to account for the economic situation during the depression. Keynes (1923: 80), by contrast, argued that this adaption process is irrelevant for real public policy issues because it takes too long – "in the long run we are all dead," as he famously put it. Crucially, he maintained that economic output and, hence, employment critically depends on aggregate demand and demonstrated how the situation could be ameliorated in the short run already: either by means of government spending or by adopting an expansive monetary policy, aggregate demand could be manipulated in order to enhance investments and production (see Keynes 1936: 23f., Backhouse 2010: 118). Consequently, under Roosevelt, the US government indeed turned into "a major economic investor," and "roads, dams, auditoriums, airfields, harbors, and housing projects blossomed" (Heilbroner 2000: 274). Yet, ultimately neither the New Deal nor Keynesian measures succeeded in eliminating unemployment so that the Great Depression did not come to a halt before the beginning of World War II (see Morgan/Rutherford 1998b).

This verdict notwithstanding, the idea of "fine-tuning" the economy heralded a fundamental shift within economic policy and the hegemony of Keynesianism exerted an enduring influence on the economists' role in the public sector. This is because the implementation of New Deal policies increased the demand for economic advice and opened up every aspect of the economy "to economic attack" (Morgan/Rutherford 1998b: 12; see Colvin 1985: 2; Coats 1989: 109). Although economics was still "held in relatively low repute, at least among those in power" (Goodwin 2008), this changed profoundly in the course of World War II when economists entered government service, not only in agencies such as the Treasury, but also in bodies more directly concerned with military activity (see ibid. Backhouse 2010: 101f.). As their work proved useful, the economists' public salience and their reputation increased significantly. To quote Morgan and Rutherford (1998b: 13):

> Economists found that by using tool-kit economics and the developing neoclassical technical expertise they could answer questions in very different fields. Economics emerged from the war covered in glory, perhaps launching the 'economic imperialism' in social sciences over the last half century.[6]

Politicians regarded the economists' contribution as so expedient that they eventually sought to integrate economics in government activities in peacetime as well (see Amadae 2003: 158; Goodwin 2008). Additionally, during the 1950s and 1960s, Keynesian measures continued to be employed more or less successfully so that this era can be regarded as "the high period of the economist as engineer, advising the government on how to set the levers of economic control" (Morgan 2003: 294; see Orlans 1986: 184; Harpham/Scotch 1988: 224). All in all, since 1945, the world saw a growing institutional integration and, concomitantly, a rising public influence of economists (see Coats 1989: 112).[7]

The ascent of the economist as a public figure was paralleled by the expansion of the welfare state. After World War II, countries "wanted to reward themselves for years of struggle. Quasi-socialist governments elected after the war wanted to expand the role of the state in the provision of basic needs" (Cutler 2007: 387). This aim was advanced by the fact that, back then, major industrialized countries experienced a phase of unprecedented growth and prosperity.[8] In health care, medical progress such as innovations in antibiotics "convinced people that medical care was valuable" (ibid.) and, consequently, changed the attitude toward health care and public insurance. The first implementation of a national medical care system took place in the UK, where the *National Health Service* (NHS) was founded in 1946 (see ibid., McMaster 2001: 113). In line with the generally sound financial situation, resources in the health care sector were quite abundant, so that rationing had not become an issue yet. Therefore, early health economic research was primarily engaged with "the search for methods to enhance the supply of health care-resources and to improve the productivity of resources" (Reinhardt 1998: 1). Reflecting the general positive attitude to state intervention, health economists focused on the phenomenon of market failure in health care and scrutinized issues of health insurance (see ibid.).[9] Nonetheless, the discipline of health economics and its methods are generally regarded as having been in a "relatively primitive" condition back then (Culyer/Newhouse 2000b: 3).[10]

While the postwar period was characterized by a decidedly pro-interventionist attitude, the climate changed in the late 1960s when a firm belief in the market mechanism started to gain hold (see Blumenschein/Johannesson 1996: 114; Backhouse 2005: 358, 2010: 159). In the 1960s and early 1970s, the major industrialized countries were governed by democratic parties fostering welfare-enhancing programs. In the US, President Lyndon B. Johnson (1963–1969) tried to perpetuate Roosevelt's New Deal policy by launching the War on Poverty and Great Society projects (see Kelley 1997: 16; Berg 1999: 160f.; Backhouse 2010: 127). In 1964 and 1965, Johnson advanced an amount of social legislation "unprecedented since the New Deal" (Orlans 1986: 195). In particular, he implemented the public health programs Medicaid for the poor and Medicare for the elderly and established the highly contested *National Commission on Guaranteed Incomes* (see Berg 1999: 161; Pressman 2005: 84). The growing complexity and the rising costs of welfare programs required for a more severe controlling so that alongside the extension of welfare policies, the Johnson administration adapted methods of rational policy analysis.

As to the development of these methods, the US military think tank RAND (Research and Development) played a key role. RAND was originally set up in 1946 in order to continue the fruitful cooperation of scientific and technical expertise established during the war and it soon advanced to one of the most important research sites in the US (see Leonard 1991: 269; Amadae 2003: 32).[11] In the 1950s, RAND became increasingly dominated by economists and the research focus shifted to abstract studies and "rigorous quantitative analysis" (Amadae 2003: 41). In particular, researchers at RAND became dedicated to so-called systems analysis, a vague term denoting management techniques rooted in rational choice theory, which could be applied to private firms and the state alike (see Leonard 1991: 276; Amadae 2003: 39ff.; Backhouse 2005: 367, 2010: 144) This method meshed with RAND's decidedly technocratic and elitist stance, as Amadae (2003: 36) points out: "Policy advice should come in the form of objective analysis or expert consultation" so that "partisan controversy" could be replaced with "objective fact."

When Robert S. McNamara – who was closely affiliated with RAND and a fervent adherent to "quantitative reasoning" and "economic efficiency" – was appointed Secretary of Defense by Kennedy (1961–1963), both RAND's technocratic ideal and its management methods entered the Pentagon as well (Amadae 2003: 58).[12] In particular, McNamara introduced the so-called Planning–Programming–Budgeting System (PPBS) into the Department of Defense (see Amadae 2003: 60f.).[13] PPBS was based on CBA and designed for "the allocation of the defense budget among its various components" (Leonard 1991: 279). Pursuant to its adherents, it promised that decisions on resource allocation could be made "rational, objective, quantitative, depersonalized, de-bureaucratized, [and] de-politicized" (Mosher quoted in Amadae 2003: 64; see Orlans 1986: 193).[14] In 1965, Johnson extended PPBS to all federal agencies and thereby heralded the measuring of "benefits and costs of almost every form of government activity" (Porter 1996: 187).[15] When Nixon (1969–1974) later abolished the device, economic reasoning in terms of costs and benefits had already become an irrevocable part of public policy (see Harpham/Scotch 1988: 224; Amadae 2003: 71). Note that the concomitant shift in authority from military and political personnel to economists meshed neatly with the current *Zeitgeist*. Since, during the

Cold War, public trust in both politicians and the military was low, the fate of the world should rather "rest on cool heads and calculating minds" of the economists, instead: "Scarcity was their stock in trade. Pure reason was their method – and they were incorruptible. They accepted neither ideology nor sentimental appeals to service loyalty or norms other than the public welfare" (Goodwin 2008; see Leonard 1991: 278).

At the beginning of the 1970s, the effects of Johnson's welfare programs became visible and it turned out that some of them had been successful while others had failed to reach the intended results (see Osberg 1995: 26). Although the programs did succeed in reducing numbers of the poor, the War on Poverty was generally perceived a failure: the "political climate has been chilled by disappointments about the housing, manpower, urban and education programs of the 1960s" (Okun 1975: 117).[16] Additionally, empirical studies on the effects of a guaranteed income revealed that government subsidies exerted an inverse effect on incentives to work and led to a decrease in overall GDP (see Pressman 2005: 85). The attainment of equity, so it seemed, comes at the expense of efficiency. Consequently, the political focus began to shift to the inefficiencies caused by social programs. It was in this climate – the critical evaluation of the welfare state and the trend toward rational policy analysis – that Arthur Okun, Chairman of the *Council of Economic Advisers* under Johnson, introduced the famous image of the leaky bucket (see Kelley 1997: 16). Okun (1975: 8, 96–100) compared money transfers from the rich to the poor with water carried in a leaky bucket in so far as some of the transfers will get lost during the transit. Such dead-weight losses especially result from the fact that redistribution reduces the workers' incentives to work and, finally, their productivity so that the economy's efficiency in terms of total output diminishes. Therefore, modern capitalist societies have to reach a compromise between the aims of efficiency in terms of GDP on the one hand and equality in terms of its distribution on the other hand: "In such cases, some equality will be sacrificed for the sake of efficiency, and some efficiency for the sake of equality"; in short, "society faces a trade-off between equality and efficiency" (Okun 1975: 88, 1) – a cliché was born.[17] In the 1990s, empirical research refuted the assumption that a high level of redistributive policy measures hampers efficiency (see Osberg 1995: 3; Pressman 2005: 86). Nevertheless, the equity-efficiency trade-off notion proved pervasive and is still present in the economic literature.[18]

In the late 1970s, the pendulum finally swung toward the ideal of efficiency. This encompassing "shift in worldview" (see Backhouse 2005: 355) in favor of the market mechanism needs to be considered against the background of the oil-crises of 1973/1974 and the subsequent slow-down in economic growth in all industrialized countries which created a condition of stagflation, i.e., a situation of economic stagnation and inflation at once (see Blinder 1987: 32f.). These circumstances challenged policy makers because Keynesian instruments now proved useless. While fighting stagnation demands a low interest rate to trigger investments, reducing inflation requires a high interest rate to slow down the rise in money supply (see Morgan 2003: 294). In effect, the stagflation of the 1970s annihilated the belief in the governments' ability to manage the economy and ended the era of Keynesianism's dominance in economic policy. Simultaneously, in economic theory it became acknowledged that while government may be "the solution to some problems," it is "the source of others" and the research interest shifted from market failure to government failure (Tullock 2008; see Backhouse 2010: 138f.).[19]

As government intervention was increasingly perceived as "creating perverse incentives and distorting resource allocation," the market regained popularity and the achievement of efficiency was henceforth considered as requiring "private ownership of assets" and "competitive prices for goods and services" (Backhouse 2005: 359).[20] Accordingly, democratic governments were replaced by center-right regimes, which began "to subject their public expenditures to much more stringent economic scrutiny," and cut down public spending to a great extent (Wolff/Haubrich 2006: 748f.).[21] Industries were privatized and regulations removed in order to "create competitive markets" and to "minimize the role of state-organized and state-funded economic activity" (Backhouse 2005: 359).[22] This demand for deregulation did not lead to a decline in the request for economic advice, though (see Harpham/Scotch 1988: 216; Coats 1989: 112). Quite to the contrary, economists had already become securely established in different government departments and their influence continued to expand in the course of the deregulation.[23]

For the time being, the rise of the market ideal in the private economy, government administration, and policy making culminated in the market-liberal Reagonomics of the 1980s (see Blinder 1987: 12, 33, 90ff.; Backhouse 2010: 182). An early executive order of Ronald Reagan empowered the *Office of Management and Budget* "to review all significant new regulations and to block those whose benefits were not demonstrably superior to their costs" (Porter 1992: 42).[24] By the end of the 1980s, markets had advanced to "a central pillar of almost every social structure throughout the modern world" and CBA, the epitome of the market ideal and "one of the most important symbols of the economic profession's new status in the public sector" (Colvin 1985: 2) had become firmly established in public policy (Powers/Faden 2006: 100).[25] Consequently, economic methods and, especially, rational choice theory spread "into leading financial, policy, educational, and legal institutions" (Amadae 2003: 5).

3.2.2 Changing public rhetoric and the ascent of health economics

This development manifested in and was reinforced by a profound transformation of public rhetoric.[26] While before, welfare programs had been justified as being "right, good, and proper," the 1970s and 1980s saw a growing influence of efficiency dominated language in the policy making process (Harpham/Scotch 1988: 224f.).[27] In particular, public policy increasingly became conceived of in terms of costs and benefits and the respective institutions adopted the economic "language and approaches to decisionmaking problems," leading to the "nearly universal presence" of the terminology of CBA (Amadae 2003: 5). At the same time, as the previous chapter illustrated, the ideal of "good" economics changed and so did its terminology. This development is particularly relevant when it comes to the application of economic methods to public policy issues.[28] To sum it up beforehand, the formalization of economic jargon, first, further buttressed the authority of economics, second, made economic theory less intelligible for lay persons, and third, hedged economics from criticism.

As to the rising authority of economists, it needs to be pointed out that the mathematization of the economic discipline and the concurrent rise of statistical techniques after World War II came along with a changing image of science and objectivity.[29] In the course of this development, numbers increasingly gained relevance and power (see McCloskey 1998: 112) and results derived by using mathematical methods came to be regarded as "unambiguously scientific on the grounds that they had to be used in a technical, i.e. nonsubjective, way" (Morgan/Rutherford 1998b: 9, see Backhouse/Medema 2009a). It seems safe to say that mathematics is still considered the paradigm example "of objectivity, explicitness, and demonstrability," in which "only truth counts, not human words" (McCloskey 1998: 165).[30] This pretension to objectivity and the use of intricate mathematics reinforced the image of economics as a hard science – harder, at least, as other social sciences – and thus served to build academic reputation (see Sagoff 2004: 73; Kliemt 2009: 26). Simultaneously, the high esteem and authority of mathematics devolved upon persons capable of dealing with them. While, in former times, the ability of reading Greek or Latin was considered a sign of a strong and virtuous character, nowadays it is the use of difficult mathematics which constitutes an emblem for "honest and careful work" (Porter 1996: 201f.), evoking the image of an intelligent and virtuous scholar.[31] By the same token, the intricacy of mathematics serves as a gate keeper, helping to select the appropriate economics claimants.[32] When it comes to public policy, economists claimed that "the objectivity of their methods warranted the objectivity of the results of the policy analysis and of the associated policy advice" (Morgan/Rutherford 1998b: 9).[33] Thereby, CBA virtually presented itself as "the soul of rationality, an impartial, objective standard for making good decisions" (Ackerman/Heinzerling 2004: 35).

As a consequence of both the spread of mathematics and an increasingly technical terminology, non-economists became excluded from the economic discourse. Nowadays, economic analysis "is the language of the expert, not the masses" (Harpham/Scotch 1988: 220) so that most economic textbooks "are no longer even superficially accessible to lay people" (McCloskey 1998: 140). By shutting out non-economists from the discourse, economics hedges from any critique from outside the discipline which again serves to reinforce the economists' authority (see Blaug 2007: 200; Richardson/McKie 2007: 795; Lübbe 2009d: 461f). This is especially worrying when it comes to public decisions with a significant normative-ethical dimension and a profound effect on the individuals' lives, such as prioritization in health care (see Lübbe 2011: 101). Couching the matter in a highly technical vocabulary may put a veil on decisions which otherwise would be considered as outrageous (see ibid.). In view of these characteristics of economic rhetoric, it becomes apparent that economic arguments might be welcomed by decision makers when it comes to the explanation and legitimization of political decisions. For one thing, referring to "hard numbers" (Smith 2006: 742) derived from rigorous economic theory might help delegating the responsibility for disagreeable decisions.[34] For another, a political case couched in authoritative, apparently simple and objective economic terms confers a strong persuasive force to the argument (see Colvin 1985: 3; McCloskey 1998: 3; Reinhardt 1998: 2).

An additional factor that makes economic terms attractive for decision makers but, at the same time, further impedes the understanding of economic arguments is the fact that economics frequently applies terms carrying a decidedly positive connotation in colloquial speech.[35] This is especially true as to the modern utility concept, as demonstrated in the previous chapter. To give another example borrowed from Reinhardt (1998: 6), while the word optimal is usually taken to mean the best in the vernacular, to economists "the word connotes no such thing." As will become clearer below, a more efficient allocation might even be regarded as worse in the colloquial understanding (see Reinhardt 1998: 9). Decision makers might "appreciate the economist's ability to couch tough policies in felicitous language" in order to draw the curtain over the real nature of some hard choices (Reinhardt 1998: 2). To quote Hurley (2000: 109):

> The terms 'efficiency', 'optimal', 'welfare', 'net social gain', etc. have specific technical meanings within economics that do not correspond to general usage. Policy makers and the general public are likely to think that 'optimal' means 'best' in some overall sense. [...] Of course, many Pareto optimal allocations can be judged to be socially inferior to non-Pareto optimal allocations. Within economics, optimal means Pareto efficient, not best. Similarly, the concept of efficiency in general refers to 'not wasting resources', in which case it is hard to be against efficiency. Even when economists use such jargon in a purely descriptive way in conversations with policy makers and the general public [...] the professional jargon constitutes persuasive, emotional language in general usage that has clear, unavoidable and often misunderstood normative undertones.

The assumed political power of economic jargon plays a crucial role when it comes to the flourishing of health economics.

When the "the economic worldview" (Colvin 1985: 2) achieved full intensity during the 1980s, the stage was set for the rise of health economics to an influential subdiscipline (see Keaney 2001: 143). Back then, debates in the UK, resembling the dispute in the US, were shaped by worries about "public intrusion" into the private realm and people expressed worries about inefficiencies in the public sector and low economic growth (see Colvin 1985: 1)· Against the backdrop of a strained economic situation, they especially believed that the percentage of spending on medical care to GDP was too high (see Colvin 1985: 148). Indeed, rising health care expenditures had become a central issue for public policy all over the world (see Reinhardt

1998: 2; Cutler 2007: 393ff.; Wolfe 2008). This was the momentum of health economics, as Ashmore *et al.* (1989: 2) observe:

> In the 1970s and 1980s, as the cost of health care in Britain continued to rise, there was a growing concern on the part of government to reduce the rate of growth and to ensure that the resources devoted to health were used to maximum efficiency. Within the health care system, participants increasingly had to monitor their own economic performance, to cut costs, to rationalize services and to make difficult choices between alternative ways of spending the funds made available by central government. It was in this climate that the community of health economics came into being and began to contribute in various ways to the running of the health care system. Its members appeared to have a major opportunity to put their economic theories to work in the service of a crucially important social organization desperately in need of helpful economic guidance.

Advocating the deregulation of health care and the implementation of market mechanisms "for the sake of greater efficiency," health economics mirrored both the political climate and the atmosphere in the main discipline (Reinhardt 1992: 305).[36] In effect, the economic ideal of getting "better 'value for money'" turned into "the mantra of health care planners and policy makers" (Hurley 1998: 374).[37]

Since then, "health economics has been a remarkably successful," "thriving" subdiscipline – at least according to some health economists (Culyer/Newhouse 2000b: 1f.). As far as research is concerned, health economics came into being at a time when decision analysis and predictive modeling on the basis of economic evaluation was becoming increasingly popular (see Cohen/Ubel 2001: 95; Forget 2004: 623; Williams *et al.* 2012: 47) and it is indeed in the field of economic evaluation that the discipline has been most innovative and has evoked "considerable policy interest" (McMaster 2007: 11).[38] Notwithstanding the initial and, in part, enduring resistance from within the health care system (see Ashmore *et al.* 1989: 10–29), health economics exerted an extraordinary impact on policy making and "is displaying increased currency among policy makers" (McMaster 2007: 9).[39] As Culyer and Newhouse (2000b: 2) maintain:

> over the past three decades health economics had had an impact that is at least as great in its sphere of policy as that of any other branch of economics in its. The policy impact of health economics has also been heightened by the policy impact that the individual policy-oriented health economists have had, where personal skills in political networking, chairing important committees, and so on, supplement the usefulness of economics.

This quote makes the normative intention of health economists abundantly clear. Obviously, they do not simply aim at positively describing their subject, but seek to give advice to decision makers.[40]

Just as the rising esteem of economics and the market ideal led to a change in the general public rhetoric, so the growing influence of health economics modified the vocabulary used to speak of health care; health became "a product, patients consumers, doctors health care providers, the hospital a product delivery system, and care managed" (Cohen/Ubel 2001: 95; see Reinhardt 1998: 19). Whereas the use of such terminology is observed with some unease by non-economists, health economists consider it a sign of their discipline's encompassing success. Culyer and Newhouse (2000b: 2), for instance, praise the fact that health economics "has introduced the common currency of economics (opportunity cost, elasticity, the margin, production functions) into medical parlance" and highlight that "the language of health economics has permeated the thinking of policy makers and health service managers at all levels." It needs to be emphasized that this is not just a matter of style or rhetoric. The use of certain concepts is never normatively neutral in so far as the latter not only describe reality but structure the perception of the phenomena in the first place (see McCloskey 1998: 10).[41] Thus, the economization of public rhetoric can be regarded as simultaneously expressing and causing fundamental changes in the way the nature of public policy in general and health care issues in particular are conceived. By colonizing the minds of decision makers and the public, health economics exerts a subtle and therefore all the more profound influence on society and policy.[42]

In view of the regaining strength of the belief in the market mechanism, the rising esteem of the economists, and the authority and persuasiveness of economic rhetoric, it becomes intelligible why health economics has come to dominate the discourse on health care to a major extent. Nowadays, it appears to be "commonly recognised that rationing is best done using the economic framework of costs and benefits" (McKie/Richardson 2005a: 1). Concurrently, economists have substituted physicians as opinion leader in the public debate on health policy (see Schlander 2009: 118). It is against this background that the adherence to economic evaluation in the face of serious fairness problems has to be considered.

3.3 The *raison d'être* of economic evaluations: mimicking markets

3.3.1 Pareto efficiency, the market, and the Kaldor–Hicks criterion

Having sketched the rising influence of economists, economic arguments, and concomitantly, the ascent of the ideal of the market and CBA as its epitome within public policy during the last century, the second part of this chapter turns to considering economic evaluations from the vantage point of economic theory. Thereby, the aims are, first, to clarify the meaning of the central concept of efficiency, second, to illustrate the normative framework of CBA and its *raison d'être*, and especially, third, to hint to a fundamental problem of the approach.

As to the efficiency concept, it already became clear in the previous considerations that it plays a pivotal role in the context of economic thinking in general and in the realm of economic evaluation in particular.[43] Especially due to its positive connotations – "Efficiency is like motherhood and apple pie; no one can admit being against it" (Harris 1997: 104) – the term demands close investigation. Presumably, the first association with efficiency is the idea of avoiding waste (see Reinhardt 1992: 302; Kelleher 2014: 259). Efficiency in this sense refers to the achievement of a certain goal with the least expenditure of resources and is referred to as technical efficiency in economics (see Reinhardt 1998: 26f.; Powers/Faden 2006: 100; Schlander 2009: 118). Taking an example from health care, a treatment is technically efficient if it cures a disease using the least expensive medicine. According to the less familiar notion of allocative efficiency, by contrast, resources are to be allocated to those uses which generate most value (see Schlander 2009: 118). Crucially, this concept takes the opportunity costs of a certain resource allocation into account, that is, the benefit that could be obtained by the next best use of the resources in question. In health care, the opportunity costs of treating one patient consist of the benefit *another* patient could derive from the same treatment. Allocative efficiency in health care resource allocation thus asks "which patient or group of patients is it beneficial to treat" (Harris 1997: 103). Whereas technical efficiency is intuitively compelling, it does not go without saying that an efficient allocation of medical resources in the latter sense is equally desirable. The claim that it is not indeed lies at the heart of the present study.

Economists usually interpret both technical and allocative efficiency in terms of Pareto efficiency and, thereby, make these notions even more opaque to lay persons. A distribution is Pareto optimal or Pareto efficient when it is impossible to redistribute resources in a way that makes at least one person better off without making anybody worse off (see Little 1957: 84; Boadway/Bruce 1984: 11ff.). Although, strictly speaking, a Pareto efficient equilibrium is only reached when both conditions of technical and allocative efficiency are met, Pareto efficiency is usually understood in terms of allocative efficiency only (see Reinhardt 1992: 307). A Pareto improvement is a change which makes at least one person better off without making anybody worse off. In accordance with the microeconomic premise of consumer sovereignty, an individual is regarded as being worse or better off to the extent that her preferences are satisfied. That is, well-being is defined in terms of preference satisfaction.[44] A Pareto improvement thus enhances overall welfare by definition.

The concept of the Pareto optimum came to the fore in welfare economics during the ordinal revolution. As outlined in the preceding chapter, Robbins argued that value judgments in general and interpersonal comparisons of satisfaction in particular had no place within economic science. This posed a major obstacle to welfare economics because making propositions about aggregate social welfare without introducing value judgments "is like running a race with your feet tied together" (Hausman/McPherson 2008: 241). The concept of Pareto efficiency was supposed to solve this problem since assessing whether a Pareto improvement has taken place does not require interpersonal comparisons of satisfaction. Due to the fact that a Pareto improvement makes no one worse off in terms of his own preferences, it can be expected that it meets "with unanimous approval" by all persons affected by the change (Blaug 1997: 573).[45] Hence, the so-called Pareto principle, that is, the normative assumption that Pareto efficient states of affairs are "morally better" than non-efficient ones (Hausman/McPherson 2006: 137), is generally regarded as a "rather weak" and "widely accepted" value judgment (Boadway/Bruce 1984: 2f.).

At first glance, Pareto efficiency seems to be an appealing concept indeed. Note, however, that for a given amount of resources and a given scale of preferences, there always exist various, mutually incomparable Pareto optimal outcomes (see Hicks 1939: 701; Samuelson 1947: 214), which are not necessarily regarded as optimal from the vantage point of commonsense (see Arrow 1963b: 942). If, for instance, we have two persons (A and B) and ten units of bread to be distributed among them, *any* distribution of the disposable bread leads to a Pareto efficient state of affairs (see Hausman/McPherson 2008: 241). Even if person A receives all the bread and person B ends up with nothing, this situation is optimal since it cannot be altered without making A worse off. The same is true for a system of slavery because it cannot be changed without making the slave owners worse off.[46] Thus, it can be said, according to Hausman and McPherson (2008: 241), that the only "praiseworthy" feature of a Pareto optimum is that it "does not pass up any opportunities to satisfy some people's preferences better without sacrificing the preference satisfaction of somebody else."[47]

In the present context, the concept of Pareto efficiency is particularly relevant due to its close theoretical connection with the competitive market. Since notions such as free market, consumer sovereignty, or enhanced economic welfare are "felicitous," persuasive terms, their meaning and their theoretical underpinnings need to be scrutinized closely, as Reinhardt (1998: 9) emphasizes:

> A point always to remember, then, is that it pays to be skeptical whenever economists speak of 'value' and 'efficiency'. It is useful to explicate the ethical importance of the free-market approach in their full detail, because that approach is so often marketed not with the blunt candor that so controversial a doctrine warrants, but instead with the highly seductive language and imaginary of economics. Who could possibly be against 'consumer sovereignty', 'consumer choice', 'consumer empowerment', 'individual responsibility', 'economic efficiency', 'enhanced economic welfare' and similarly felicitous terms into which the approach is so often wrapped?

In the 1950s, the aforementioned existence proof established that a freely working market mechanism meeting certain assumptions – such as complete information of all market participants, no transaction costs, and perfect competition – guarantees a Pareto efficient equilibrium. This finding constitutes the first fundamental theorem of welfare economics (see Hurley 2000: 61).[48] The underlying rationale is straightforward: if two self-interested individuals are to enter a market transaction voluntarily, each party has to expect a gain from the exchange for otherwise they would not have agreed on the trade in the first place. Thus, the first theorem can be regarded as "a generalization of the case of bilateral exchange, which, being voluntary, must be welfare-enhancing for both parties" (Blaug 2007: 187).[49] The second fundamental theorem demonstrates that any Pareto efficient distribution of income can be considered as an outcome of a perfectly competitive market given the appropriate (re)distribution of initial wealth (see Hurley 2000: 62).[50] Taken together, the theorems constitute the "cornerstone of postwar normative economics" and "secured Pareto efficiency's ascendancy" (Mandler 1999: 151).[51] In the present context, especially two effects on the economic discipline are interesting. First, the theorems established a separation of the economic sphere of the market on the one hand and the realm of distributional questions on the other. At least since then, "economists have felt free to analyze only questions of efficiency, leaving the questions of the right distribution of resources to the political process" (Hurley 2000: 62).[52] To be sure, this separation makes the counterfactual presumptions that redistribution is costless and does not exert adverse effects on the achievement of the optimum (see Arrow 1963b: 943). Second, by providing a close link between Pareto optimality and the competitive market equilibrium, the theorems established the free market as a "moral ideal" and as a benchmark for allocating resources (Hausman/McPherson 2008: 243).

Against the background of these considerations, within neoclassical economics, government intervention in the market is only warranted in so far as at least one of the stated premises for perfect competition is violated so that the market mechanism is unable to guarantee an efficient outcome. Among the reasons for such market failures are, first and foremost, the presence of externalities and public goods (see Boadway/Bruce 1984: 13f.; Powers/Faden 2006: 105ff., 144ff.). And yet, also the government needs information on the citizen's preferences in order to make sure that an efficient outcome will be reached (see Powers/Faden 2006: 145). It is at this point that economic evaluations come into play since it is their purpose to "approximate the economic efficiency of markets" (see Powers/Faden 2006: 142) and "to ensure welfare maximization" (McGuire 2001: 1).[53] Hence, this is also the economic rationale behind *health* economic evaluation. Due to, for instance, informational asymmetries between providers and consumers and the existence of externalities, the health care and health insurance markets fail (see Hurley 2000: 67ff.).[54] Beyond that, health care is usually regarded as a merit good that ought to be consumed by everyone regardless of his or her ability to pay (see Reinhardt 1998: 2).[55] Thus, both for reasons stemming from microeconomic theory and on the basis of a value judgment, health care is generally not, or at least not completely, bought and sold on a free market.[56] Instead, nearly all industrialized countries provide their citizen with a public health care system so that, from the vantage point of neoclassical welfare economics, economic evaluations become necessary.

Given CBA's aim to mimic markets, it needs to identify possible Pareto improvements (see Mishan 1972: 14). However, even if the issue of how to obtain the required information on preferences is put aside for the time being, this undertaking faces a severe problem. Since policy changes typically produce winners and losers, Pareto improvements are virtually never feasible in reality (see Mitchell/Carson 1989: 21). Confronted with this issue, Nicholas Kaldor and

John R. Hicks came up with the conception of the potential Pareto improvement, also known as the hypothetical compensation principle or the Kaldor–Hicks principle (KH principle), as a pragmatic alternative.[57] According to this principle, an increase in social welfare takes place whenever the winners of a redistributive policy gain enough to be able to compensate the looser and still remain better off than before (see Mishan 1972: 14).

In order to illustrate the concept, it is helpful to consider its original formulation by Kaldor (1939). In the paper "Welfare Propositions of Economics and Interpersonal Comparisons of Utility," he seeks to show that a case for abolishing the Corn Laws need not rely on interpersonal comparisons of satisfaction.[58] He points out that the effects of repealing the Laws on income were basically twofold: for one thing, dismantling the Corn Laws would lead to a reduction in the price of corn so that everyone's real income rises. For another, it would alter the income distribution to the effect that the landlords lose income while the income of other people increases, given that aggregate income remains constant. However, this distributional effect could be offset "by compensating the 'landlords' for every loss of income and by providing the funds for such compensation by an extra tax on those whose incomes have been augmented" (Kaldor 1939: 550).[59] After the compensation, nobody would be worse off than before in terms of income and, due to the lower corn prices, everybody would be better off in his capacity as a consumer. Hence, free trade would be beneficial overall (see ibid.). Stated more generally:

> In all cases, therefore, where a certain policy leads to an increase in physical productivity, and thus of aggregate real income, the economist's case for the policy is quite unaffected by the question of the comparability of individual satisfactions; since in all cases it is possible to make everybody better off than before, or at any rate to make some people better off without making anybody worse off.
>
> (Ibid.)

It deserves emphasis that the KH principle does not offer a *test* of whether an increase in welfare has taken place, but rather *defines* what counts as an increase in social welfare (see Little 1957: 91; Sugden/Williams 1978: 93). Crucially, this definition refers only to the possibility of compensation, not to actual compensation. That is to say, whereas the Pareto principle focuses on policy changes making no one worse off, the KH principle abandons this proviso, making the definition of an increase in welfare totally independent from the resulting distribution of income.[60] In doing so, the KH criterion seems to fulfill "one of the oldest dreams of economics," namely, the separation of equity and efficiency and the legitimization of the exclusive focus on the latter (Blaug 1997: 576). This is completely in line with Robbins' ideal of the positivist science of economics, of course. While intricate and value-laden decisions on distributional issues fall into the realm of philosophy and politics, the "economist is on sure ground" when it comes to the production of economic benefits (Kaldor 1939: 551).[61] Here, economics' "scientific status is unquestionable" (ibid.). Kaldor and Hicks thus claim to have rendered economic advice "approximately innocuous from the distributive point of view" and welfare economics "capable of the same logical precision and the same significant elaboration as its twin brother, Positive Economics" (Hicks 1939: 712).

The compensation criterion was heavily criticized and its alleged normative innocuousness as to distributional issues was refuted eventually.[62] Nevertheless, the principle found "remarkable wide acceptance" in economics (Mitchell/Carson 1989: 22) and still plays a pivotal role for CBA (see Davis 1990: 144). Most likely, its popularity stems from the previously considered separation of the sphere of distribution on the one hand and a decisively economic domain of inquiry on the other. Given that welfare economics seeks to answer the question "What do we mean when we say that one state of a social system is better than another in strictly economic terms?" (Boulding 1969: 5), there has to be an area describable "in strictly economic terms" in the first place:

> The idea that there is, thus, a specifically economic dimension of evaluation determines the character of mainstream normative economics. It is this idea that makes it possible to envision normative economic theory, as opposed to a set of normatively motivated inquiries into consequences and properties of economic policies and institutions. Welfare Economics depends not only on a specific view of welfare but also on the view that inquiries into welfare can be separated from inquiries into freedom, rights, equality and justice.
>
> (Hausman/McPherson 2008: 240)[63]

Beyond splitting-up the spheres of inquiry, Hicks elaborated measures to elicit costs and benefits of non-market goods in terms of the individuals' willingness to pay (WTP) and, thereby, made an important contribution to the methods of economic evaluation (see Mitchell/Carson 1989: 23ff.; Schlander 2009: 120). In effect, Kaldor and Hicks embedded CBA in the theoretical framework of new welfare economics so that CBA could henceforth be regarded as application of economic tools to public policy programs (see Tsuchiya/Williams 2001: 22).[64]

This "takeover by the economists" of CBA in the 1940s aggravated "the pursuit of unbounded quantification" and "the spread of cost-benefit techniques to all kinds of government expenditures" (Porter 1996: 188).[65] Referring back to the deceiving nature of felicitous economic language, it now becomes clear why the results of CBAs based on the KH criterion have to be handled with care (see McGuire 2001: 7). To quote Mishan (1972: 15), a CBA revealing a net gain of $100,000 does by no means imply that the policy in question makes everyone better off. It only means "that it is conceptually possible, by costless redistributions, to make everyone better off, in total by an amount equal to $100,000" (ibid.). Having outlined the basic rationale and the normative foundation of CBA as well as the reasons for its authority and the need to scrutinize the underlying assumptions closely, the following section elaborates the methods of preference elicitation applied within CBA and provides a first account of why the use of economic evaluations in health economics is connected with fundamental problems.

3.3.2 Cost-benefit analysis in health economics

As pointed out above, the aim of economic evaluations is to mimic markets in cases of market failure, the prime example being the provision of public goods, such as building a bridge or a highway. Its theoretical objective is thus to "determine whether a potential project produces a favorable ratio of benefits to costs" (Powers/Faden 2006: 142). Evidently, a critical issue is how to define the monetary value of the respective costs and benefits in the absence of a market. To this extent, economists generally favor revealed preference methods. In line with the economists' "informal behaviorism" (Mandler 1999: 88), they rely on what people are actually preferring, not what they merely state they prefer (see Richardson 2002: 633f.). An example for the revealed preference method is the study of wage-risk trade-offs, which analyzes the relationship between health risks associated with a dangerous job and the wage rates the individuals require to accept the job (see Drummond *et al.* 2005: 218).[66] Disregarding the fact that revealed preference methods are facing problems of their own,[67] they are hardly ever viable when it comes to the evaluation of intangible values in environmental or health economics, though (see Viney *et al.* 2002: 319; Wolff/Haubrich 2006: 750f.). Hence, economists have to revert to stated preference methods, predominantly those going under the heading of contingent valuation (CV) (see Mitchell/Carson 1989: 9).[68] The name *contingent* valuation stems from the fact that the respondents are asked for the maximum they would be willing to pay for obtaining or retaining a good under the contingency that an actual market existed (see Mitchell/Carson 1989: 2f.).[69] Alternatively, respondents are asked for the minimum amount they would accept as compensation for a negative outcome (willingness to accept (WTA)) (see Copp 1985: 130).[70]

The contingent valuation method (CVM) had already been proposed in 1947, but did not gain popularity until the 1980s. To see why this is, it is instructive to take a short look at one catalyzing factor behind this development, namely, an environmental disaster in the US (see Portney 1994: 6ff.). In March 1989, the oil-tanker *Exxon Valdez* ran aground on the Bligh Reef, "spilling 11 million gallons of crude oil into the icy blue waters of Alaska's Prince William Sound" (Ackerman/Heinzerling 2004: 153).[71] The accident resulted in "1300 miles of oiled shoreline, the deaths of 250,000 birds, 2800 otters, over 250 seals, and destruction of nearly uncountable salmon and herring eggs" and heralded a public debate on the appropriate compensation of environmental damages (Kling *et al.* 2012: 3).[72] This is when CV came "to meet the real world" (Portney 1994: 7). Methodological debates on the evaluation of non-market goods, which had formerly been of mere academic interest, suddenly turned into a matter worth billions of dollars when it came to litigation over liability and damages (see Kahneman/Knetsch 1992: 57; Ackerman/Heinzerling 2004: 154). In particular, the amount of compensation Exxon would have to pay crucially depended on the methodological question of whether only use-value, such as the economic loss suffered by the fishermen, or also existence value assigned to the Reef by those people who have never been there and are not planning to go either is taken into account. This question is important since including the latter in the estimation of damages leads to much higher costs than a focus on use-value only, of course.[73] The effect of this methodological choice in monetary terms is striking indeed. Ackerman and Heinzerling (2004: 155f.) report that "based on estimates of their actual economic losses," fishermen and local residents were awarded $300 million, whereas a telephone survey measuring the existence value of the Prince William Sound revealed a national total WTP of $9 billion.[74]

Details of the CVM thus became the subject of a fierce political controversy: while environmentalists heavily endorsed the use of existence values for evaluating the damage caused, the oil companies fervently opposed the application of CVM to measure existence value; Exxon even funded research attacking the method (see Portney 1994: 7). In view of the high stakes involved, the National Oceanic and Atmospheric Administration, directed to regulate damage assessments, commissioned an expert panel to investigate whether the CVM was capable of generating non-use values that were sufficiently reliable to be used in natural resource damage assessments. As a result, the panel recommended the use of CV given that certain conditions were met (see Knetsch 1994: 352ff., Portney 1994: 9). Although in the end, no results of any CV study have "ever stood up as credible evidence in litigation" (Sagoff 2004: 109), the Exxon oil spill and its political consequences initiated a discussion within economics on the appropriate methods for valuing public goods and "launched a thousand surveys" (Ackerman/Heinzerling 2004: 154). The concurrent advancements of CV, in turn, "increased the role of monetary valuation in public policy" more generally (Spash 2000: 453).[75] Hence, it does not seem a stretch to assume that these developments in environmental economics enhanced the rise of health economics in the early 1990s.

Equipped with the CVM, a CBA now proceeds as follows:

> Each person who would lose from the project is asked what is the minimum payment of money he would consider full compensation for his loss. This amount is defined as the value of his loss. [...] Each person who would benefit is asked how much money he would be prepared to pay to get the benefit. This amount is defined as its value. Then, if the value of the benefits adds up to more than the value of the losses, the project can be carried out, the gainers can compensate the losers, and no one will end up worse than when he started.
>
> (Broome 1978: 91f.)

Making the data on individuals' WTP the units of value, CBA adheres to the principle of welfarism.[76] Following Sen (1979: 468), welfarism means that the "judgment of the relative goodness of alternative states of affairs must be based exclusively on, and taken as an increasing function of, the respective collections of individual utilities in these states." In order to provide propositions as to "whether society as a whole will become better off" by undertaking a certain project (Mishan 1975: xiii), CBA needs to be "as all-encompassing as possible" (Hansson 2007: 168). That is, CBA adopts a *societal perspective*, taking into account all costs and benefits connected with a certain policy measure.[77] In reality, the accomplishment of this goal is restricted by several factors, such as the demand for efficient information-gathering or the existence of cognitive boundaries, of course (see Hansson 2007: 169). Nonetheless, from the vantage point of neoclassical welfare economics, the major advantage of using CBA in health care resource allocation consists in its encompassing scope. First, as CBA does not restrict what counts as a benefit, it is able to tackle what the individuals actually value so that it is entirely in line with the assumption of consumer sovereignty (see Drummond *et al.* 2005: 214).[78] Second, due to the fact that CBA assigns a monetary value to all benefits, it allows the comparative evaluation of all kinds of medical interventions. Third, the benefit of investing in health can in principle be compared with non-health benefits in other areas (see Schöffski 2012b: 59).[79] For these reasons, CBA is generally regarded as "the most powerful" of the existing health economic evaluation techniques (Drummond *et al.* 2005: 214).

Having said that, the following examples cast doubt on the claim that achieving "overall efficiency" (Powers/Faden 2006: 145) is really such an attractive ideal when it comes to health care resource allocation. To begin with, discussing the issue of whether future costs of unrelated illnesses should be included in a CBA, Garber *et al.* (1996: 45) offer the following case in point:

> Suppose, for example, that we contemplate instituting a suicide prevention program in high school. It is highly effective and reduces teenage suicides by 50%. Students who would otherwise have died now lead lives of average length and have medical care utilization comparable to those of average persons of their age. Should the future cost of health care that they consume be counted as costs of the intervention?

Given the aim of calculating the true costs of the treatment, it is only straightforward to include the costs of future health care needed.[80]

By the same token, all future costs accruing to the public budget, such as transfer payments or pensions, would have to be incorporated as well. This is illustrated by the example of smoking-cessation programs presented by Powers and Faden (2006: 146f.):

> In one of the more controversial examples of how CBA might be used, some studies of the costs and benefits of governmental programs for discouraging smoking took into account the economic losses to the national treasury that would accompany success in smoking-cessation programs. While the unmistakable public health benefit of reduced smoking might be achieved, an important item in the 'cost' side of the ledger is the added expenditure for retirement and medical care of those who, because of increased longevity, would live longer and cost more.

Additionally, smoking cessation on a broad scale would certainly influence the tobacco industry so that the respective CBA has to include the "benefits of increased sales of tobacco products," the associated "greater employment opportunities in manufacturing, marketing, and retail sales, together with greater tax revenue from the sale of cigarettes" (Powers/Faden 2006: 147). As a result, it is well possible that a smoking-cessation program would reduce overall welfare. Ackerman and Heinzerling (2004: 72) quote a study revealing that smoking indeed saves the government money. Because in general, smokers die earlier than non-smokers, both costs for providing them nursing home care and other medical costs are saved. In view of the high financial benefit to the state, the author of the quoted study suggests that "cigarette smoking should be subsidized rather than taxed" (Viscusi quoted ibid.).

Finally, Richardson and McKie (2007: 788–790) consider the hypothetical decision between treating one out of two individuals whose lives can both be prolonged by ten years at a cost of $100,000. One of the patients is a multi-millionaire without any relatives who owns $40 million, whereas the other is an ordinary citizen. Wondering which patient should be treated, they state:

> The treatment of the magnate will cost the taxpayer $100,000 directly plus $40 million which, if treated, she will consume, but which would otherwise revert to society. It is reasonable to assume that society would obtain greater benefit from the money than a single, aged person with limited capacity to enjoy benefits from her money. Subject to minor caveats, taxpayers would be much better off if C [the millionaire] died and the service was provided to the other patient.
>
> (Richardson/McKie 2007: 790)

In all the examples presented, it seems inapt to strive for overall efficiency by actually incorporating *all* costs and benefits induced by a program. But why exactly is this?

The first reason presenting itself is the rough intuition that the allocation of health care resources should not aim at benefitting the tobacco companies or the taxpayer but the patient in need. The fact that an overt appeal to the value of a persons' health *to society* leads to troublesome consequences has already been acknowledged in the health economic literature some decades ago when the human capital approach was used to estimate costs and benefits in monetary terms (see Blumenschein/Johannesson 1996: 115; Sassi *et al.* 2001: 4). To put it pointedly, this approach basically regards individuals "as a type of machine with costs of maintenance and expected output" (Murray 1994: 435). Accordingly, it considers spending on health care as an investment in a person's human capital and regards health care benefits as "the estimated reductions in subsequent treatment costs plus increases in production due to improved health" (Johannesson 1996: 1).[81] The increase in production, i.e., "the pay-back" on the "investment" in human capital is determined by the present value of the individual's future earnings, using market wage rates (Drummond *et al.* 2005: 215f.).[82]

Obviously, according to the human capital approach, the value attached to a life year is directly proportional to the person's income.[83] As a corollary, it assigns small values to the health of people not working on the labor market – such as housemen, children, students, and pensioners – and to those whose productivity is low. By the same token, higher weights have to be attached to the health of physicians or exceptionally skilled workers and, vice versa, lower weights to the health of unskilled workers.[84] Beyond that, the "logical extension of the human capital approach would be to weight time by other human attributes that correlate with productivity such as income, education, geographical location or even, in some economies, ethnicity" (Murray 1994: 435). This focus on the value of the individual's health to society, however, hardly squares with "ideals of democracy and equal treatment under the law" (Ackerman/Heinzerling 2004: 72). The ethically unacceptable implications of the human capital approach have been recognized within the health economic literature as well. Murray (1994: 435), for instance, points out that its application leads to "obvious inequity,"[85] and Greiner and Damm (2012: 33) concede that different treatment on the basis of productivity violates the principle of equal access to health care. When the human capital approach became more and more criticized in the 1970s, researchers turned to the WTP method to value economic costs and benefits and developed cost-effectiveness analysis (CEA) as a form of economic evaluation better tailored to the subject of health care (see Drummond *et al.* 2005: 217).[86] Yet, the serious objections leveled against the human capital approach notwithstanding, it is still regarded as an appropriate measure to assess the indirect costs of ill health.[87]

Abandoning the use of the human capital approach did not eliminate the ethical issues arising as soon as the value of a person's health is considered within a framework striving for overall efficiency, as the examples considered above show.[88] Indeed, some of the authors point toward the ethically unacceptable consequences an all-encompassing CBA would have in the respective cases. Powers and Faden (2006: 147) assess a policy based on the depicted CBA of a smoking-cessation program as "unethical," not least due to the fact that in this case, the quest for efficiency comes at the "price of some falling short of a sufficiency of health for a decent life" and Richardson and McKie (2007: 790) surmise that their "argument for letting the magnate die would be universally rejected as unfair" so that the "efficiency of the policy (the greater social benefits) would be irrelevant."[89] It becomes apparent that the issue of which costs and benefits to include in CBA is in fact no methodological problem, but a question of fairness requiring an ethical instead of a technical analysis (see ibid., Cookson *et al.* 2009: 235). Pursuant to Richardson and McKie (2007: 794), the ethical issues connected with applying CBA's societal perspective in medical resource allocation also seem to be recognized in applied health economics, implicitly though this might be. They point out that "important elements of fairness are already included in the practice, as distinct from the theory, of economic evaluation"; applied economic evaluations, for instance, commonly ignore "the indirect benefits of increased production, despite current theoretical arguments for their inclusion" (ibid.).[90] That is, the value maximizing logic of CBA is not strictly adhered to in praxis;

it seems as if economists "have not been willing to stomach the implications of cost-benefit analysis," which present a "radical collision with everyday morality" (Hausman 2000b: 334).[91]

Including some cost and benefits of health care resource allocation and excluding others constitutes a significant departure from both the theoretical foundation and the original aim and rationale of CBA, though (see Powers/Faden 2006: 147). Hence, this endeavor raises the question as to the normative justification for such a truncation of CBA. If the aim is to achieve overall efficiency, why and when exactly are exceptions warranted? This fundamental normative-theoretical issue remains unreflected within the health economic discipline (see Lübbe 2015: 18f.). In fact, it points to the inappropriateness of adopting the value-maximizing perspective of economic evaluations in health care to begin with (see ibid.). This is also indicated by the problems stemming from the use of WTP data as units of value. Since stated WTP values are heavily hooked on the respondent's ability to pay, "a unit in health would be valued more if it went to a rich person than to a poor person" (Tsuchiya 2012: 407). In effect, a resource allocation based on these data would be tilted toward the preferences of the wealthy (see Olsen/Smith 2001: 46).[92] In the face of such unacceptable consequences, CBA became substituted by other forms of economic evaluation more suited to the area of health care, first and foremost CUA.[93] This amounts to a "conceptual drift" away from CBA's initial underpinnings in welfare economics "in part to become more useful to program administrators, and in part to avoid ethical objections" (Powers/Faden 2006: 155). But while the ideal of market efficiency was abandoned, the concepts and methods used within economic evaluation and, thereby, the general value-maximizing framework remained intact, leading both to conceptual ambiguities and to new fairness issues, as the following chapter shows.

Notes

1 Italics added. Strictly speaking, Robbins' definition denies any difference between economic or noneconomic means and alternatives, of course.

2 Likewise, Richardson/McKie (2007: 792) report that the NHS was primarily "established to achieve fundamental fairness objectives." Actually, equity considerations still provide the "fundamental reason for interventions in the health sector in virtually every country in the world with a functional government," as Richardson (2009: 247) points out. See McMaster (2001: 113).

3 See also Kelley (1997), Morgan/Rutherford (1998b), and Amadae (2003). The following considerations basically refer to the US due to the facts that, first, this is where the pivotal event of the Great Depression had its origin and, second, economics conducted in the US became dominant in the profession after World War II, especially in the course of the Cold War. See Morgan (2003: 296).

4 Note that I do by no means intend to claim that all advocates of equity weighting, or all health economists for that matter, endorse market-liberal politics. What I do claim is that the shift to the right at the end of the twentieth century mirrored and simultaneously fostered a strong belief in the free market as allocation device and, in doing so, set the stage for the rising popularity of economic imperialism on the one hand and economic evaluations in public policy on the other.

5 See also Kelley (1997: 29, 31f.) and Backhouse (2010: 182).

6 See also Leonard (1991: 262).

7 In the US, one important turning point as to the public role of the economists was the creation of the *Council of Economic Advisers* in 1946, which was especially expected to give economic advice to the President on how to prevent economic depression.

8 Between 1947 and 1970, the general real income in the US increased by astonishing 80 percent (Berg 1999: 148).

9 See especially Arrow (1963b), one of the earliest contributions to the emerging field.

10 See also Blumenschein/Johannesson (1996), Reinhardt (1998: 1), and Cookson *et al.* (2014: 29). Note that the development of health economics happened with different paces in different countries. Culyer (1981: 3) observes that in the US, a special session of the American Economic Association Meeting was dedicated to the economics of medical care already in 1951, whereas in Germany, the first meeting of economists discussing health economic issues did not take place until 1978. Presumably, this delay is connected with the country's history. Although the Holocaust was motivated by racism, both the killing of inmates in the concentration camps and the euthanasia program was motivated by concerns for productivity and the utility of the respective persons *for society* . As the rhetoric of especially the early contributions to CBA in health care shows a striking resemblance with such reasoning, it is no wonder that the prioritization discourse in Germany is conducted much more cautiously than in other countries. See on rationing as a taboo in Germany also Lübbe (2011: 99f.). For an overview of the development of health economics in Germany and the US see Schulenburg (2012: 17–19).

11 RAND attracted scholars such as Schelling, von Neumann, Buchanan, and Arrow. See Amadae (2003: 9, 10–12, 40). Arrow's seminal *Social Choice and Individual Values,* for instance, resulted from a task he was assigned with during his time at RAND, namely the definition of a collective utility function for the Soviet Union. See Amadae (2003: 103).

12 Backhouse (2010: 144) states: "Symbolic of the idea that efficient management systems developed in business could also be applied to government activities was the application of systems analysis to the conduct of the Vietnam War under Robert McNamara." See also Goodwin (2008).

13 See on the PPBS more extensively Amadae (2003: 62ff.) and Orlans (1986: 193ff.).

14 Amadae (2003: 63) points out that by way of removing budget ceilings, PPBS put the policy process upside down: "instead of fiscal appropriations being handed down from Congress to meet operational needs, defense planners would articulate their needs using presumptively *objective* and thus *incontrovertible* cost-effectiveness studies" (italics added).

15 See also Orlans (1986: 193), Leonard (1991: 280), and Amadae (2003: 68).

16 Pursuant to Okun (1975: 117), "the main fault of those programs lay in 'overpromising' rather than in 'underperforming'."

17 Osberg (1995: 24) explicitly regards Okun as the "originator of the trade-off cliché." See Porter (1996: 156).

18 See e.g. Mankiw/Taylor (2014: 3). Further examples are provided by Schefczyk/Priddat (2000: 428). According to Lukes (1996: 38), Okun's equality-efficiency trade-off owes its popularity to Samuelson who adapted it "to support the idea that there is a tension between democracy and market capitalism."

19 This was especially emphasized by public choice theory. See Kelley (1997: 44ff.), Backhouse (2005: 359f.), and Tullock (2008). The pivotal importance of public choice theory for the consolidation of rational choice theory after World War II is stressed by Amadae (2003).

20 Wolff/Haubrich (2006: 748) observe that welfare-enhancing programs became more and more regarded as having "adverse effects on economic efficiency and international competitiveness." See Morgan/Rutherford (1998b: 10).

21 See also Porter (1996: 198), Keaney (2001: 143), and Backhouse (2010: 150f., 156).

22 See also Kelley (1997: 16ff.), Morgan (2003: 294), and Backhouse (2010: 124–129).

23 Colvin (1985: 2) reports regarding the UK:

> beginning in the mid 1960s the number of professional economists within central government increased dramatically (from less than 25 in 1964 to more than 350 in 1975). By the end of the 1970s the economics profession had come to be represented in virtually all parts of Whitehall, and government economists were engaged in work ranging across all aspects of the discipline.

See regarding the US Orlans (1986: 192).

24 See also Harpham/Scotch (1988: 225f.) and Ackerman/Heinzerling (2004: 18ff., 195ff.).

25 See also Mishan (1975: 1–23), Spash (1999: 130), Drummond *et al.* (2005: 214), and Wolff/Haubrich (2006: 749).

26 See Harpham/Scotch (1988: 224f.), Blumenschein/Johannesson (1996: 114), Keaney (2001: 144), Backhouse (2005: 358), and (2010: 159).

27 Colvin (1985: 11ff., 44–76) analyzes how economists became integrated into various branches of government in the 1970s and 1980s and demonstrates how profoundly economic thinking came to permeate public policy debates. By the end of the 1980s, Harpham/Scotch (1988: 216) aver: "We live in the age of the economist. Economic language has become one of the principal languages through which we discuss public affairs in the modern democratic state."

28 The rhetoric of health economics and the role of metaphors are scrutinized in Chapter 5 of this study.

29 On the rise of statistics see the references given in Section 2.2.2.

30 See also Mirowski (1988: 119f.). As to the question of whether "numbers tell," McCloskey (1998: 100) maintains: "According to the official rhetoric, yes: only numbers. Most economists believe that once you have reduced a question to numbers you have taken it out of human hands." Likewise, Goldenberg (2005) avers: "if it is neutrality that is desired, numbers are the pinnacle."

31 According to McCloskey (1998: 36) this is irrespective of whether the mathematics is actually necessary for the task set or not. See Morgan (2003: 277) and Porter (1992: 28). To give an example, McCloskey (1998: 36) argues regarding Samuelson's *Foundations of Economic Analysis*:

> The air of easy mathematical mastery was important for the influence of the book [...]. Samuelson's skill at mathematics in the eyes of his readers, an impression nurtured at every turn, is itself an important and persuasive argument. He presents himself as an authority, on good grounds. That the mathematics is sometimes pointless [...] is beside the point. Being able to do such a difficult thing [...] is warrant of expertise.

32 Put the other way round, "it helps to keep the profession free of 'admixture with all baser matter'," as an actuary quoted by Porter (1996: 202) uttered in the nineteenth century.

33 See also Mandler (2001: 398).

34 Nygaard (2000: 123) avers:

> Introduction of health indicators and 'mechanical' measures of health care evaluation can also release politicians from the responsibility of making difficult decisions, on the grounds that 'Research has shown that programme X should be prioritized above programme Y' or 'WHO recommends that the priorities should be this or that'.

35 On the relevance of adopting a proper terminology in the context of public policy see Fisher (1918: 335): "In all sciences, and particularly one like economics, which

appeals to the general public and which uses concepts and terms already at least partial familiar, it is a matter of some practical importance to select a suitable terminology."

36 The quote in the main body refers to American health economists but other sources, for instance Keaney (2001), report the same for the UK.

37 By then, economists and others were "in regular informal contact about matters which they themselves described as 'health economics'" (Ashmore *et al.* 1989: 5). The first international conference was organized in 1973 and the first widely used textbook published in 1979 (see Fuchs 1987). University courses as well as professional associations were established (see Schulenburg 2012: 17ff.) and the first international journal dedicated to health economics, the *Journal of Health Economics* was founded in 1982 (see Forget 2004: 623). By the end of the 1980s, the quantity of health economic conferences had grown enormously, and so had the number of their participants: "Instead of booking merely a room or two for a small luncheon, they book entire hotels!" (Reinhardt 1998: 2)

38 Mooney (2009: 64) points out that health economics had its greatest influence in the use of economic evaluation in pharmaceuticals, whereas its policy impact as to priority setting at the level of, for example, investments in different client groups had been low. He traces this difference back to the power of the medical profession.

39 By contrast, Mooney (2009: 27ff., 64) evaluates the discipline's policy impact much more negatively.

40 On the normative claim of health economic evaluation see Lübbe (2009d) and Chapter 4 of this study.

41 See Section 5.2 of this study.

42 In a chapter entitled "Colonizing the Mind," Ashmore *et al.* (1989: 10–29) scrutinize how the health economists Mooney and Drummond tried to overcome the unexpected resistance from within the medical profession to their ideas and show that they explicitly aimed at persuading the medical staff of the importance of economic analyses.

43 On efficiency as the dominating rubric of (health) economics see Reinhardt (1992: 305), Morgan/Rutherford (1998b: 10), Backhouse (2005: 355), and McMaster (2007: 11).

44 See on critical discussions of the preference-satisfaction view of well-being Sagoff (1986: 303), Hurley (1998: 377), Mongin/D'Aspremont (1999: 388ff.), and especially Hausman (2000a, 2012: 75ff.) and Hausman/McPherson (2006: 118ff., 2009). The crucial issue is what these preferences are supposed to refer to. See therefore Chapter 5 of this study.

45 Culyer (1998: 364f.) points out that it was the Pareto criterion's "commendable object to minimize the intrusion of personal values into economic analysis" and to impose "political modesty on economics."

46 The constitution of a slave society could even constitute a Pareto improvement for all parties involved if the slaves were worse off in an alternative system and consented to their enslavement. See Buchanan (1975: 85f.).

47 See also Reinhardt (1992: 306). Even this praiseworthy implication becomes questionable as soon as the preferences at stake are sadistic or racist, though.

48 See also Boadway/Bruce (1984: 3) and Hausman (2008b: 24).

49 See also Smith (2006: 731). Note that the ethical attractiveness of this reasoning hinges on a specification of what characterizes a voluntary action.

50 See also Richardson/McKie (2007: 792) and Hausman/McPherson (2008: 242).

51 See also Culyer (1989: 37) and Hurley (2000: 62). Note that the theorems only hold provided that all conditions of perfect competition are met. In reality, however, this is never the case. See Blaug (1997: 557) and Hausman/McPherson (2008: 242). For a conceptual critique of the theorems see Mandler (1999: 153ff.). Recall that the existence proof falls into the tradition of Bourbaki. Being a completely axiomatic exercise, Blaug (2003: 397) characterizes it as "formalism run riot." In another paper, Blaug (2007: 200) raises the obvious question of how "something that is so patently

impractical [can] be a useful reference point?" and gives an answer that is particularly interesting in the context of the previous considerations of economic rhetoric:

> Well, actually, it cannot, and so there must be some other reason for both asserting mathematical theorems to be valid while simultaneously denying their practical import. I believe that it is a methodological fear that no one will separate equity from efficiency unless that separation is enshrined in mathematical theorems, mathematical theorems that the uninitiated cannot comprehend but that the initiated will be inclined to accept as a hallmark of their professional competence.

52 Richardson/McKie (2007: 792) state that the theorems provided for "a compelling reason to ignore ethical analysis." The separation between production and distribution was already foreshadowed by Mill (1871a: 21, 199, 200) (see Schabas 2007: 125ff.) and Pigou (see Kaldor 1939: 551 and Mandler 1999: 131). The contribution by Kaldor and Hicks also plays an important role in this development, as will become clear immediately.

53 See also Hurley (2000: 57, 67ff.), Powers/Faden (2006: 144), and Hansson (2007: 166).

54 See also Culyer (1989: 37ff.), Powers/Faden (2006: 105ff.), and Wolfe (2008).

55 As the notion of merit goods, which are provided regardless of individual preferences, violates the premise of consumer sovereignty, it is not in line with neoclassical economics. Therefore, extra-welfarism is suggested as an alternative normative framework for health care resource allocation. See Chapter 4.

56 Note that these considerations focus on the *economic* reasons for a public provision of health care. From the vantage point of social justice, by contrast, a public health care system is frequently grounded in the characterization of health as a transcendental or conditional good. These terms express the idea that health is the prerequisite for attaining all other goods that are needed for leading a flourishing life. From the perspective of social justice and the normative ideal of equality of opportunity, gross inequalities in health thus present a considerable problem, as Schlander (2005: 84f.) and Huster (2011: 12f.) point out.

57 Kaldor (1939) was the first to propose the principle, whereas Hicks (1939), (1941) elaborated and clarified the meaning of compensation in a series of later articles. See Mandler (1999: 141).

58 The example of the Corn Laws may require a short comment. At the beginning of the nineteenth century, the population of England had grown so fast that demand for grain exceeded supply. This led to rising prices for wheat and to growing agricultural profits. Hence, merchants started to import cheap grain from abroad and sold it at a price below the domestic price level, which did not please the landlords at all. Because they dominated parliament, the landlords were able to meet the problem of falling prices by passing the so-called Corn Laws "which imposed a sliding duty on the importation of grain; the lower the foreign price fell, the higher went the duty" (Heilbroner 2000: 80). This policy led to extraordinary grain prices by 1813 which were met with enraged reactions by the capitalists. Contrary to the landlords, the capitalists were interested in cheap grain, as the price of grain largely determined the wages they had to pay for labor. The Corn Laws were not abolished completely until 1846. See Heilbroner (2000: 79ff.).

59 See also Kaldor (1940: 385).

60 See Kaldor (1939: 550f.), Hicks (1939: 700), Little (1957: 87), Mishan (1972: 15f.), (1975: 15, 392f.), Copp (1985: 131), and Hausman/McPherson (2009: 144). For a critique of this "unrequited-punch-in-the-nose criterion of social welfare" see Reinhardt (1992: 312f.).

61 See also Hicks (1939: 711).

62 In particular, it was pointed out that Kaldor and Hicks implicitly assume the value of a dollar as being the same for everyone, so that real income and utility could be treated

as exchangeable concepts. See Cooter/Rappoport (1984: 526). Beyond that, it was demonstrated that the criterion can lead to contradicting policy advice. See Samuelson (1947: 251f.), Little (1957: 96), Mishan (1972: 16f.), Mandler (1999: 141, 147f.), and Hausman/McPherson (2009: 147ff.).

63 See also Dobb (1973: 242), Reinhardt (1992: 313), and Hausman/McPherson (2006: 145).

64 See also Sugden/Williams (1978: 91), Boadway/Bruce (1984: 1, 292), Mitchell/Carson (1989: 21f.), Reinhardt (1998: 30), and Coast (2004: 1233f.).

65 See also Porter (1992: 39).

66 Further examples are provided by Schöffski (2012c: 377f.). The endeavor of inferring economic values from observed choices is criticized in Chapter 5 of this study.

67 See for instance Ackerman/Heinzerling (2004: 75ff.), Drummond *et al.* (2005: 218f.), and (Hansson 2007: 180). Recall that, strictly speaking, neither choices nor preferences as such can be observed, as Chapter 2 argued.

68 See also Portney (1994: 4f.), Blumenschein/Johannesson (1996: 117), Spash (1999: 128ff.), Drummond *et al.* (2005: 220), Wolff/Haubrich (2006: 751f.), and Kling *et al.* (2012: 7f.). Another stated preference method, the discrete choice experiment (DCE), is discussed in Chapters 5 and 6.

69 See also Kahneman/Knetsch (1992: 57), Portney (1994: 3), Spash (1999: 128), and Drummond *et al.* (2005: 219).

70 See also Mitchell/Carson (1989: 30ff.) and J. Hausman (2012: 46).

71 For details see http://evostc.state.ak.us/index.cfm?FA=facts.home, July 22, 2014.

72 See also Portney (1994: 7) and Ackerman/Heinzerling (2004: 153).

73 As Kling *et al.* (2012: 4) point out, in the case of pristine wilderness areas, existence values are likely to be the largest component of value. On the concept of use-value in environmental economics see Sagoff (2004: 40ff.).

74 See for a similar example Kling *et al.* (2012: 4). Another example is the decision of whether to use WTP or WTA. Although, according to economic theory, both measures should elicit roughly the same answers, it is well established in the literature that the WTA approach systematically leads to higher values than WTP questions. See Mitchell/Carson (1989: 30ff.), Arrow (1993: 480), Baron (1997: 80), Diamond/Hausman (1994: 46), Knetsch (1994: 352), Kling *et al.* (2012: 11, 19), and J. Hausman (2012: 46). The disparity between WTA and WTP values has also been observed in CV studies in health care. See Whynes/Sach (2007).

75 See also Kahneman/Knetsch (1992: 57), Ackerman/Heinzerling (2004: 154, 157), Sagoff (2004: 188), and Kling *et al.* (2012: 7).

76 See on CBA's welfarism Sugden/Williams (1978: 90f.), Boadway/Bruce (1984: 143), Hurley (1998: 375), (2000: 60f.), Richardson (2002: 629), Richardson/McKie (2005: 266), McGuire (2001), Tsuchiya/Williams (2001), Drummond *et al.* (2005: 217), Brouwer *et al.* (2008: 327), and Williams *et al.* (2012: 49).

77 See on CBA's societal perspective Mishan (1972: 11), Brouwer/Koopmanschap (2000: 441), Sculpher (2001: 95), Powers/Faden (2006: 145), Wolff/Haubrich (2006: 746), and Hansson (2007: 165). CBA can thus be regarded as an extension of private management techniques to society as a whole, as Mishan (1975: xii) points out.

78 See also Olsen (1997a: 604), Olsen/Donaldson (1998: 1), Reinhardt (1998: 2), and Olsen/Smith (2001: 39, 42).

79 Yet, Marckmann/Siebert (2002b: 179f.) note that carrying out a CBA on this level is virtually impossible. See Drummond *et al.* (2005: 214). The different levels of resource allocation are considered in Chapter 4.

80 See on the debate on which costs to include in economic evaluation Garber *et al.* (1996: 36ff.), Weinstein/Manning (1997), Sculpher (2001), Brock (2004: 208f.), and, for a review, McKie/Richardson (2005b: 3–7).

81 See also Murray (1996: 56), Drummond *et al.* (2005: 215), McKie/Richardson (2005b: 3f.), and Greiner/Damm (2012: 32ff.).

82 See also Sculpher (2001: 99). Some authors cite Sir William Petty (1623–1687) as earliest reference for the human capital approach. See Culyer (1981: 3), Johannesson (1996: 1f.), Blumenschein/Johannesson (1996: 115), Sassi *et al.* (2001: 4), and Forget (2004: 618), who quotes Petty as follows:

> 100,000 persons dying of the Plague, above the ordinary number, is near 7 million pounds loss to the Kingdom: . . . how well might 70,000 pounds have been bestowed in preventing this Centuple loss? [...] Petty valued an Englishman at 69 pounds and a Frenchman at 60 pounds. He allowed the latter to be an underestimate because he could buy an Algerian slave for 60 pounds.

83 As Greiner/Damm (2012: 33) put it, seeking an efficient allocation implies that a working person would have to be the more favored the higher her income, a proposition also discussed by Lübbe (2010b: 278, 2011: 101, 2015: 17f.).

84 See for this line of criticism Anand/Hanson (1997, 1998), Lübbe (2010b), and (2011).

85 Murray (1994: 435) explicitly rejects the human capital approach, but endorses the attachment of age-weights on the basis of different social roles at different ages so that high weights would be given to the middle ages and lower weights to the very young and the very old (see Tsuchiya 1999: 268). Although on this account, the weights do not depend on income, they still mirror the value of a person's health to others. In the face of ongoing objections leveled against age-weights and time-discounting (see Anand/Hanson 1997, 1998), the weights have finally been abandoned in the GBD 2010 (see Murray *et al.* 2012: 2064).

86 CEA measures the benefit of a medical intervention in disease-specific natural units, such as reduction of blood pressure in mm Hg or the number life years saved. See Drummond *et al.* (2005: 12) and Schöffski (2012b: 59f.).

87 See Weinstein/Stason (1977: 717), Johannesson (1996: 2), McKie/Richardson (2005a: 4), and Greiner/Damm (2012: 33). Note that the *German Recommendations on Health Economic Evaluation* explicitly postulate that economic evaluation should adopt a social perspective and incorporate *all* incurred direct and indirect costs such as absence from work and lower productivity. See Schulenburg *et al.* (2007: 288).

88 See for this line of criticism Lübbe (2010b) and (2010c).

89 This quote is especially interesting for the present study since it contradicts the idea of an equity-efficiency trade-off: given the unfairness of letting the millionaire die, the efficiency sacrificed apparently does not constitute a consideration to bear in mind at all. This aspect will be put up again in Chapter 5.

90 See also Cookson *et al.* (2009: 235) and Lübbe (2010a: 584).

91 The perhaps best-known example for an ethically objectionable CBA from outside health care is the case of the Ford Pinto car. See therefore Lukes (1996: 45f.).

92 See on the problems of the WTP measure Weinstein/Manning (1997: 127), Drummond *et al.* (2005: 230ff.), Powers/Faden (2006: 149), Hausman/McPherson (2006: 149), Tsuchiya (2012: 407), and Williams *et al.* (2012: 50).

93 CBA has not been the method of choice in health care resource allocation. See Sculpher (2001: 100), Sassi *et al.* (2001: 4), and Powers/Faden (2006: 146). More recently, a resurge of CBA and WTP can be observed, as noted by Olsen/Donaldson (1998: 1), Drummond *et al.* (2005: 214f.), Richardson *et al.* (2005: 1), Smith/Richardson (2005: 82f.), and Schöffski (2012b: 59).

4 The empirical failure of CUA and the approach of equity weighting

4.1 Introduction

Cost-utility analysis currently constitutes the gold standard of health economic evaluation (see Sculpher *et al.* 2005: 14). In contrast to CBA, it couches medical benefits in terms of health-related quality of life (HrQOL), usually measured by the quality-adjusted life year (QALY).[1] The first attempt to actually allocate resources on the basis of CUA in Oregon famously failed, though. This event and the debate it provoked made it abundantly clear that the application of CUA faces serious fairness issues as well. The first part of this chapter scrutinizes the QALY concept and illustrates the happenings in Oregon. Thereby, the reaction to CUA's empirical failure on part of the health economists is of particular interest: they generally argued that the fairness problems could be accounted for *within* the framework of economic evaluation by means of a further modification of the outcome measure, i.e., by equity weighting of QALYs (see Lübbe 2015: 35). The second part of the chapter connects the discussion on health economic evaluation with a fundamental issue of moral philosophy by characterizing economic evaluation as applied consequentialism. It points out that the path from CBA to the weighting approaches resembles the development from hedonic utilitarianism to different types of consequentialism, applying ever more sophisticated theories of value. Both consequentialist moral theories and the equity approaches thus present attempts to surmount counterintuitive distributional implications of utilitarianism and CUA respectively by means of modifying the axiology while leaving the value maximizing framework intact (see Lübbe 2015: 33, 35).[2] These considerations provide the conceptual background for the critique of the weighting approaches and social value maximization in Chapters 5 and 6.

4.2 Cost-utility analysis and its fairness issue

4.2.1 Cost-utility analysis and the QALY

The QALY can be regarded as the "most sophisticated" HrQOL measure (Wolff/Haubrich 2006: 758) and, as such, constitutes the linchpin of CUA's current attractiveness in health economics.[3] By attaching a quality weight to the time spent in the respective health state, the QALY is capable of simultaneously representing an intervention's effect on both quality and quantity of life. The empirically elicited weights are anchored on 1 expressing perfect health and 0 representing death, so that one year spent in perfect health produces one QALY, whereas a year spent in a health state with a weight of 0.5 generates 0.5 QALYs. To borrow a concrete example from McKie and Richardson (2005a: 6),

> if a year of life on hospital dialysis is considered to be worth only 60 per cent as much as a year of normal health, other things being equal, then 20 years on dialysis would be equivalent to 20 x 0.60 = 12 QALYs.

As to the allocation of resources, it was initially taken for granted that "society" chiefly aims at QALY maximization, as Weinstein and Stason (1977: 717) explicitly state: "The underlying premise of cost-effectiveness analysis in health problems is that, for any given level of resources available, society (or the decision making jurisdiction involved) wishes to maximize the total aggregate health benefits conferred."[4] Hence, traditional CUA's "measure of benefit" was "the sum of individual health gains in terms of QALYs" (Schwappach 2002: 210f.) and maximizing QALYs was supposed to maximize the social value of a resource allocation (see Nord 1995: 202; Dolan *et al.* 2008: 21; Tsuchiya 2012: 408).

To exemplify what exactly the QALY is measuring, the techniques used to gauge the quality weights shall be considered briefly. The three most popular preference elicitation methods are the standard gamble (SG), the time trade-off (TTO), and the rating scale (RS), also called analog scale (AS).[5] To begin with, the SG asks the respondents to put themselves in a certain chronic health state and to consider a hypothetical choice between two alternatives. In the first alternative, they undergo a treatment restoring perfect health with probability x and leading to immediate death with probability $(100 - x)$. In the second alternative, no treatment is undertaken, producing the certain outcome of the chronic health state for lifetime (see Drummond *et al.* 2005: 150). The probability x is then varied until the respondent expresses indifference between the two alternatives, as the following example from a survey conducted by Oliver (2004: 275) illustrates:

> Imagine that you were born without a sense of sight; that is, you are, and always have been, totally blind. On visiting your doctor, she or he informs you that there is a new cure for your blindness, but the treatment entails a risk. There is a chance that the treatment could kill you, but the size of this chance is unknown. Therefore, if you take the treatment, there is a chance that you will be fully sighted for your remaining life expectancy, but there is also a chance that you will die more or less immediately. If you do not take the treatment, you will be completely blind for your remaining life expectancy.

Figure 4.1 summarizes these options.

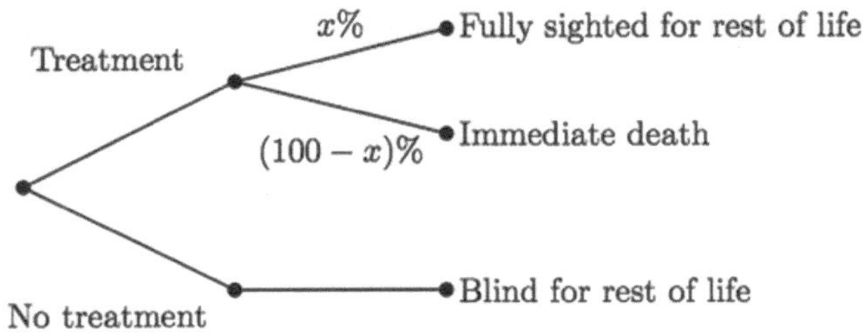

Figure 4.1 Standard gamble.

Source: adapted from Oliver (2004: 275).

The study then asked the respondents to mark "the minimum of chance of treatment success (that is, the minimum *x*)" they would require for accepting the treatment on a scale from 0 to 100 (see Figure 4.2).

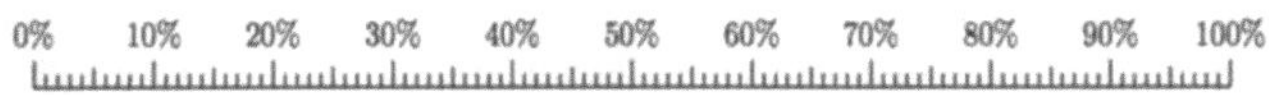

Figure 4.2 Scale of probabilities.

Source: adapted from Oliver (2004: 275).

If, using the present example, death is assigned 0 and full health 1, the value of the health state "blind" can be calculated by converting the probabilities accordingly. For instance, if the respondents indicated a probability of 80 percent at the indifference point, blindness would be assigned a quality weight of 0.8. The SG is generally regarded as "the most theoretically appealing" method (Green *et al.* 2000: 159) because it is grounded in the axioms of expected utility theory of VNM and is thus supposed to measure cardinal utilities (see Torrance 1986: 20).[6] However, respondents apparently have difficulties in dealing with probabilities and explaining and administering the method is time-consuming (see Bognar/Hirose 2014: 38).[7] These findings led to the development of the TTO (see Torrance 1986: 22).

The TTO requests the respondent to choose between two certain, hypothetical alternatives: in the first, the subject suffers from a certain condition, health state *i*, for the rest of her life *t*; in the second option, she will be completely healthy for time *x*, with $x < t$, followed by death (see Gold *et al.* 1996a: 113). Basically, the respondent is asked how much lifetime she would be willing to sacrifice in order to be cured from the condition, or, put differently, to trade a health improvement for a reduction in lifetime (see Brazier *et al.* 1999: 26). The following example taken from Ubel *et al.* (1996a: 110) illustrates the task:

> We would like you to rate how you feel about a few different health conditions. We will describe each condition and ask you to tell us how many seconds, minutes, hours, days, weeks, months, and/or years of your life you would be

> willing to give up in order to rid yourself of the condition. Assume that you can expect to live until the age of 75. Imagine that you are in the following state of health: You have a growth in the tissue lining the brain called a meningioma. It causes you to have constant headaches. The pain is often severe. It can be decreased with medicines, but it cannot be eliminated without interfering with your ability to concentrate. You must take pain medications to sleep at night. The meningioma is not cancerous and will not affect how long you live.

After making the respondents familiar with the task by confronting them with some choices between living a certain time in perfect health and a longer period in a worse health state, Ubel *et al.* (1996a: 110) ask: "How much time would you be willing to give up in order to eliminate the meningioma pain and remain in perfect health?" The value of the respective health state is then given by the fraction x/t.

Finally, the RS asks subjects to rank different health states according to their desirableness. The scale can adopt different forms but it usually ranges from zero for the least desirable health state or death to 100 indicating perfect health (see Gold *et al.* 1996a: 116). It has been developed within psychophysics in order "to measure people's response to sensory stimulation, such as light, sound and heat" (Brazier *et al.* 1999: 23). Hence, the RS decidedly aims at the elicitation of feelings, as the wording of an RS exercise presented by Ubel *et al.* (1996b: 109) shows:

> We would like you to rate how you feel about a few different health conditions. We will describe each condition and ask you to rate it on a scale from 0 to 100, where 0 is as bad as death and 100 is perfect health. If you think a condition is about halfway between death and perfect health, give it a score of 50. You can use any numbers you want from zero to 100, and you can include decimal points. Imagine that you are in the following state of health: You have a ganglion cyst on one hand. This cyst is a tiny bulge on top of one of the tendons in your hand. It does not disturb the function of your hand. You are able to do everything you could normally do, including activities that require strength or agility of the hand. However, occasionally you are aware of the bump on your hand, about the size of a pea. And once every month or so the cyst causes mild pain, which can be eliminated by taking an aspirin. On a scale from 0 to 100, where 0 is as bad as death and 100 is perfect health, how would you rate this condition?

The phrasing of the question neatly shows that the RS – just like the SG and the TTO – seeks to elicit the subjects' individual preferences regarding *their own* health states.[8] It becomes obvious that the respondents are facing a tremendously difficult task, regardless of which elicitation procedure is employed (see Hausman 2012: 121). Although the RS task is comparably easy to understand, it is of crucial importance that the distances between the placements on the scale actually represent the perceived difference between the health states at stake (see Torrance 1986: 18f.; Drummond *et al.* 2005: 147). That is, the numbers assigned to the health condition have to reflect the strength of preferences on an interval scale, but it is doubtable whether the RS is capable of generating such numbers.[9]

In contrast to the ratio scale, an interval scale is characterized by the lack of a natural zero-point. An example for the former is provided by the measurement of lengths in meters: measuring 0m indicates the actual absence of length (see Drummond *et al.* 2005: 176). Gauging a temperature of 0°C on an interval scale, by contrast, does not imply the lack of any temperature. Rather, the assignment of 0°C to a certain temperature is essentially arbitrary (see ibid.). Due to this feature, the differences between the values on an interval scale are meaningful, but the ratios of scale quantities are not (see Torrance 1986: 16).[10] When it comes to the QALY, the properties of the interval scale make sure that equal differences between the scale values represent equal differences in preferences, that is, "a gain from 0.2 to 0.4 on the scale represents the same increase in desirability [or HrQOL] as a gain from 0.6 to 0.8" (Drummond *et al.* 2005: 177; see Cookson *et al.* 2009: 235).

Given the connection between individual preferences and the QALY's quality weights, the question arises as to whether the latter can be regarded as a *utility* measure in the sense of modern economic theory. At first sight, this interpretation is indicated by the terminology surrounding the QALY – after all, it is a measure within cost-*utility* analysis. Accordingly, Nord *et al.* (2009: S11) argue that "the standard QALY expresses value in terms of individual utility" and Wolff and Haubrich (2006: 757) state that the "greater the preference for a particular health state, the greater the 'utility' associated with it."[11] This jargon notwithstanding, strictly speaking, the quality weights do not represent utilities (see Drummond *et al.* 2005: 188).[12] Recall that CUA was adopted for the very reason that the application of CBA in health care led to problems CUA was supposed to overcome. Thus, the QALY was particularly designed to measure the value of health instead of utility or well-being (see Culyer 1989: 51; Wagstaff 1991: 22f.; Ubel 2001: 67f.; Drummond *et al.* 2009: S31).[13] Accordingly, the preference elicitation methods seek to measure *health-related preferences,* whereas in economics, preferences are generally regarded as preferences all things considered (see Richardson 1994, Brouwer *et al.* 2008: 328, Hausman 2010: 284). Note in this context that although health usually forms an important part of well-being, people's preferences all things considered need not coincide with their evaluation of health states (see Hausman 2010: 284).[14] A person might, for instance, very well prefer a minor disability to perfect health because it disqualifies her from military service (see ibid.). The shift from the focus on well-being to health as such expresses the value judgment that health is not only instrumentally valuable as a means for promoting well-being, but also desirable for its own sake:

> Indeed, health has become seen as the central (if not exclusive) focus of evaluations, given that health care policy makers, as clients of economic analysts, are interested mainly in this aspect of human life. Health is pursued and valued by policy makers for its own sake (and possibly because of its impact on productivity) rather than because it yields utility or merely to the extent that it yields utility. Although good health certainly also contributes to welfare [...], it is valuable in itself as an important characteristic of human beings.
>
> (Brouwer *et al.* 2008: 332)[15]

In this respect, CUA is not only preferred to CBA for methodological reasons, but is regarded as "morally superior" (Ubel 2001: 67).

The focus on health has an important implication for CUA's normative foundation. Since it does not incorporate all possible preferences, CUA abandons the premise of welfarism and, hence, the framework of Paretian welfare economics (see Culyer 1989: 51).[16] This deviation also becomes apparent in the standardization of the quality weights on the 0–1 scale and the subsequent application of QALYs to all individuals concerned (see Brouwer/Koopmanschap 2000: 449). Thereby, it is assumed that the value difference between being in perfect health and being dead is equal for everyone and that all health states in between have the same HrQOL for all persons (see Torrance 1986: 17; Olsen 1997b: 632f.). In reality, however, diverse health states certainly affect persons differently depending, for instance, on their specific life-plans (see Dolan 2001: 49).[17] Thus, while the outcome measure of CUA is better tailored to the application in the area of health care resource allocation, it does not rest on a firm foundation in economic theory (see Brouwer/Koopmanschap 2000: 450). Note that CUA also gives up the original aim of economic evaluations to mimic the efficiency of markets, as maximizing QALYs does not necessarily coincide with maximizing social welfare. In other words, by not taking into account *all* costs and benefits associated with a certain policy measure, CUA does not lead to overall efficiency.

This raises the question how health maximization can be legitimized within economic theory instead. As an alternative normative framework for CUA, Culyer (1989, 1990, 1997, 1998) proposed extra-welfarism. There is no consensus in the literature as to how exactly extra-welfarism is to be defined, though.[18] Suffice it to stress at this point that extra-welfarism and welfarism share a value-maximizing framework (see Hurley 1998: 373, 380ff.), but differ in terms of the maximand: whereas in Paretian welfare economics, the maximand embraces only individual utilities, extra-welfarism can adopt any maximand that seems fit (see Culyer 1998: 366). This framework paves the way for both CUA and the weighting approaches, but it also appears very much *ad hoc*.[19]

4.2.2 The Oregon experiment and its interpretation

Having characterized the QALY as a measure of value, this section turns to the distributional implications of QALY maximization. Beforehand, a few remarks on the different levels of resource allocation in health care are in order. Based on Marckmann and Siebert (2002b: 179f.), four levels of resource allocation can be distinguished: the upper and lower macro-level and the upper and lower micro-level. On the upper macro-level it is decided which percentage of GDP is allocated to the health care system as a whole in comparison with other branches of public policy such as education and defense. On the lower macro-level the distribution of the health care budget on different subareas of health care and different indications takes place. The decisions on this level include choices between the investment in different branches of research, in curative or preventive measures, and in ambulant or stationary treatment in hospitals. The distribution of resources to the treatment of different groups of patients, for example according to guidelines specifying certain condition/treatment pairs, takes place at the upper micro-level. Finally, decisions about the treatment of the individual patient occur at the lower micro-level.

Which of these levels is relevant for the application of CUA, then? To begin with, the upper macro-level can be disregarded for two reasons: first, focusing on the production of health, CUA is unsuitable for comparing investments in the health care sector with investments in areas not or not only aiming at the improvement of health. Beyond that, economic evaluations on such a broad scale are virtually impossible anyway. The other levels allow for the application of CUA, but do not all give rise to distributional conflicts. On the lower micro-level, a CUA could for instance be conducted in order to examine which of two drugs for one and the same patient or group of patients is more cost-effective. In such cases of seeking technical efficiency, no distributional issues emerge in the first place. The circumstances are different when the allocation of resources on different groups of patients in the same (upper micro-level) or in different conditions (lower macro- and upper micro-level) is at stake. It is in such cases of tackling allocative efficiency, that is, when CUA is used to allocate resources across indications and different (groups of) patients that QALY maximization raises issues of distributive justice (see German Ethics Council 2011: 66f.). Unquestionably, reaching allocative efficiency is the aim of rationing medical resources and the fact that CUA allows for cost-effectiveness comparisons across indications is one of the major reasons for the attractiveness it enjoys among health economists.

The first attempt to ration medical resources "explicitly, systematically, and openly" (Oberlander *et al.* 2001: 1583) in strict accordance with the logic of cost-effectiveness occurred in Oregon in 1990 – and famously failed. The "Oregon experiment" (Nord *et al.* 1995b: 80) aroused much attention on both national and international scale (see Brock 2000: 224). As it put the issues of distributional justice and public participation in the prioritization process irrevocably on the decision makers' and health economists' agenda, it marks a "crucial turning point" in the rationing debate (Powers/Faden 2006: 178).[20] The Oregon experiment needs to be considered against the background of a recession on the one hand (see Bognar/Hirose 2014: 60) and rapidly increasing health care costs, creating a firm pressure on the Medicaid budget on the other (see Brock 2000: 223).[21] Since improving access to basic health care for low-income citizens was sought, cutbacks in other areas of health care became inevitable. As the few cases of organ transplantation in Oregon had been very expensive and rather unsuccessful, leaders of The Division of Adult and Family Services urged the legislators "to choose between continuing transplant coverage for a few and investing in more basic health needs for the many" (ibid.).[22] On June 1st, 1987, the Joint Ways and Means Committee unanimously voted for the latter option, albeit without much discussion and public debate (see Welch/Larson 1988: 171; Dixon/Welch 1991: 891). Subsequently, the Medicaid program no longer covered bone marrow, pancreas, heart, or liver transplants (see Hadorn 1991: 2219). This step marked a completely new strategy of dealing with limited health care resources.

Whereas previously, Oregon had cut Medicaid costs by limiting eligibility or lowering provider reimbursement, it now limited the benefits provided. That is, Oregon proposed to "ration services rather than people" (Brock 2000: 223).[23]

While the Committee's decision was met with very little public reaction, in November 1987, the case of the seven-year-old boy Coby Howard aroused the nation's interest (see Japenga 1987).[24] He suffered from acute lymphocytic leukemia but was denied a bone marrow transplant under Medicaid so that his mother tried to raise the required $100,000 to pay for the treatment in a transplant facility on her own (see ibid.). Howard had raised about $80,000 when her son died in December. The highly salient case of Coby Howard put the issue of rationing medical resources and, especially, the preceding decision process in the center of public attention. As a consequence, the State Senate President Kitzhaber eventually acknowledged the "arbitrary nature" of the decision and prepared the Senate Bill 27 (SB 27) to make sure that distributive decisions as to public issues "would be made more rationally and openly" in the future (quoted in Dixon/Welch 1991: 891). The SB 27 and two other Bills passed in 1989 constituted the *Oregon Basic Health Service Act* (see Capron 1992: 18), which aimed at expanding Medicaid coverage to all Oregonian citizens below the federal poverty line by financing only health care services of high priority (see Hadorn 1991: 2218).[25] In order to reach this goal, the SB 27 created the Oregon Health Service Commission (OHSC) and charged it with generating a priority list of health services.

In the process of establishing the list, different health states were evaluated by means of the quality of well-being scale (QWB), a multi attribute health state classification system, which describes a health state in terms of a number of attributes varying on different levels (see Drummond *et al.* 2005: 155).[26] The QWB applied in Oregon comprised the three attributes mobility, physical activity, and social activity as well as 25 symptom/problem complexes (see Kaplan/Anderson 1988: 213f.).[27] The weights attached to the different health states within the classification system were elicited by means of the RS approach in a representative telephone survey (see Eddy 1991: 2137).[28] Additionally, public hearings and town meetings, in which the participants were asked why a certain health care service seemed important to them, accompanied the process of preparing the list. In order to calculate the cost-effectiveness of different interventions, the OHSC condensed over 10,000 medical procedures to a list of condition/treatment pairs, identified the costs of the services, and determined the condition/treatment pairs' net benefit. Finally, the cost-effectiveness measure of 709 condition/treatment pairs was established by applying a formula, taking into account the costs of the treatment, its expected net benefit, and the benefit's expected duration (see Eddy 1991: 2136f.).[29] Note that the benefit in question here refers to the incremental QALY gain. Hence, the crucial figure is the incremental cost-effectiveness ratio, that is, the "incremental price of obtaining a unit health effect [...] from a given health intervention when compared with an alternative" (Garber *et al.* 1996: 27). It allows for the ranking of all condition/treatment pairs on a so-called QALY league table. The lower the incremental cost-effectiveness ratio, the more health can be produced by spending the resources on the respective intervention and the higher the latter's ranking on the list.[30] Given the aim of maximizing overall health benefits, the decision maker should start financing programs from the top of the list and continue to the point at which the resources are extinguished "or at which society is no longer willing to pay the price for the benefits achieved" (Weinstein/Stason 1977: 717). This threshold ratio separates the cost-effective from the cost-ineffective interventions (see Drummond *et al.* 2005: 330).[31] Resting entirely on cost-effectiveness ratios, the OHSC's preliminary priority list was supposed to "create an objective and scientific vehicle for setting priorities" (Oberlander *et al.* 2001: 1584) by revealing "how to buy the greatest amount of medical benefit" with Medicaid dollars (Ubel 2001: 5).[32]

However, the list led to a very counterintuitive ranking and, hence, was "met with immediate and overwhelming rejection" (Ackerman/Heinzerling 2004: 99), "made repeated headlines," "provoked strong criticism" (Bodenheimer 1997: 651), and "touched off a firestorm of national controversy" (Oberlander *et al.* 2001: 1585). The indignation particularly resulted from the fact that the list ranked highly beneficial and life-saving interventions below routine procedures (see Nord 1993a: 46). To give some examples, reconstructive breast surgery was ranked higher than treatment for open fractures of the thigh (see Dixon/Welch 1991: 892), dental cups for pulp or near pulp exposure had a higher priority than appendectomy (see Hadorn 1991: 2219), and the treatment for thumb sucking ranked before the treatment for AIDS (see Tengs *et al.* 1996: 101). In 1992, the Bush administration rejected the list, especially because the Health Care Financing Administration had pointed out that CUA discriminated against the disabled and thus threatened to violate the *Americans with Disabilities Act* (ADA) (see Brock 2000: 225).[33] In the course of amending the ranking procedure, the OHSC abandoned CUA and continually diminished the role of costs. When the plan was finally approved by the Clinton administration in 1993, any reference to costs and all marks of the QALY had been eradicated.[34]

In the present context, the interesting question is why the initial cost-effectiveness list led to such counterintuitive results in the first place, of course. While the OHSC primarily blamed faulty data stemming from methodological errors for the counterintuitive ranking,[35] another interpretation of CUA's failure gained currency eventually. The lessons learned from the Oregon experiment were chiefly twofold. First, it revealed that no rationing policy could be successful without taking the opinions of the persons concerned into account (see Powers/Faden 2006: 178f.). Whereas before, the people had basically been considered as consumers of medical services, they now became regarded as a "collection of citizens" (Price 2000: 273).[36] From that time on, governments in the United States, New Zealand, Sweden *et al.* have assigned public consultation a central role in the process of priority setting (see ibid.).[37] The second key message was that people do not endorse QALY maximization as an allocation rule for medical resources; apparently, *beside* efficiency, they care about the distribution of QALYs as well (see Schwappach 2002: 210). To illustrate the relevance and scope of the latter finding, the systematic reasons behind the failure of the Oregon list, that is, the distributional implications of CUA need to be considered.[38]

Most fundamentally, due to its focus on maximizing the overall sum of QALYs, CUA cannot account for the distribution of QALYs on the different persons concerned, a trait called "distributive neutrality" in the literature (Nord *et al.* 1995a: 1429). Consequently, CUA disregards both the overall pattern of the resulting distribution and the specific characteristics of the patients and their health states (see Schwappach 2002, Dolan/Olsen 2002: 124ff.). As to the latter, the most salient issue consists in the fact that CUA neglects the severity of an illness as such. If both a severely ill patient and a moderately ill patient can gain the same amount of QALYs, from the vantage point of CUA it does not matter who receives treatment. This inability to account for a special concern for the worse off has been labeled the "priorities problem" (Daniels 1993: 228).[39] In the Oregon experiment, it became manifest in the ranking of life-saving treatments below comparably trivial procedures. This ranking also reveals another issue of CUA, namely the "aggregation problem" (Daniels 1993: 229), which consists in the question of whether small benefits to a large group of patients can outweigh huge benefits to a few (see Brock 2005: 43f.). Within value-maximizing frameworks, no limits are set on aggregation. In the Oregon experiment, the counterintuitive ranking partly resulted from the fact that the condition/treatment pairs are ranked according to "the amount of benefit they deliver per unit of cost," as Eddy (1991: 2138) emphasizes. Instead of making one by one comparisons, "one: many comparisons" are required (Daniels 1993: 229). To give an example, this means

> that the benefit of providing ten people with a utility gain of 0.1 for the rest of their life (corresponding to sildenafil treatment for men with erectile dysfunction) is [...] equivalent to saving the life of a single (otherwise healthy) person.
>
> (Schlander 2007: 537)

The logic of the ranking furthermore implies that the priority of a condition/treatment pair is inversely proportional to its cost (see Nord *et al.* 1995a: 1430). Hence, a person happening to suffer from a high-cost illness may end up without receiving any treatment at all. Finally, QALY maximization systematically gives priority to patients with a higher potential to benefit from an intervention.

The impression that people do not approve the consequences of QALY maximization triggered further empirical research on how they want resources to be allocated instead.[40] As a result, all the implications delineated above were rejected. It turned out, for instance, that the respondents want to give priority to severely ill patients (see Nord *et al.* 1995b; Richardson *et al.* 2011),[41] disregard costs (see ibid.), are reluctant to discriminate against patients with low potential to health (see Nord 1993c; Nord *et al.* 1995a; Dolan/Cookson 2000), especially in case of life-saving treatment (see Ubel *et al.* 1999b), and approve of egalitarian patterns of the final distribution of health benefits (see Ubel/Loewenstein 1996; Richardson *et al.* 2010). In view of these results, Nord *et al.* (1995a: 1435) conclude "that QALY maximization receives very limited support when the consequence of the maximizing strategy is a perceived loss of equity." The crucial point to note is that although these results are fundamentally at odds with the premises of CUA, they have not been interpreted as a rejection of CUA as such (see Lübbe 2009b, 2009c, 2010c). Instead, it was argued that by focusing exclusively on individual preferences concerning the individuals' own health states, peoples' distributional or social preferences as to how they want health care to be distributed on other persons had been neglected. Contrary to the initial assumption, these social preferences turned out to "deviate considerably from the ranking that consideration of costs per QALY would suggest" (Drummond *et al.* 2009: S32). As the subjects apparently value not only health gain, important sources of value had been ignored (see Ubel *et al.* 2000c: 130; Schwappach 2002: 210). Accordingly, it was argued that the mistake made by the OHSC in preparing the list consisted in eliciting individual preferences via the RS on the one hand and applying the results to the completely different matter of allocating resources on the other hand (see Eddy 1991: 2140).[42] Basically, traditional CUA had maximized the wrong measure.

The empirical data were thus interpreted to the extent that the respondents attach a "high value" (Nord 1993a: 47) to life-saving in comparison with health-improving programs and that society "places extra value" (Schwappach 2002: 215) on rescuing identifiable patients.[43] Also, "health gains are valued less when they are concentrated among few people, and valued more when they are distributed more widely" (McKie/Richardson 2005a: 3).[44] Finally, Menzel *et al.* (1999: 10) state that "palliative measures for patients with terminal conditions produce an extra value not possessed by palliative measures to other patients."[45] These differential valuations of QALYs generated in different circumstances could be accommodated for by incorporating social values into CUA's maximand. This basic conviction is expressed by Ubel *et al.* (1996b: 115) as follows:

> Our subjects did not agree with the social consequences of their utility elicitation. [...] This does not necessarily mean that our subjects have rejected a utilitarian notion of health care justice, although that is one possibility. Instead, the discrepancy between people's utility responses and their rationing choices may indicate that the method of utility elicitation does not capture the social utilities of treating different conditions.

They conclude that "a better measure might be acceptable to people, thereby salvaging utilitarianism" (ibid.). Note that especially in the early reactions to the Oregon experience, the phrasing in the literature strongly suggests a hedonic reading of the term social value. Nord *et al.* (1995a: 1436), for instance, explicitly refer to the "benefit" individuals obtain from a just allocation of resources and Eddy (1991: 2140f.) explains CUA's failure by pointing out that "people other than the patient can derive benefit or utility" from a treatment.[46] This "vicarious utility (happiness)" mirrors the "desirability of the outcome to people other than the patient" (ibid.). Henceforth, the major approach to incorporate concerns for equity into CUA had been to elicit people's prioritization preferences empirically and to attach the corresponding equity weights to QALYs. In doing so, the "individual level maximand" of QALYs became substituted by a "social maximand" (Kelleher 2014: 259). By maximizing equity-weighted QALYs, or "EQALYs" (Nord 2014: 139), CUA could encompass concerns for both efficiency and equity at once and, thereby, maximize the actual social value of a resource allocation (see Nord *et al.* 1999: 25).[47] The next section elaborates this basic thread of equity weighting, discusses its normative claim, and sketches its current implementation.

4.3 Equity weighting: basic idea, normative claim, and state of the art

> [D]o we not feel impelled to cherish the life-years of the very young and the very old? [...] do we not feel differently about the person whose poor health is the result of her own reckless or feckless behaviour from the way we feel about the person who is more 'responsible'? [...] do we not have a special attitude to those in important social positions, and so on.

This is how Culyer (1990: 25) couches the basic intuition behind equity weighting.[48] Basically, the weights express the idea that a QALY is "worth more than 1.0 for those individuals for whom society values health improvements more highly" (Dolan *et al.* 2005: 202).[49] In so doing, the approach rejects the assumption that a QALY is a QALY is a QALY and raises the question as to whether "a particular improvement in health [is] to be regarded as of equal value no matter who gets it; and if not, what precisely is its relative value in accruing to one kind of person as opposed to another?" (Williams 1988: 112)[50] A QALY's value has henceforth been regarded as being context-dependent and varying with factors such as the age of the patient or the severity of his illness. Note that equity weights are explicitly assigned the role of a corrective device supposed to ameliorate unpalatable results of the efficiency calculus (see McMaster 2007: 12). Williams (1997: 118), for instance, postulates that any undesired discrimination whatsoever could be eliminated by means of equity weights:

> Those who do not like the implication that *in the efficiency calculus* the quantum effect may discriminate against some group whom they regard as particularly deserving (e.g. the old, or the poor, or smokers or those with serious concurrent medical conditions) are, of course, free to pursue some countervailing argument as an *equity argument* [...].

In the same vein, Williams and Cookson (2000: 1907) aver that equity weights allow for integrating concerns for equity systematically "when the results of an efficiency calculus are up for consideration."[51] It becomes clear again that the authors do not drop the assumption that the sum of health as such is a good; they seek to correct unacceptable results of QALY maximization by complementing the axiology instead (see Lübbe 2015: 20f.).

The question of how exactly the units of value are to be modified is regarded as a matter of socio-empirical research. As outlined above, economists are generally disinclined to introduce their own value judgments into economic analysis. Since they lack any scientific means to decide on fairness issues in health care resource allocation, health economists thus refer to the preferences of the persons concerned instead (see Lübbe 2015: 23, 64).[52] This proceeding neatly mirrors the separation of the spheres of efficiency and equity and the economists' concentration on the former. A popular method to elicit prioritization preferences is the person trade-off (PTO), which asks subjects for the number of patients in one group that would make them indifferent between treating that group and a certain number of patients in another group (see Nord 1995: 201).[53] Using the words of Ubel *et al.* (2000c: 129), people are "asked how many patients cured of condition Y *brings* the same *amount of benefit* as curing ten people of X."[54] Although initially, PTO had been designed to gauge individual utilities of different health states and is still used in this manner (see Torrance 1986),[55] Nord regards it as the most straightforward method for measuring social preferences. This is because, in his view, prioritization in health care basically means dealing with person trade-offs anyway: "choosing to spend a given amount of resources on a number of patients of one kind is to trade off specific numbers of patients of other kinds who also could have used those resources" (Nord 1999a: 13). Therefore, he argues, it becomes possible to bypass the process of measuring individual health-related utilities altogether and to infer the QALY directly from the PTO exercise. As a result, the QALY itself becomes a measure of "social valuation," taking both equity and efficiency into account (Nord 1994: 89).[56] Thereby, a concern for the severity of illness is mirrored by compressed upper-end values of the QALY scale: the values of relatively good health states move closer to one, that is, to full health, whereas the disvalues of severe conditions and, hence, the value of their treatment increase significantly, as Table 4.1 illustrates. The compressed scale also accounts for limited potential for health. Because the values at the lower part of the table are higher than the individual utilities for the respective health states, the relative value of bringing an individual from level 7 to level 5 to a rise from level 7 to level 3 increases in comparison with the normal QALY scale (see Nord 2014: 140).

Table 4.1 Upper-end compression of the QALY scale

Problem level	*Value*
Healthy	1.00
Slight problem	0.9999
Moderate problem	0.99
Considerable problem	0.92
Severe problem	0.80
Very severe problem	0.65
Completely disabled	0.40
Dead	0.00

Source: Nord *et al.* (1999: 30).

However, compressing the QALY scale does not allow for disentangling different concerns for equity that may have influenced the respondents' answers.[57] As an alternative, Nord *et al.* (1999: 30) thus propose the decomposed approach of cost-value analysis (CVA). By attaching equity weights to QALYs, CVA is supposed to make "the nature and the extent of the efficiency-equity trade-off explicit" (ibid.). Note that CVA is not a well-defined theory, but rather constitutes a broad research project to integrate previously neglected values into CUA.[58] At its heart lies the conviction that QALY gains are one thing, but "societal value is another" (Nord *et al.* 1999: 31).[59] Accordingly, a two-step procedure of preference measurement is adopted: the first step consists of eliciting individual preferences as to different health states whereas the second step amounts to measuring the "distributional preferences" of the general public (ibid.).[60] Once social preferences are collected, weights can be assigned to different health gains according to the patients' severity of illness, the potential for health or on the basis on "whatever other factors the public might consider of importance in an overall judgement of societal value" (ibid.). The social value of a health gain accruing to one person is then determined by an algorithm of the following form: $SV = dU \times SW \times PW$, with dU as the health-related utility gained by the intervention, SW as a weighing factor for severity of illness, and PW as a weight determined by the potential for health (see Nord *et al.* 1999: 32). As a result, equity-weighted QALYs become "measures of health related societal value" (Nord *et al.* 1999: 25).[61]

To sum it up, both the compression of the QALY scale and the direct weighting approach present attempts to solve the fairness issue by means of modifying the valuable units, i.e., "the distribuendum" within CUA (Tsuchiya 2012: 406; see Lübbe 2015: 35f.). As Nord (2014: 139) points out, the difference between CUA and CVA is that in the latter, "concerns for equity are included in the determination of value." The resulting social value serves as an "equity-sensitive social maximand" (Kelleher 2014: 261), "incorporating trade-offs between conflicting objectives" (Schwappach 2002: 211).[62] These trade-offs are encapsulated in the multiplicative connection of the different weighted factors ($dU \times SW \times PW$) while the overall social value of a distribution is determined by the additive aggregation of the social values accruing to different individuals (see Lübbe 2015: 36). Since the early 1990s, the weighting approach has become increasingly popular and research on social preferences in health care resource allocation reverberated. In the view of its popularity, the normative claim of equity-weighted CUA deserves investigation.

To begin with, some extra-welfarist accounts, such as the decision-maker approach (DMA), regard the results of economic evaluations as providing crucial information to the decision maker, who in turn has to evaluate them carefully "in light of the circumstances and values that cannot be included in the analysis" (Russell *et al.* 1996: 10).[63] Thereby, the term decision maker stands for "someone responsible for making decisions in the public interest," legitimized by a political process (Sugden/Williams 1978: 91). The DMA substitutes CBA's objective of maximizing economic efficiency in terms of preference satisfaction by the social objectives of the respective decision maker. These objectives incorporate "anything that the decision maker regards as relevant" (Williams 1991: 63). To be sure, the specification of the social objectives is highly controversial so that the legitimacy and reasonableness of the DMA ultimately depends on the legitimacy of the objectives chosen (see Sculpher *et al.* 2005: 11). Obviously, the objectives cannot actually include "anything" the decision maker regards as relevant for this might include idiosyncratic preferences and personal relationships (see Lübbe 2015: 34f., 223). Within the DMA, economic evaluations are supposed to provide the decision maker with one piece of information he might want to consider (see Sugden/Williams 1978: 91ff.). While this stance seems to acknowledge CUA's principle inability to capture all relevant equity concerns, it does not spell out in detail which aspects cannot be included. Instead, the authors usually refer broadly to special circumstances or the concrete context of the situation without giving a hint as to which circumstances exactly they have in mind.[64] Cookson *et al.* (2009: 242), for instance, aver:

> equity weight data may merely be used to help inform decision makers about what equity considerations are generally valued most highly by the general public, while leaving plenty of room for deliberation and judgement on the part of the decision-maker about how much weight to place on these data in particular circumstances.

Apparently, the decision maker has to weigh the weights again. Thereby, it is still assumed that the decision maker seeks to maximize the social value of a resource allocation.[65] But if he contextualizes the results of equity-weighted, i.e., already contextualized, CUA, what is he maximizing, then? (See Lübbe 2015: 78.)

Apparently, the normative status of social value maximization remains unclear. That being said, the general rhetoric of economic evaluation is in stark contrast to the modest claims presented above, anyway (see Lübbe 2009b, 2015: 23ff.). Richardson (1994: 14), for instance, argues that the "end point of economic evaluation should be information that is *persuasive*: it should help *convince* decision makers that a program is, or is not, *desirable*," and Bobinac *et al.* (2013: 1272) maintain that economic evaluation should "inform decision makers on *optimal* resource allocation."[66] Such quotes do not sound as if economic evaluations merely provide the decision maker with a piece of non-binding information; instead, they indicate that the result of economic evaluations determines the unquestionably *best* allocation of resources (see Lübbe 2015: 25f.). The underlying idea seems to be that economists are the experts to turn to when it comes to the optimal use of scarce resources. But if CUA is supposed to serve as an all-encompassing and decisive decision rule for allocating medical resources and if it is acknowledged that simple QALY maximization is untenable, all relevant concerns for fairness have to be incorporable into CUA. Although the positions as to the potential of equity weighting to actually surmount CUA's fairness issue diverge in the literature, a clear pattern emerges: objections against CUA are frequently answered by pointing to the possibility of improving it by means of equity weighting.[67] Culyer (1990: 25), for instance, explicitly utters very high expectations:

> And now suppose that you have those weights right. [...] Is there any distributional concern left that has not been embodied? If not, the maximizers day (though not the 'simple utilitarians'). If so, then we are perhaps at the heart of what it is that the egalitarians fear most about the maximizers. But what it can be I cannot discern!

If all relevant aspects of equity were "built into outcome data in this way, then a full integration of equity and efficiency will have been achieved in health policy" (Culyer 1989: 53).[68]

It can be concluded that regardless of whether equity-weighted QALYs serve as arguments in an encompassing final decision rule or are regarded as one piece of information for the decision maker, they are ultimately supposed to influence decision making. That is, they are normatively relevant either way. This conclusion is reinforced by considering the sheer amount of research on the social value of a QALY which reveals the trust in the approach and the actual relevance of the topic. There can be no doubt that the improvement of the methods and, sooner or later, the implementation of the approaches in public policy are clearly sought. Therefore, the topic of the present study is not only interesting from an academic vantage point, but is of pragmatic importance for actual public policy as well. This verdict is reinforced by considering the effect of quantifying ethical concerns.

In the health economic literature, the quantification of concerns for equity is usually proposed on decidedly ethical grounds. Whereas mere verbal arguments do not present "a commitment to do anything effective" (Williams 1997: 120), but are prone to be used in an "arbitrary and capricious" way, quantitative weights are supposed to allow for treating equity concerns in a "systematic" fashion (Williams/Cookson 2000: 1907). Additionally, verbal arguments can obfuscate the hard choices required in medical resource allocation, while the quantification of ethical concerns honestly uncovers the opportunity costs of equitable choices in terms of the QALYs forgone.[69] Numbers furthermore embody rigor and transparency and have "the potential for clarification, for performance measurement, for accountability, and for policy formulation, analysis and reappraisal" (Williams/Cookson 2000: 1901).[70] Therefore, they are believed to foster transparency and consistency in decision making (see Cookson *et al.* 2009: 241), particularly by shielding the decision-making process from "ad hoc influences of media, patient organisations, [and] lobbyists" (Nord 1993b: 236).[71] To this extent, allocation on the basis of numbers is considered a genuinely ethical endeavor, as Williams and Cookson (2006: 2) highlight:

> economists see themselves as standing up for the silent majority: the diffuse and unidentifiable groups of patients whose care is delayed, diluted, deterred, or denied whenever decisions are made to fund a costly new technology that will be loudly supported by the relevant industry and professional and patient groups.

Finally, Drummond *et al.* (2009: S32) point out that decision makers are far more likely to consider concerns for equity when they are integrated into the economic evaluation than when they are just presented as "something else" to consider, presumably due to the political "power of quantification."

The quantification of concerns for equity – even if it was possible in the first place – faces some serious drawbacks, though. It is, for instance, doubtable whether equity weighting actually contributes to the transparency of decision making. The QALY already relies on lots of questionable assumptions which are not easily intelligible to lay persons. In fact, it has been pointed out in the literature that the decision makers' difficulties with understanding the QALY present a major hindrance to CUA's implementation (see Drummond *et al.* 2009: S32).[72] The incorporation of progressively more information into the QALY is thus more likely to decrease than to increase its transparency and applicability (see ibid.), CUA would become "more mystical" (Dolan/Olsen 2002: 132) and, concomitantly, less attractive to both decision makers and the public.[73] Another, more fundamental issue of quantifying concerns for fairness consists in the danger that aggregated numbers can disguise controversial moral debates. An instructive example is provided by Powers and Faden (2006: 186f.) who reconsider a study by Nord.[74] The survey asked Norwegian health politicians to choose between the treatments of two different groups of patients. In each case, one of the options available guaranteed the maximization of health benefit. As a result, this alternative was only chosen by a minority of the participants, so that Nord entitled the paper "Health Politicians do not Wish to Maximise Health Benefits." A closer look at the data revealed that the majority of the politicians having chosen the health-maximizing alternative were conservatives, while the respondents rejecting health maximization mainly stemmed from social democratic parties. In view of these results, Nord concludes that the sample needs to be enlarged in order to erase such political biases. That is, he regards the issue as a mere methodological one, whereas it actually indicates a fundamental moral controversy. This conflict "needs to be featured in public debate, rather than buried in large samples and summary statistics" (Powers/Faden 2006: 187). The pretended exactness of the weights is not only methodologically worrisome but also treacherous when it comes to actual policy making. Recall that decision makers are more likely to take concerns for fairness into account when they are incorporated into the economic evaluation already. This entails the risk that weighted CUA creates an "illusion of completeness" (Ubel *et al.* 2000b: 899). Decision makers may think that equity has already been taken care of so that they do not bother with distributional considerations any further. Thus, even if the weighting approach was conceptually sound, quantifying concerns for equity might actually do more harm than good.

Having discussed the normative claim of equity weighting and the problems associated with the quantification of concerns for fairness, a remaining question concerns the actual implementation of weighted CUA. Although the need for incorporating concerns for fairness into economic evaluation is generally acknowledged in the theoretical literature and despite the fact that equity weighting currently seems to present the most promising account of doing so, the weighting approaches are at a developmental state and have barely been used in applied economic evaluation yet.[75] Studies actually modelling equity weights are rare and the existing attempts to do so largely remain at an explorative level, using small scale or convenience samples.[76] The few studies deriving weights have led to results that are considerably diverging from each other so that, up to now, it has not been possible to establish a consistent set of equity weights.[77] Not only do the data diverge between different studies, but they also vary within one and the same study when different methods are used.[78] In addition, a pivotal obstacle to modeling broadly applicable weights consists in the inconsistencies and instabilities frequently observed in respondents' stated preferences.[79] On the whole, these phenomena have predominantly been assigned to unresolved methodological issues, as the following conclusion by Wailoo *et al.* (2009: 984) illustrates:

> The equity-weighted QALY approach may be appealing to some but has not been considered viable to date because of uncertainties about relevant equity characteristics, insufficient data and a lack of agreement on methods with which to estimate the required weights.[80]

By contrast, the present study takes it that both the diversity of the empirical results and the observed preference inconsistencies cast doubts on the very possibility of inferring a consistent set of weights from elicited prioritization preferences in the first place. In fact, this endeavor rests on much stronger assumptions than generally acknowledged in the literature. To establish this claim, the philosophical debate on consequentialism needs to be considered.

4.4 Economic evaluation as applied consequentialism

The preceding parts of this chapter presented CUA as an alternative to CBA. While the former is particularly designed to meet the demands of health care resource allocation, it drops CBA's welfarist foundation by defining the outcome measure in terms of health. It turned out, though, that maximizing QALYs also violates strong fairness intuitions, a finding having given rise to further modifications of CUA's outcome measure by means of equity weights. This section seeks to illustrate that this development resembles the development in moral philosophy from hedonic utilitarianism to modern consequentialism and, hence, faces the same difficulties. In doing so, the applied debate on fairness within health economics is connected with a fundamental debate in moral philosophy and the following considerations provide the conceptual framework for the subsequent critique of the weighting approaches.

To begin with, it needs to be clarified what is meant by "consequentialism."[81] At the most general level, consequentialism can be defined as a moral theory which determines the normative status of acts, motives, rules, etc. solely with regard to their consequences (see Sinnott-Armstrong 2011).[82] That being said, in the following, the focus is on act consequentialism. According to the famous definition by Sen (1979: 464), act consequentialism holds that an "action α is right if and only if the state of affairs x resulting from α is at least as good as each of the alternative states of affairs that would have resulted respectively from the alternative feasible acts."[83] It is thereby assumed that states of affairs are the bearers of the good so that "an act is right if and only if that act maximizes the good" (Sinnott-Armstrong 2011). The wording of the definitions indicates that a consequentialist theory embodies two parts: first, the theory of the right postulates that we ought to act so as to maximize the good, that is, to reach the best available states of affairs.[84] Second, in order to discern which act maximizes the good, one certainly needs to know what the good is in the first place. Therefore, any consequentialist theory requires for a theory of value or a theory of the good providing a principle according to which different outcomes can be ranked "from best to worst" (Scheffler 1988b: 1).[85] A closer look at this ranking task reveals that the theory of the good in turn has to embrace two kinds of information as well.[86] First, it needs to spell out the valuable properties of a state of affairs which are to be taken into consideration when its goodness is to be judged. Second, the theory of the good has to provide a principle for the aggregation of these items so that the whole state of affairs can be evaluated (see Sumner 1989: 172). These different elements of consequentialism are usually regarded as being independent of each other.[87] In the following, they are illustrated using utilitarianism as an example.

Not only is the classical, hedonic version of utilitarianism the paradigm case of a consequentialist theory, but it is also consequentialism's historical and systematical ancestor. Hence, anyone engaging in an informed discussion of consequentialism should be familiar with utilitarianism and its problems in the first place. In general terms, utilitarianism is a moral theory according to which an act is right if and only if it maximizes the sum of individual utilities either in terms of pleasure or in terms of preference satisfaction.[88] Referring to Sen (1979) again, it can be said that utilitarianism combines a consequentialist theory of the rightness of acts with a utilitarian principle for evaluating the goodness of states of affairs. According to the latter principle,

> [a]ny state of affairs x is at least as good as an alternative state of affairs y if and only if the sum total of individual utilities in x is at least as large as the sum total of individual utilities in y.
>
> (Sen 1979: 464)

This principle in turn comprises the premises of welfarism and sum-ranking. As quoted above already, the principle of welfarism holds that "[t]he judgment of the relative goodness of alternative states of affairs must be based exclusively on, and taken as an increasing function of, the respective collections of individual utilities in these states" (Sen 1979: 468). Pursuant with the principle of sum-ranking, one "collection of individual utilities is at least as good as another if and only if it has at least as large a sum total" (ibid.).

By first specifying certain non-moral units of goodness and then defining the right action as the one maximizing these units, utilitarianism represents the prime example of foundational consequentialism, to adopt a term coined by Scanlon

(2001: 39). Foundational consequentialism "starts with some notion of value and explains notions such as right, wrong, rights, duty and obligation in terms of the production of the best states of affairs as measured by this standard" (ibid.). That is to say, it is characterized by the priority of the good to the extent that the good "is defined independently of the right, and then the right is defined as that which maximizes the good" (Rawls 1971: 24). This priority has two dimensions: for one thing, it has a temporal element in so far as a theory of the good is required in order to know what the right act in a certain situation consists of. For another, the good is normatively prior to the right to the extent that an act is right *because* it maximizes the good (see Sumner 1989: 167; B. Williams 1988: 24). Presumably, it is this priority of the good which provides foundational consequentialism and, thus, utilitarianism with its attractiveness. As Scanlon (2001: 39f.) surmises, its appeal roots in the belief that deontic notions "are in need of explanation and justification" whereas the good "has clearer and more obvious justificatory force than 'the right'." Adherents to foundational consequentialism may think that

> we have strong reason to promote the good, but that, by contrast, it is unclear why we should be concerned not to violate principles of rightness, especially insofar as this requires something different from promoting the good and can even conflict with it.
>
> (Scanlon 2001: 39)[89]

In order to serve its "explanatory and justificatory aims," the axiology of foundational consequentialism should be kept free of any "deontic notions, such as rights or duties" (ibid.).

Apparently, the classical utilitarians shared the conviction that the notion of the good as such already provides for a reason to act in a certain way. Recall that Bentham regarded pleasure, broadly considered, as the only commendable end of government action and legislation. Once this goal was set, the question as to "whether one ought to maximize utility was a silly question. It was like asking 'Ought one to do what one ought to do'" (Little 1957: 7). Bentham obviously believed "that it followed from the very concept of welfare that it ought to be maximized" (Little 1957: 9).[90] It can be said that the fact that people can be better and worse off provides utilitarianism for "an obvious motivational force" (Scanlon 1982: 108). Indeed, happiness and well-being are universally desirable: whatever different persons seek, it seems safe to assume that they at least share the aim to be happy so that the normative significance to avoid pain and suffering and to enhance pleasure seems intelligible from anyone's point of view (see Williams 1972: 95).[91] The finding that utilitarianism's attractiveness stems from the reason-giving and motivating character of the notion of the good bears important implications for the relationship between the elements of consequentialist theories. To quote Scanlon (2001: 40):

> Although these theses [consequentialism, welfarism, sum-ranking] are logically independent, it seems to me that their appeal is not independent, and

> that in fact it is welfarism (or, historically, hedonism) that provides the support for the other two. Although hedonism does not entail sum-ranking, it is plausible that if pleasure and the absence of pain is the sole ultimate value, then since more of it is better than less, the value of states of affairs should be determined by the amount of happiness they contain. More important [...] is the relation between hedonism and consequentialism. If pleasure and the absence of pain are the sole ultimate values (or the only morally relevant ultimate values), then all (moral) value adheres in states of affairs, and what morality requires is that we produce those states of affairs with the greatest possible value.

Put in more general terms, once it is acknowledged that certain units of good exist, it seems only straightforward to infer that more of the good is better than less,[92] so that it indeed appears paradoxical not to maximize the good (see Scheffler 1988c: 243).

At this point, it is worth reconsidering Sen's definition of welfarism and his claim of the independence of utilitarianism's elements. Sen (1979: 471) regards welfarism as constraining the informational basis for assessing states of affairs: "If all the personal-utility information about two states of affairs that can be known is known, then they can be judged without any other information about these states." This phrase as such neither restricts the possible ways of aggregating individual utilities, nor does it constrain the possible theories of the right. On the basis of the individual utility information, the decision maker could, for example, adopt a priority-view and choose to act so as to maximize the utilities of the worse off members of society. In the definition of welfarism quoted above, however, Sen (1979: 468) states that the goodness of a state of affairs is an "increasing function" of the individual utilities in this state. This claim is much more demanding and rules out certain modes of aggregation. The same is true for the definitions of welfarism offered by other authors. Schroth (2008: 127), for instance, takes welfarism to be the view that "well-being is the only thing that is intrinsically valuable" and according to Sumner (1996: 3), welfarists hold that "welfare is the only value which an ethical theory need take seriously, ultimately and for its own sake." If this is true, how can a consequentialist theory prescribe an action that does not lead to the realization of as much of the *only* valuable property as possible? Crucially, both any non-additive aggregation of units of value and any non-maximizing decision rule require an axiological interpretation as well (see Lübbe 2015: 32f.). In the present example, something else of value must have been added; that is, "anything other than maximizing seems to require admission of some other good" (Shaver 2004: 238, 250).

The claim that the specification of units of goodness naturally leads to the principle of sum-ranking and the allocation rule of maximization is reinforced by considering an objection leveled against this argument by Schroth (2008: 130). He argues that the position presented has the "consequence that nonconsequentialists do not understand the concept of the good" and considers this as "obviously implausible" (ibid.). And yet, this result is not implausible at all, since according to some non-consequentialists, their theories indeed do not require any notion of *the* good to judge the overall goodness of states of affairs.[93] Foot (1988: 238), for instance, stresses the fact that the abstract concept of the good or of "the best outcome standing outside morality as its foundation and arbiter" does not make any sense to her. Where consequentialists see "the best states of affairs from an impersonal point of view," there is simply a "blank" for the non-consequentialist (Foot 1988: 232, 242). Certainly, the latter can also speak in a loose way of better or worse situations or outcomes, but these evaluations derive from a certain notion of the rightness of acts in the first place. In other words, the action in question is not right because it leads to the best outcome, but the best outcome can only be identified as such because it resulted from the right action.[94] Hence, it is erroneous to claim that any moral theory needs a theory of the right and a theory of the good by necessity.[95] The alleged challenge for the non-consequentialist to explain how it can ever be right to prefer a worse state of affairs to a better already presupposes a consequentialist framework (see Foot 1985: 29f.; 1988: 227). From a non-consequentialist perspective, by contrast, it is meaningless right from the start.

Having considered the structure of consequentialist theories, it becomes clear that economic evaluations can be regarded as a type of applied consequentialism (see Hansson 2007: 164).[96] While they differ with respect to the specification of the units of value, the approaches discussed so far all adopt the principle of additive aggregation and the decision rule of maximization. Using the words of Tsuchiya and Dolan (2009: 147), the "basic tenet of economic evaluation is that we should seek to maximize benefits, however they are conceived." Interestingly, consequentialism and CUA not only share the same structure, but their development was motivated by the same distributional concerns as well. Thereby, due to their structural similarity, the problems of utilitarianism broadly resemble the distributional issues of CUA. Put in a nutshell, because utilitarianism also focuses on generating the greatest possible sum of utilities over and above all persons concerned, it cannot account for an independent normative status of rights, liberties, or the distribution of utilities on different persons. As a corollary, utilitarianism may not only allow for, but in fact require the moral agent to carry out terrible actions: if the overall good can only be promoted by torturing or murdering an innocent individual or by neglecting a certain group of citizen basic human rights, so be it.[97] Furthermore, utilitarianism is generally considered an extremely demanding moral theory because the requirement of always acting so as to maximize utility is both cognitively challenging (the moral agent frequently has to consider all future consequences of all possibly available actions for all persons concerned (see Scheffler 1988b: 2ff.)) and morally arduous (there is no space left for individual projects).

Although these implications contradict widely held moral convictions (see Scanlon 1982: 103), they have not led to a wholesale rejection of utilitarianism as such. The reason for utilitarianism's irresistibility, it is said, lies in the "spellbinding force" of the "seductive idea" that it simply cannot be wrong to bring about the best states of affairs (Foot 1988: 226f.). In a similar vein, it is argued that the notion of maximizing the good is taken to embody the ideal of rationality, as Rawls (1971: 24f.) claims: "It is natural to think that rationality is maximizing something and that in morals it must be the good."[98] Although the accounts of what exactly utilitarianism's spellbinding trait consist of differ in detail, they all share the basic idea that its merit is located in its theory of the right. Utilitarianism's counterintuitive results, by contrast, are regarded as stemming from its theory of the good and, hence, are taken to be surmountable by means of constructing more sophisticated axiologies (see Foot 1988: 225).[99] This idea of sticking to utilitarianism's maximizing theory of the right and improving its hedonic theory of the good lies at the heart of consequentialism's *raison d'être* (see Griffin 1995: 154).[100] It should be noted that the popularity of both the notion of maximization and the focus on consequences is presumably connected with an increasing attractiveness of decision theory which, as we saw in Chapter 2, focuses on the consequences of actions instead of the underlying reasons. If individual rational choice involves maximization, it only seems straightforward to assume that the morally right choice should do so as well (see Fehige/Wessels 1998: xxxviii).

By now, there is widespread agreement in the literature that individual utility can at the utmost serve as *one* value among others within a pluralist theory of value (see ibid.; Lübbe 2009c: 100, 2015: 23). Just as in the case of CUA, it is thus assumed that the relevant concerns for fairness could be incorporated into consequentialism by amending the axiology accordingly. In order to meet the overdemandingness objection, for instance, agent-centered options are introduced, and the conception of agent-relative value is supposed to avoid the requirement of committing atrocities (see Scheffler 1988b; Sen 1988; B. Williams 1988). Likewise, "the compliance with the law of nature," "human freedom, social solidarity, the autonomous development of nature, or a combination of such features" could be accounted for by modifying the axiology correspondingly – in fact, "the possibilities are endless" (Pettit 1991: 230). Currently, so-called consequentializers even maintain that any consideration deemed relevant for the evaluation of the normative status of an act could be encompassed by consequentialism, so that, in the end, any non-consequentialist moral theory could be turned into a consequentialist theory (see Dreier 1993; Louise 2004; Portmore 2007). Hence, the analysis of the weighting approaches in the following chapter, which draws on the conceptual considerations of this section, has implications for the philosophical debate on the scope and limits of consequentialism as well.

Notes

1 For other measures see Murray (1994, 1996), Gold *et al.* (1996a: 93), Drummond *et al.* (2005: 178ff.), and Schöffski/Greiner (2012: 99ff.).
2 See also Lübbe (2005, 2009b, 2009c).
3 See on the QALY Gold *et al.* (1996a: 89, 91, 94), Johannesson (1996: 173), Schlander (2005: 53), Drummond *et al.* (2005: 173ff.), Weinstein *et al.* (2009), and Schöffski/Greiner (2012: 71).
4 See on the virtually self-evident status of the maximization-rule also Williams (1985a: 326, 1995: 222), Wagstaff (1991: 22), Garber *et al.* (1996: 27), Culyer

(1997), Weinstein *et al.* (2009: S5), Schöffski (2012a: 4f.), and Schöffski/Greiner (2012: 73).

5 Surveys are offered by Torrance (1986), Richardson (1994), Baron (1997: 80f.), Murray (1996: 27–29), Gold *et al.* (1996a: 113–117), Brazier *et al.* (1999), Green *et al.* (2000), Drummond *et al.* (2005: 147ff.), Schöffski (2012c), and Richardson *et al.* (2014: 794).

6 This is a controversial issue, though, as will become clear below. See Richardson (1994: 11, 17), Green *et al.* (2000: 159), McGuire (2001: 9), and Kahneman (2011: 267ff.).

7 See also Brazier *et al.* (1999: 26) and Green *et al.* (2000: 153).

8 Note that the results of the different techniques differ in a systematic fashion to the extent that the SG usually leads to higher values than the TTO and both methods produce significantly higher values than the RS. See Baron (1997: 81), Richardson (1994: 19), Nord (1999a: 90f.), Dolan (2001: 56), Drummond *et al.* (2005: 146), and Schlander (2005: 58).

9 For the need of measuring the QALY's quality weights on an interval scale, see Torrance (1986: 16f.), Richardson (1994: 14), Gold *et al.* (1996a: 90), Johannesson (1996: 206f.), Dolan (2001: 52), Drummond *et al.* (2005: 177), and Weinstein *et al.* (2009: S5). On the issue of whether RS values meet the interval properties see Richardson (1994: 16), Nord (1999a: 92ff.), Green *et al.* (2000: 158), and Bognar/Hirose (2014: 36).

10 In more technical terms, an interval scale is unique under a positive linear transformation so that "any interval scale x can be transformed to a scale y using a function $y = a + bx$, where a can be any constant and b can be any positive constant" (Drummond *et al.* 2005: 176).

11 Likewise, Weinstein and colleagues state that the value of health is "ultimately subjective" (Weinstein/Stason 1977: 719) and should therefore be measured in terms of "preferences or desirability" (Weinstein *et al.* 2009: S8). See Gold *et al.* (1996a: 83, 90), Johannesson (1996: 174, 183, 2001: 574), Hawthorne/Richardson (2001: 216), and Weinstein *et al.* (2009: S5).

12 For a detailed discussion of this issue see Richardson (1994).

13 Note that the quality weights could only be interpreted as VNM utilities if the preferences are elicited by means of the SG and satisfy some quite severe assumptions. See Richardson (1994: 11, 17), Johannesson (1996: 186f.), Garber *et al.* (1996: 31), Dolan (2001: 50), Green *et al.* (2000: 159), McGuire (2001: 9), Drummond *et al.* (2005: 188f.), Schlander (2005: 55), and Tsuchiya/Dolan (2005: 461). Some authors nevertheless regard the QALY as a good approximation of utilities under certain conditions, as Drummond *et al.* (2005: 189) point out. Examples are Garber *et al.* (1996) and Weinstein *et al.* (2009).

14 See also Williams (2001b: 583).

15 For critical remarks on this focus on health see Hurley (1998: 380) and Mooney (2009: 16ff.).

16 See also Wagstaff (1991: 23), Brouwer/Koopmanschap (2000: 449), Tsuchiya/Williams (2001: 37), and Brouwer *et al.* (2008: 330ff.).

17 Defenders of the QALY frequently counter this plea by pointing to the size of the sample: in a large sample, the differences counterbalance each other. See Torrance (1986: 26f.).

18 Even the characterization of CUA as extra-welfarist is not uncontested. An extra-welfarist approach to CUA is, for instance, endorsed Brouwer *et al.* (2008), whereas Birch/Donaldson (2003) argue for the supremacy of welfarism. Also, Garber *et al.* (1996) and Weinstein *et al.* (2009) embed CUA in a welfarist framework. For overviews of the debate on welfarism and extra-welfarism see Weinstein/Manning (1997), Culyer (1998), Hurley (1998), Brouwer/Koopmanschap (2000), Tsuchiya/Williams (2001), Coast (2004), Schlander (2005), and Coast *et al.* (2008).

19 Accordingly, critics of extra-welfarism like Mooney (2009: 34) consider it "less an alternative theory and more an attempt to justify health maximisation and in turn QALY maximisation in the health care objective function."

20 Reviewing the health economic literature, Williams and Cookson (2000: 1867) observe an "increasing use of the word 'fairness', which failed to get a mention in connection with health during the 1980s, but logged around 10 mentions a year during the 1990s." Nevertheless, Richardson (2009: 247) reports that equity still "represents only 2.5% of the cumulative total keywords used in the *Journal of Health Economics* in its first 25 years."

21 See also Capron (1992: 19).

22 See also Menzel (1990: vii) and Daniels (1991: 2232).

23 See also Daniels (1991: 2232), Eddy (1991: 2135), Dixon/Welch (1991: 891), and Oberlander *et al.* (2001: 1583).

24 See on Coby Howard also Welch/Larson (1988: 171f.), Hadorn (1991: 2219), and Oberlander *et al.* (2001: 1583).

25 See also Capron (1992: 18), Bodenheimer (1997: 651), Brock (2000: 223), and Oberlander *et al.* (2001: 1584).

26 For an example of a QWB classification system and a scoring formula see Drummond *et al.* (2005: 158–161). On other popular multi attribute health state classification systems see Hawthorne/Richardson (2001).

27 See also Eddy (1991: 2136), Kaplan (1992: 67), and Nord (1993a: 45).

28 See also Kaplan (1992: 70), Nord (1993a: 45f.), and Brock (2000: 224).

29 See also Hadorn (1991: 2219), Dixon/Welch (1991: 892), Tengs *et al.* (1996: 101), and Oberlander *et al.* (2001: 1584).

30 See on the league table approach Drummond (1989: 68ff.), Russell *et al.* (1996: 11), Drummond *et al.* (2005: 327), McKie/Richardson (2005a: 6), Schlander (2005: 69), McGregor/Cato (2006: 949), Mooney (2009: 17), and Schöffski/Greiner (2012: 81ff.).

31 The question certainly is where to set the threshold. See Schlander (2005: 69). NICE implements the approach but rejects to set an absolute threshold. Instead, decisions are made "on a case by case basis" whereby the threshold value for a QALY ranges between £20,000–30,000 (NICE 2008: 18). See therefore Rawlins/Culyer (2004: 224f.), Schlander (2007: 536), Baker *et al.* (2010: 4f.), Donaldson *et al.* (2011b: 1), and Schöffski/Greiner (2012: 82).

32 See also Eddy (1991: 2136) and Tengs *et al.* (1996: 99).

33 See also Menzel (1992: 21), Brock (2000: 225, 2009: 28f.), and Bognar/Hirose (2014: 84f.). On CUA's issue of disability discrimination see Chapter 6 of this study. It should be noted that critics surmise that the ADA merely served as a "smoke screen" used to avoid "confronting any of the fundamental issues surrounding the national health care debate" during the year of presidential elections, though (Kitzhaber quoted in Bjornstad 1992: 4A). See Capron (1992: 19), Menzel (1992: 21), and Bjornstad (1992: 1A).The plan may have been actually denied "because George Bush, about to wage a presidential campaign against Bill Clinton, was afraid to be labeled the 'rationing president'" (Bodenheimer 1997: 652). See also Tengs *et al.* (1996: 100f.), Brock (2000: 225), and Bognar/Hirose (2014: 61).

34 For the developments in Oregon after 1994 see Tengs *et al.* (1996), Bodenheimer (1997), and Marckmann/Siebert (2002a: 1603f.). Although different evaluations of the final Oregon Plan's success prevail in the literature, the general tenor is negative. See Eddy (1991: 2136), Bodenheimer (1997: 651f.), Oberlander *et al.* (2001: 1585), Marckmann/Siebert (2002a: 1602), and Ackerman/Heinzerling (2004: 99f.).

35 "The data are so inadequate … if we want to use the formula system, we have to start collecting data all over again," Commission member Wopat stated (quoted by Dixon/Welch 1991: 892). Other authors confirm that the prioritization process was characterized by lots of technical problems. See Eddy (1991: 2138), Kaplan (1992: 70, 73), and Marckmann/Siebert (2002b: 182–184).

36 See also Lengahan (1999: 45f.).

37 See also Lengahan (1999: 46), Bruni *et al.* (2008: 17), and Johri *et al.* (2009: 57).

38 For overviews see Daniels (1993), Brock (2004), Tsuchiya (2012), Cookson *et al.* (2014), and Kelleher (2014).

39 See also Brock (2004: 212ff., 2005).

40 Reviews of empirical studies are presented by Sassi *et al.* (2001), Ubel (2001: 67ff.), Schwappach (2002), Dolan *et al.* (2005), McKie/Richardson (2005a), (2005b), Green (2007: 83ff.), Baker *et al.* (2010), Bobinac *et al.* (2012), and Tsuchiya (2012).

41 A review is offered by Shah (2009).

42 See also Nord (1993a, 1995), and Nord *et al.* (1999).

43 Nord *et al.* (2009: S11) claim that society values interventions "the more highly" the worse off an individual would be without it and Bognar/Hirose (2014: 71) state that "a given benefit has more value if it goes to those who are more severely ill."

44 Olsen (1994: 40) concludes that additional QALYs have a diminishing social value.

45 For similar wordings see Nord *et al.* (1999: 29), McKie/Richardson (2005a), (2005b), and Weinstein *et al.* (2009: S7).

46 Nord *et al.* (1995a: 1436) state:

> The rejection of simple utility maximization does not necessarily imply a similar rejection of the utilitarian basis of economic theory. While respondents revealed a strong preference for egalitarianism, there is clearly a benefit from the knowledge that the society is 'just' and that its rules of social justice correspond with personal values. This 'distributional' source of individual utility would, ideally, be included in a simple utilitarian calculation.

47 See also Nord (1993a: 52), Nord *et al.* (1995a, 1995b), Ubel *et al.* (1996b), and Schwappach (2002: 211).

48 The concept of equity weights goes back to Williams (1988) and Culyer (1989).

49 Dolan *et al.* (2008) state that "'equity weights' refer to any conscious departure from the assumption that all QALYs should be valued equally". See Sassi *et al.* (2001: 20).

50 See also Williams (2001a: 252).

51 See also Williams (1995: 225).

52 See also Gaertner/Schokkaert (2012: 14) and Lübbe (2013: 251f.).

53 See also Nord (1991, 1993a, 1993b, 1994, 1995). Before 1992, he referred to the approach as the equivalence of number technique (see Nord 1995: 201).

54 Italics added. See also Olsen (1994: 41) and Ubel *et al.* (2002: 190).

55 See also Robinson (2011), Salomon *et al.* (2012), and Robinson/Bryan (2013).

56 See also Nord (1994: 89, 1995: 201f., 1999a: 30f.), and Nord *et al.* (1999: 30).

57 See Dolan (1998: 41):

> Responses to PTO questions contain the relative weights a respondent attaches to at least four things: (1) the severity of the pre-intervention health state; (2) the severity of the post-intervention health state; (3) the health gain as a result of intervening; (4) the number of persons treated. It is impossible from the answers to PTO questions to disentangle what are the relative weights attached to each of these considerations [...]. While all four are likely to be important, different weights attached to each may have quite different implications for resource allocation decisions.

See also Williams/Cookson (2000: 1903).

58 The term CVA refers in a comprehensive sense to "any evaluation that takes into account relevant concerns for fairness (equity) in the weighting of individual benefits" (Nord 2014: 139). See on CVA Nord (1993b, 1995a, 1999a), Nord *et al.* (1999), Menzel *et al.* (1999), and Ubel *et al.* (2000b, 2000c).

59 See also Nord (2014: 139).

60 While Nord endorses the PTO, distributional preferences can also be elicited by means of CV and DCE. See Dolan (2001: 47), Cookson *et al.* (2009: 238) and Nord (2014: 141). For attempts to elicit the social WTP for a QALY see Baker *et al.* (2010), Donaldson *et al.* (2011a, 2011b), and Bobinac *et al.* (2012, 2013).

61 In order to solve the issue of disability discrimination, Nord (1999a: 118ff.) and Nord *et al.* (1999: 36) suggest the equal value of life approach as further modification of CUA. See Chapter 6 of this study.

62 See also Nord *et al.* (1999: 25) and Nord (2014: 139).

63 See also Garber *et al.* (1996: 31), Daniels (1998: 41) and, with explicit reference to equity weights, Nord (1993b: 235ff.), Ubel (2001: 170f.), Cookson *et al.* (2009: 242), and Edlin *et al.* (2012: 1425).

64 Nord (1993b: 237) argues that the decision maker has to "make necessary adjustments in actual decisions." See also Richardson *et al.* (2011: 172) and Bognar/Hirose (2014: 74).

65 Brouwer/Koopmanschap (2000: 445) state: "Implicit in the DMA is the general notion that society wishes to maximize a social welfare function." And Sugden/Williams (1978: 183) regard it as "plausible to assume that a decision maker [...] sees his role as being to maximize the social value of the medical care provided by that part of the health service for which he is responsible."

66 Italics added.

67 See e.g. Bognar/Hirose (2014: 74). It is generally assumed that "every utility affecting characteristic and any equity preference could in principle be built into the QALY as weights" (Dolan/Olsen 2002: 47).

68 See also Williams (1995: 225, 1997: 118), and Williams/Cookson (2000: 1907).

69 Williams (1997: 128) emphasizes that a major reason for equity weighting

> was to impose some quantitative rigour upon the assertions made by non-economists about what is equitable, so that whenever it is argued that more weight should be given to one class of persons, it has to be acknowledged that this means that some specified other class of person [sic] is going to suffer. There is a regrettable tendency for equity arguments to be conducted within a rhetorical framework in which it appears possible to 'do good' at no opportunity cost whatever. It generates a great deal of righteous self-satisfaction for the romantic escapists and it puts economists back in the role of the dismal scientists always stressing the sacrifices, but it does not help the hard-pressed decision makers who grapple with the issues in real-life every day.

Likewise, Neumann/Weinstein (2010: 1496) argue that those criticizing the QALY adhere to "magical thinking," suggesting "that the country can avoid the difficult trade-offs that cost-utility analysis helps to illuminate."

70 See also Nord (1999a: 3), Wailoo *et al.* (2009: 988), and Bognar/Hirose (2014: 74).

71 See also Murray (1994: 429f.).

72 See also Nord *et al.* (2009: S13). Due to unresolved methodological issues and a lack of reliability and accuracy of the QALY, some even argue that it is of no help for the decision maker at all. See for instance McGregor/Cato (2006). For a critique of the "highly worrisome subjectivity and diversity in the ways in which the QALY gains of different interventions are calculated in applied health economics" see Nord (1999a: 79ff.). It deserves to be noted that the research project ECHOUTCOME, funded by the European Commission and constituting the "largest survey ever undertaken to specifically validate the [QALY's] underlying assumptions," concludes that the QALY calculation is seriously flawed and suggests that the member states should *not* use it to assist health care decision making. See http://www.echoutcome.eu/, October 10, 2014.

73 Dolan/Olsen (2002: 133) state the general rule: "the fewer the parameters, the better." See Johannesson (2001: 577).

74 Nord, E. (1993) Health Politicians do not Wish to Maximize Health Benefits. *Tidsskrift for den Norske Laegeforening* 113: 1171–1173. As the paper is only available in Norwegian, the considerations refer to Powers/Faden (2006: 186f.).
75 See Sculpher *et al.* (2005: 23), Cookson *et al.* (2009: 238, 2014: 29), Bobinac *et al.* (2012: 1122), Tsuchiya (2012: 412f.), and Bognar/Hirose (2014: 73). As to the research on equity, Mooney (2009: 17) states:

> Today it remains the case that the distance between where we are and where we want to get to with equity is much greater than that between where we are and where we want to be with respect to efficiency.

76 Overviews of studies calculating weights are offered by Sassi *et al.* (2001: 21ff.), Dolan *et al.* (2005), Haninger (2006: 74ff.), Lancsar *et al.* (2011), Bekker-Grob *et al.* (2012), and Bobinac *et al.* (2012: 1122). Very small samples are used by Nord (1993b) (ten employees of the National Institute of Public Health in Oslo), Ubel *et al.* (1996b) (53 economics undergraduate), Dolan (1998) (35 economics undergraduates), and Dolan/Green (1998) (28 members of university staff). Note that although these studies were conducted some time ago, they are still frequently quoted in more recent texts.
77 Compare, for instance, the diverging data on the relevance of age in priority setting elicited by Nord *et al.* (1995a, 1996), Tsuchiya (1999: 270f.), Cookson *et al.* (2009: 238), Johri *et al.* (2009), and Richardson (2009: 249).
78 To give an example, Baker *et al.* (2010: iii, 33f.) used both DCEs and PTOs to elicit social preferences as to age and severity. While the DCEs revealed a negligible effect of these features, the PTO results indicated a strong influence of age and severity on prioritization choices. In fact, "gains to some groups were weighted three or four times more highly than gains to others." See Sassi *et al.* (2001: 28).
79 See Ubel (2001: 86), Dolan/Cookson (2000: 20), Dolan *et al.* (2003: 547), Tsuchiya/Dolan (2005: 460), and Bobinac *et al.* (2012: 1122). This problem is tackled in Chapter 6.
80 See also Williams/Cookson (2006: 3), Richardson/McKie (2007: 786), Baker *et al.* (2010: 5), and Donaldson *et al.* (2011a: 6).
81 A different type of consequentialism will be presented in Chapter 5.
82 This formulation immediately raises the question as to how a consequence is to be defined and, in particular, how consequences are to be distinguished from acts. See Lübbe (2015: 84, 97ff.). On different versions of consequentialism see Sen (1979: 465), Sumner (1989: 167), Griffin (1995: 154), and Portmore (2007: 45).
83 Similar definitions are offered by Rawls (1971: 24), Foot (1988: 224f.), Pettit (1991: 230), Griffin (1995: 154), Scanlon (2001: 49), and Sinnott-Armstrong (2011).
84 Whether consequentialism necessarily involves the requirement of maximizing the good is discussed below. See Griffin (1995: 154).
85 See also Lübbe (2009c: 100).
86 This systematization follows Sen (1979), but the general structure has been adopted widely. See Sen/Williams (1982b: 3f.), Foot (1988: 225), Sumner (1989: 168ff.), and Pettit (1991: 232).
87 See e.g. B. Williams (1988: 23), Sumner (1989: 170), Rawls (1971: 25), Sen (1979: 464ff., 1988: 187), Scheffler (1988b: 6), Broome (1991a), Pettit (1991: 231), Portmore (2007), and Riley (2008).
88 Sen's (1979: 463) account explicitly allows for both readings.
89 See also Rawls (1971: 24f.), Scanlon (1982: 108), and Shaver (2004: 240). Note that the alleged connection between value and the reason to act so as to maximize it draws on a parallel with the reason-giving character of the notion of good *for*, as Foot (1985: 30) points out.
90 See Bentham (1823: 4ff.) and for a similar case Shaver (2004: 239f.).
91 See also Nagel (1986: 160), Scanlon (1998: 101), and Shaver (2004: 248, 249).

92 Scanlon (1982: 110) avers:

> If all that counts morally is the well-being of individuals, [...] and if all that matters in the case of the individual is the degree to which his or her well-being is affected, then it would seem to follow that the basis of moral appraisal is the goal of maximising the sum of individual well-being.

See Nagel (1979: 110).

93 See Taurek (1977), Foot (1985, 1988), and Lübbe (2005, 2015).

94 See Foot (1985: 33), B. Williams (1988: 24f.), Lübbe (2005, 2013: 249, 2015: 226).

95 Beside Schroth (2008: 130), this claim is also made by Pettit (1991: 230).

96 The characterization of CUA as aggregative consequentialism is essential to Lübbe's work. See especially Lübbe (2015: 30ff.).

97 See B. Williams (1988: 34). This is not to say that either Bentham or Mill would have approved of such consequences, of course. Utilitarianism, as it is used here, does not refer to any historical theory, but to the analytical structure of utilitarianism in terms of utility maximization.

98 See also Foot (1985: 29f., 1988: 227), Scheffler (1988c: 252, 1988b: 1), and for an overview Portmore (2007: 47ff.).

99 Examples are Sen (1988) and Broome (1991a).

100 See also Sen (1979), Scheffler (1988b: 6), and Portmore (2007: 41).

5 Values, weights, and trade-offs
The conception of choice in economics

5.1 Introduction

Chapter 4 demonstrated that the weighting approach presents an attempt to solve CUA's ethical problems by means of axiological modifications while leaving the maximizing framework intact. This chapter scrutinizes the implicit assumptions connected with this account and especially focuses on the economic conception of choices as trade-offs according to which any decision whatsoever reveals the subject's relative valuation of the alternatives at stake. By transferring this understanding of decision making to the realm of prioritization choices it is implicitly assumed that equity judgments resemble consumer choices to the extent that they are susceptible to the same methods of inquiry. And yet, it does not go without saying that concepts and tools stemming from consumer choice analysis – such as utility maximization, indifference curves, and MRS – are appropriate for tackling the issue of health care resource allocation. As a structuring heuristic, the genuinely metaphorical character of such notions is emphasized – unquestionably, there is no entity called society having preferences or being capable of enjoying any benefit and there certainly are no virtual weights attached to QALYs either. The question of whether the weighting approaches are promising can thus in part be reformulated as the query of whether these metaphors are apt for considering the issue of health care resource allocation. It turns out that the economic conception of choice is much more demanding than generally acknowledged in the literature. While the problems associated with the notions of social preferences and social value maximization root back to consumer choice theory, the weighting approach makes requirements on the nature of equity judgments which can be regarded as a heritage from classical utilitarianism. Crucially, the assumptions considered here are not buttressed by argument in the health economic literature. As it seems highly unlikely that they actually hold, the equity weights derived from social preference studies most likely lack any validity.

5.2 Choices in economics and the role of metaphors

The way in which health economists interpret and try to solve CUA's fairness issue – that is, as a matter of values, weights, and trade-offs – mirrors a conception of choice deeply ingrained in the economic discipline. Recall Robbins'

(1935: 16) definition of economics as the science studying "human behaviour as a relationship between ends and scarce means which have alternative uses." An economic problem thus exists whenever an act "which involves time and scarce means for the achievement of one end involves the relinquishment of their use for the achievement of the other" (Robbins 1935: 14). Resembling Robbins' definition, the health economist Williams (2001a: 252) argues that different objects become interesting for the economist as soon as "in order to gain them some other valuable thing has to be sacrificed, or, in plainer terms, when they are costly," that is, when they have an opportunity cost. These costs reveal the value of the chosen alternative so that economics is essentially "about what people value and how much they value different things" (Williams 2001a: 251). Economists generally take it for granted that human actions comprise these characteristics so that they are describable in terms of trade-offs (see McPherson 1987: 45; Okun 1975: 1; Le Grand 1990: 564; Schefczyk/Priddat 2000; Amadae 2003: 5).[1] This assumption indeed lies at the heart of economics:

> The discipline is premised on the notion that *every decision* made by a consumer, producer, bureaucrat or politician involves some kind of *trade-off* between the different bundles of attributes that make up each choice. *Implicit trade-offs* can be revealed from decisions made by policy-makers in the public sector, e.g. how the benefits from additional education are *weighed* against the benefits from using those resources to reduce the risk of death or serious injury. By studying such choices, it is possible to infer the implied *value* of different goods.
>
> (Dolan 2001: 46)[2]

When it comes to medical resource allocation, it is accordingly assumed that each prioritization decisions inevitably reveals an equity-efficiency trade-off which allows for inferring the relative value of the equity concern at stake (see Lübbe 2015: 58ff.). This is because any non-health-maximizing decision involves the sacrifice of a certain amount of efficiency in terms of QALYs. These QALYs forgone constitute the opportunity cost of the chosen alternative and, hence, indicate "how much weight a particular equity concern is deemed to merit" (Williams/Cookson 2006: 1).[3] The "central ethical question" then becomes:

> How much sacrifice to efficiency (e.g., in terms of sum total population QALYs forgone) is it worth making to achieve a particular improvement in equity? This central question can be asked in relation to *any* reduction in *any* kind of health inequality, however defined. It can also be asked in relation to equitable procedures. In short, it can be asked (and answered) in relation to any equity concern deemed to warrant a departure from a strict cost-effectiveness approach.
>
> (Williams/Cookson 2006: 6)

Analogously, when different concerns for equity conflict in a particular choice situation, the choice made reveals the relative values of the equity factors at stake; an "equity-equity trade-off" exists (Cookson *et al.* 2009: 234; see Williams 2001a: 252). Equity weights can thus be regarded as expressing "the extent to which society is prepared to sacrifice health gain in the pursuit of fairness" (Sassi *et al.* 2001: 20).

In order to illustrate the underlying, value-maximizing framework, consider the following prioritization problem: suppose a respondent has to choose between the treatment of a severely ill patient A and a patient B who suffers from a relatively mild disease but would nevertheless gain slightly more QALYs from the treatment than A. Assume the respondent chooses to treat A, that is, the option *not* maximizing the number of QALYs generated. To make any sense of such a decision within a value-maximizing framework it has to be presumed that the respondent considers the QALYs generated in A as more valuable than the QALYs would have been if they were generated in B. Otherwise, the sacrifice of a certain amount of QALYs would have been higher than the value realized by treating A.[4] Hence, although the respondent did not maximize QALYs, he nonetheless made a value-maximizing choice.[5] In view of this example the question arises as to whether the trade-off is indeed in "the very nature of things" (McPherson 1987: 45) and, in particular, whether it is in the nature of rationing decisions. As the second chapter of this study made clear, the concepts of trade-offs, opportunity costs, and value maximization stem from the framework of consumer choice theory (see McPherson 1987: 46; Amadae 2003: 5). By transferring these concepts to the consideration of choices of all kinds it is tacitly assumed "that the market provides an appropriate model for understanding decision-making" in general (Lukes 1996: 37). In order to investigate whether the market indeed provides for a good model when it comes to prioritization decisions, the central concepts need to be investigated closely. As they originally stem from a different context, they can be characterized as metaphors.

The publication of McCloskey's monograph *The Rhetoric of Economics* in 1986 is generally regarded as the starting point of the "'rhetoric of economics' movement" (George 1996: 28).[6] At its core lies the conviction that in spite of the scientific image of economics, economic argumentation involves the application of all kinds of literary devices. Indeed, economists make use of "the whole rhetorical tetrad: fact, logic, metaphor, and story" (McCloskey 1992: 1).[7] This is not meant as a critique of economics, though, since the use of rhetoric in its ancient meaning of "writing with intent" is regarded as an essential characteristic of any science (McCloskey 1998: 5). Rather, the focus on rhetoric highlights the need "to read with understanding" in order to grasp "the depth and the surface of the text" (ibid.). An important rhetorical device is the metaphor, i.e., "a figure of speech in which one thing is talked about in terms of language and attributes drawn from another" so that "what is said is not literally meant" (Henderson 1998: 289).[8] Metaphors indeed abound in economics. Consider, for instance, the watery images derived from hydraulics such as "liquidity, floating exchange-rates, [...] circulation, leakages, injections, trickle-down effects" (Henderson 1994: 359), or mechanistic metaphors, such as market forces, equilibrium, or the price mechanism.[9] McCloskey (1992: 1) also regards the most basic economic tools of supply and demand functions as essentially metaphorical in character: "The market for apartments in New York, says the economist, is 'just like' a curve on a blackboard. No one has so far seen a literal demand curve floating on a sky above Manhattan. It's a metaphor." To be sure, this use of the term metaphor is very broad and incorporates similes, analogies, and personifications. Such a comprehensive application of the term can be criticized and a systematic analysis of the role of metaphors in economics would certainly require a more elaborate theory of metaphors (see Henderson 1998: 289).[10] For the present concern, a rough notion of the term is sufficient, though.

Crucially, metaphors are neither "mere ornament," nor just "textual decoration," but constitute an essential part of both ordinary thinking and scientific argument (McCloskey 1992: 56).[11] They reflect worldviews, simultaneously constitute "means whereby a world is constructed" (Henderson 1998: 290),[12] and have the capacity to change the meaning of the signified. By transferring the language and the respective attributes and connotations from one thing to another, metaphors highlight those aspects of their subject which are in accordance with the initial signified and downplay others (see McCloskey 1998: 47).[13] In doing so, metaphors adopt a genuinely new meaning, which results from the interaction of the different contexts (see Bicchieri 1988: 104). Therefore, the use of metaphors bears chances as well as risks (see Henderson 1994: 355). On the one hand, the skillful invention of a metaphor has "a capacity to astonish us with implications formerly unseen" and can convey new insights by disrupting established ideas (McCloskey 1998: 42).[14] Metaphors can thus be regarded as "indispensable" for science in so far as they provide a means for expanding and adapting a theory to changing circumstances (Mirowski 1988: 138).[15] On the other hand, a metaphor can also suppress or altogether dismiss important aspects of the subject just because these facets are inconsistent with the chosen image (see Henderson 1994: 355). Consequently, these aspects may cease to be perceived so that, in the end, the signified adopts a new meaning. In short, a metaphor frames and constrains our perception at once or, to say it metaphorically, it "is capable of both illuminating dark areas and casting shadows" (ibid.). Hence, although metaphors cannot be right or wrong, they can be more or less appropriate for illuminating their subject (see McCloskey 1992: 64f., 1998: 41, 46; Henderson 1994: 357f.). The task of rhetorical analysis is to reveal their implications and to critically reflect their suitability (see McCloskey 1998: 46; Henderson 1998: 291).

This is not always an easy task, though, since the salience of metaphors comes in varying degrees. At one end of the spectrum are the highly visible ones. When Gary Becker speaks of the family as a little firm or regards children as durable goods like refrigerators, it is quite obvious that this is not to be taken literally (see McCloskey 1994: 327f., 1998: 42). At the other end of the continuum are so-called dead metaphors, which are no longer recognized as metaphors at all but have come to be taken literally (see Henderson 1998: 293). When it comes to economics, notions such as the market, demand curves, or the price mechanism are so deeply ingrained in the discipline that they presumably do not invoke any association with their original context any more. And yet, once this happens, the parts of a concept's meaning illuminated by the metaphor become identical with its total meaning. To quote an example from Henderson (1994: 345), if the human capital metaphor "is so successful in its implications that we slip into the assumption that education is *nothing but* investment in human capital [...] then we are being used by the metaphor rather than using it." Another example from the realm of health care is provided by the debate on organ donation. In this case, the mismatch between the number of patients waiting for a transplant on the one hand and the available organs on the other hand is frequently couched in terms "of 'organ shortage', 'organ scarcity', 'low organ supply' or an 'unfulfilled organ demand'," as Schicktanz and Schweda (2009: 473) carve out. Critically, the "economic subtext" (ibid.) of these terms is not ethically neutral. Instead, by transferring economic concepts to the issue of organ donation, the latter is put into an economic framework right from the beginning so that economic solutions to the issue of organ shortage, such as financial incentives (see ibid.), naturally present themselves.[16] Because the metaphorical nature of terms such as organ supply is not recognized anymore, alternative approaches of dealing with the issue do not even come to mind.

This example reveals that "[m]atters of form, usually viewed as ornament, are commonly in fact matters of argument" (McCloskey 1992: 56). In the following, it is argued that the health economic discourse on resource allocation to a certain extent resembles the case of the debate on organ donation since trade-offs, social preferences, social benefit, utility maximization, etc. can be regarded as dead metaphors as well. Couching the whole prioritization debate in such terms from consumer choice theory, however, makes it impossible to solve CUA's fairness problem.

5.3 Social preferences and social value maximization

5.3.1 The social preference concept in welfare economics

The concepts of social value, social preferences and equity weights lie at the heart of the health economic interpretation of CUA's fairness issue and the corresponding attempts to solve the latter. Yet, as pointed out at the outset of this study, they remain particularly vague.[17] What exactly does it mean to value "QALYs in others" (Donaldson *et al.* 2011b: 4) and how can it be determined which states of affairs are "equally good for society" (Dolan/Tsuchiya 2009: 213)? The present section argues that the reference to the good *to* or *for* society is inextricably tied to the use of the social preference concept in the first place since the latter transfers the link between *preference* and *value* from consumer choice theory to the evaluation of states of affairs. In order to buttress this claim, the use of the social preference concept in welfare economics is considered in more detail. Thereby, a special focus is on the question of how and where the different conceptions take individual concerns for the welfare of others into account.

In general, modern welfare economics "can be viewed as an investigation of methods of obtaining a social ordering over alternative possible states of the world"

(Boadway/Bruce 1984: 1). The branch of modern welfare economics applying SWFs differs in a crucial respect from Paretian welfare economics. Recall that the Pareto criterion is supposed to minimize the use of value judgments in welfare economics, primarily by avoiding the necessity of interpersonal comparisons of utilities (see Culyer 1998: 364). These comparisons are necessary for establishing a complete ranking of states of affairs, though, so that Paretian welfare economics cannot accomplish this task (see Samuelson 1947: 214; Boadway/Bruce 1984: 4f., 138). This challenge is met by the branch of welfare economics in the tradition of Bergson and Samuelson. It allows for interpersonal comparisons of utility, but stresses the need to formulate explicitly outlined, transparent societal value judgments on how utilities should be distributed. These value judgments determine the shape of the SWF, i.e., "the means by which a complete social ordering is obtained" (Boadway/Bruce 1984: 4). In line with their liberal spirit, welfare economists embrace the premise of normative individualism, stating that "[s]ocial states are to be judged 'good' to the extent that the individuals concerned judge them to be good" (Vanberg 1986: 115). This postulate is not unambiguous, as will become clear immediately.

Initially, the social preference ranking of different states of affairs was conceptualized as resulting from an aggregation of each individual's preferences as to how he or she fares in the respective setting. The most straightforward example is provided by the Utilitarian SWF which ranks social states according to the sum of individual utilities attained in the particular state: $SW = U^1 + U^2 +, \ldots, + U^n$ (see Mandler 1999: 124). In the 1930s, the Utilitarian SWF became embedded in the theoretical framework of the Bergson–Samuelson SWF. According to Abram Bergson and Paul Samuelson, social welfare is some function of the individual utilities attained in a social state, albeit not necessarily an additive one: $SW = SW\ (U^1, U^2, \ldots, U^n)$ (see Boadway/Bruce 1984: 17). Although at first, Bergson endorsed a more general stance as to the arguments of the function, he and subsequent writers soon "restricted analysis to private consumption and required social welfare to be an increasing function of agent utilities" (Mandler 1999: 136). Individual utilities thus became defined in terms of preference rankings on the basis of the individual's direct consumption (see Arrow 1963a: 23, Pattanaik 2008). However, it remains an open question where the value judgments required for establishing the concrete shape of the Bergson–Samuelson SWF are supposed to come from since in a pluralistic and democratic society, it is quite unlikely that a unique ranking of states of affairs exists (see Harsanyi 1955: 315).[18]

An alternative way of conceiving a social preference ranking in the spirit of normative individualism consists in regarding it not as the result of an aggregation, but as a different *kind* of preference the individual has – an individual social preference, as it were (see Thurow 1973: 63f.). This view entails that there are "as many (vague) welfare functions as there are individuals" (Little 1957: 122); individual *i* has her own SWF: $SW^i = SW^i\ (U^1, U^2, \ldots, U^n)$, as does individual *j*: $SW^j = SW^j\ (U^1, U^2, \ldots, U^n)$, and so forth. Yet, this conception immediately raises the question of how to distinguish between an individual social preference on the one hand and an individual personal preference on the other (see Thurow 1973: 63f.). In *Social Choice and Individual Values,* first published in 1951, Arrow (1963a: 18) proposes the following solution:

> In general, there will, then, be a difference between the ordering of social states according to the direct consumption of the individual and the ordering when the individual adds his general standards of equity (and perhaps his standards of pecuniary emulation). We may refer to the former ordering as reflecting the *tastes* of the individual and the latter reflecting his *values*.[19]

He thus allows individuals "to have preferences over end states that precisely qualify how all individuals fare" (Amadae 2003: 241). Arrow (ibid.) argues that the more encompassing ranking on the basis of values should be decisive when it comes to the overall assessment of social welfare, because it is "the ordering according to values which takes into account all the desires of the individual, including the highly important socializing desires, and which is primarily relevant for the achievement of a social maximum." Thus, in contrast to the Bergson–Samuelson conception, the arguments within Arrow's SWF are the individuals' orderings based on values, not tastes (see Arrow 1963a: 23).[20] Put differently, the elements constituting the overall social preference are individual social preferences. This is a crucial turning point in the history of economic thought since Arrow's definition of the ranking of social states on the basis of values changed the interpretation and the subsequent reception of the Pareto optimum to a major extent.

Although the Pareto optimum proved especially fecund in the realm of welfare economics, Pareto himself was not concerned with redistributive policy measures. Instead, he sought to establish the optimum conditions of production and exchange, that is, the conditions under which the market mechanism benefits each party participating in voluntary exchange (see Amadae 2003: 241). To this extent, Pareto (1927: 261) maintains:

> We will say that the members of a collectivity enjoy maximum ophelimity in a certain position when it is impossible to find a way of moving from that position very slightly in such a manner that the ophelimity enjoyed by each of the individuals of that collectivity increases or decreases.

He focuses on the ophelimity derived by each economic agent from *his own* commodity bundle here (see Amadae 2003: 242). Interpreted this way, there is no place for unanimous consent to begin with, because each actor is only concerned with his own decision to enter, continue, or stop engaging in voluntary exchange (see ibid.). The reading of the Pareto criterion changed when Arrow constructed individual preferences so as to refer to whole states of affairs (see Amadae 2003: 241f.). While before, each person was confined to evaluating the state of affairs with reference to *her own* commodity bundle, preferences on the basis of values now refer to "social states affecting all members of society" (Amadae 2003: 242). In this vein, Boadway and Bruce (1984: 2f.), for instance, interpret the Pareto principle as requiring that "if state A is ranked higher than state B for one person, and all other persons rank A at least as high as B, then A should be ranked higher than B in the social ordering."[21]

Arrow's differentiation between preference rankings based on values and preference rankings based on tastes was criticized by John C. Harsanyi (1955: 315), who argues that due to external effects, the individual utility function depends "not only on this particular individual's economic (and noneconomic) conditions but also on the economic (and other) conditions of all other individuals in the community." Then, however, the dissimilarity between the concept of individual preferences on the one hand and of social preferences on the other is in danger of vanishing altogether again. This is something Harsanyi (ibid.) does not want to happen either, as becomes clear in the following:

> We cannot allow the distinction between an individual's social welfare function and his utility function to be blurred if we want (as most of us do, I think) to uphold the principle that a social welfare function ought to be based not on the utility function (subjective preferences) of *one* particular individual only (namely, the individual whose value judgments are expressed in this welfare function), but rather on the utility functions (subjective preferences) of *all* individuals, representing a kind of 'fair compromise' among them.

Apparently, Harsanyi seeks to stick to the idea that the social welfare function results from aggregating individual utility functions. Instead of incorporating concerns for others in the preferences of the individuals already, this approach includes the interests of other persons on the level of aggregation, as Lübbe (2015: 158f.) points out.[22] The conception that individual preferences determine the arguments of the social welfare function, whereas equity concerns influence the latter's shape is indeed characteristic for traditional social choice theory (see Gaertner/Schokkaert 2012: 141).

Having emphasized the importance of this separation, Harsanyi (1955: 315) continues by making the following proposition to differentiate between social and individual preferences:

> Even if both an individual's social welfare function and his utility function in a sense express his own individual preferences, they must express preferences of different sorts: the former must express what this individual prefers (or, rather, would prefer) in the basis of *impersonal social considerations* alone, and the latter must express what he *actually* prefers, whether on the basis of his *personal interest* or on *any other basis*. The former may be called 'ethical' preferences, the latter his 'subjective' preferences. Only his 'subjective' preferences (which define his utility function) will express his preferences in the full sense of the word as they actually are, showing an egoistic attitude in the case of an *egoist* and *altruistic attitude* in the case of an altruist. His 'ethical' preferences (which define his social welfare function) will, on the other hand, express what can in only a qualified sense be

> called his 'preferences': they will, by definition, express what he prefers only in those possibly rare moments when he forces a special *impartial and impersonal attitude* upon himself.[23]

Individual and social preferences are hence distinguished with reference to the reasons or attitudes motivating the individual's preference rankings (see Lübbe 2015: 71). While the former constitute the individuals' actual preferences, whatever these may be, the latter are of a hypothetical character and are formed from an impersonal point of view.[24] In effect, Harsanyi transforms an issue of justice into a problem of individual rational choice (see Mandler 1999: 139).

Both Arrow and Harsanyi try to differentiate individual from social preferences by means of the considerations influencing the individual's ranking. This approach has an important methodological corollary, for it inhibits the inference of preferences from overt choices and, thus violates the axiom of choice determination (see Lübbe 2015: 71). In order to know whether an observed choice expresses an individual or a social preference, information on the subject's underlying reasoning is required. Yet, recall that the formalization of the utility concept had been driven to a large extent by the very desire to evade any assumptions on the individuals' reasons behind their choices. Reintroducing such restrictions in order to keep individual and social preferences distinct is to partly withdraw this development. But even if these methodological qualms are put aside for the time being, Harsanyi does not provide for a clear-cut separation between individual and social preferences anyway.

Consider the example of altruism. In the quote above, Harsanyi (1955: 315) explicitly subsumes altruistic concerns under the category of personal preferences. A similar conception still prevails in modern economics when it is argued that in making choices, a person may "take into account the interests of all others in the community"; these interests, then, "enter as arguments in the choice calculus internally to the participant" (Brennan/Buchanan 1985: 37). Consequently, acting on the basis of altruism – or envy, for that matter – is tantamount to individual preference satisfaction and maximizes the individual utility function (see Dolan *et al.* 2003: 548).[25] Making concern for others an argument in the individual utility function leads to a serious problem, though. For if the SWF is derived from such encompassing individual utility functions, some individual preferences may be counted several times. On Harsanyi's account, subjective and ethical preferences can indeed completely merge if the individual actually bases his choices on his impartial preferences (see Lübbe 2015: 160). In both cases, the SWF no longer establishes a fair compromise between the preferences of different individuals.

In view of these difficulties to define the social preference concept in welfare economics, it is not surprising that the term is characterized by serious ambiguities in health economics as well. For example, consider a debate between Dolan and Johannesson. Grounded in a decidedly welfarist stance, Johannesson (1999: 382) objects that the PTO method endorsed by Dolan (1998) only measures altruistic preferences. Responding to this criticism, Dolan (1999: 388) points out that the reasons behind the PTO responses can be legion so that if person A was asked to trade-off the QALYs gained in individuals B and C,

> A's response to such a question need not be based on her altruistic concerns for B or C at all. She may simply think that it is *better for society* (according to some notion of fairness) to give priority to B over C, say, and may not feel anything for B or C per se. Moreover, she may simply think this because she would want the decision about her own treatment to be made on exactly the same grounds. And she may think this out of self-interest. Therefore, it is not at all clear to me that my approach measures only A's altruistic preferences (if this were the case, then my approach would not be picking up preferences over equity at all since altruism is an efficiency consideration: if A feels good when B is well treated then this is a utility benefit to A).

That is, if an individual endorses a distribution of QALYs because it is "better for society," she acts on the basis of equity preferences, whereas if the distribution makes her feel good, she acts out of altruism, an efficiency consideration. The evaluation of what is good for society apparently requires a disinterested perspective and may be based neither on feelings for the persons concerned nor on self-interest (see ibid.).[26]

These considerations reveal that the literature on social preferences is marked by grave haziness. In addition to the methodological difficulties of referring toward inner states of the individual, three further aspects deserve to be highlighted: first, the reference to the individual's feeling in the passage taken from Dolan (1999: 388) quoted above is utterly unwarranted once a hedonic utility concept is dropped. Second, it seems virtually impossible to establish a clear-cut separation between what is good for others and what is good for oneself, or, as it were, between "self-regarding" and "other-regarding" preferences (Griffin 1986: 24).[27] A father's self-regarding preferences, for instance, will certainly take the well-being of his children into account, just as a lover's welfare depends on the well-being of the beloved one (see Griffin 1986: 24f.). Third, the statement that a certain allocation of resources was "better for society (according to some notion of fairness)" (Dolan 1999: 388) lacks a clear meaning, as the following subsection further elaborates.

5.3.2 Preferences and value – the consumer choice framework

> Welfare economics can be viewed as an investigation of methods of obtaining a social ordering over alternative possible states of the world. A social ordering permits one to compare all states of the world and rank each one as 'better than', 'worse than', or 'equally good as' every other.
>
> (Boadway/Bruce 1984: 1)

This quote points toward the fundamental reason for the terminological difficulties associated with the social value and social preference concepts: the idea that states of affairs are to be judged according to their goodness stems from a category error to the extent that considering distributional judgments in terms of preference rankings of states of affairs transfers the individual conception of rational choices and the corresponding connection between preference and value to equity judgments just like that. If a social preference is to express a valuation, the personified society and the latter's "organic and metaphysical" well-being need to enter the equation (Harris 1990: 397). In the following, this claim is illuminated by considering the SWF in health economics.

Using an SWF to determine the optimal resource allocation resembles the way economists generally consider distributional issues: they "typically approach optimisation problems by listing the options to be considered (the 'opportunity set') and then choosing between them by applying some maximand (the 'objective function')" (Williams/Cookson 2000: 1867). When it comes to medical resource allocation, the opportunity set is commonly presented as a health possibility frontier indicating the feasible distributions of health on the two groups of individuals given the resource-constraint (see ibid.). The objective function, i.e., the health-related social welfare function (HrSWF),[28] in turn, is defined over different health states as measured by the QALY (see Wagstaff 1991: 35f.). It represents combinations of the health of patients in group A and the health of patients in group B which "society regard [sic] as equally desirable (or in other words between which they are indifferent)" (Williams *et al.* 2005: 68).[29] Adopting an HrSWF to model the trade-off between efficiency in terms of the sum of QALYs and equity in terms of their equal distribution was initially proposed by Wagstaff (1991).[30] In his view, the HrSWF has an edge over the approach of maximizing directly weighted QALYs because, in contrast to the latter, it can account for a societal aversion to unequal patterns in health outcomes (see Wagstaff 1991: 33).[31] As it also allows for attaching different weights to the health of patients according to some personal or health-related characteristic, the HrSWF is regarded as the appropriate normative economic framework for attaching equity weights to QALYs.[32] The HrSWF and the health possibility frontier are represented in Figure 5.1.

The positions and slopes of the curves allow for the following inferences. To begin with, the health possibility frontier is not symmetrical to the 45° line, but indicates that group B has a higher potential to benefit from the available resources. In other words, by allocating an identical amount of resources to B instead of A, more health can be produced. The health possibility frontier thus mirrors a trade-off in *terms of production* (see Le Grand 1990: 556). The HrSWF contour is not symmetrical to the 45° line either, but tilted to the vertical axis. This implies that a unit of health generated in group B is regarded as more important or more valuable by society than a unit of health generated in group A. The slope in each point of the curve indicates the MRS between the health of A and the health of B, showing how much of A's health society would be willing to sacrifice in order to improve B's health by a certain amount and still "keep the total level of social welfare constant" (Dolan *et al.* 2008: 5).[33] Hence, the larger the curvature of the HrSWF is, the higher the societal aversion to inequality (see Wagstaff 1991: 36).

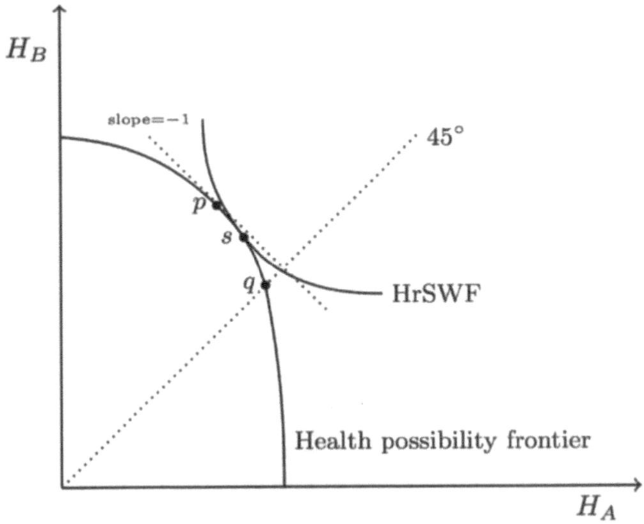

Figure 5.1 HrSWF and health possibility frontier.

Source: adapted from Wagstaff (1991: 37).

Since it illustrates the socially desired combination of equity and efficiency, the HrSWF represents a trade-off in *terms of value* (see Le Grand 1990: 555f.). Williams (1997: 118) emphasizes the different meaning of the curves as follows:

> a careful distinction needs to be drawn here between personal characteristics of the beneficiary which affect the *quantum* of benefit to be expected from a treatment and personal characteristics which affect the *value attached to any given quantum* of benefit. [...] The quantum effect will influence the shape and position of the production possibility frontier. The valuation effect will influence the shape of the social welfare function. I regard the former as an efficiency issue and the latter as an equity issue.

The tangent point between the HrSWF and the health possibility frontier at point *s* mirrors the "best" combination of equity and efficiency for the respective society, which "among all feasible combinations [...] is the one that yields the highest possible level of welfare" (Le Grand 1990: 558). If society's solitary aim was equality in health, the optimal distribution would be at point *q* on the 45° line (see Wagstaff 1991: 36). By contrast, if society targeted health maximization only, the optimum would be reached at point *p* because if "better [overall] health means higher social welfare," the further away the SWF is from the origin, the higher the social welfare (Williams *et al.* 2005: 68). The tangent point in *s*, lying in between the extremes of a maximum of health and a maximum of equality again shows that the respective society strives after a trade-off between equity and efficiency. Yet, the question arises as to what exactly is meant by saying that society desires this or that outcome or by referring to a trade-off in terms of value between equity and efficiency. In fact, these terms have to be interpreted metaphorically, as a look at the origin of the equity-efficiency trade-off notion illustrates.

The concept of the equity-efficiency trade-off in terms of value goes back to the political philosopher Brian Barry.[34] At the outset of his monograph *Political Argument,* Barry (1965: 2f.) differentiates between "justification" and "evaluation" and claims that while the former implies being able to give reasons for a decision, an evaluation could be reached without being capable of verbalizing the underlying principles. In the passage relevant for the present concern, Barry (1965: 3–8) argues that evaluations can be rational even though they are made on the basis of incommensurable principles or values which cannot be reduced to a third, ultimate principle. This is the case if the choices based on the evaluations "show a consistent pattern of preference" (Barry 1965: 4). Interestingly, Barry quotes Hicks' indifference curve analysis of consumer choices as a blueprint. Using an example, Hicks' account does not demand to inquire how much potatoes and grapes respectively contribute "to the quantity of a homogeneous entity of 'pleasure' or 'utility'"; rather, it is sufficient to know how many grapes the individual would have to be given to compensate him for the loss of one potato (ibid.). Barry's crucial methodological move consists of applying this economic reasoning with respect to individual preferences over different bundles of consumption goods to choices based on values and principles in the political realm (see Le Grand 1990: 556). In doing so, Barry (1965: 6) considers the indifference curve analysis particularly apt for his concern because while incommensurable political values, such as equity and efficiency, are usually not reducible to a single value, they could be "expected to be to some extent substitutable for one another." The goodness of a state of affairs to be evaluated, then, "is not a quantity to which efficiency and equity contribute but merely a shorthand expression for the total set of the man's indifference curves expressing the trade-offs between equity and efficiency which would leave him equally satisfied" (Barry 1965: 7).

But is the indifference curve analysis really an appropriate tool when it comes to the evaluation of social states in terms of different principles? To be able to answer this question, the assumptions implicit in the trade-off image need to be uncovered. These are basically four: first, the trade-off notion presumes that the individual's choices reveal the relative values of the goods at stake. Second, the notion of a *relative* valuation requires for the comparability of the items according to some standard (see Sassi *et al.* 2001: 20). Third, both elements have to be regarded as valuable or desirable by themselves and, finally, cannot both be reached to full extent, but are, at least after a certain point, conflicting, making an either-or choice inevitable (see Barry 1965: 7). To this extent, the slogan "You can't have your cake and eat it too" captures the essence of the trade-off notion

(Okun 1975: 1).[35] Summing it up with Lukes (1996: 40), the trade-off notion presupposes that the items to be traded off against each other are

> discrete, free-standing, and independently characterizable values the extent of whose realization can in any case be measured according to some scale that enables the agent engaged in evaluation to express a preference between such 'extents' or else indifference between them.

These assumptions usually hold when it comes to consumer choices.[36] To use Barry's example again, both grapes and potatoes can each be considered as valuable by themselves and, given stable preferences and rational choice behavior, a series of choices between different bundles of grapes and potatoes allow for deducing the individuals' relative valuation of these edibles. Furthermore, taking a budget restriction into account, the consumer cannot have any amount he wishes of each, but has to allocate his resources to the purchase of a certain quantity of potatoes and a certain number of grapes. Regarding the common measure, grapes and potatoes could be compared by taste or nutritional value. Crucially, the trade-off in question refers to a literal trade, as Little (1957: 17) points out: "The object of the [indifference] map is to demonstrate what quantities of *X* and *Y* our consumer will purchase if we give him a certain quantity of *Y* and then let him trade X for Y at a given price." In this context, it also makes perfect sense to say that the increase in the amount of grapes compensates the consumer for the sacrifice of some potatoes, so that he retains the same satisfaction level. The goods at stake are goods for him *because* he values them (see Little 1957: 16; Griffin 1986: 28). That is to say, preferences "make it the case that x is better or worse than y rather than reporting on what is independently the case" so that they are not open to criticism (Hausman 2000a: 27).

Having traced the notion of the equity-efficiency trade-off in terms of value back to the indifference curve analysis of consumer choice theory, it now becomes obvious why welfare economists frequently invoke the personified 'society': it fills the gap left by the consumer. It is for this reason that the welfare economic language used to analyze distributional issues is so very tainted by hedonic concepts, such as compensation, sacrifice, or desirability.[37] Nord (1999a: 16), for example, defines the MRS as "the number of additional persons receiving outcome Y that would be required to compensate for the loss of outcome X in one person."[38] But who gets compensated here, for and by what? Likewise, no decision maker literally has to "sacrifice" (Nord *et al.* 1999: 34) anything because the goods at stake are not goods for him. The fundamental problem is that both the trade-off notion and the very concept of indifference require a common standard according to which the items at stake can be evaluated (see Nagel 1979: 128). As to trade-offs, Lukes (1996: 41) states that they "occur when one [alternative] is exchanged for another because they are taken to be equal in value." Assessing this equality would certainly be impossible if the goods were completely incommensurable in the first place (see Lukes 1996: 42f.). Note that although Barry (1965: 4f.) endorses the indifference curve analysis because it does not require a "common yardstick" to evaluate a state of affairs so that it is capable of accounting for the "plurality of ultimate values," he nevertheless makes use of such a common measure when he refers to the *satisfaction* yielded by a certain combination of equity and efficiency (see Barry 1965: 7). But if in the case of public policy issues, any hedonic interpretation of indifference is ruled out, which kind of standard remains? (See Lübbe 2015: 28f., 228.) As long as the value-maximizing consumer choice framework is left intact, it is indeed hard to come up with a satisfying answer to this query. This is because considering public policy issues within this realm amounts to a category error and so does the invocation of the utterly fictitious image of a society as a distinct subject (see Sagoff 1986: 305f., 313).

To sum it up, Arrow's conception of preferences based on tastes on the one hand and on values on the other allows individuals "to have preferences over end states that precisely qualify how all individuals fare" (Amadae 2003: 241). By nevertheless sticking to the connection of preferences and value, however, current welfare economics in general and health economics in particular are in a situation of considerable terminological turmoil. The basic problem is a fundamental category error: the value-maximizing consumer choice framework is transferred to issues of justice, which have to be considered within a framework of rights instead (see Lübbe 2015: 34f., 226).[39] Couching the debate on medical resource allocation in terms of value maximization is also beside the point when a formal understanding of value is explicitly adopted, as the following section demonstrates.

5.4 Equity weights and representational consequentialism

5.4.1 Representational consequentialism and value atomism

It could be objected that the considerations in the previous section rely on a mistaken understanding of the concepts involved. The apparently hedonic notions, the critic might argue, are in fact to be interpreted in a formal manner. The claim that all choices can be regarded as trade-offs, revealing the relative values of the alternatives at stake, then turns into the assertion that any choice whatsoever can be *represented* as a value-maximizing decision, irrespective of the individual's actual reasons. Accordingly, the notions of social value and value maximization in health care resource allocation would have to be understood metaphorically, since there is no substantial value that could possibly be maximized in the first place. At first glance, this conception of social value maximization seems normatively innocuous. Yet, a closer look at the ultimate purpose of economic evaluations reveals that they cannot get along without any reference to the reasons behind observed prioritization preferences. As it turns out, the weighting approaches imply rather strong assumptions on the nature of people's fairness preferences in particular and on the way moral judgments are reached in general. In the following, these claims are buttressed by taking a closer look at the concept of equity weighting. In order to scrutinize the idea of equity weights, the weighting approaches first need to be pigeonholed into a consequentialist framework. After all, weighted CUA still seeks to maximize benefits, "however they are conceived" (Tsuchiya/Dolan 2009: 147). However, weighted CUA cannot be embedded in a consequentialist framework as easily as traditional CUA, since the two accounts differ in an important respect: While the latter proceeds by *first* identifying QALYs as the units of value and *then* recommending the QALY maximizing course of action, the weighting approaches start by eliciting what the public regards as fair allocation decision and specify the "social maximand" afterwards (Kelleher 2014: 259). In other words, the weighting approaches do not derive the right action from a previously defined notion of the good, but start with rough ideas about what is right and seek to make up the corresponding theory of the good after that. By thus putting the cart before the horse, equity-weighted CUA cannot be regarded as a form of foundational consequentialism.

This is not to say that it does not qualify as a consequentialist theory, though. Consider the initial characterization of consequentialism presented above again: consequentialism "is the claim that an act is right if and only if that act maximizes the good" (Sinnott-Armstrong 2011). Taken literally, this definition only requires the morally right act and the maximization of the good to coincide but does not say anything about their causal relation.[40] Hence, an approach starting with an account of right actions and deriving a fitting theory of value afterwards falls under the category of consequentialism as well. This is indeed the basic idea of the consequentializing project, as the following "recipe" for consequentializing moral theories illustrates:

> Take whatever considerations that the non-consequentialist theory holds to be relevant to determining the deontic status of an action and insist that those considerations are relevant to determining the proper ranking of outcomes. In this way, the consequentialist can produce an ordering of outcomes that when combined with her criterion of rightness yields the same set of deontic verdicts that the non-consequentialist theory yields.
>
> (Portmore 2007: 39)[41]

As a result, "all moral theories can be brought under the umbrella of consequentialism" (Louise 2004: 518).

Both the weighting approaches and consequentialized theories can be characterized as forms of "representational consequentialism," to adopt the terminology introduced by Scanlon (2001: 39). Representational consequentialism

> starts with widely shared intuitions about right and wrong, and shows how a conception of value can be constructed so that these intuitions can be squared with the thesis that an act is right if and only if it is productive of the best consequences.
>
> (Ibid.)

As it obviously does not share foundational consequentialism's capacity to explain and justify actions, the question arises as to what is gained by pressing already existing intuitions into the axiological straightjacket of consequentialism at all. Or, to quote Scanlon (2001: 42):

> Why should it be an advantage to represent rights, duties, and other deontic notions in terms of the value of outcomes, even if in so doing one does not explain them in terms of an independent and allegedly clearer notion of value?

In order to shed light on this issue, it has to be clarified what kind of representation of actions is required if representational consequentialism is to constitute an appropriate framework for equity weighting.

To begin with, representational consequentialism could simply determine the right action in every single situation on the grounds of any reason or intuition whatsoever and rank the outcomes afterwards so that the right action coincides with the maximization of goodness. This type of consequentialism is even acceptable for a devoted non-consequentialist. If he assigns higher values to the outcomes stemming from the right action and lower values to those outcomes resulting from unjust actions, his choice could certainly be regarded as value maximizing in a trivial sense (see Foot 1985: 33; B. Williams 1988: 24; Lübbe 2013: 249, 2015: 31). However, the values generated on such a case-to-case basis cannot be transferred to new choice situations just like that and it is indeed doubtable whether this kind of consequentialism presents a meaningful moral theory for, presumably, the latter should not only systematize moral intuitions as to specific choice situations after the choice was already made, but should also provide for some account of what we are to do in new situations. Beyond that, it should offer a generally valid standard for legitimizing and criticizing actions (see Scanlon 2000: 307). This is clearly something the *ad hoc* representation of actions cannot accomplish.

For the same reason, such an *ex post* representational consequentialism cannot provide an appropriate foundation for equity weighting either. It pays to stress that the aim of economic evaluation consists in providing the decision maker with a "general allocation rule" (Bleichrodt *et al.* 2004: 158), a "formula, which would then be applied impartially, transparently, and fair-mindedly to all future decisions" in order to reach the optimal resource allocation (Williams/Cookson 2006: 1).[42] Therefore, general statements of the type "outcome X is normally appreciated ten times as much by society as outcome Y" have to be established (Nord 1993b: 237). This purpose obviously implies that the values elicited in one particular survey are transferable to future decision contexts. By contrast, if

> all values used in a CBA [or CUA] had to be derived from the precise context of the particular CBA, then the practice of performing CBAs would come close to that of performing opinion polls on the topic to be analyzed.
>
> (Hansson 2007: 179)

When it comes to equity weights, Nord (1993b: 228) explicitly regards them as "explanatory variables," which "predict social preferences much better than a pure QALY-like model." Once stable weights are elicited, it becomes possible to leapfrog the investigation of public preferences and to infer the just allocative decision directly from the value of the outcomes' parts in the first place (see Lübbe 2012: 249f., 2015: 31f.). To give an example, if a survey reveals that the respondents regard a gain of one QALY for a patient at the age of 30 as 1.5 times as valuable as one QALY gained by a 60-year-old, this social value should enter the corresponding decision rule in any new choice situation as well.[43] Due to this explanatory and predictive function of the weights, the numerical representation of observable preference patterns is not enough. Instead, the weighting factors, that is, the arguments in the decision rule, actually have to mirror the reasons the respondents have for their choices (see ibid.).

This necessity has also been recognized in the health economic literature. As to the PTO method, Williams and Cookson (2000: 1903) maintain:

> the great difficulty lies in defining the value elicitation questions tightly enough to elicit precisely targeted information on equity-efficiency trade-offs of a kind which can be used in economic analysis. [...] PTO questions, for instance, are likely to contain the relative weights a respondent attaches to a number of potentially relevant equity factors (in particular, the severity of the pre- and post-intervention health states, the health gain as a result of intervening, and the number of persons treated) and it may be impossible to disentangle what are the relative weights attached to each of these considerations. The weights attributed to these different equity considerations may have quite different implications for resource allocation decisions.[44]

The disentanglement of different underlying motives indeed proves difficult as one and the same preference can express a lot of considerations, of course (see Hurley 1998: 386). To give an example, Nord *et al.* (1996: 103) differentiate between three kinds of age-related preferences, all stemming from very diverse motivations. An uttered preference for treating the young rather than the old could reflect a concern for the person's value to society in terms of her productivity ("productivity ageism"), it could result from the aim to maximize health because the younger are expected to live longer ("utilitarian ageism"), and finally, it could reflect a concern for some kind of equality ("egalitarian ageism").[45] Likewise, a preference for treating the more severely ill patients may either result from a concern for equality in final health or from the aim to maximize health (see Williams 2000: 741). The latter becomes possible if respondents misunderstand the interval properties of the QALY scale and believe, for instance, that a move from health level 2 to level 3 actually represents a *larger* treatment effect than the move from level 5 to 6 (see Shah 2009: 81). In both cases, the observed preference does not express a concern for the worse-off patient at all.

More fundamentally, without knowing how the individual defines the alternatives, even the choice and, concomitantly, the preference as such cannot be witnessed in the first place. These considerations show that the mere observation of preferences, or rather, overt choice behavior, does not provide any information on the underlying reasons and, hence, the proper equity weights. Recall furthermore that the consistency axioms of rational choice theory apply to the ranking of whole alternatives. This ordering does not allow for deriving any conclusion about how the alternatives' attributes influenced the individual's choices, though. By the same token, the overall ranking does not tell us anything about the value of the alternatives' parts, either. Yet, this is exactly the inference drawn in the case of social value measurement since in order to be able to identify the correct equity weights, the respondents' reasons have to be consistent and stable not only as to whole alternatives but also with regard to the alternatives' parts, i.e., the individual factors in which the options are supposed to be dissectible.

Assuming stable reasons for equity judgments across situations, the weighting approaches implicitly adopt an atomistic conception of reasons and values.[46] Atomism of reasons means that "a feature that is a reason in one case must remain a reason, and retain the same polarity, in any other" (Dancy 2004: 7). Dancy (2004: 105) refers to this concept as the "kitchen scale model" of reasoning according to which "each consideration has a practical weight, which it keeps irrespective of what it is combined with – just as a kilogram of butter weights a kilogram whatever it is added to." When it comes to values, atomism postulates "that the moral value of any object is ultimately determined by simple features whose contribution to the value of an object is always the same, independently of context" (Alm 2004: 312). In a nutshell, it is assumed that reasons and values "behave like butter" (Fehige 2005: 12). Precisely the same connotations are carried by the metaphor of equity *weights* already. Since genuine weights do not change their heaviness on a case-to-case basis, this notion suggests independent and stable values of the equity relevant factors. In effect, concerns for justice are supposed to behave like butter as well.[47]

The assumption that respondents make up their choice by considering the value of the alternative's different equity relevant attributes and by aggregating these "partworth utilities" (Diekmann *et al.* 2009: 201) into an overall value of the alternative at stake indeed underlies discrete choice experiments (DCEs). The DCE is an attribute-based stated preference valuation technique, which, since its first use in 1994, has gained increasing popularity in health economics (see Viney *et al.* 2002: 319f.; Drummond *et al.* 2005: 236). While, up to now, the majority of DCE studies focus on patient experiences and individual valuations of health outcomes, they became applied to measure social preferences recently as well.[48] In contrast with other elicitation methods, such as PTO and CV, the DCE is said to be capable of shedding light on the relative value of the different concerns for equity, that is, on the trade-offs between different social values (see Cookson *et al.* 2009: 238; Green/Gerard 2009: 952; Lancsar *et al.* 2011: 467; Nord 2014: 141). It basically confronts respondents with several choices between "bundles of attributes" differing in two or more characteristics (Ryan *et al.* 2006: 406). Analyzing the answers by means of statistical methods allows for inferring how much relative value the respondents assign to the attributes (see Drummond *et al.* 2005: 234; Ryan *et al.* 2006: 406; Amaya-Amaya *et al.* 2008: 13f.; Baker *et al.* 2010: 19). The basic idea that subjects consider the alternatives at stake in terms of their features stems from

Lancaster's (1966) theory of demand (see Koslow 1999: 102; Bennett/Blamey 2001b: 5; Viney *et al.* 2002: 320; Amaya-Amaya *et al.* 2008: 14).

Lancaster (1966: 132f.) starts from the observation that traditional consumer choice theory only considers 'goods' as such but is mute with respect to their "intrinsic properties" so that it can neither account for consumer reactions to the implementation of new commodities, nor for their behavior in the face of quality differences.[49] He describes his core idea as follows:

> The chief technical novelty lies in breaking away from the traditional approach that goods are the distinct objects of utility and, instead, supposing that it is the properties or characteristics of the goods from which utility is derived. [...] Utility or preference orderings are assumed to rank collections of characteristics and only to rank collections of goods indirectly through the characteristics that they possess.
>
> (Lancaster 1966: 133)

The approach does not focus on the value goods as a whole have for the consumer, but rather on the services they generate (see Blaug 1980: 171). To give an example, the utility of a computer can be considered "as the sum of your utility for memory size and your utility for price" (Baron 1994: 339). Note the hedonic language used here: consumers are supposed to *derive* utility from the goods' characteristics. According to random utility theory, utility is explicitly regarded as "a latent construct that exists (if at all) *in the mind* of the consumer, but cannot be observed directly by the researcher" (Louviere 2001: 15).[50] Although the consumer is assumed to choose in accordance with his utility function, i.e., to "select the alternative with the highest utility" (Green/Gerard 2009: 953), the observer never knows all factors that might have influenced a particular choice (see Tay 1999: 157). This "unexplained" part of choice is captured by a random factor so that the random utility function takes the following form:

$$U_{an} = V_{an} + \varepsilon_{an}$$

U_{an} denotes the

> latent, unobserved utility for choice alternative a [sic] held by consumer *n*, V_{an} is the systematic, observable or 'explainable' component of the latent utility that consumer *n* has for option *a*, and ε_{an} is the random or 'unexplainable' component of the latent utility associated with option *a* and consumer *n*.
>
> (Louviere 2001: 15)

Due to the fact that part of the choice remains unexplained, preferences can only be predicted with a certain probability so that the researcher faces an "inherently stochastic" problem (ibid.).[51]

Using statistical techniques, DCEs allow for modeling the different attributes' marginal values in terms of WTP (see Baker *et al.* 2010: 19; Bekker-Grob *et al.* 2012: 155). Baker *et al.* (ibid.) sum it up as follows:

> In a discrete choice study, respondents are presented with a series of choice sets (usually pairwise). Each scenario in the set is defined according to some predefined attributes [...] and levels of such attributes. The attribute levels vary across scenarios and choice sets. In each choice set, the respondent is asked which scenario they prefer or would choose. Faced with a series of such choices, respondents essentially *reveal how much weight they attach* to each of the attributes, the actual weights being derived through statistical analysis of the data.[52]

It becomes possible to predict people's choices under different circumstances and to estimate "the impact on utility of changing the attributes of alternatives" (Viney *et al.* 2002: 320). Of particular interest in the context of the present inquiry are the demands DCEs put on the respondents' preferences.[53] Beside the axioms of completeness, stability, and rationality of preferences – 'rational' here means that "an individual should prefer more of a good thing rather than less" (Ryan *et al.* 2006: 411f.) – it is assumed that the respondents choose between the alternatives presented to them by considering the value of the alternatives' characteristics and aggregating these "partworth utilities" into the overall value of the alternative at stake (Diekmann *et al.* 2009: 201; see Amaya-Amaya *et al.* 2008: 13). The crucial premise underlying this approach is the continuity assumption which postulates "unlimited substitutability" (Ryan/Bate 2001: 61) of the different attributes and "compensatory decision making" on part of the respondents (Ryan *et al.* 2006: 411f.).[54]

These premises imply that all the parameter values of the different characteristics are independent of each other and, hence, allow for unrestricted trade-offs (see Ryan/Bate 2001: 61). This means that "a vegetarian will accept a leather cover of the helmet if the price is low enough for the cover not being made of a preferred non-leather material" (Koslow 1999: 101). If the vegetarian refuses to accept leather under any condition, he violates the assumption of compensatory decision-making. This case illustrates that the premise of continuity is not innocuous even if it is applied to individual consumer choices. A comprehensive discussion of whether it is a reasonable assumption when it comes to *distributional* decisions is lacking in the literature, though (see Ryan/Bate 2001; Lloyd 2003; Lancsar/Louviere 2006; Lancsar *et al.* 2011). An exception is provided by Haninger (2006: 85) who points out that it does not go without saying that the continuity assumption holds in the case of prioritization decisions:

> consider an equity weighting function over age, sex, and health. The additive representation of these attributes implies that the effects of differences in age and sex do not depend on health, the effects of differences in age and health do not depend on sex, and the effects of differences in sex and health do not

> depend on age. Concerns for equalizing the quality-adjusted survival curves of men and women, which might be a legitimate goal of equity weights, would likely violate the assumptions of preferential independence.

While it would be theoretically possible to include interaction terms in the function, such an endeavor would obviously significantly complicate the derivation of equity weights from the results of DCEs. Additionally, it cannot be ruled out that "tradeoffs between two attributes might depend on other attributes omitted from the survey design" (Haninger 2006: 86). By the same token, the pooling of results from different surveys could be utterly misleading and, in effect, the transferability of equity weights would be seriously at stake. Chapter 5 demonstrates that the assumptions coming along with the DCE are indeed very often violated in actual empirical studies. At this point, we return to the consequentialist framework of the weighting approach.

5.4.2 Are all choices trade-offs?

It turns out that DCEs in particular and the weighting approach in general assume that "which consequences are best is some function of the value of parts of those consequences" (Sinnott-Armstrong 2011). In doing so, weighted CUA constitutes a form of aggregative consequentialism.[55] Presumably, the conviction that the value of outcomes has an aggregative structure stems from the utilitarian origin of consequentialism; it can be regarded as a utilitarian atavism of economic evaluation. Within classical utilitarianism, states of affairs are "more or less valuable depending on the amount of pleasure and pain they contained" (Scanlon 1998: 80). This additive structure of utilitarianism implies, first, that "the value of a state of affairs is the sum of the values of its component parts" (ibid.) and presupposes, second, the transferability of values. Now, even though hedonism is generally rejected by modern consequentialists, the latter still stick to the belief that "whatever the correct account of value" is, it will have an aggregative structure (Scanlon 1998: 100).[56] Undoubtedly, this is a normative assumption the appropriateness of which has to be established by argument in the first place. To quote Hansson (2007: 179), the argument of the transferability of values

> is based on the value assumption that our evaluations of a consequence should be the same irrespective of the context in which that consequence appears. We can call this the sameness-thesis. According to this widely held view, a life lost in a workplace accident and a (hypothetical) life lost due to arsenic drinking water should be assigned the same value.

While the premise of the transferability of values and the corresponding conception of moral reasoning apply to hedonic utilitarianism, there is no reason to assume that they generally hold true. In fact, if "there is no general value that can be transferred, but all values are holistic and context-dependent, then the additive structure of utilitarianism is not meaningful" (ibid.). As to equity weighting this means that if the different equity factors were not context-independent and if the respondents evaluated each choice situation in a holistic fashion, there would be no stable preferences as to the parts of the alternatives and, thus, no equity weights in the first place.

It deserves emphasis that the questions of how different reasons work together in moral reasoning and of whether values are holistic or context-dependent refer to a broad and ongoing debate within moral philosophy.[57] Some accounts even reject the assumption that diverse moral judgments can or should be derived from general principles at all. Instead, they take the pluralism of rules and principles applying in different contexts or spheres at face value without striving to integrate them "into a coherent whole" (Birnbacher 1999: 322). When it comes to moral judgments in the vernacular, Hansson (2007: 179) surmises that "when evaluating consequences we do not normally separate them from their contexts, and it is far from obvious why we should do so."[58]

A look at the respondents' actual reasons for their prioritization choices reveals that they indeed usually do not mention the value of the alternatives' attributes, but rather frequently refer to non-consequentialist categories such as rights, duties, claims, and equal chances. To give an example, Ubel (1999) conducted a study on social preferences as to the allocation of resources either to a group of severely ill patients who would benefit little from the treatment or to a group of less severely ill patients who would gain considerably. Ubel (1999: 899) found that the majority of respondents opted for distributing the resources equally among the two groups, giving the following rationales for the choices: "'Everyone *deserves* proper funding and treatment', 'Even though money is limited, it is everyone's *right* to have the best medical care possible', or 'Because everyone should be *treated equally'*."[59] The concern to treat everyone equally was also repeatedly invoked in other qualitative studies, in which respondents remark that the patients concerned had "equal rights to treatment" (Oliver 2004: 277) or were "equally *entitled* to treatment" (Nord *et al.* 1995b: 85).[60] Moreover, subjects refer to "the 'moral' point of view, which tries to give everyone an *equal chance* of being treated" (Dolan/Cookson 2000: 24).[61] Other explanations elicited by Ubel (1999: 899) emphasize "the importance of not abandoning patients: 'No one should be overlooked for health treatment', 'Health care funding should be evenly spread so no one is left out'." This finding is buttressed by other studies which found that respondents neither want "to abandon people" (McKie *et al.* 2011: 951), or whole groups (see Ubel/Loewenstein 1996), nor to remove hope from high-cost patients (see Nord *et al.* 1995b; McKie *et al.* 2011). The question of whether such decidedly non-consequentialist reasons can be represented as values of the alternative's parts at all remains unreflected in the health economic literature. Yet, as Lübbe (2009a: 14, 2009c: 102, 2015: 191ff.) shows, the postulate of treating everyone with equal respect cannot be represented within a value-maximizing framework. Hence, it cannot be embodied in equity weights either.

All in all, it is by no means clear that the assumptions of atomism in values and reasons, which are tacitly taken for granted by the weighting approaches, actually apply when it comes to equity judgments in general and to prioritization decisions in particular. In fact, there is much evidence to the contrary. Hence, the equity weights derived from the respondents' choices may represent the particular choices in that particular survey, but most likely are not transferable to new allocation situations. Returning to the question of what should be gained by representing "rights, duties, and other deontic notions in terms of the value of outcomes, even if in so doing one does not explain them in terms of an independent and allegedly clearer notion of value" (Scanlon 2001: 42), it can now be concluded that the mere *ex post* representation of particular choices based on fairness intuitions is pointless. A meaningful representation must aim at establishing a *consistent axiology* which allows for deriving the right action in new choice situations as well. Therefore, it has to tackle the respondents' actual reasons for their choices. It can hence be said that while the weighting approaches start as a form of *ex post* representational consequentialism, they have to end up as a type of aggregative, foundational consequentialism.

It remains to be emphasized at this point that the health economic concept of choices as trade-offs, expressing relative values, differs crucially from the general manner of speaking about value in the vernacular.[62] If one speaks of valuing friendship, beauty, good food, etc., in most cases this basically expresses the importance of the valued items to the individual (see Barry 1965: 9f.). It certainly does not imply that the object at stake can be assigned consistent and stable values, though. This ambiguity of the value notion is not sufficiently acknowledged in the health economic literature. Papers entitled "Toward a broader view of values" (Menzel *et al.* 1999) or phrases like the "goal should be to capture the most important values that will affect most people" (Ubel *et al.* 2000b: 900) suggest the quotidian meaning of values in terms of highly valued things or ideals. Once this fundamental conceptual difference is recognized, it becomes obvious that it is implausible to regard any choices whatsoever as trade-offs expressing valuations in the strong sense delineated above. In fact, choice situations exist in which it is neither the decision maker's aim nor his task to focus on any kind of value, nor can his choice be reasonable represented as such (see Lukes 1996: 45ff.; Lübbe 2010a: 583, 2015).

This case is exemplified by the following example borrowed from Lübbe (2010a: 584).[63] Patient A suffers from multiple organ failure and is in need of both a kidney and a lung transplant. Giving him these two organs implies that two other patients, B and C, one in need of a kidney and another in need of a lung, will die while they are on the waiting-list. That is, saving patient A comes at the opportunity cost of two lives. In accordance with the economic understanding of choice, putting A on the list implies that the person doing so – implicitly or explicitly – values the life or the health of A twice as much as the life of the other two patients. As pointed out above, it is without a doubt possible to represent this specific choice to put A on the list and to transplant a kidney and a lung to the patient as a value-maximizing choice *ex post*. Still, it cannot be assumed without further ado that the decision maker put A on the list for the very *reason* that this action generates more value. Hence, the alleged value inferred from this particular choice cannot be transferred to other situations. Considering the choice to put the patient on the list in terms of the value of his life seems to be beside the point anyway. Following Lübbe (ibid.), it seems safe to assume that patients in general do not receive organ transplants – or any other treatment, as it were – for the reason that their survival is assigned a certain value but because they have an equal claim to health care (see Lübbe 2015: 61f.).

Hence, the assumption that all choices necessarily reveal the valuation of the chosen alternative and, thereby, the "benefit forgone" is unsubstantiated so that there is "no good reason for assuming that all our choices are to be understood as trade-offs" (Lukes 1996: 47). To do so is to neglect a whole range of reasons people can have for their decisions and "to subscribe to a dogma which deflects us from paying attention to the ethical and explanatory significance, in personal and institutional life, of choices that are not trade-offs" (Lukes 1996: 48).[64] Decisions could just as well stem from the desire to respect or corroborate the rights of the persons concerned (see Lübbe 2010a: 584). Similarly, inferring the value of a human life from past decisions of the bodies in charge or from government legislation more generally is unwarranted, too, as Sagoff (2004: 150f.) points out:

> Risk regulation does not necessarily provide an implicit economic valuation of 'intangibles' such as human life. Decisions in this area more typically respond to public attitudes, statutory guidance, and relevant legal history. [...] To impute a value-per-life/year to any regulation or policy, such as highway construction, is to create an epiphenomenon, a statistical abstraction, or descriptive convention, but not to identify a value judgment that necessarily affected the program.

In conclusion, it can be said that the metaphor of equity weighting makes strong and unwarranted assumptions on the nature of the respondents' distributive judgments so that instead of expediently illuminating the subject, the weighting metaphor is actually leading astray.

5.5 On the equity-efficiency trade-off, or whose benefit is it anyway?

Having considered the concepts of social value, social preferences, and equity weighting, the "master metaphor" of the rationing debate, the equity-efficiency trade-off, remains to be scrutinized. For this purpose, recall the implications of the trade-off metaphor outlined above. In the words of Lukes (1996: 40), the items to be traded off against each other have to constitute conflicting,

> discrete, free-standing, and independently characterizable values the extent of whose realization can in any case be measured according to some scale that enables the agent engaged in evaluation to express a preference between such 'extents' or else indifference between them.

As pointed out in the previous chapter, health economists generally take it for granted that these assumptions apply to efficiency and equity. The present section challenges this conviction by investigating whether efficiency in terms of QALY maximization can indeed be considered a separate goal of its own (see Le Grand 1990: 555; Lübbe 2005). This query remains relevant even though it is usually acknowledged in the literature by now that efficiency cannot be the *only* aim of allocating resources, since also multi-dimensional axiologies presume that efficiency is at least *one* normatively relevant factor (see Lübbe 2009c, 2011, 2015: 23).[65] This section argues in line with Lübbe (ibid.) that units of value and, hence, efficiency *as such* have no normative-ethical relevance at all and that the attempts to solve CUA's fairness problem by means of weighting QALYs and trading-off equity and efficiency seriously misconceive the relationship between efficiency and fairness. The considerations reveal that the health economic interpretation of CUA's failure was beside the point in the first place. In so far as the problems of QALY maximization stem from the aggregative, value-maximizing framework of CUA, they will keep reappearing as long as this paradigm remains intact.

The normative arguments provided in the health economic literature for health maximization – if provided at all – chiefly fall into one of two categories, both of which closely resemble utilitarian arguments for utility maximization. One thread refers to the sum of health as a good to society, whereas the other focuses on the egalitarian, non-discriminatory nature of QALY maximization. As to the latter case, it is generally argued that maximizing QALYs is "in line with a particular egalitarian view that everybody's health should be valued equally" (Tsuchiya 2012: 407).[66] Whereas the use of WTP data systematically favors the rich, QALY maximization regards every QALY as being of equal value, no matter how it is generated or who gets it – "a QALY is a QALY is a QALY."[67] According to Williams (1988: 117), the ethical appeal of QALY maximization derives from its "strong non-discriminatory flavor": it "is free of judgments about people's worth, or deserts, or influence, or likeability, or appearance, or smell, or manners, or age, sex, wealth, social class, sexual beliefs, race, colour, sexual orientation, or general or particular life-style."[68] This case bears striking similarity to utilitarianism's claim that in determining the overall sum of utility, everyone counts for one and no one for more than one (see Nagel 1979: 113). It thus becomes apparent that both utilitarianism and traditional CUA are based on a certain account of egalitarianism, i.e., a certain conception of justice already (see Lübbe 2015: 92f.). Hence, *if* there is a trade-off between equity and efficiency, it is a trade-off between different conceptions of justice (see Schmidt 1994: 48; Schefczyk/Priddat 2000: 459). It does not go without saying that any theories of justice whatsoever can be consistently combined with each other, though (see ibid.). In the present case, utilitarianism's specification of the ideal of equality is incompatible with simultaneously interpreting equality as equal distribution of well-being (see ibid.). This point will be taken up below again.

The second line of argument for the "morality of efficiency in health care" can be illustrated by considering Culyer's (1997: 95) claim that there could "be no doubt that a principle objective of the NHS is to maximise health."[69] As a basic premise, Culyer (1997: 96) assumes that the individuals' "flourishing" constitutes an "ultimate good" and an "ethically commendable end." Since health is a necessary condition for realizing this aim and because health care is a means for achieving better health, individuals not only "want" health care, but "need it in an ethically persuasive sense of the word" (Culyer 1997: 97). He draws the conclusion that "maximising the health of the populations becomes an ethical objective" (ibid.). His rationale thus boils down to the assertion that because health is a good for the individual, the sum of health is a good for society (see Schlander 2007: 535). This argument sounds familiar as it closely resembles Mill's (1871b: 269f.) proof of utilitarianism. It deserves to be quoted at length:

> The only proof capable of being given that an object is visible, is that people actually see it. The only proof that a sound is audible, is that people hear it: and so of the other sources of our experience. In like manner, I apprehend, the sole evidence it is possible to produce that anything is desirable, is that people do actually desire it. If the end which the utilitarian doctrine proposes to itself were not, in theory and in practice, acknowledged to be an end, nothing could ever convince any person that it was so. No reason can be given why the general happiness is desirable, except that each person, so far as he believes it to be attainable, desires his own happiness. This, however, being a fact, we have not only all the proof which the case admits of, but all which it is possible to require, that happiness is a good: that each person's happiness is a good to that person, and the general happiness, therefore, a good to the aggregate of all persons. Happiness has made out its title as one of the ends of conduct, and consequently one of the criteria of morality.

Notably, this reasoning from the good for the individual to the good for society is explicitly adopted in the health economic literature. To this extent, Hadorn (1992: 1458) maintains that the "utilitarian 'greatest good for the greatest number' approach seems reasonable in the abstract – and indeed is the ideal toward which we should strive" and Cubbon (1991: 182) argues:

> [Mill's] argument can be interpreted or reconstructed as a move from the premise that giving someone what he or she wants is good to the conclusion that the maximum good will be produced by satisfying as many desires as possible. Likewise the defender of QALY maximisation can claim that the principle rests on the judgement that raising someone's stock of QALYs is a good for him or her.

The inference from the individual good to the good of an aggregate of persons is unwarranted, of course, as has been demonstrated time and again in the philosophical literature. It is worthwhile to reconsider the basic thread of the objections levelled against utilitarianism here since the previous quotes indicate that the philosophical literature is not sufficiently received in health economics. It is thus important to make the arguments accessible to a broader, non-philosophical audience. The seminal paper arguing that there is no entity for whom the sum of good actually constitutes a good so that the former does not have any normative-ethical relevance at all is Taurek's "Should the Numbers Count?"[70] His starting point is the following allocation scenario: one person, called David, and five other persons are in need of a drug without which they are going to die soon. These individuals do not differ in any relevant way except for one thing: whereas David requires the whole amount of the drug to be cured, each of the other five needs a fifth of the medication. Hence, either David or the five other persons can be saved – a trade-off situation *par excellence*. Taurek (1977: 303) challenges the view that "other things equal, it is a worse thing that these five persons should die than that this one should." As long as it remains unspecified "to whom or for whom or relative to what purpose it is or would be a worse thing," he is unwilling to commit himself to such a claim (Taurek 1977: 304). It would certainly be a worse thing for each of the five persons if they were to die and David were to survive, but for David, it would be the other way round. The five losses never "add up to anyone's experiencing a loss five times greater than the loss suffered by any of one of the five" (Taurek 1977: 307). Pointing to the sum of value generated by saving the five, he argues, conflates the issue at stake with the treatment of objects: in the case of objects that are valuable *for* an individual, it makes perfect sense to preserve five objects instead of one from being destructed by a fire. Because the overall value of the five objects is five times as great as the value of one object, saving five objects preserves more of value to the individual (see Taurek 1977: 306). When it comes to persons, however, it "is the loss *to* the individual that matters to me, not the loss *of* the individual" (Taurek 1977: 307). Therefore, each person's loss is to be regarded as equally significant, "only as a loss to that person alone" (ibid.). Expressing *equal concern* for each person in the allocation scenario described at the outset, Taurek (1977: 306f.) concludes, requires giving each individual an equal chance to survive.

This is not the place to spell out in detail what exactly "expressing equal concern," treating everyone equally, or, as Dworkin (1977: 272) puts it, treating each person "as an equal," with "the same respect and concern as everyone else," requires in different situations.[71] Suffice it to emphasize that giving everyone an equal chance to survival is seriously at odds with the normative basis of utilitarianism. Recall that within utilitarianism, equality is specified as counting everyone's utilities equally. In doing so, however, it basically reduces persons to containers of utility and does not assign any primary normative relevance to their rights or liberties as such (see Sen/Williams 1982b: 4).[72] As the latter only serve as means for maximizing overall utility, there is no reason in principle "why the greater gains of some should not compensate for the lesser losses of others; or [...] why the violation of the liberty of a few might not be made right by the greater good shared by many" (Rawls 1971: 26).[73] The same is true when it comes to health maximization, for CUA does not take seriously the distinction between persons either (see Harris 1987: 118; Lübbe 2005, 2009b; Huster 2010: 1075, 2011: 46). Actually, it does not take persons into account at all because that "which is to be given equal weight is not persons and their interests and preferences, but quality-adjusted life-years" (Harris ibid.). The ethically unacceptable distributional effects of this approach were delineated above.[74]

The crucial point is that neither the production of utility nor of health *as such* has any normative relevance at all.[75] Just as pleasure, health obviously resides in persons and

> if it is people and not units of life-span that matter, if the QALY is advocated because it is seen as a moral and efficient way to fulfil our obligation to provide care for our fellows, then it does matter who gets the QALYs – because it matters how people are *treated*.
>
> (Ibid.)[76]

That is to say, any QALY induced in ways violating individual rights and liberties or denying persons equal concern and respect should not count to begin with. The example of the ill millionaire presented in Chapter 2 is a case in point. Richardson and McKie (2007: 790) surmised that their "argument for letting the magnate die would be universally rejected as unfair" so that the "efficiency of the policy (the greater social benefits) would be irrelevant." Remarkably, they do not argue that the policy's efficiency is outweighed by or traded off against the unfairness; instead, they consider it as completely irrelevant in the first place.[77]

The claim that efficiency as such is not normatively relevant also extends to multi-criterial schemes, as Lübbe (2015: 46ff.) demonstrates.[78] If a treatment's cost-efficiency is regarded as one prioritization criterion among others – such as medical need and expected medical benefit – it will be decisive as soon as the patients concerned do not differ with respect to the other criteria. Again, the example of multiple organ failure points to the inappropriateness of this conception counter-example: assume that three patients are in need of an organ transplant. While the patients do not differ as to medical need and expected benefit, their treatments diverge with respect to cost-efficiency: patient A needs a heart, patient B needs a liver, and patient C needs both. Hence, the multi-criterial prioritization scheme would delete C, or any patients in need of multiple transplants, from the waiting list. This seems unfair. To anyone sharing this intuition, the example shows that efficiency should not serve as an independent prioritization criterion of its own. Instead, the production of QALYs can only be regarded as normatively relevant if it happens in ways compatible with the demands of justice (see Lübbe 2009d). Therefore, the aims of equity and efficiency in health care resource allocation are not on a par and cannot be considered independent goals of their own. Instead, the former defines what counts as a normatively relevant production of value in the first place so that the equity-efficiency trade-off notion is seriously misleading (see Lübbe 2015: 225ff., 233ff.).

To make it worse, couching the problem of resource allocation in terms of the preferred equity-efficiency trade-off is not only deceptive, but also dangerous. As it "appears to put complicated issues into a clear-cut manageable shape" (McPherson 1987: 45), it obscures the normative-ethical dimension of the issue at stake. Thereby, the trade-off image bears the hazard of legitimizing any allocative decision whatsoever (see Lübbe 2015: 227f.).[79] As the transplantation example illustrates, once fairness is considered even with efficiency, basic rights and liberties of the persons concerned can no longer be guaranteed. Justice, that is, cannot serve as a safeguard against obviously unfair policies if its requirements can always be counterbalanced by demands of efficiency. The precise shape of this trade-off becomes a matter of mere preferences, then (see ibid.). Cookson *et al.* (2009: 231), for instance, aver that "policy makers *may place rather little value* on health outcomes achieved by infringing individual liberties or discriminating on the basis of age, sex, or race."[80] Regardless of how "little" the respective values are, the aggregated sum might be considerable.[81] In addition, without giving a reason for the specific value placed these outcomes, i.e., without specifying the benchmark against which equity and efficiency are to be traded off against each other, there is no reason why policy makers might not as well place rather high value on "health outcomes achieved by infringing individual liberties." Hence, to avoid such capriciousness, the debate on resource allocation in health care needs to be embedded into a normative framework which makes concrete allocation proposals accessible to rational arguments (see Lübbe 2015: 228).

To resume, the value-oriented metaphors applied in the debate on health care resource allocation illegitimately transfer assumptions from the field of consumer choice theory to issues of distributive justice without reflecting their appropriateness. The *dead* metaphors used, however, prove inapt since they restrict the perspective on the subject far too much (not all choices are value-maximizing choices), lead to the usage of meaningless concepts (social value, good for society, etc.), imply high demands on the individuals' distributive judgments and the working of equity considerations (stable equity weights, atomism of reasons and values), and suggest a fundamentally mistaken relationship between equity and efficiency (trade-off). The following chapter supports the assertion that CUA's fairness issue cannot be solved within the value-maximizing framework of economic evaluation by considering inconsistencies arising in empirically elicited preferences and in the theoretical attempts to solve the problem of disability discrimination.

Notes

1 For a textbook example see Mankiw/Taylor (2014: 3).
2 Italics added. Likewise, Ryan *et al.* (2006: 405) state: "The notion of value used, based on economic theory, implies sacrifice or trade-offs. That is, the value of a particular choice is revealed by what we are prepared to give up in order to make that choice."
3 Pursuant to Culyer (1990: 24), the opportunity cost gives information on "the acceptable price [in terms of QALYs] that one should pay for greater equality." See Cookson *et al.* (2014: 32).
4 See for this reasoning Ubel/Loewenstein (1995: 149) and Schwappach (2002: 214).
5 Likewise, when a respondent disregards costs in his allocative choice, he apparently values the (health of the) respective patients differently:

> Economic theory postulates that competing projects should receive a priority that is inversely proportional to their cost. In other words if projects of type A are twice as costly as projects of type B, then society should choose As rather than Bs if and only if each A is considered more than twice as valuable as each B. This follows from the definition of cost, which is the value sacrificed by not putting resources to the best alternative use.
>
> (Nord *et al.* 1995b: 79f.)

6 See also Backhouse (1998b: 419) and Lagueux (1999: 2). Another pioneer is Mirowski (1989).
7 See also McCloskey (1998: 40, 51). On story-telling in economics see McCloskey (1992).
8 See also McCloskey (1992: 12).
9 See also Henderson (1994: 356, 1998: 292), and Colvin (1985: 6). Ample examples are offered by Bicchieri (1988) and McCloskey (1992, 1998).
10 See also Henderson (1994) and Lagueux (1999).
11 On the importance of metaphors for daily life see Lakoff/Johnson (2003: 3, 158).
12 See also McCloskey (1992: 63) and Henderson (1994: 355).
13 In this respect, they are similar to scientific theories. See Henderson (1994: 345, 1998: 293), McCloskey (1998: 47), and Lakoff/Johnson (2003: 10ff.).
14 See also Henderson (1998: 290).
15 See also Bicchieri (1988: 104ff,).
16 Note that although the metaphor organ *donation* falls outside the market framework, this does not cause any conceptual tension, which is a further evidence for the claim that the metaphors considered here are dead.
17 See Section 2.1.
18 See also Little (1957: 117, 121f.), Blaug (1997: 576), and Mandler (1999: 124).
19 The sections referred to here are identical in the first and second edition of *Social Choice and Individual Values.*
20 On the difference between the Bergson-Samuelson and Arrow SWF see Pattanaik (2008).
21 See also Hausman/McPherson (2009: 136).
22 See also Lübbe (2013: 252f.).
23 Italics added.
24 This becomes clear in Harsanyi's (1953: 434) following example:

> If somebody prefers an income distribution more favorable to the poor for the sole reason that he is poor himself, this can hardly be considered as a genuine value judgement on social welfare. But if somebody feels such a preference in spite of his being wealthy himself, of [sic] if somebody who is in fact poor expresses such a preference, but does it quite independently of the fact of being poor himself, this may well be a value judgment of the required kind.

25 In modern welfare economics, such "reciprocal consumption externalities" can be represented by interdependent utility functions (Boadway/Bruce 1984: 114). See Hurley (2000: 87) and Davis (2003: 31f.).
26 Dolan *et al.* (2003: 549) recognize that the researcher has to understand the motivation behind the stated fairness preferences to make sure that the choice is not tainted by self-interest.
27 See also Dworkin's (1977: 281, 1978: 134) attempt to distinguish between "personal preferences" and "external preferences for the assignment of goods and opportunities to others."
28 The term health-related social welfare function was coined by Dolan (1998: 41).
29 See also Wagstaff (1991: 37).
30 Drawing on Culyer (1989, 1990), Wagstaff (1991) presents an important contribution to kick off the debate on the integration of equity into health economic evaluation (see Richardson *et al.* 2010). Since then, the SWF has been extensively applied and elaborated in the health economic literature. See Johannesson/Gerdtham (1996), Williams (1997), Dolan (1998), Bleichrodt *et al.* (2004), Dolan/Tsuchiya (2009), and Tsuchiya/Dolan (2009).
31 Direct equity weighting cannot incorporate an aversion to unequal patterns of distributions because "the concern here lies with inequality in the distribution of health, not

with the question of whether or not A happens to be a compulsive smoker, a parent of a 2-year old child, or whatever" (Wagstaff 1991: 33). See Ubel (2001: 167f.) and Schwappach (2002: 219). More precisely, the pattern of the resulting distribution cannot be accounted for by direct equity weighting *ex ante*. Once the distributional pattern is known, the fitting weights can certainly be attached to the QALYs received by those individuals who end up in a lower health state than most others. In this vein, McKie/Richardson (2005a: 3) for instance state that "a number of studies suggest that health gains are valued less when they are concentrated among few people, and valued more when they are distributed more widely." The necessity to specify the weights *ex ante* is delineated in the following section.

32 The HrSWF permits trade-offs "between all of the various ethical desiderata," as Williams/Cookson (2000: 1869) put it. See Wagstaff (1991: 35f.), Williams (1997: 118), Dolan/Olsen (2002: 129), Bleichrodt *et al.* (2004: 158), and Williams *et al.* (2005: 70). On the SWF as normative framework for equity weighting see Sassi *et al.* (2001: 7f.), Dolan/Olsen (2002: 121ff.), and Cookson *et al.* (2014: 30).

33 See also Williams (1997: 118), (2001a: 252), Williams *et al.* (2005: 68f.), and Dolan *et al.* (2008: 5).

34 Barry is regarded as the originator of the trade-off in terms of value by Le Grand (1990: 555f., 559), Lukes (1996: 41), and Schefczyk/Priddat (2000: 431). The notion was taken up by Rawls (1971: 37f.) and rapidly entered public discourse so that in the midst of the 1980s, it was already used widely, as McPherson (1987: 44) reports: "'Trade-off' is a fairly recent addition to the English language but it is now in common use in business and labour circles and by economists, politicians, and political commentators." By now, it has become "almost a truism" for economists and political scientists that "equity-efficiency trade-offs prevail in virtually all areas of social policy" (Schmidt 1994: 45). See Lukes (1996: 36).

35 See also Le Grand (1990: 564) and Amadae (2003: 5).

36 Exceptional cases such as perfect substitutes or complementary goods are disregarded.

37 The SWF is "a social indifference map" (Blaug 1997: 576), mirroring the combinations of goods society regards "as equally good in terms of social welfare" (Dolan *et al.* 2008: 7).

38 According to Dolan *et al.* (2008: 5),: the MRS "represents the relative social value of a marginal change in the social value of health to one group relative to the other, keeping the total level of social welfare constant."

39 See also Lübbe (2005, 2009b, 2009c, 2010c, 2011).

40 According to Brown (2011: 753), the definition of consequentialism

> claims only that, among possible actions, certain properties, namely those of being morally right and of maximizing the good, are necessarily coinstantiated. It makes no claim of causation, determination, or explanation; it doesn't say that acts are right because their outcomes are best. Nor (if this amounts to a distinct claim) does it make a claim of priority; it doesn't say that the good is prior to the right.

41 See Dreier (1993: 23f.): "The main strategy for 'consequentializing' any given moral theory is simple. We merely take the features of an action that the theory considers to be relevant, and build them into the consequences."

42 See also Culyer (1989: 53), Lancsar *et al.* (2011: 467), and Gaertner/Schokkaert (2012: 139f.).

43 This is true although, speaking within the value-framework different factors could outweigh each other.

44 See also Dolan (1998: 41).

45 See also Tsuchiya (1999: 267). According to Wailoo *et al.* (2009: 984), the former two preferences cannot be regarded as equity preferences since productivity and utilitarian ageism are apparently motivated by concerns for efficiency. See also Williams/Cookson (2000: 1904).

46 See on value atomism extensively Lübbe (2015: 129ff.).
47 Richardson (2002: 635) seems to regard this assumption as trivially true: "There is no ethical complexity in accepting that severity *per se* may of *independent* importance in prioritizing health services" (italics added).
48 For the use of DCEs to elicit social preferences see Green/Gerard (2009), Baker *et al.* (2010), Lancsar *et al.* (2011), and Norman *et al.* (2013). Yet, the number of social DCEs is still very limited. See Green (2007: 149ff.) and Bekker-Grob *et al.* (2012: 1153ff.).
49 As Lancaster's approach seeks to overcome these deficiencies, it is especially relevant for the field of marketing. See Nelson (1999: 392f.) and Bennett/Blamey (2001b: 6).
50 Italics added. The foundation in random utility theory is a central trait of DCEs and distinguishes it from conjoint analysis. See Koslow (1999: 102), Louviere (2001: 23f.), Viney *et al.* (2002: 320), and Diekmann *et al.* (2009: 200). Note that hedonic utility concepts are frequently invoked in the literature on DCEs as well. Ryan/Gerard (2003: 55), for instance, maintain that for "each choice he/she chooses the alternative that leads to the highest level of utility." See also Diekmann *et al.* (2009: 201) and Bekker-Grob *et al.* (2012: 149).
51 For more details on the procedure see Ryan *et al.* (2006: 408).
52 Italics added.
53 The concrete assumptions on preferences differ depending on the econometric models used for analyzing the data. See Ryan/Gerard (2003: 60). For the present concern, it is sufficient to consider the basic premises.
54 See also Lloyd (2003: 394).
55 See on aggregative consequentialism Lübbe (2015: 30ff.).
56 To be precise, Scanlon (1998: 101) states that it is still assumed that whatever the theory of the good, it will have a teleological form. The latter implies that the axiology is of an aggregative form, though, which is relevant in the present context.
57 See for instance Dancy (2004) and Lübbe (2015).
58 See also Price (2000). The question of whether respondents in empirical surveys share the consequentialist framework of the surveys will be discussed in Section 6.2.
59 Italics added.
60 Italics added. See also Johri *et al.* (2009: 62).
61 Italics added.
62 As to the loose form of talking about "weighing" in the vernacular see Lübbe (2015: 27f.).
63 The example is also provided in Lübbe (2010b: 281, 2015: 49f., 61, 79).
64 See also Lübbe (2010b: 281f.).
65 Examples are provided by Williams (1995) and Weinstein *et al.* (2009).
66 See also Torrance (1986: 17), Drummond (1989: 71), and Dolan/Tsuchiya (2006: 383).
67 This claim was dubbed "QALY egalitarianism" by Culyer (1991: 144). See Williams (1985b: 5) and Culyer (1990: 10).
68 See also Williams (1995: 225) and McKie/Richardson (2005a: 6f.).
69 See also Culyer (1991).
70 Taurek's argument is discussed by Lübbe (2008, 2009a, 2015: 97ff.).
71 See therefore Lübbe (2015: 224ff.). In particular, treating everyone as an equal is not always tantamount to giving everyone equal chances, as Dworkin (1977: 273) points out:

> If I have two children, and one is dying from a disease that is making the other uncomfortable, I do not show equal concern if I flip a coin to decide which should have the remaining dose of a drug.

This example illustrates that regarding the requirement of equal respect as fundamental does not imply the total neglect of consequences, as Lübbe (2015: 226) stresses.
72 See also Rawls (1971: 26f.).

73 See also Nagel (1979: 113).
74 See Section 4.2.3.
75 This claim is spelled out by Lübbe (2011, 2015: 23, 227ff). See also Harris (1987), Powers/Faden (2006), Lübbe (2005, 2009a, 2009b, 2010a), and Huster (2010).
76 Italics added.
77 This argument is buttressed by the example of disability discrimination in Section 6.3.
78 See also Lübbe (2011).
79 See also Lübbe (2013: 247f.).
80 Italics added.
81 Recall CUA's aggregation problem presented in Section 4.2.3.

6 Inconsistencies in the determination and measurement of social values

6.1 Introduction

The previous chapter argued that if equity weighting is to be a promising endeavor, the respondents' prioritization preferences have to meet very strong demands. In particular, they have to be stable and consistent as to the different equity relevant factors, that is, they have to rely on a consistent atomistic axiology, so that the resulting allocation rule can be regarded as a type of aggregative foundational consequentialism. The present chapter seeks to reinforce the claim that these assumptions are unwarranted by taking a closer look at, first, actual empirical studies to elicit fairness preferences and, second, the unsuccessful attempt to deal with the issue of disability discrimination by means of adjusting CUA's theory of value. As to the first issue, it was already pointed out above that inconsistencies in prioritization preferences pose a major obstacle to establishing a consistent set of equity weights. An inconsistency well documented in the health economic literature is multiplicative intransitivity of PTO answers; a finding resembling a persistent problem of stated preference studies in general, namely the insufficient sensitivity of preferences to the size of the good in question. The lack of so-called scope effects can be characterized as a kind of measurement bias. Measures are biased when "responses are insensitive to manipulations that should affect them," or when "responses are sensitive to what should not affect them" (Baron 1997: 72). In such cases, preferences depend on how the question is framed, i.e., they are prone to framing effects (see Kahneman 2011: 364). Biases arising in stated preference studies especially have been investigated in environmental economics. Considering this research thus provides insights for the health economic debate.

As pointed out above, deriving preferences from observed choice behavior requires assumptions on how the individual frames the choice and how she conceives of the alternatives. Beyond that, preferences over total options do not tell anything about the different reasons motivating the choice. Considered against this background, it becomes apparent that the identification of preference inconsistencies hinges on substantial assumptions on the individual's subjective considerations. Therefore, whether a particular result of a social preference study is interpreted as expressing a true preference or as stemming from a framing effect crucially depends on the paradigm adopted by the researcher (see Fischhoff 1991;

Powers/Faden 2006: 186; Gaertner/Schokkaert 2012: 27). This chapter argues that preference inconsistencies witnessed in prioritization studies actually point to the inappropriateness of the value maximizing framework presumed by the surveys. Once the narrow framework of rational choice theory is abandoned, the observed inconsistencies disappear as well. The review of theoretical attempts to solve CUA's issue of disability discrimination, in turn, shows that none of them has been successful up to now. This is no coincidence. By contrast, the persistent problem of disability discrimination actually points to the fundamental conceptual difference between the value-oriented paradigm of economic evaluation on the one hand and the attempt to account for non-consequentialist interests in non-discrimination and equal respect on the other (see Lübbe 2015: 75ff.; Klonschinski/Lübbe 2011). In addition, it fosters the claim that efficiency has no normative relevance as such.

6.2 Preference anomalies in empirical studies

6.2.1 Scope insensitivity of stated preferences

A preference anomaly frequently observed in PTO answers is the lack of multiplicative transitivity (see Klonschinski 2013, 2014). Pursuant to Ubel (2001: 168), the postulate of multiplicative transitivity can be described as follows:

> Imagine a person who thinks that curing one person of condition A is equally beneficial as curing ten people of condition B, and that curing one person of condition B is equally beneficial as curing ten of condition C. To be consistent, this person ought to think that curing 1 person of condition A is equally beneficial as curing 100 people of condition C.

That is: (a) 1 person cured of A ~ 10 people cured of B, (b) 1 person cured of B ~ 10 people cured of C, and (c) 1 person cured of A ~ 100 people cured of C. If, by contrast, a respondent reveals preferences (a) and (b), but then considers curing one person of A as equally valuable as curing 50 or 200 persons of condition C, his choice is multiplicatively intransitive. This "systematic inconsistency" (ibid.) in PTO responses was first witnessed by Ubel *et al.* (1996b: 109) who primarily seek to test "whether people's utilities for health care conditions, as commonly elicited through established methods [...] are consistent with the judgments they make in rationing scenarios." In order to do so, they conduct two different written surveys. The first aims at measuring individual valuations of different health states by means of AS, SG, and TTO. The health states to be valued are, first, a ganglion cyst on the hand, second, ligament knee damage, and third, a meningioma causing severe and constant headache. As a result, all three methods generated the same ordering of health states, with the cyst receiving the highest utility and the meningioma receiving the lowest. The second survey is designed to elicit the rationing preferences of the respondents via PTO. A further health state, acutely fatal appendicitis, is introduced as a reference case and the subjects are presented with different choices between two groups of patients. The concrete wording of the questions was as follows:

> Suppose that we had only enough money to pay to cure either ten people of appendicitis or ** people of knee ligament damage.
>
> A. Which do you think would bring the most benefit?
>
> ____ten people cured of appendicitis
> ____** people cured of knee damage
> ____Indifferent
>
> B. How many people would have to be cured of knee damage to equal the benefit brought by curing ten people of appendicitis?
>
> (Ubel *et al.* 1996b: 111)

The double asterisks were replaced by the number at which the respective subject "would be indifferent between the two rationing choices if the subject's answers to the utility survey captured his or her social priorities" (ibid.).

As a result, rationing choices differed from the individual valuations to the respect that the subjects "placed values on treating severely ill people that were tenfold to one-hundred-thousand-fold greater than would have been predicted by their utility responses" (Ubel *et al.* 1996b: 108). The study's most interesting finding was the multiplicative intransitivity of the respondents' rationing choices. In the present case, multiplicative transitivity requires that if a person is indifferent between treating ten patients with meningioma and 100 patients with knee damage, and also between curing ten patients of the knee damage and 100 patients of the cyst condition, then this person should also be indifferent between curing ten persons of meningioma and 1,000 persons of the cyst condition (see Figure 6.1).

When asked to trade-off 10 persons cured of meningioma against x persons cured of the cyst, however, subjects stated indifference points that were three times less than predicted by the chaining of previous responses. To be precise, for the median respondent, 333 persons with the cyst condition would have to be cured in order to *equal the benefit* conveyed by curing ten people of meningioma (see Ubel *et al.* 1996b: 114). Remarkably, a significant number of respondents indicated "that it would take an infinite number of people cured of the less severe condition to equal the benefit of treating ten in the more severe condition" (Ubel *et al.* 1996b: 113). These respondents seemed unwilling to make any person trade-off at all. Later research confirmed the finding of multiplicatively intransitive PTO

a)	10 persons cured of meningioma	~	100 people cured of knee damage
b)	10 persons cured of knee damage	~	100 people cured of the cyst
c)	10 persons cured of meningioma	~	1,000 people cured of the cyst

Figure 6.1 Multiplicative transitivity in person trade-offs.

Source: adapted from Ubel *et al.* (1996b: 113f).

answers (see Baron/Ubel 2002; Dolan/Tsuchiya 2003; Schwarzinger *et al.* 2004; Baker *et al.* 2010).[1] It generally revealed the pattern that the "extreme judgments were not extreme enough" (Baron *et al.* 2001: 32). That is, multiplying the nearer values typically leads to higher values than direct measurement (see Ubel 2001: 169).

This systematic error is worrisome as it violates the assumption of "a constant social value of increasing numbers of persons" (Olsen 1994: 41). As the respondents' answers do "not reflect a consistent relative value" (Green 2001: 238), it becomes impossible to infer the relative value of treating individual patients in one of the three health states described. It remains unclear, for instance, whether curing one patient of meningioma is as "equally beneficial" as curing 100 people with the cyst *or* whether curing one patient with meningioma is as "equally beneficial" as curing 33 patients with the cyst condition (Ubel 2001: 168f.). Note that the researchers apparently not only seek to *represent* the elicited preferences in terms of values. By contrast, the framing of the questions suggests that they are indeed regarding the subjects as *aiming* at maximizing the resulting value or benefit of the allocation at stake. To give a further example, Baron *et al.* (2001: 21) introduce their PTO as follows:

> The state cannot pay for everything, but it wants to do the *most good* with what it has. So it wants to determine the *benefits* of curing different numbers of people of different conditions. It will then try to get the *most benefit for its money*.[2]

Subsequently, the subjects were asked to complete the following statement, where 'Blind' means blindness in both eyes and 'One-blind' denotes blindness in one eye: "Curing 10 people with Blind *does as much good* as curing __ people One-blind."[3] The authors seemingly understand the PTO as a task of value maximization and, by phrasing the questions accordingly, assume without further ado that the respondents adopt the same mindset.

Both such framing of the questions and the very demand for multiplicative transitivity carry a clear signature of consumer choice theory. The surveys assume that the respondents are valuing parts of the alternatives, aggregate these values, and, finally, choose the most valuable option – or they assume, at least, that the respondents' choices can be represented *as if* they were choosing in this manner. Recall, however, that the inference from the ranking of wholes to the ranking of parts is not backed by rational choice theory. Thus, deriving the relative value of treating one patient of each group from the respondents' decisions on the treatment of whole groups of patients is entirely unwarranted (see Lübbe 2015: 79). This endeavor resembles Lancaster's (1966: 133) idea that preferences "rank collections of characteristics and only [...] rank collections of goods indirectly through the characteristics that they possess." In the present case of the PTO method, it can be said that the collection of goods amounts to the group of patients, whereas the characteristics correspond to the individual patients. In adopting this conception of choices, the PTO rests on a "purchase model" (Kahneman *et al.*

1993: 310). In line with the economic notion of choices as revealing values, this model assumes that the respondents' task in a stated preference study is to indicate how much a particular good "is worth to them" (ibid.). It is only under the concomitant assumption that there is no difference in principle between distributive choices between persons on the one hand and consumer choices between consumption packages on the other that the observed PTO answers can be assessed as inconsistent to begin with.

This premise also lies at the bottom of the CVM, which explicitly derives its "theoretical justification" from consumer choice theory (Baron 1997: 73). Indeed, the measurement of existence values, for which the CVM had been developed in the first place, was undertaken by extending "the standard theory of consumer choice," as Kahneman *et al.* (1993: 310) point out. Hence, the stated WTP is regarded as "a measure of the economic value associated with that good, which is fully comparable to values derived from market exchanges on the basis of which allocative efficiency judgements can be made" (Kahneman/Knetsch 1992: 58). A certain health improvement, the preservation of fisheries, or the protection of the whooping crane are considered on a par with any other consumption good the individual might value. Yet, the purchase model is not even adhered to by WTP answers, as the following case in point elucidates.

In line with the purchase model and the corresponding premise of neoclassical consumer choice theory that more is better, WTP values should vary with the size of the good in question: the higher the amount of the good, the higher the WTP should be and *vice versa* (see Olsen *et al.* 2004: 446). This relationship goes under the heading scope effect or scope sensitivity of WTP values. Multiplicative transitivity can be regarded as a particular type of this phenomenon. For the purpose of illustration, consider an example borrowed from Knetsch (1994: 361). For a certain individual, the economic value of one liter of milk is $2 and the value of one muffin is $1. If this person was asked for her WTP for one muffin, for two muffins, and for milk and two muffins respectively, she can be expected to state a WTP of $1 in the first case, $2 in the second, and $4 in the third. That is, the "value of a single muffin is $1 whether considered by itself, as one of two muffins, or as part of a bundle with another muffin and a carton of milk" (ibid.). However, the actually observed scope effects in CV studies are usually "not nearly large enough to make contingent valuation results credible" and it is a common finding indeed that respondents express the same WTP for vastly different amounts of goods. Frequently, that is, WTP values reveal no scope effect at all (J. Hausman 2012: 48).[4]

A particular instance of such insensitivity to scope is the "embedding effect," which consists in the observation that "the same good is assigned a lower value if WTP for it is inferred from WTP for a more inclusive good rather than if the particular good is evaluated on its own" (Kahneman/Knetsch 1992: 58). As to the milk and muffin example, embedding would generate WTP data as depicted in Table 6.1. The second column represents the different WTP values elicited from a respondent who is asked for the valuation of all the different bundles in turn, starting at the top with milk and two muffins and ending at the bottom with the valuation of one muffin (R_1). The last two columns show the WTP values of

Table 6.1 Embedding effect in the valuation of consumption goods

Goods to be valued	WTP_{R1}	WTP_{R2}	WTP_{R3}
Milk + 2 muffins	$4	–	–
2 muffins	$3	$4	–
1 muffin	$1	$2	$4

Source: adapted from Knetsch (1994: 361).

respondents only asked for the valuation of two muffins and one muffin (R_2) and for one muffin (R_3) respectively. As the values assigned to one muffin differ in the three scenarios, the valuation apparently depends on whether the muffin is valued in isolation or whether it is embedded into the larger set of goods. Actual CV studies are replete with examples for insensitivity to scope and the embedding effect. To give an example, in a now famous study in environmental economics, Desvousges and colleagues demonstrate that the stated WTP for solving a problem killing 2,000, 20,000, or 200,000 waterfowl was approximately the same in all three cases (see Diamond/Hausman 1994: 51). Similarly, in a telephone survey asking three groups of subjects how much they would be willing to pay for maintaining the fisheries in different regions of Ontario, the respondents expressed roughly equal WTP numbers to preserve the fish stocks in one Ontario lake, in several Ontario lakes, and in all of the lakes in Ontario, irrespective of the extremely different numbers of lakes and fish at stake (see Kahneman 1986: 191).[5]

These findings are relevant for the area of health care since the WTP measure is increasingly regaining attraction in health economic evaluation as well. It has been argued, for instance, that while traditional methods of preference elicitation in health care confront the respondents with unrealistic and unfamiliar tasks, the WTP approach "employs a widely used and simple metric, namely the sacrifice of money" (Richardson *et al.* 2014: 793). That being said, results from both environmental economic and health economic surveys cast doubt on the metric's alleged simplicity. To give an example, Olsen *et al.* (2004) test whether the stated WTP for a health care program varies with the number of persons treated and with the size of a program's effect in terms of different reductions in the risk of heart attack. The results of within-sample comparison of mean WTP reveal that doubling the number of cancer patients treated increased mean WTP for the program by only 10 percent and doubling the reductions in risk for heart attack led to an increase in WTP of merely 18 percent. Even when the researchers explicitly referred the respondents to the doubling of the size of the health effect, the majority stuck to their initial WTP (see Olsen *et al.* 2004: 454). The across-sample comparison exposes that the mean WTP for a helicopter ambulance program actually decreased by 13 percent when the size of the effect increased by 50 percent (see Olsen *et al.* 2004: 452). The authors conclude that their results "lend no support to the hypothesis based on neo-classical theory of consumer behavior that WTP should increase with the size of the good" (Olsen *et al.* 2004: 457).[6] Another example for scope-insensitivity in WTP for health care is provided by Bobinac *et al.* (2013). They asked a sample of 1,004 respondents for their

WTP for a treatment eliminating a hypothetical risk of health deterioration. As a result, the elicited WTP values "did not vary proportionally with the size of the QALY gain on offer [...] indicating poor sensitivity to scale" (Bobinac *et al.* 2013: 1275).

6.2.2 Explaining preference anomalies

The crucial issue certainly consists of explaining these preference anomalies. To begin with, it needs to be pointed out that the observed inconsistencies in environmental and health economic surveys cannot be accommodated for by neoclassical consumer choice theory.[7] On the whole, "the rate at which WTP-values have been shown to diminish with increased size of the good is too great to be theoretically plausible" (Olsen *et al.* 2004: 446). It thus seems as if WTP data to a large extent cannot be regarded as reflecting the goods' "real economic values" to the individual (Kling *et al.* 2012: 10; see Knetsch 1994: 362). Hence, there are basically two possibilities left to proceed in the face of a mismatch between theory and preferences: either the theory is questioned, or the elicited preferences. As to the latter option, again two alternatives arise: first, the respondents may be incapable or unwilling to answer the questions correctly or, second, the survey may be deficient to the extent that the questions do not tackle the answers appropriately. An explanation along the former line is offered by Gyrd-Hansen *et al.* (2012: 109) who surmise that respondents "grow tired" when they are asked to answer more than one CV question. Scope insensitivities could hence result from "weariness" or "perhaps the cognitive limitations of the respondents" (ibid.). To this extent, Mitchell and Carson (1989: 251) argue that embedding is evadable by incorporating the explicit description of the bigger unit combined with a "warning not to confuse the larger entity with the amenity changes being valued" into the survey. Furthermore, the authors suggest asking the respondents to value the largest entity first and continue with ever more specific goods afterwards. However, Olsen *et al.* (2004: 457f.) observe that even a very strong emphasis of the differences in outcomes in the survey did not ameliorate scope insensitivity in CV studies. In view of this result, they postulate that further research should focus on the "cognitive capacity of the respondents" (ibid.). Especially in the early days of CV, it was also assumed that preference anomalies stem from strategic behavior on part of the respondents (see Sagoff 1988: 62; Fischhoff 1991: 840f.; Spash 2002: 205). Taking into account the fact that the respondents to CV questions report serious difficulties with grasping the task, the hypothesis of strategic behavior on their part seems quite unlikely, though (see Ackerman/Heinzerling 2004: 178; J. Hausman 2012: 45).

The most common explanation of arising inconsistencies in elicited preferences argues that although the respondents do their best when answering the questions presented to them, the surveys still do not succeed in eliciting what they are supposed to elicit. Inconsistencies are hence regarded as a methodological problem. Referring to the study by Ubel *et al.* (1996b) again, the authors surmise that the internal preference inconsistencies are "correctable by modifying the way person tradeoffs are elicited." As the lack of consistency is a sign for the invalidity of the method, improved consistency may also enhance validity (see Baron *et al.* 2001: 19). The validity of a measurement instrument is defined as the extent to which it in fact measures what it is supposed to measure (see Brazier *et al.* 1999: 12). As to preference elicitation methods in general and the PTO in particular, this means that the elicited preferences actually correspond to the respondents' "underlying preferences" (Lloyd 2003: 394) and their "true values" (Baron/Ubel 2002: 111).[8] In CV studies, the term "true values" is usually taken to be "synonymous with behaviour because such values are revealed by market transaction. Thus, true value will correspond perfectly with market behaviour when biases are removed" (Jorgensen *et al.* 1999: 134). And yet, CV and PTO studies in environmental and health economics enter the scene for the very reason that there is no actual market in the first place. Accordingly, there is no standard against which the truth of elicited values could be checked so that the cited definition does not apply. In sharp contrast to the informal behaviorism of the economic discipline, the notion of true value apparently points toward an unobservable mental construct and is interpreted in terms of some kind of inner value scale, instead. In this vein, Baron *et al.* (2001: 19) argue that a convergence of the elicited and the true preferences can be expected

> if the subject has an *internal scale of disutility* which obeys the consistency requirement but the subject distorts this scale when expressing it through certain kinds of questions. When the distortions are removed, different kinds of questions will tap the same *underlying scale.*[9]

In order to eradicate these "distortions," they propose the introduction of consistency checks into preference elicitation surveys. To this respect, Baron *et al.* (2001) confront the respondents with the inconsistencies resulting from their AS and PTO answers and ask them to eliminate the discrepancies, if possible. As a result, the check improved consistency, though only to a small extent, and increased agreement between AS and PTO answers.

The authors quoted in the previous paragraph obviously believe that the respondents possess "some in-built master utility function" (Dolan/Olsen 2002: 130) waiting to be discovered by the accurate questions. This assumption is explicitly spelled out by Lloyd (2003: 394):

> Preference elicitation methods assume that individuals have access to well-formed preferences regarding the commodity that is being valued or are able to form such preferences based upon information they have. It is assumed that the preference elicitation exercise produce an accurate reflection of underlying preferences.

When it comes to the interpretation of empirically elicited preferences, the purchase model of stated preference methods thus embodies a "philosophy of articulated values," which is typically adopted by economists and resembles the premise of complete and given preferences (Fischhoff 1991: 835).[10] The respondents are held to be capable of stating their true preferences as to "the most diverse topics" (Fischhoff 1991: 839); they just have to consult their underlying preference order, as it were, and retrieve the values asked for (see Kahneman *et al.* 1993: 310; Spash 2000: 456). Within this framework, the way the questions are formulated gains pivotal importance. In particular, the researcher needs to take care "that evaluative questions are formulated and understood exactly as intended" (ibid.). And yet, the question arises as to whether assuming a "stable, well-defined, consistent, and context-independent" (Clark/Friesen 2008: 197) preference order from which true valuations of environmental goods or health care programs can be retrieved is actually plausible. This leads to the second possible account of preference anomalies in terms of questioning the theoretical framework of stated preference methods, that is, the value maximizing purchase model and the corresponding conjecture of the "existence of a coherent preference order at the individual level, which is waiting to be revealed by the market" (Kahneman 1986: 192).

As said in Chapter 2, a stated preference is not an expression of mere whim or desire, but has to be regarded as the result of a demanding reflective process. Hence, preferences are not given just like that, waiting to be discovered. Thus, instead of postulating an "existing order" (Kahneman *et al.* 1993: 310), it seems much more likely "that people lack well-differentiated values for all but the most familiar evaluative questions" (Fischhoff 1991: 835) and have to construct their answers in the course of the elicitation process.[11] On the basis of this "philosophy of basic values" (ibid.), the survey design does not aim at hitting the intended answer as precisely as possible, but at helping the respondent forming his preferences in the first place (see Spash 2000: 458). In doing so, the researcher needs to avoid putting any pressure on the subjects that could induce them to give meaningless answers to questions they actually have no opinion about (see Fischhoff 1991: 841). Although this interpretation does not deny the existence of relatively stable basic values, it highlights the "lability of preferences" and their dependence on the particular surroundings (Kahneman *et al.* 1993: 310f.). Such a perspective seems much more suitable when it comes to the evaluation of very particular environmental issues or to hypothetical prioritization tasks in health care. Most likely, the respondents have never – or at the utmost very rarely – thought about the matter at stake before and have to infer their answers from quite basic values and opinions. The crucial point to note in the present context is that once the articulated value perspective of the value-maximizing purchase model is dropped, there is no need to regard scope insensitivities and other deviations from the consumer choice paradigm as inconsistencies or anomalies to begin with.

But how can the observed preference patterns be explained instead? A prominent explanation stemming from Kahneman and Knetsch (1992: 64) claims that instead of mirroring the economic value of a good, respondents' answers in CV studies "express a willingness to acquire a sense of moral satisfaction (also known as 'the warm glow of giving')."[12] This hypothesis could account for the insensitivity to scope since, arguably, the "moral satisfaction" derived from the knowledge of having supported a good cause does not depend on the particular cause and the size of the good at stake (see ibid.). The authors point out that it might indeed be the case that contributing to a more narrowly defined cause (saving the panda from extinction) is more satisfying than contributing to the more comprehensive issue (saving endangered species) (see ibid.). Bobinac *et al.* (2013: 1276) offer an explanation along these lines for the observed scope insensitivity of WTP for different QALY gains. They suggest that instead of indicating "the monetary value of the underlying gains" in health, the WTP data might "reflect the worth of having a collective healthcare system as such" or may buy "moral satisfaction" (ibid.). And yet, accounting for insensitivity to scope with reference to the warm glow hypothesis interprets WTP data in entirely hedonic terms.[13] In doing so, it draws a cynical image of human motives and disregards the wide range of decidedly ethical and political reasons people can actually have for their choices.

To illustrate this claim, consider the waterfowl study again, which resulted in equal WTP answers irrespective of whether the program saved 2,000, 20,000, or 200,000 birds. Instead of stating the economic value of saving a certain numbers of birds, respondents may have actually answered the question of how important the issue at stake is to them (see Kahneman 1986: 191). This does not necessarily mean that they misunderstand the task, though. Instead, it may well be the case that "people quite rationally believe in saving birds, but cannot and need not convert that belief into a dollar price per saved bird" (Ackerman/Heinzerling 2004: 163).[14] In fact, a qualitative study by Schkade and Payne (1994: 99) on the reasons behind the stated WTP numbers in the waterfowl study reveals that it is a common concern of the respondents that "something should be done." A substantial group of respondents also regarded their WTP as a means to signal their concern for environmental issues in general (see Schkade/Payne 1994: 100). By contrast, there were almost no statements "indicating that respondents considered how much they valued the birds or how much the birds were worth" (Schkade/Payne 1994: 100f.). A similar observation is made by Sagoff (1988: 69f.) in a CV study on air quality:

> In measuring the value of visibility, we need to know, first how a loss of atmospheric clarity or quality is caused. A mist or fog hanging on the mountains, for example, can be very beautiful, perhaps more beautiful than a clear view [...] Even a volcano which distributes ash over hundreds of miles may be viewed as an aesthetic marvel [...]. If soot and precipitates from a power plant impede visibility, however, the resulting loss of air quality, even if undistinguishable from that caused by a volcano, has a completely different meaning.

If the subjects are aware of the fog's cause, their answers might "express a political opinion" rather than a valuation of clear sight as such (Sagoff 1988: 70).[15]

These considerations suggest that the respondents regard the causes of the issue to be evaluated as important. Several studies reveal, for instance, that individuals state a higher WTP for preventing damage caused by humans than for the same damage caused by natural forces, indicating that human responsibility for the calamities plays an important role in the evaluation process (see Baron 1997: 80; Spash 2000: 458). In this vein, Diamond and Hausman (1994: 57) interpret the results of the waterfowl study as follows: "The finding seems much more likely to reflect a feeling that it is a shame that people do things that kill birds rather than a preference over the number of birds." Evidently the subjects do not, or at least not only, focus on the different outcomes to be evaluated, but pay attention to the kind of action generating the outcomes in the first place. In view of the importance of whether environmental damage is caused by human action or by a natural catastrophe, Baron (1997: 83f.) surmises that deontological rules play a role in the evaluation process:

> An example of such a rule is 'Do not destroy natural processes irreversibly'. Such a rule would prohibit people from destroying species, but it would not, for example, oblige them to prevent natural extinctions. When people who try to follow such rules are asked about their values, they are reminded of the rules. They take the value questions to bear on the actions that the rules prohibit.

Crucially, if the values apparently attached to states of affairs ultimately apply to the actions at stake and, hence, depend on the outcome's history in general and on the responsibilities involved in particular, the respective preferences are not subject to the consistency requirements of rational choice theory (see Diamond/Hausman 1994: 57). In particular, if respondents focus on the type of action instead of the outcome, the latter's size may not be important at all (see Spash 2002: 207). In effect, the issue of scope insensitivity evaporates.

All in all, it cannot be assumed without further ado that subjects reach their answers by counting the numbers of birds saved, fisheries protected, or persons treated and make the "precise trade-offs" required to reach their final decision (Fischhoff 1991: 838). Most likely, they take a wide range of also decidedly non-consequentialist reasons and the broader context into account and, in doing so, specify the opportunity set in a different manner than the survey presuppose. As they do not actually refer to the outcomes at stake, the values elicited cannot be transferred across different choice situations, that is, they cannot serve as inputs to economic evaluation (see Baron 1997: 80).

Before returning to the initial example of multiplicatively intransitive PTO answers, this intermediate result will be further illustrated by considering the two additional preference anomalies of anchoring and priming. Anchoring, "one of the most reliable and robust results of experimental psychology" (Kahneman 2011: 119), describes the observation that people's estimation of a certain quantity tends to depend on any random number formerly presented to them.[16] To give an example, Knetsch (1994: 358) describes a survey on the WTP to preserve fish populations in an area near Toronto. The respondents were divided into subsamples and each of these groups was asked whether they were willing to pay a certain sum of money; afterwards, all individuals were asked to pay $50. Knetsch (ibid.) illustrates the setting as follows: "One group, for example, was first asked if they would be willing to pay $100 to preserve fish populations; those saying 'No' were then asked if they would be willing to pay $50 for the purpose." If the questions tackles the 'true preferences' of the respondents, the first question should exert no influence on the latter. And yet, this is exactly what happened: "Of the respondents first asked if they would pay $200, 63 per cent indicated a WTP of $50. Of those first asked if they would pay $25, only 18 per cent said they would pay $50!" (Ibid.) Apparently, the answers were anchored on the sum mentioned in the first question. This effect can be explained as a sort of priming effect (see Kahneman 2011: 52, 122). Priming means that a certain concept temporarily evokes certain associations influencing the subsequent perception. In the present example, the respondents who were first asked whether they would pay, say, $200 for protecting the fisheries may have been primed on a high value, whereas those asked for a lower amount were primed on a lower sum.

Such priming effects are detected in a series of studies on prioritization preferences by Ubel and colleagues (1996a, 2000a, 2001).[17] Ubel *et al.* (1996a) asked a sample which of the following two screening tests for a population at low risk for colon cancer they would choose: the first test saves 1,000 lives and can be offered to the whole population of Medicaid enrollees (100 percent), the second, more effective test saves 1,100 lives but since it is more expensive, it can only be offered to half the population (50 percent), whereupon the persons receiving the test are selected randomly. As a result, the majority of respondents chose Test 1, generally arguing that they considered it unfair to offer Test 2 to only half the people (see Ubel *et al.* 1996a: 1175f.). As a participant of a follow-up survey explained his choice: "It is better to give bread to everyone than giving brioche to only a percentage of the population" (Ubel *et al.* 2000a: 369). With this study, Ubel *et al.* (2000a) sought to test whether the preference for Test 1 depends on the fact that it could be offered to *more* people than Test 2, or whether it rests on the aspect that it could be offered to *everyone*. Put differently, they wondered whether preferences for equity over efficiency are "all or nothing" (Ubel 2001: 87; see Ubel *et al.* 2000a: 366). Therefore, Ubel and colleagues randomly assigned the participants (physicians and prospective jurors) one of three questionnaires (Q1, Q2, and Q3). The scenarios depicted in each survey had in common that, just as before, the first screening test can be offered to more persons and saves 1,000 lives while the second can be made available to fewer people and saves 1,100 lives. The questionnaires differed with respect to the percentage of Medicaid enrollees that could be treated, as Table 6.2 illustrates. As a result, in accordance with the

Table 6.2 Questionnaires on colon cancer screening test

	Q1	*Q2*	*Q3*
Test 1: saves 1,000 lives	100%	50%	90%
Test 2: saves 1,100 lives	50%	25%	40%

Source: adapted from Ubel *et al.* (2000a: 367).

previous findings, almost 60 percent of the respondents to Q1 chose Test 1, but the preference pattern reversed for Q2 and Q3, where roughly 70 percent of the subjects chose Test 2. Along with Ubel (2001: 86), this "dramatic reduction" in people favoring Test 1 suggests "that some people's preferences for fairness over efficiency may be all or none: fairness loses value when a health care intervention cannot be offered to an entire population."

Ubel *et al.* (2001: 181) call this greater "preference for equity" when 100 percent of the community can be tested "all-tested equity premium." As the whole community is a contingent construct, the all-tested equity premium is likely to constitute a mere measurement bias. Hence, the authors surmise: "If we call the subjects' attention to the broader population, their judgments may reverse" (ibid.). In order to test this hypotheses, Ubel *et al.* (2001: 88) present both the 100 percent/50 percent and the 50 percent/25 percent scenario to the same sample of respondents, but vary the order in which the groups receive the "all-tested" and the "half-tested" example. In line with the two previous studies, the majority of respondents in the group receiving the all-tested scenario first preferred Test 1 in this case (61 percent) and a smaller majority still favored Test 1 in the half-tested scenario (53 percent). By contrast, only a minority of the second group chose Test 1 in the half-tested example (25 percent). When they received the all-tested scenario afterwards, however, some respondents changed their mind and almost half of the subjects endorsed Test 1 (49 percent). It turns out that the bulk of those respondents having received the all-tested scenario first chose the less effective test, whereas those having answered the half-tested scenario first, more often preferred the more effective treatment.

The result of the study is twofold. For one thing, a significant number of respondents exhibited the all-tested equity premium (see Ubel *et al.* 2001: 183). For another, the answers were susceptible to an ordering effect for which the authors offer two possible explanations. First, the effect could stem from arbitrary "numerical anchoring" in so far as the respondents 'anchored' on their answer to the first choice and "insufficiently adjusted" to the second (Ubel *et al.* 2002: 191, 187). And yet, this description does not explain the divergence amid the answers for the same scenarios between the groups. This latter finding rather points toward the second explanation in terms of a priming effect exerted by the first task. While the respondents receiving the all-tested example first were primed "to favor fairness over efficiency," the other group might have been "primed by the half-tested example to favor efficiency over fairness" (Ubel 2001: 90). In a later paper, Ubel *et al.* (2002: 191) slightly modify this interpretation and argue that the second group may have been "less inclined to see the scenario as a trade-off between equity and efficiency; since neither test could be offered to everybody, both tests may have been seen as being inequitable." The equity-efficiency trade-off preferred by the respondents thus seems to depend tremendously on the framing of the questions so that Ubel (2001: 90) concludes: "people's ideas of fairness and efficiency are, to put it bluntly, a mess."

It deserves emphasis again that the respondents most probably have never thought about prioritization questions before. Interpreted within a basic values framework, it thus seems safe to assume that they have to infer their answers from very basic values and opinions during the elicitation procedure. Therefore, it is not surprising that the preferences on equity and efficiency are highly susceptible to framing-effects. By the same token, the studies conducted by Ubel and colleagues do not necessarily reveal that people's "preferences for equity versus efficiency" are a sloppy mess (Ubel *et al.* 2001: 186). Instead, they may very well indicate that the respondents are struggling to come up with meaningful answers, clutching at straws. In the case of prioritization questions, these straws may be the intuition that it is unfair to leave a significant part of the community untreated, a distrust to randomization, or the feeling that the more lives saved the better, just to mention some possibilities. Asked for the reasons behind their choice between Test 1 and Test 2, the respondents indeed raised such concerns (see Ubel *et al.* 2000a: 368ff.). Also, they are probably committed to the basic values of human dignity, equality, and solidarity, as other qualitative studies show (see *Bürgervotum* 2014: 138). In the face of this mélange of relevant aspects, it is expectable that the framing of the task focuses the respondents' attention on either the number of persons saved or the percentage of persons treated.

Additionally, if the subjects consider such a broad range of aspects, they may define the situation quite differently than the researchers presume. As to the evaluation of health states, Baker and Robinson (2004: 37) demonstrate that in answering SG questions, the subjects frequently ponder on "inappropriate" considerations, such as a concern for the well-being of others, personal duties, and responsibilities. Similarly, in the case of prioritization preferences, Dolan and Cookson (2000: 25) point out that the participants of a group discussion on the relevance of the size of the health gain considered factors "which the questions were deliberately designed to set aside and which the moderator repeatedly asked not to be taken into account." In both cases, the respondents were actually answering quite different questions than presumed by the surveys so that the observed choices do not allow for inferring the subjects' preferences or relative valuations in the first place. It becomes apparent that once the articulated values, value-oriented perspective is dropped, the conclusion that "people place special value on benefitting a high proportion of a population" or that saving a certain number of persons is "more valuable" (Ubel 2001: 187) the more persons have already been tested before becomes unwarranted.

Coming back to multiplicative intransitivity in PTO studies, it is reasonable to assume that trading-off different persons is an even less familiar task for the respondents than a simple prioritization question so that a basic value account is the most appropriate framework to consider their answers. A straw they are clutching at when making the required trade-off may, for instance, be a particular concern for the patients in the worse condition. It can be surmised in line with Baron (1997: 82) that when asked for their indifference point, the subjects transform this basic concern into some high number, without counting the exact number of persons at stake in each alternative. Put differently, they might treat great numbers metaphorically rather than literally so that "1000" does not describe a quantity of precisely 1000 units, but means very much instead (see Richardson *et al.* 2011: 170). If this is true, great numbers "lose their cardinal meaning and become deflated," as Schwarzinger *et al.* (2004: 178) state. Lacking a cardinal meaning, the numbers stated cannot meet the demand for multiplicative transitivity in the first place. But while the authors quoted regard this metaphorical handling of the numbers as the respondents' failure to answer the PTO task correctly, it can be argued by contrast that this is an entirely reasonable way of dealing with PTO questions *if* the subjects have only basic opinions to the issue at stake and, crucially, do not consider resource allocation as a value maximizing endeavor. To conclude with Ackerman and Heinzerling (2004: 178): "It is not the people in these studies who are confused; it is instead the analysts who insist that every value can be fit into the market paradigm who are misguided."

6.2.3 Protest responses, attitude change, and coerced answers

Summing it up so far, it seems unreasonable to interpret preferences elicited via CV, PTO, and other prioritization questions in environmental and health economics along the lines of consumer choice theory within an articulated values framework. Instead, the answers are not read off an existing consistent preference scale, but are most likely constructed on the basis of a small set of basic values in the course of the study and encompass a broad range of also decidedly *non-consequentialist* concerns for rights, responsibilities, etc. The present section reinforces this claim by considering so-called protest responses, that is, "unreasonably" high or low numbers stated by the respondents. Such answers may in fact indicate that a significant number of subjects in each survey do not come to terms with the narrow, value-oriented framework forced upon them. As it turns out, the pressure to adopt a societal perspective they are not acquainted with is also present in deliberative elicitation procedures and is reinforced when consistency checks are introduced.

To begin with, it is well-known that CV studies are characterized by a "high rate of refusals to provide acceptable responses" to the questions posed to them (Fischhoff 1991: 841). In each study, a certain percentage of subjects expresses unreasonably high WTP values, up to the point of 25 percent of their income, others state a WTP of zero for goods they actually regard as important, and yet others entirely refuse to answer the CV questions (see ibid., Kahneman/Knetsch 1992: 61, 66).[18] When it comes to PTOs, protest manifests in the subjects' denial to make any trade-off at all or in the statements of very high numbers as indifference points. The central problem certainly consists of determining what counts as "(un)reasonable" answer in the first place. In fact, there is no common standard according to which the reasonableness of stated numbers can be assessed so that the judgment of whether an answer qualifies as a protest response is ultimately determined by the respective researcher (see Jorgensen *et al.* 1999; Ackerman/Heinzerling 2004: 164; Gyrd-Hansen 2013: 853, 857). To give an example, zero responses are usually regarded as "true" zeros when they stem from reasons in line with economic theory, such as the lack of income or the true unimportance of the issue at stake (see Spash 2000: 467). They are defined as protest responses, by contrast, when the subjects consider the good in question as important, but reject a certain aspect of the hypothetical choice scenario. To give an example, under the assumption that "individuals have access to well-formed preferences regarding the commodity that is being valued" (Lloyd 2003: 394), the manner of how a good is paid for should not exert any influence on the WTP. And yet, respondents apparently react to different kinds of payment vehicles, such as out-of-pocket payments at the time of consumption or increased taxes. In the case of earmarked taxation, for instance, some people may give zero responses to WTP questions not because they do not value the good at stake, but due to a general tax aversion (see Olsen 1997a: 607). In doing so, they exhibit so-called payment vehicle biases (see Gyrd-Hansen 2013: 853).[19]

The common way of dealing with such protest zeros or extremely high values is to exclude them from the analysis. And yet, alongside the element of capriciousness in the identification of protest responses, the exclusion of deviating answers is problematic in an even more fundamental manner, for it dismisses the potentially informative value of the protesters' opinions (see Ackerman/Heinzerling 2004: 162). If a respondent states an extremely high WTP number, this might very well indicate that he regards the issue at stake as exceptionally important;[20] so important that it cannot and should not be assigned a monetary value at all. For example, stating a WTP of 10,000 euros for preserving the whooping crane may mean that protecting the bird is actually regarded as priceless. Likewise, a respondent indicating that it would take 100,000 patients cured from a sore throat to outweigh the loss of another person's life might want to express that *no* number of cured sore throats can be traded off against the loss of a life. To illustrate this hypothesis, consider the PTO study by Ubel *et al.* (1996b) again wherein a significant number of subjects stated "that it would take an infinite number of people cured of the less severe condition to equal the benefit of treating ten in the more severe condition" (Ubel *et al.* 1996b: 113). Overall, this occurred in 20 percent, i.e., in 49 of 252 rationing choices. Crucially, the percentage of respondents stating infinity was highest in the case of the choice between treating appendicitis and cyst patients, that is, when a life-saving treatment was at stake (see Nygaard 2000: 121). Apparently, the respondents reject the assumption of compensatory decision making when it comes to rationing judgments so that protest responses might tell us something about the acceptability of the value-oriented framework as such.

This conjecture is also buttressed by evidence from DCEs. To give an example, Norman *et al.* (2013: 570) conduct a DCE including the dimensions gender, smoking status, income, healthy lifestyle, carer status, and total life expectancy. As a result, from the total number of 553 respondents, 106 never chose the option with fewer life years gained and the authors draw the conclusion that "the remaining 447 respondents were willing to trade aggregate LY's [life years] to focus health towards a specific member of society," especially toward carers and non-smokers (Norman *et al.* 2013: 575). And yet, it does not go without saying that the respondents actually reached their decision by trading-off the different attributes. To give an example, their choices could also stem from lexicographic preferences. This means that the individuals order the different attributes according to their importance and decide on the basis of the highest ranked attribute. If the characteristic of the most important attribute is the same in both scenarios, the individual turns to the second most important and so on.[21] Although lexicographic preferences cannot be regarded as irrational, they violate the continuity assumption so that when such non-traders are identified, they are usually deleted from the sample (see Lancsar/Louviere 2006: 800f.). Just as in the case of the PTO, however, this course of action possibly removes valuable information from the data set because non-traders may have particularly strong preferences as to one or more attributes (see Lancsar/Louviere 2006: 802). If, on the other hand, non-traders are not identified as such and, concomitantly, are not excluded from the sample, the validity of the results is seriously challenged. The conjecture that the weights derived are artefacts of the framework is buttressed by the striking differences in the results of DCE studies. While, all in all, Baker *et al.* (2010) and Lancsar *et al.* (2011) found little empirical support for attaching equity weights to QALYs, Norman *et al.* (2013) derived weights significantly differing from 1. In principle, such divergences in the results could have methodological reasons, but considered against the background of the previous considerations, they are probably pointing to the inadequacy of the assumptions on people's equity judgments at the bottom of DCEs. Most likely, the respondents do not consistently value parts of the alternatives and form their equity judgment accordingly.

The refusal to trade when it comes to life-threatening conditions is frequently explained as a bias stemming from the respondents' endorsement of the rule of rescue (see Robinson 2011: 1388, Gaertner/Schokkaert 2012: 156, Robinson/Bryan 2013: 811). It incorporates the observation that "people cannot stand idly by when an identified person's life is visible threatened if effective rescue measures are available" (Hadorn 1991: 2219). To this extent, the wish to save lives might function as a heuristic, that is, a simple and practical procedure of reaching decisions (see Kahneman 2011: 98). Due to their generalizing and simplifying character, the use of heuristics leads to an insufficient sensitivity of the answers to the precise question asked. In the present case, this means that the respondents disregard the substantial opportunity costs of their choice not to trade (see Robinson 2011: 1388; Robinson/Bryan 2013: 811). Being an irrational bias, the "issue" of unwillingness to trade hence needs to be overcome (ibid.).

And yet, given that the aim of the studies is the investigation of how individuals make choices, it seems "somewhat paradoxical, if not paternal, for researchers to impose their own preferences on choice data by deleting responses that do not conform to expectations of how the individuals 'should' behave" (Lancsar/Louviere 2006: 801). At this point, it pays to recall that the people's unwillingness to aggregate small benefits across persons until the sum of these abstract benefits outweighs the loss of a life was one of the problems traditional CUA had faced already and that the incorporation of such social values was the basic rationale for eliciting social preferences in the first place. However, somewhat contradictorily, the approach to overcome the issues connected with traditional, QALY-maximizing CUA by means of social preference elicitation requires that these preferences are in line with the very value-maximizing framework of economic evaluation the people had rejected to begin with. This is because "any solution to the problem of multiplicative intransitivity would entail that there is some noninfinite number of mild headaches that would be granted priority over a cure of appendicitis" (Kelleher 2014: 262). Thus, non-traders in PTOs and DCEs are not just stubborn or too sensitive to make tough decisions. More likely, they refuse the unlimited aggregation of values, that is, they are non-consequentialists, unable or unwilling to come to terms with the efficiency-oriented framework of the surveys, "which may appeal to no one but the economists" (Sagoff 1988: 62).

Analogous considerations apply to the CVM, as Spash (1997: 404) argues:

> [W]hen environmental cost-benefit analysis is conducted, implicitly assuming that everybody is utilitarian, the results will be biased by utilitarian justifications for non-utilitarian reasoning. For example, individuals holding a rights-based belief system would be forced to adopt a utilitarian mind-set as they answer a contingent valuation method questionnaire. These individuals will then be likely to refuse to participate in the willingness-to-pay or accept procedure. The rejection could show up in non-response, zero bids, or outliers, and the data would erroneously be regarded as respondents placing no value on the public good in the first two cases or acting irrationally in the third case.[22]

The respondents may believe that decisions about health care financing and environmental protection include ethical, political, and cultural concerns, which need to be tackled in the process of political deliberation within the institutions of representative democracy (see Sagoff 1988: 57, 62; Ackerman/Heinzerling 2004: 213). This interpretation is strengthened by the observation that one reason commonly given for zero bids refers to the government's responsibility for the issue at stake (see Jorgensen *et al.* 1999: 137; Spash 2000: 468).[23] Since such considerations cannot be accounted for in the "artificially quantified vocabulary" (Ackerman/Heinzerling 2004: 165) of economic evaluation, protest responses may indeed be the only way subjects "can begin to make their values known" (Sagoff 1988: 74).

In view of the previous considerations, it could be concluded that the danger of pressing the respondents into a narrow, value-oriented framework they cannot identify with calls for the use of more open, deliberative preference elicitation methods. Based on the objection that large-scale surveys are unsuitable for generating useful information on how people want health care resources to be allocated because these studies "are superficial and reflect uninformed views of the public" (Lengahan 1999: 50), deliberative studies with a small number of participants are gaining more and more acceptance.[24] Note that in this context deliberation is to be understood in a broad manner and takes place whenever the subjects have the possibility to discuss the issue at stake with each other and sometimes with third parties, such as invited experts (see ibid.). In particular, the term refers to a method of preference elicitation and is not regarded as an element of the political process within deliberative democracy (see Friedrich *et al.* 2012: 415). Proponents of deliberative methods argue that the latter have an edge over quantitative surveys in so far as the participants can be informed quite extensively on the subject, can exchange arguments, reflect on the issue and, ideally, get to more informed and considered judgments (see Robinson/Bryan 2013: 806). Giving them room for discussing and reflecting on the issue at stake, deliberative methods are presumably apt to reveal the participants' actual reasoning instead of producing meaningless numbers (see Schicktanz *et al.* 2012: 136).

A closer look at deliberative studies casts doubt on whether this hope is warranted, though. Having scrutinized various citizen juries conducted in the UK on different health care allocation issues, Price (2000: 276) argues that instead of involving a "rational enquiry" of the issues and values at stake, they basically present an exercise in "attitude change" from an individual to a social welfare perspective.[25] Price (2000: 274) observes that some of the subjects were initially reluctant to make the required decisions and that several participants had to be "reassured that they were competent or entitled" to make the judgments at stake.[26] Price surmises that this initial disinclination at least in part stems from the clash between the respondents' quotidian manner of considering questions of justice on the one hand, and the consequentialist framework implied by the questions presented to them on the other. The latter, he points out, tackle "social welfarist considerations" and represent variants of the prototype: "what state of affairs will ensue from this decision and will society be better or worse off as a result" (ibid.). And yet, respondents have difficulties with handling such questions for the following reason:

> As a matter of fact, our everyday evaluative language, at least so far as personal health care is considered, is unlikely to be wholly or even mainly consequentialist. When we talk about health care we are as likely to talk about what people do to or for us. We evaluate actions as much as consequences or states of affairs. We talk about our rights, our dignity, out autonomy; about kindness, rudeness, or attentiveness. And even when we talk about consequences, this is likely to be in personal rather than social welfare terms. In evading evaluations of actions, question-framing served to suppress a commonplace evaluative language.
>
> (Price 2000: 274f.)

The important point to note is that their initial qualms notwithstanding, the subjects got more and more used to the unfamiliar welfare-oriented framework in the course of the studies until they finally adapted a "new evaluative structure" (Price 2000: 272f.). To give an example, one citizen jury was supposed to discuss the case of a girl who had been denied a second bone marrow transplant. Although initially, the participants were "sympathetic" to the child, Price (2000: 273) observes that during the four days of discussion, the subjects' "moral objections to the decision dissolved once they learned that the implications of the decision had to be understood in terms of their consequences for social welfare."[27] Eventually, the jury "was induced to use descriptive terms which it at first found alien and adopted reluctantly" (Price 2000: 275). The author concludes that the results of the deliberation exercise are "corrupted" by the form of reasoning "in the language of social welfare" required by the setting (ibid.).

The change of the participants' evaluative frameworks in the course of the study is not only a side-effect of the deliberative approach; quite to the contrary, it is the latter's explicit aim. Murphy (2005: 173) even defines citizen deliberation "as reasoning about collective values or common good(s)." This is because it is generally taken for granted that prioritization decisions require for a societal perspective, as the following examples illustrate. To begin with, Lengahan (1999: 48, 53) assumes that "[p]ublicly funded health care require health care choices to be made in the interest of the wider community" and argues that deliberative exercises have the potential of giving the participants the "opportunity to consider why rationing must take place" and to accept this fact.[28] Likewise, Williams *et al.* (2012: 32) are convinced that deliberative methods are particularly well suited for fostering the understanding and the acceptance of the "unpalatable realities of rationing." This acceptance is promoted by focusing the respondents' attention to "the public good that resource allocation should support" (Williams *et al.* 2012: 27). While "patient and consumer involvement foregrounds individual rights, experiences and preferences, public involvement is primarily a collective model of engagement" in which "the participant is required to consider benefits to a population rather than advancing his or her own concerns" (Williams *et al.* 2012: 29, 30). To give a final example, Bowie *et al.* (1995: 1157) state that the deliberative approach "enables people to focus more easily on common – rather than individual – benefits. [...] It is clear from the discussion that panel members made the conceptual leap to the common concern."[29] This is not to say that the depicted change in perspective is to be condemned in any case.[30] Rather, the point is to emphasize that deliberative approaches are by no means normatively neutral. Instead, by framing the whole deliberation exercise in a certain way, they implicitly prescribe a particular viewpoint. In order to be able to perform the required leap from an individual to a societal perspective, the respondents often seem to require a nudge, though, as will be demonstrated in the following.

As pointed out above, respondents' refusals to trade-off hypothetical patients are frequently interpreted as their reluctance to make tough but nonetheless necessary decisions. On the basis of this understanding, some authors explicitly acknowledge the need to 'force' the respondents to make "'hard choices' involving quantitative trade-offs between competing values" (see Williams/Cookson 2006: 7).[31] To give another example, Lengahan (1999: 53) maintains with regard to deliberative groups that the cases presented "force the jurors to make the trade-offs between competing values." Also, it has to be guaranteed that the participants "understand the notion of opportunity costs" (ibid.). And yet, recall that within the basic value perspective the researchers have to carefully avoid exerting any pressure on the respondents. The danger is that in the absence of actual preferences on the matter at stake, the subjects give meaningless answers.[32] This problem is aggravated by the common observation that once the subjects agreed to participate in a survey, they are inclined to please the interviewer.[33] Using the words of Fischhoff (1991: 841):

> In this regard, an inherent problem with most surveys and experiments is that there is little cost for misrepresenting one's values, including pretending that one has them. By contrast, offering no response may seem like an admission of incompetence. Why would a question have been posed of (prestigious?) individuals who created it did not believe that one ought to have an answer? With surveys, silence may carry the additional burden of disenfranchising oneself by not contributing a vote to public opinion. With psychological experiments, it may be awkward to get out, or to get payment, until one has responded in a way that is acceptable to the experimenter.

An example of an essentially meaningless response is provided in the colon cancer study discussed above. One respondent did answer the health care resource allocation question, but when asked for the reason behind his choice he said: "I selected [test] 2 only because an answer is required. However, neither is correct. Screening tests are indicated in high-risk groups" (Ubel *et al.* 2000a: 370).[34] The danger of exerting pressure on the respondents to give meaningless answers is aggravated when consistency checks are introduced because the participants will probably answer as suggested by the survey or the interviewer. Consequently, "those investigations most concerned about testing for consistency may also be most vulnerable to generating what they are seeking" (Fischhoff 1991: 843).[35]

Against the background of these considerations, it is insightful to consider a WHO proposal to calculate the DALY by means of two versions of the PTO (see Murray 1996: 35f.; Murray/Acharya 1997: 714). The DALY can be characterized as the counterpart to the QALY in so far as it adjusts life years lived by a disability instead of a quality weight. It combines time lost due to premature death and time lived in less than optimal health and can hence be regarded as a measure of ill-health (see Murray 1994: 441). The first PTO variant, PTO1, asks the respondents to trade-off life expansion of healthy individuals for one year with the life extension of individuals in a certain state of ill-health: "would you as decision maker prefer to purchase, through a health intervention, 1 year of life extension for 1000 perfectly healthy individuals or 2000 blind individuals?" (Murray/Acharya 1997: 714) In PTO2, by contrast, respondents have to trade-off extending the life of a healthy individual for one year with the *cure* of a certain disease in another individual. Murray and Acharya (ibid.) presume that both PTO versions are equally apt to elicit the disability weights of the health state in question. Nevertheless, the disability weights derived from PTO1 turned out to be inconsistent with those inferred from PTO2. Consequently, the researcher confronted the respondents with tables illustrating the presumed equivalence of the questions and instructed them "to resolve the inconsistency in their own valuations" (Murray 1996: 36).

It is doubtable, however, whether the different disability weights derived from the two versions of PTO imply any inconsistency at all. Rather, the respondents may understand the two PTOs as querying different things: while PTO2 asks for the evaluation of a health state, PTO1 presents an allocation scenario (see Arnesen/Nord 1999). In the latter case, respondents might think that disabled persons have the same "claims" to the life-saving procedure as healthy persons. In a value-maximizing framework, this means that they regard prolonging the life of 1,000 healthy persons and prolonging the life of 1,000 disabled persons as "equivalent," thereby implying a disability weight of zero (Arnesen/Nord 1999: 1424). When the method was used in a training session on a workshop of European researchers working with DALYs (see Nord 1999b), this answer was regarded as "unreasonable," though:

> Anyone who chose this option was told that he or she was implying that being disabled is as good as being non-disabled and that there is no need to spend resources on disabled people. It was suggested that he or she should therefore indicate a number higher than 1000.
>
> (Arnesen/Nord 1999: 1424)

Especially interesting in the present context is the following finding: in a follow-up survey, seven out of eight respondents indeed stated that they regarded the two PTOs as asking for "different things" (Arnesen/Nord 1999: 1425). Nonetheless they acknowledged the need for consistency and amended their responses accordingly.[36] As to the reasons for this choice behavior, Arnesen and Nord (ibid.) report:

> Four subjects felt that they were led 'to some extent' to answer in a particular way, and two subjects felt they were led 'to a great extent'. [...] Some explained that they felt they were participating in a game of little practical consequence. Other reported that rather than making person trade-off judgments, they picked disability weights that 'looked reasonable' and then selected corresponding person trade-off numbers. Perhaps some also accepted the authority of the facilitators and assume that they were right in what they were demanding, or tried to avoid unpleasantness.

It deserves emphasis that the respondents – researchers working with the DALY themselves – were acquainted with summary measures of health and the corresponding preference elicitation methods already. If even they feel some pressure to answers in a particular way, ordinary respondents most probably do so as well. Moreover, Nord (1999b) reports as to the study conducted at the workshop that the PTO was considered "difficult to understand" by the subjects, which is indeed a common observation in the empirical literature. For instance, Ubel *et al.* (2002: 197) excluded two thirds, that is 609 of their subjects "because they had demonstrated that they did not understand (or were confused by) the PTO elicitations."

The crucial point to note is that both the answers given despite an insufficient grasp of what the PTO asks for and those answers elicited by means of forced consistency are essentially meaningless. Hence, the inferred disability weight "does not correspond to any actual preference of the respondent," but "is basically an artefact," generated either "by the requirement for consistency" (Arnesen/Nord 1999: 1424), or by the pressure to answer the value-maximizing questions even though the respondent cannot identify with the presumed vantage point at all. To resume, two findings of this section deserve emphasis. First, the different preference elicitation methods presented all adhere to a consumer choice framework and foist this paradigm on the respondents without further ado. Second, the analysis of inconsistent stated preferences, protest responses, and qualitative studies indicates that the presumed framework is in fact not shared by the respondents. In all likelihood, the data elicited and the corresponding equity weights are futile.

6.3 Disability discrimination and the equal value of life approach

6.3.1 The equal value of life approach and its critics

Having considered inconsistencies in empirically elicited prioritization preferences, the present section turns to inconsistencies arising in different theoretical accounts of meeting CUA's issue of disability discrimination. The problem of disability discrimination is the following: the allocation of resources on the basis of QALY maximizing CUA disproportionally affects the disabled and the chronically ill in different ways (see Brock 2000, 2004: 218ff., 2009). Given that these distributional consequences are regarded as ethically unacceptable, the discrimination against the disabled is *unfair*. For instance, already existing disabilities often function as co-morbidity, making treatments less effective so that fewer QALYs are generated by treating the disabled than by treating an otherwise healthy person. Beyond that, disabilities can make the cure of a disease more complex or extended and, thereby, lead to higher costs. The most serious problem arises when it comes to live-saving treatments. Because disabled persons have by definition a lower quality of life than otherwise healthy persons, prolonging the life of a disabled person by *x* years can never generate as much QALYs as extending the life of a non-disabled person by the same number of years. Since "the value of life extensions depends on the QALY weight in the added years" (Johannesson 2001: 573), saving the lives of persons with disabilities has to be considered "less valuable" (Ubel *et al.* 2000b: 894). In the words of Nord *et al.* (1999: 36): "If the logic of the conventional QALY analysis is directly translated into policy, life years gained by disabled people will be regarded as less valuable than life years gained by healthy people."[37]

To give an example, if paraplegia is assigned an HrQOL of 0.8, "then saving the life of a person with paraplegia for a year must be judged as having a societal value of 0.8 QALYs" (Ubel *et al.* 2000b: 896). Saving a paraplegic person with a remaining life expectancy of 30 years thus generates 24 QALYs, whereas saving the life of a healthy person produces 30 QALYs. Unsurprisingly, empirical evidence reveals that people apparently do not endorse a QALY-maximizing allocation in these cases (see Nord 1993c; Nord *et al.* 1995a; Dolan/Cookson 2000). Ubel *et al.* (1999b: 741), for instance, confront respondents with an allocation choice between Treatment A, which saves the patients' lives and returns them to full health, and Treatment B, which saves the life of persons with pre-existing paraplegia and returns them to their previous health state. By means of the PTO method, Ubel *et al.* (1999b: 740) seek to elicit the "value people place on saving the lives" of the patients in these two groups. The concrete wording of the question was as follows: "How many people with paraplegia would have to be helped by Treatment B so that you would have difficulty choosing which treatment to offer? If 100 patients could helped by Treatment A or __ people with paraplegia could be helped by Treatment B, I could not decide which treatment to choose" (Ubel *et al.* 1999b: 742). As a result, the bulk of the respondents considered live-saving Treatment A and B as "equally valuable," stating indifference points of 100 (Ubel *et al.* 1999b: 743). Apparently, they do not want discriminate against the disabled (see Ubel *et al.* 1999b: 740).

The issue of disability discrimination indeed gets to the heart of CUA. This is because providing fewer resources to those who have a lower HrQOL stems from "the very fact of ranking-by-outcome itself" (Capron 1992: 20). This procedure entails the supposition "that certain outcomes – that is, certain qualities of being – are to be preferred over others" (ibid.).[38] If unequal treatment on the basis of worse outcomes and, hence, the discrimination of some group of patients due to their low expected HrQOL were prohibited, a "virtual roadblock" to any prioritization based on measures of health would be erected (ibid.). Thus, a strict adherent to CUA has to bite the bullet and needs to postulate that rationing procedures considering quality of life "must be allowed to go forward even if at times it happens to disadvantage some persons with disabilities" (Menzel 1992: 25).[39] Yet other authors consider the issue of disability discrimination a fundamental obstacle to CUA's implementation, but do not regard it as a vital challenge to CUA as such (see Johannesson 2001: 573; Nord *et al.* 2003: 876). In line with the general thread of the weighting approaches discussed so far, it is assumed that the problem is correctable within the realm of economic evaluation by means of the appropriate axiological modifications. However, the problem of disability discrimination constitutes quite a particular case in so far as it cannot be amended by the differential weighting of QALYs (see Ubel *et al.* 2000b: 895). Instead, in the case of life-saving treatment of disabled and non-disabled persons, the QALYs thereby generated seem to make no difference *at all* (see Lübbe 2010c: 584, 2015: 74).

In order to solve the issue of disability discrimination, Nord *et al.* (1999: 36) propose the equal value of life approach (EVL) according to which each life year saved is counted as one QALY, as long as the health state is "good enough to be desired by the individuals concerned" (Nord 2014: 140).[40] This solution is "not difficult to achieve technically," as the authors claim (Nord *et al.* 1999: 36). And yet, although the EVL obviously eliminates the arising disability discrimination in the case of life-saving treatment and thus accommodates for prioritization preferences such as those elicited by Ubel *et al.* (1999b), it runs into serious consistency problems as soon as the broader picture of health care resource allocation is taken into account. Note that counting each life year gained as one QALY means that the disability at stake is assigned the same HrQOL as full health. This rescaling entails that curing the disability does not improve the person's HrQOL, though (see Menzel 1999: 257).[41] Thus, it cannot be consistently claimed "that saving the life of a paraplegic is equal to saving the life of a person who can be returned to full health while simultaneously saying that there is still some benefit from curing paraplegia" (Ubel *et al.* 2000b: 896). "The QALY model has us trapped," Ubel *et al.* (2000b: 895) conclude:

> In it, the HRQOL of any health condition determines not only the benefit of curing the condition but also the benefit of saving the life of someone with that condition. This forces us to decide whether we think that saving the life of a person with paraplegia is equally as important as saving anyone else's life or instead whether we think that curing paraplegia brings some benefit.

By the same token, implementing the EVL makes it impossible to assign different values to a treatment that saves the life of a disabled person and a treatment that saves her life and simultaneously cures the disability (see Ubel *et al.* 2000b: 899). "Thus, whether people can be offered miserable extra years or healthy extra years would make no difference… the benefits of each intervention would be regarded as equally valuable!" Williams (2000: 741) wonders.

Consequently, the EVL sparked a controversial debate in the health economic literature. To begin with, Johannesson (2001: 573) raised the plea that the EVL is at odds with individual preference rankings. A person in a health state with an HrQOL of 0.1, for instance, would prefer a cure of her condition to life extension of one year, but the EVL reverses this preference. From this point of view, too many resources would be spend on life-saving programs at the expense of programs improving the individual HrQOL. Hence, Johannesson (2001: 574) proposes a different way to avoid disability discrimination within CUA which is consistent with individual preference rankings:

> This can be achieved by giving the same relative change in expected QALYs the same weight irrespective of the number of expected QALYs (controlling for age and gender). With this approach, the 'equity weight' to multiply a marginal change in expected QALYs for a patient group is: the average expected number of QALYs for the population of that age and sex divided by the number of expected QALYs for the patient group before the intervention.

According to this approach, the lower the individuals' expected QALYs without treatment and the higher the average number of expected QALYs in the reference group, the larger the equity weight. Johannesson (2001: 575) argues that without controlling for age and gender, older patients would receive higher weights than younger patients and men higher weights than women due to their lower remaining number of expected QALYs. Such unequal weighting, however, is unwarranted since it violates the preferences of the individuals (see ibid.). Table 6.3 provides a numerical example for this approach. QALE means quality-adjusted

Table 6.3 Johannesson's equity weights

Person	*Age group*	*QALE for group*	*QALE for person*	*Johannesson's equity weight*	*Health gain*	*Equity-weighted health gain*
A	70	4	1	4.00	2	8.00
B	70	4	8	0.50	2	1.00
C	50	16	8	2.00	2	4.00
D	50	16	20	0.80	2	1.60

Source: Williams (2001b: 584).

life expectancy and is thus tantamount to the expected number of QALYs for the respective individual (see Williams 2001b: 584). Pursuant to Johannesson, patient A receives the highest equity weight and, in effect, would have to be prioritized.

And yet, Williams (2001b: 584) doubts whether this is actually the fairest option. He counters Johannesson's consideration by emphasizing the advantages of the fair-innings approach according to which "everyone is entitled to some 'normal' span of health" or healthy life years so that "anyone failing to achieve this has in some sense been cheated, whilst anyone getting more than this is 'living on borrowed time'" (Williams 1997: 119). In its original version, proposed by Harris (1985: 91), the fair-innings argument refers to the plain number of years lived. A "fair share of life" is supposed to be reached at the age of 70, and anyone who does not reach this age "suffers, on this view, the injustice of being cut off in their prime." By contrast, referring to a "normal span of health," Williams (1997: 119) endorses a generalized type of the fair-innings argument, which takes the *quality of life* experienced in these live-years into account (see Nord 2005: 261). This account is exemplified by Table 6.4. The table is based on the assumption that, up to now, persons A to D have led a perfectly healthy life so that their number of life years reached corresponds to their experienced QALYs. The numbers in the first two rows resemble the example used to illustrate Johannesson's approach, but the equity weights now result from dividing 70 (the fair innings) by the expected lifetime QALYs of the patient without treatment (see Williams 2001b: 585). Whereas before, patient A was prioritized, now, patient C receives priority. Viewed from the vantage point of the fair-innings argument, this is fair because all patients

Table 6.4 Williams' equity weights

Person	*QALYs so far*	*Expected lifetime QALYs*		*Williams' equity weight*
		Without treatment	*With treatment*	
A	70	71	73	0.99
B	70	78	80	0.90
C	50	58	60	1.21
D	50	70	72	1.00

Source: Williams (2001b: 585).

except for C will still enjoy their fair innings even if they are not treated (see ibid.). The additional life years A, B, and D could gain from treatment thus constitute a "bonus which may be cancelled when this is necessary to help others reach their threshold" (Harris 1985: 91). One basic difference between the fair innings argument and both the EVL and Johannesson's proposal lies in the acknowledgment of a person's past health experiences. The latter two approaches, Williams (2001b: 584) objects, neglect "a person's whole lifetime experience of health" and "are still locked into efficiency type thinking, in which bygones are forever bygones, and only the future prospects are relevant."[42] When it comes to CUA's issue of disability discrimination, the generalized fair-innings argument implies that prolonging the life of a person with a history of disability is not only equally important as saving an otherwise healthy persons' life; *ceteris paribus* it is even more significant (ibid.).[43] To sum it up until this point, "the Nord and Johannesson rules imply that we ought to be indifferent between individuals with different levels of health, and the fair innings argument might well prescribe that we prioritize those who are chronically ill or disabled" (Oliver 2004: 273).

Coming back to the EVL, Johannesson and Williams basically object that it requires a separate valuation of improvements in HrQOL on the one hand and life years gained on the other. That is, they focus on axiological inconsistencies in the determination of value. The EVL's proponents, however, overrule this plea by pointing to the fundamentally different decisions at stake:

> When we think about saving the life of a person with paraplegia, we are making a separate decision than when we think about curing paraplegia. When we decide about the benefit of curing paraplegia, our decision is not dictated by the value we think should be placed on saving the life of a person with paraplegia.
>
> (Ubel *et al.* 2000b: 897)

Apparently, axiological consistency across these decision contexts is not sought. Instead, it is argued that once the fundamental difference between individual preferences as to HrQOL and social preferences with regard to the social value of a resource allocation is recognized, the inconsistency embodied in the QALY trap evaporates (see Ubel *et al.* 2000b: 896, 2000c: 129; Menzel 1999: 257). Ubel *et al.* (2000b: 896) illustrate this claim by means of the following example of three possible medical programs. Program A saves the lives of otherwise healthy patients and returns them to full health, whereas program B saves the lives of paraplegic patients with a HrQOL of 0.8. Program C, in turn, cures paraplegic patients from their disability, thus increasing their HrQOL from 0.8 to 1.0. If, in line with the EVL, the outcomes of A and B are assigned a social value of 1 and the effect of C is given a social value of 0.16, it becomes possible to infer that saving the lives of the disabled and the healthy patients is "equally valuable" *and* that curing the disability produces an additional value because the values of program B and C add up to 1.16 – the QALY trap is escaped.

In the same vein, Nord *et al.* (2003: 874) repudiate Johannesson's (2001) objection that the EVL clashes with individual preferences. They present the following hypothetical preference structure: first, persons with a certain disability D prefer the cure of their symptoms for a number of years to having their lives prolonged by the same number of years (P_1: *ReliefD* > *GainedYearsD,* with ">" meaning "is preferred to"). Second, as to the allocation of resources, the general public regards saving the lives of otherwise healthy persons as more important than keeping people with D free of symptoms (P_2: *GainedYearsHealthy* > *ReliefD*). Finally, the public also thinks that saving the lives of persons with D is equally important as saving the lives of otherwise healthy persons (P_3: *GainedYearsD* = *GainedYearsHealthy*). At first sight, it might seem that these preferences are inconsistent because P_2 and P_3 establish that *GainedYearsD* > *ReliefD,* while P_1 states exactly the opposite. Yet, Nord *et al.* (2003: 874) emphasize that the preferences actually "speak to different matters": while P_2 and P_3 constitute social preferences, ordering resource allocations to different persons, P_1 is an individual preference, referring to different forms of benefit for one and the same person. The alleged inconsistency spotted by Johannesson (2001) thus stems from "the structure of preferences in the real world" and does not pose a challenge of their model – "No mathematical modelling can do away with this fact" anyway (Nord *et al.* 2003: 874, 875).

As to Williams' (2000: 741) objection that the EVL prohibits the differentiation between offering people "miserable extra years or healthy extra years," Nord (2001) argues that if the EVL was meant to guide decisions between different interventions for a single patient, this critique would be sound. And yet, this is not the case since the EVL is "only concerned with priority setting between life extending interventions for different diagnostic groups with different levels of functioning" (Nord 2001: 579). Axiological consistency across these decision contexts cannot and need not be expected (see Nord 1999a: 120; Nord *et al.* 1999: 36).[44] Those who suppose otherwise are failing to recognize an important conceptual distinction:

> We need to distinguish between the *desirability* of a condition to people who are not in it themselves (*ex ante* judgements), the experienced *well being* [sic] of people with the condition (*ex post* judgements) and the *worth* of those people. [...] A single score for a health state, of the kind used in QALY calculations, cannot express all these three types of value.
>
> (Nord 2001: 579f.)

While the lack of coincidence between *ex ante* and *ex post* evaluations of health states is well established and still widely discussed in the literature,[45] the concept of the worth of persons is particularly interesting in the present context because pursuant to Nord (2001: 579), the EVL is supposed to capture "the equality in the worth of persons." However, it does not become clear what exactly Nord means when he refers to a person's worth. He tries to illustrate the mutual independence of desirability, well-being, and worth by pointing out that while it may not be desirable to end up in a wheelchair, the subjective well-being of a person in this condition could be comparable to the well-being of an otherwise healthy person (Nord 2001: 580). And if a person in a wheelchair suffered from "a life threatening organ failure of some kind, most people would consider him just as worthy of an organ transplant as a non-disabled person" (ibid.). Apparently, the equal worth of persons is meant to denote something like each person's equal right or equal claim to treatment.[46] It thus refers to decidedly non-consequentialist notions. This change of the normative-conceptual framework is scrutinized in the following subsection.

6.3.2 Values vs. rights

A closer look at the health economic discourse on disability discrimination reveals that it is in fact permeated by such non-consequentialist categories. Nord *et al.* (1999: 36), for instance, surmise that respondents want to treat the healthy and the disabled "*on completely equal terms* on the grounds that people's interest in, and *entitlement* to, continued life is largely independent of their health," Nord (2009: S16) emphasizes that the disabled and the healthy have "the same *right* to live," and Nord (1999a: 27f.) considers the worse off as having "a *stronger claim* to being helped" than the better off.[47] That being said, it remains unreflected in the literature how these rights-oriented notions relate to the value-oriented framework of economic evaluation (see Klonschinski/Lübbe 2011: 692f.). As pointed out by Lübbe (2005, 2009b, 2009c, 2010a, 2010b, 2010c) and as indicated in the preceding parts of this study as well, these frameworks cannot be consistently combined without further ado. Instead, there is a fundamental difference between considering health care resource allocation within a normative paradigm based on rights and a paradigm predicated on values:

> An ethical consideration of the evaluation of medical benefits and cost-effectiveness analysis in connection with the distribution of scarce resources in health care can be based on the one hand on the notions of value and medical benefits and on the other on that of rights and claims. If one takes the view that the cost-effectiveness of medical interventions should be used as the criterion for priority setting – [...] – one is necessarily opting at the same time for embodying the insured population's entitlements in such a form that the resources used produce the greatest value in aggregated terms. Considerations of value theory in this case thus represent the basis for the determination of rights and entitlements.
>
> (German Ethics Council 2011: 68f.)

A system based on rights, by contrast, determines what counts as a just 'production of value' in the first place.

In the face of this fundamental incompatibility of these accounts, it needs to be decided "which of the two should form the ethical foundation of the public health care system and which should be considered at most on a subordinate basis" (German Ethics Council 2011: 70). As became clear above, the debate on disability discrimination refers to concepts from both frameworks simultaneously. This poses the question, however, as to why in the particular case of discriminating against the disabled, the latter's entitlements to treatment render the cost-effectiveness of a treatment moot, whereas in other cases, it is the cost-effectiveness which determines claims and entitlements in the first place. Indeed, the EVL very much appears like an *ad hoc* modification of CUA in order to avoid obviously unacceptable consequences of the value-maximizing perspective (see Lübbe 2010c: 583, 2015: 75, 78; German Ethics Council 2011: 69). It fails to offer a coherent explanation for the fact that the production of QALYs is axiologically relevant in one instance (improving HrQOL) but completely irrelevant in another (life-saving treatment), though.

While the proposals by Williams and Johannesson avoid the obvious invocation of incompatible frameworks, the difficulties they are facing point toward the limitations of the value-oriented framework again. To begin with, Nord *et al.* (2003: 875) point out that Johannesson's account itself leads to inconsistencies. Using the preference pattern presented above, they argue that his proposal requires attaching a higher value on both *GainedYearsD* and *ReliefD*. While this modification conforms to P_3 (*GainedYearsD* = *GainedYearsHealthy*), it violates P_2 (*GainedYearsHealthy* > *ReliefD*). Nord *et al.* (ibid.) conclude that Johannesson "ends up respecting individual preferences at the price of violating a reasonable and defensible societal distributive preference instead." As to the fair-innings approach, in turn, Nord (2005) contends that it is not convincing in its generalized form since the approach implies that persons who have not reached their fair innings yet are not only to be favored in the case of life-saving treatment, but also in the case of ameliorating suffering. Hence, when it comes to a choice between treating a patient who is currently in a relatively good, though not perfect health state and has suffered considerably in the past on the one hand and a patient in a very bad health state who has lived his life in full health up to that point on the other hand, the former has to be prioritized. Thus, the generalized fair-innings argument is at odds with a special concern for the worse-off. This example hints to the conclusion that the fair-innings approach embodies a much too narrow conception of health equity, as Sen (2002: 664) demurs. As a further case in point he objects that given the uneven life expectancies of men and women, the fair-innings argument leads to the prioritization of men in order to "redress the balance" (ibid.). And yet, it is doubtable whether unequal provision of health care on the basis of gender would be considered as equitable. This example elucidates a more general problem, "namely that differences in quality-adjusted life expectancy need not give us ground enough to ignore the demands of non-discrimination in certain vital fields of life" (ibid.). This intermediate conclusion points toward the conceptual tension carved out above again.

The claim that none of the proposals offers a satisfying rule for allocating medical resources is reinforced by empirical evidence. Oliver (2004) conducted a survey in order to test Nord's, Johannesson's, and William's approaches by eliciting the thought processes underlying the subjects' prioritization decisions between disabled and non-disabled patients. Therefore, 25 respondents were first confronted with an SG to measure the HrQOL associated with blindness, deafness, and paraplegia. Afterwards, they had to answer a prioritization question concerning a patient in the respective health state since birth on the one hand and a healthy patient on the other. The priority setting question with regard to blindness was as follows:

> Imagine that you are a medical doctor. You are deliberating over the case notes of 2 patients on your patient list. Call these patient A and patient B. Patient A has been blind since birth. Patient B is fully sighted. In all other respects, the 2 patients are identical. Both patients have an identical illness, which has nothing to do with patient A's blindness. Without treatment, the illness is fatal and, if untreated, will cause death for both patients within the next 2 weeks. However, there is a treatment for the illness. The treatment is risky and can in itself cause death, but there is also a chance that it will eradicate the fatal illness and return the patients to their usual states of health for their remaining life expectancies. The posttreatment life expectancy is the same for both patients. Unfortunately, the treatment is expensive. Your budget is such that you can afford to treat only 1 of the 2 patients. Who would you decide to treat (please circle) 1. I would treat patient A. 2. I would treat patient B. 3. I am indifferent between the 2 patients and would choose through some random device (e.g., by tossing a coin). Please explain your decision.
>
> (Oliver 2004: 275)

As a result, the majority of the respondents implicitly assigned the disability a value of less than 1 in the SG but expressed indifference between treating patient A and patient B in the prioritization question (see Oliver 2004: 276). These observed preferences are in accordance with the EVL and Johannesson's proposed weights. Hypothetically, it is also possible that these respondents considered the fair-innings argument, but balanced this consideration with the expected health benefit. Only two out of 25 respondents chose to treat patient A. Asked for their reasons in the qualitative part of the survey, they indeed referred to compensating the patient for the former bad health state, so that their preferences are in line with the fair-innings argument (see Oliver 2004: 277). As to the respondents who chose to treat A, only one subject's remarks allow for inferring that he considered the fair-innings argument (see Oliver 2004: 278). Most of them, however, referred neither to compensation, nor to health outcomes, but made use of rights-oriented terms instead and argued, for instance, that A and B had an "equal right to treatment" and that "discriminating on the basis of physical handicap is immoral" (ibid.). Oliver (2004: 278f.) thus draws the following conclusion:

> [O]n the whole, there is very little qualitative evidence to suggest that the respondents considered either compensation or future health gain as relevant in answering the priority-setting questions, and it is therefore unlikely that

> the reasoning employed by the indifference-expressing respondents was consistent with the underlying criteria of the fair innings principle. There was also no evidence that the respondents processed their priority-setting choices in the manner indicated by Johannesson [...]. It is therefore likely that these weights are something of a *mathematical convenience* that, if adopted, may often lead to decision rules that are consistent with people's preferences but do not encompass the reasoning that people employ in reaching their decisions.[48]

All in all, the previous considerations give rise to two conclusions. For one thing, it seems as if the concern for non-discrimination against the disabled cannot be accounted for within the value-maximizing framework of CUA. The very fact that piecemeal corrections on the basis of non-consequentialist reasons – such as the EVL – become necessary in the first place hints toward the fundamental inadequacy of considering medical resource allocation as a matter of maximizing any kind of value (see Lübbe 2010c: 583f., 2015: 76ff.; German Ethics Council 2011: 69f.). For another, the reflections on the different accounts of altering CUA's axiology respecting one factor or the other suggest that the search for a general, value-maximizing allocation rule might in fact be pointless regardless of how exactly the value in question is defined. Moral judgments in general and judgments on equity in health care in particular are complicated issues and might not be reducible to a unifying theory or a simple algorithm at all. As already stated in the previous chapter, if judgments on equity are holistic and context dependent, the search for the accurate social values to serve as stable arguments within a simple decision rule is doomed to fail right from the start. Indeed, this is also the major conclusion drawn by Oliver (2004: 280):

> The main message from this article is that different contexts internalize different conceptual parameters, which in turn induces people to adopt different ethical principles across the different contexts. The search for a technical decision rule to apply to all circumstances may prove elusive. It is therefore possible that those who propose an overarching decision rule are attempting to say too much and that they perhaps ought to be searching for the specific contexts that are most relevant for the application of their ideas.

Perhaps, the way to develop an alternative approach for a just allocation of scarce medical resources begins with recognizing "that there is no formula" (Ackerman/Heinzerling 2004: 209).[49] As a corollary, the diverse inconsistencies arising in the search for an all-encompassing, maximizing decision rules would disappear.

Notes

1 Baron and Ubel (2002) designate the arising inconsistency "ratio inconsistency" and Dolan/Tsuchiya (2003) call the consistency requirement "cardinal transitivity."
2 Italics added.

3 Italics added.
4 See also Kahneman (1986: 190ff.), Mitchell/Carson (1989: 250ff.), Kahneman/Knetsch (1992), Arrow (1993), Kahneman *et al.* (1993), Knetsch (1994), Diamond/Hausman (1994), Baron (1997: 74), Olsen (2001: 604), Olsen *et al.* (2004: 446), Clark/Friesen (2008), Gyrd-Hansen *et al.* (2012), J. Hausman (2012), and Kling *et al.* (2012: 18ff.).
5 Further examples are offered by Fischhoff (1991: 842f.), Kahneman/Knetsch (1992: 65f.), Diamond/Hausman (1994: 52f.), and Knetsch (1994: 360).
6 See also Gyrd-Hansen *et al.* (2012).
7 For the conditions under which scope insensitivity can be expected within consumer choice theory see Kahneman/Knetsch (1992: 59). These conditions do not apply to environmental goods and health care, though. See Arrow (1993: 480) and Diamond/Hausman (1994: 50f.).
8 Likewise, Baron *et al.* (2001: 26) speak of a "true utility judgment" and Green (2001: 236) refers to "true preferences."
9 Italics added.
10 See on the articulated values perspective Kahneman *et al.* (1993: 310), Spash (2000: 456, 2002: 207), and Robinson/Bryan (2013: 806). On the assumption of given preferences see Mandler (2001: 381ff., 398).
11 See also Kahneman *et al.* (1993: 310), Spash (2000: 456), and Clark/Friesen (2008: 197). Baker/Robinson (2004) adopt the basic value paradigm when analyzing responses to SGs.
12 On the warm glow hypothesis see Kahneman *et al.* (1993), Diamond/Hausman (1994: 56), and Baron (1997: 75).
13 For a description of the warm glow hypothesis in hedonic terms see also Olsen (1997a: 604), Olsen *et al.* (2004: 447), and Gyrd-Hansen (2013: 853).
14 See also Diamond/Hausman (1994: 58) and Ackerman/Heinzerling (2004: 165).
15 See also Kahneman *et al.* (1993: 314).
16 See on the anchoring effect Kahneman/Knetsch (1992: 58), Diamond/Hausman (1994: 49), Baron *et al.* (2001), Ubel *et al.* (2002), Kahneman (2011: 119), and Gyrd-Hansen *et al.* (2012: 102, 108).
17 For order effects in PTO studies see Ubel *et al.* (2002).
18 The study Kahneman *et al.* (1993: 312), for example, showed "a typical percentage of zero responses" of 35.2 percent. See Spash (2000: 468).
19 See also Kahneman/Knetsch (1992: 62) and Gyrd-Hansen *et al.* (2012: 102, 108).
20 Sagoff (2004: 189) reports that in a CV study on greater visibility in national parks, the inclusion of outlying bids would have raised the average bid by a third.
21 Further examples for the use of simplifying heuristics in DCEs are presented by Lloyd (2003).
22 Italics added. See also Spash (2000: 477).
23 As to health care resource allocation, respondents frequently express the view that it is the government's role to make "difficult decisions on behalf of the population," as Richardson (2002: 632f.) points out.
24 For a comparison of qualitative and quantitative preference elicitation techniques see Hasman (2003), Johri *et al.* (2009), and Friedrich *et al.* (2012).
25 Citizen juries are one type of deliberative preference elicitation methods. Usually, they consist of 12 to 16 randomly recruited participants who meet for four days in the course of which they are informed on the subject, deliberate on the issue, and have the opportunity to examine experts. See Coote/Mattinson (1997: 4), Lengahan (1999: 50f.), and Williams *et al.* (2012: 33f.).
26 In a similar vein, Lomas (1997: 105) maintains in a paper with the telling title "Reluctant Rationers": "Average citizens are, however, largely reticent about their ability to perform this collective decision-maker role. […] In our own research in Canada,

two-thirds of individuals did not want to take responsibility for priority-setting." And Richardson (2002: 632) reports that respondents frequently prefer "paternalism" to "consumer sovereignty" when it comes to decisions of health care resource allocation. See Lengahan (1999: 53) and Shah (2009: 82).

27 See also Coote/Mattinson (1997: 6).

28 Lengahan (1999: 53) states:

> Key obstacles [to citizen juries] include the initial reluctance of the public to accept that rationing is inevitable (and a desire to retreat into a recommendation for more money) and an initial assumption that all such decisions are clinical in nature, and therefore for others to make. Both obstacles can be overcome with skilled agenda development and moderation, but care must be taken not to bulldoze the jurors.

29 Stumpf/Raspe (2011: 317) also report that after the participants of a citizen's debate had met for four days, they showed a higher acceptance of the efficiency criterion than before.

30 For example, the adoption of a broader perspective can marshal the subjects to take responsibility for societal issues they had considered none of their businesses before. See Coote/Mattinson (1997: 9).

31 Williams/Cookson (2006: 8) confront the subjects with a series of questions which "forces the respondent to quantify how much efficiency they are prepared to sacrifice for the sake of reducing health inequality."

32 In Schkade/Payne's (1994: 100) study, 20 percent of the sample "said they just made up a number or guessed an answer." The general danger of empirical preference elicitation studies to generate meaningless data is also acknowledged by Gaertner/Schokkaert (2012: 23).

33 Such a "social desirability bias" (Gyrd-Hansen 2013: 858) became especially salient in the famous Milgram experiments the participants of which were apparently so "cowed by authority" that they were willing to do anything, up to the point of torturing their fellow participants (Sagoff 1988: 62).

34 Ubel *et al.* (2000a: 370) report that all in all: "Thirteen participants wrote that neither test should be offered because the enrollees are at too low a risk to deserve any kind of colon cancer screening." Unfortunately, they do not add the information how these thirteen subjects had answered the prioritization question before.

35 When proposing consistency trainings in PTO studies, Baron *et al.* (2001: 19) take this possibility into account when they state that the numbers revisited should still "honestly expresses subjects' judgments." Whether this remark is sufficient to ameliorate the presumed pressure to answer in accordance with the consistency requirement is doubtable, though.

36 In total, including the authors, thirteen persons participated in the workshop. Out of the eleven participants receiving the survey, eight answered it. See Arnesen/Nord (1999: 1424).

37 See also Harris (1987: 120), Nord (1999a: 119), and Oliver (2004: 272). For an analog criticism of DALY minimization see Anand/Hanson (1997: 700). Recall from Chapter 4 that discrimination against the disabled was offered as major rationale for rejecting the Oregon Health Plan. But whereas it is not evident whether the objections leveled against the *actual* Plan hit the mark, there can be no doubt that the *logic* of CUA disadvantages the disabled in the described manner.

38 In the context of the Oregon debate, the reference to the ADA further aggravated the importance of the objections, because the act offered an extraordinary broad definition of disabilities, including any chronic "physical or mental impairment that substantially limits one or more 'major life activities'" (Hadorn 1992: 1454). As examples, it lists "contagious and noncontagious diseases and conditions as orthopedic, visual, speech,

and hearing impairments, [...], diabetes, mental retardation, emotional illness, specific learning disabilities, HIV [...], drug addiction, and alcoholism" (ADA quoted in Hadorn 1992: 1455).

39 Note that Menzel changed his view eventually, as becomes apparent in Menzel *et al.* (1999) and Nord *et al.* (1999).

40 See also Nord (1999a: 118ff.), Menzel *et al.* (1999), and Ubel *et al.* (2000b). The term equal value of life approach was coined by Nord *et al.* (2003). The basic thread of this section is also presented in Klonschinski/Lübbe (2011), Lübbe (2010c, 2015: 75ff.).

41 This problem was at the core of the two PTO tasks examined by Arnesen/Nord (1999), as presented in Section 6.2.3.

42 Sen (2002: 664) and Nord (2005: 261) provide reasons for disregarding the past in health care resource allocation.

43 Williams (2001b: 584) points out that whether the disabled actually receive priority in health care allocation is an empirical question, as the goal of reducing health inequalities

> has to be tempered somewhat to enable us to compare the social worth of relative small gains for the disabled with much larger gains for the non-disabled. For this we need equity weights based on a rate at which the community is willing to have its resources devoted to reducing lifetime health inequalities compared with improving the lifetime health of the whole population. Whether the disabled person now gets priority will depend on that trade-off.

In view of this quote, recall the considerations on the danger of the equity-efficiency trade-off notion in Section 5.5.

44 Likewise, Nord *et al.* (2009: S14) state as to the evaluation of prevention versus treatment: "Mathematical consistency in values and preferences is not necessarily to be expected across situations that differ on such issues."

45 In particular, it is a common finding that patients suffering from a disability usually assign their health state a much higher HrQOL than persons who imagine being in the respective condition. In view of this discrepancy, the question of whose valuations should be included in CUA has important consequences for public policy. See Lomas (1997: 107f.), Nord (1999a: 82ff.), Menzel (1999), Ubel *et al.* (2000b), (2003), Hasman (2003: 44), Dolan/Kahneman (2008: 217), and Schicktanz *et al.* (2012: 134f.).

46 Williams (2001b: 584) interprets Nord as equating worth with "being deserving" or with "having an equal moral claim on the community's resources."

47 Italics added. See also Nord *et al.* (2003: 873), Donaldson *et al.* (2011a: 102), Richardson *et al.* (2011: 164), and Bobinac *et al.* (2012: 1121).

48 Italics added.

49 For similar claims see Hurley (1998: 385), Sen (2002: 664), Mooney (2009: 121), and Gaertner/Schokkaert (2012: 196).

7 On the normative status of empirically elicited prioritization preferences

7.1 Introduction

Having made a case against the suitability of a value-maximizing framework to deal with fairness issues in health care resource allocation in a satisfying manner, the present chapter challenges the weighting approach from another angle and asks whether empirically elicited prioritization preferences should be assigned any normative-ethical relevance in the academic discourse on medical resource allocation at all. In order to analyze this query, two major lines of arguments in favor of public participation offered in the literature are discussed: first, the idea that by means of correcting for biases in or filling gaps of the theoretical discourse, public involvement in priority setting somehow improves the prioritization debate and, second, the notion that in a liberal and democratic society, respecting individual autonomy requires involving public preferences on a theoretical level. The chapter argues that both threads basically rely on category errors as to the nature of the issue at stake. Consequently, even if the arguments presented up to now were wrong and equity weights indeed accurately mirrored the respondents' concerns for fairness, the weighting approach still would not constitute a promising attempt to solving CUA's fairness problem. Before establishing this claim, however, two preliminary remarks are required.

First, note that the present interest is decidedly not in pragmatic political questions such as how certain policies can be communicated or implemented, how a societal discourse on prioritization can be triggered, how participative methods could "build a habit of active citizenship" (Lengahan 1999: 47), or how the topic of prioritization can be set on the public agenda. In addition, the following considerations certainly are not meant to deny that the public should have a say in the democratic political process when it comes to the actual implementation of health policy. Therefore, it is again important to recognize that the terms participation and deliberation refer to a method of preference elicitation and are not regarded as an element of the political process within deliberative democracy (see Friedrich *et al.* 2012: 415).[1] Instead, the analysis focuses on the question of whether the empirical elicitation of the public's prioritization preferences – i.e., their opinion on what a just distribution of resources consists of – can contribute to the respective normative-ethical academic debate. In so far as the public's views on justice are supposed to be relevant for the theoretical debate on a just resource allocation, the endeavor to integrate public preferences into theory building can be subsumed under the heading of empirical ethics. The second remark concerns the subject matter of this chapter. Although the primary interest is with the weighting approaches, which assign a particularly strong normative role to elicited preferences, this chapter also considers arguments from the broader discourse on public participation in priority setting. The reason for this is twofold: for one thing, the literature on equity weighting is rather moot as to the normative-ethical legitimization of their empirical account; for another, rebutting more modest arguments for consulting the public serves to reinforce the case against equity weighting.

7.2 Two alleged dead-ends of the normative-theoretical discourse

The first line of arguments for involving the public in the discourse on prioritization expresses the hope that this endeavor provides for a way out of the alleged dead-end of the academic prioritization discourse. Thereby, two different kinds of dead-ends can be distinguished, one caused by methodological limitations, the other by a lack of consent when it comes to theoretical arguments. The first impasse is frequently invoked by economists, as was already pointed out above. Due to the discipline's positivistic self-image, economists are usually disinclined to introduce their own value judgments into economic analysis. Dealing only with facts and lacking any scientific means to tackle normative questions, they leave normative-ethical issues to others. This stance is illustrated by the explanation Williams *et al.* (2005: 65) offer for the economists' habitual neglect of concerns for fairness:

> The most fundamental [justification] is a denial that economics has any tools to handle such issues, since its current mainstream corpus of knowledge derives from a position in which interpersonal comparisons of welfare are held to be invalid and so are ruled out of consideration. But those willing and able to emancipate themselves from this strict welfarist regime still face severe problems in addressing issues of equity, because equity is an essentially contestable concept in which many rival views flourish. [2]

The quote's last sentence hints toward the second alleged blind alley of the prioritization discourse. Apparently, scholars of normative disciplines, such as political theory or philosophy, are incapable of reaching agreement as to what a just resource allocation consists of (see Williams/Cookson 2006: 3). In view of the irreversible ethical and moral pluralism in modern societies, there remains no device left to establish the superiority of one account over another. Since priorities have to be established nonetheless, public involvement is supposed to offer a way out of this impasse. This idea seems to underlie Ubel's (2001: 94) following argument:

> I am not a proponent of any single theory of distributive justice, which I cannot explain by lack of time or inclination, but can blame only on my indecisive nature or my intellectual weakness. Perhaps because I do not advocate a specific theory I am inclined to take public attitudes seriously. Many allocation dilemmas have no simple solutions, and highly trained, intellectual rigorous philosophers would completely disagree with each other about the best solution, for example, about the extent to which severely ill patients deserve treatment priority. In such situations, the public deserves a role.[3]

Two aspects are especially noteworthy. First, while Ubel states that he does not endorse a particular theory of distributive justice, it became apparent in the previous chapters that he actually adopts a quite specific account, namely, a consequentialist one (see Ubel *et al.* 1996b: 115, 2000c: 130). His claim to the contrary reinforces the impression that the value-oriented paradigm's normative content is not sufficiently reflected in the health economic literature. Instead, the structure of economic evaluation is viewed as a mere formal vehicle, allowing for the adoption of any substantive theory of distributive justice whatsoever. Second, Ubel indeed seems to attach normative priority to the arguments of "highly trained philosophers" and, concomitantly, ethical theory. When theory runs out, the public should have a say. In this respect, Walker and Siegel (2002: 267) observe: "While proponents of the use of SVPs [social value preferences] in CEA would no doubt decry the creation of philosopher kings, their own arguments may ultimately provide the crowning." On the whole, the quote evokes the impression that consulting the public offers an easy way of solving controversial issues and allows for circumventing the irreducible value pluralism. Eliciting prioritization preferences would thus provide the "key to resolve ethical dilemmas" (Williams *et al.* 2012: 27).[4]

If the elicited public preferences are to fulfill this purpose, they have to be ultimately decisive when it comes to the allocation of health care resources. In other words, the arguments presented imply a form of ethical relativism according to which what is right is defined by what the majority considers to be right (see Hausman 2002: 642f.). And yet, this account is hardly plausible (see Bognar/Hirose 2014: 21). In fact, it is generally – implicitly or explicitly – acknowledged even in the empirical literature that not all kinds of prioritization preferences should influence priority setting to an equal extent. To give an example, Menzel *et al.* (1999: 8f.) argue that population preferences should only be taken into account under the condition "that those preferences are not irrational or ethically objectionable, as when they reflect discriminatory attitudes" and according to Richardson (2002: 632), "there may be a class of population values – hopefully small – where it would be hoped that decision-makers would override population values entirely (racism, sexism etc.)."[5] Since "preferences sometimes seem 'dirty'" (Goodin 1986: 76), they have to be laundered before they come to exert any influence on policy making. One way of laundering preferences is by "responding selectively to only certain sorts of citizen preferences," that is, by excluding some preferences from the survey (Goodin 1986: 96). Note that the problem of dealing with "dirty," i.e. ethically objectionable preferences, is not merely a hypothetical issue. To give an example, a study by Ubel *et al.* (1999a) revealed that respondents were less willing to allocate organs to intravenous drug users than to smokers or persons consuming high-fat diets. This preference pattern remained stable even if the subjects were informed that the drug users had stopped using and that the drug consumption was not causally responsible for the need of the transplant. The authors draw the conclusion that the respondents "believe that such patients are simply less worthy of scarce transplantable organs" (Ubel *et al.* 1999a: 58).[6] Apparently, they want to "'punish' individuals for their 'socially undesirable' behaviour" (Gaertner/Schokkaert 2012: 162). Likewise, Mortimer (2005: 166) quotes a study on prioritization preferences in which smokers, heavy drinkers, and homosexuals received very low priority and concludes that "it is difficult to think of a motivation other than personal prejudice for some of these preferences." Such findings reveal that the "answers of the respondents may be influenced by psychological mechanisms with a rather doubtful ethical legitimacy" and, therefore, challenge the normative relevance of questionnaire studies altogether (Gaertner/Schokkaert 2012: 164).[7]

The crucial point is that once it is granted that prioritization preferences can be ethically objectionable, the preferences obviously cannot provide the benchmark for what is to count as ethically objectionable in the first place (see Walker/Siegel 2002: 267). Hence, the question arises as to why and when exactly social preferences should be considered at all. To quote Walker and Siegel (ibid.):

> If we cannot justify an appeal to SVPs [social value preferences] without first establishing that they are not ethically objectionable, then SVPs will be superfluous to the extent that we can resolve resource allocation issues through the application of ethical principles.

Instead of laundering preferences *ad hoc* on the basis of diffuse fairness intuitions, the reasons for excluding some preferences and counting others need to be spelled out systematically beforehand. The existence of preference laundering in the prioritization studies thus leads to two conclusions. First, phrases such as those quoted above indicate that the normative status of empirically elicited preferences is not sufficiently reflected and remains ambiguous in the literature. Second, preference laundering hints toward the inevitability of normative-theoretical reflections on the issue of which preferences are relevant in the first place (see Powers/Faden 2006: 183f.; Düwell 2009: 202, 208).

In view of the rationales provided for turning to empirical ethics, it could be objected that postulating more elaborate theoretical considerations immediately runs into the second impasse: as different accounts of justice prove irreconcilable with each other, consulting the public is the last resort. In reply to this case, four counterarguments can be put forward. First, if it is really the case that two equally just allocation options are available and consensus cannot be reached as to which one is preferable, the public may indeed function as a "tie-breaker" (Hausman 2002: 643; see Düwell 2009: 206). And yet, such cases do not constitute "ethical dilemmas" because if both options are equally just, there is no moral issue at stake at all and turning to public preferences does not fall into the category of empirical ethics. Hence, this argument "does not justify respecting population values in cases which do raise moral questions, where population values may conflict with what is morally permissible" (Hausman 2002: 643f.). Second, the existence of different, in part diametrically opposed accounts of what a just resource allocation consist of does not provide a *normative* argument for the relevance of the public's prioritization preferences. At the utmost, it offers a pragmatic rationale. Third, although the quote by Ubel (2001: 94) presented above suggests otherwise, the juxtaposition of a normative-philosophical account to the issue of prioritization on the one hand and a socio-empirical account on the other is erroneous since the turn to prioritization preferences is not normatively neutral either. Assigning normative-ethical relevance to the public's opinion on rationing decisions requires a substantive theoretical justification itself and so does the decision to exclude some preferences from the survey assessment, as the considerations on preference laundering pointed out already (see Düwell 2009: 208; Gaertner/Schokkaert 2012: 14).

Against the background of the previous reflections, the very premise of the argument remains to be challenged, for it is doubtable whether the limits of normative-theoretical reflections are so rapidly reached as assumed by the proponents of empirical ethics. Quite to the contrary, the present study demonstrated that the current debate on equity weights and the equity-efficiency trade-off in health care resource allocation is by no means stretched to its theoretical limits, but is rather characterized by too little theoretical and conceptual deliberation. As long as the central concepts and normative assumptions are not clarified on a theoretical level, the unresolved issues will reappear again in the course of the deliberative exercise. This claim will be buttressed by means of an example taken from Daniels (2008: 291ff.). In 2003, the Mexican government passed a law establishing a national health reform, the *Seguro Popular,* in order to offer health insurance to half of Mexico's population. The crucial question was which conditions ought to be covered in the insurance scheme. Therefore, Daniels conducted some workshops on decision-making in health care with key personnel from the central institutions. During the first workshops, it was suggested that four groups should be involved in the decision-making process:

> A clinical group would provide important information about the clinical course of the disease and the effectiveness of treatments. An economic group would provide information on the costs and cost-effectiveness of the treatments. Since conformance with ethical norms and social acceptability were *also* criteria mentioned in the law, an ethics working group, [...] and a social acceptability working group would contribute to the deliberative process.
>
> (Daniels 2008: 293)[8]

Initially, each of the groups was supposed to rate the different conditions on an ordinal scale from 0 to 5 according to some self-selected criteria. Yet, it turned out that "the two groups assessing values, the ethics group and the social acceptability group" could not quantify their deliberations' results in the required manner (Daniels 2008: 294). Hence, the process was amended to the extent that the clinical and economics group would evaluate the interventions on the basis of criteria such as prevalence, seriousness, and cost-effectiveness, whereas the "ethics group would then base its analysis of the ethical issues on this information" (ibid.). Finally, their results would be assessed by the social acceptability group.

In the context of the present study, it is especially striking that this decision-process clearly distinguishes between economic concerns on the one hand and ethical concerns on the other. While the ethics group is supposed to assess "values," the economics group's task is presented as a purely positive analysis. This endeavor tacitly assumes at least two highly questionable premises: first, that cost-effectiveness is of independent normative relevance and, second, that this criterion can be adjusted by considering other concerns for fairness. It becomes obvious that the conceptual problems arising in a theoretical discussion of what a substantial account of justice requires in priority setting are carried over to the procedural account of deliberative decision making. As a consequence, the latter does not provide a solution to the alleged "pervasive disagreements," but merely reiterates the underlying problems on another level. To make it worse, delegating the allegedly separate concerns of efficiency and fairness to different deliberative groups does not foster the required conceptual inquiry, but is likely to reinforce the unreflected persistence on the respective framework in the different groups, instead. As it turns out, "philosophical guidance of considerable moral weight does not run out quite as readily as some seem to suggest" (Powers/Faden 2006: 181). The exhaustive and troublesome clarification of concepts and the reflection of arguments about the best theory of justice cannot be avoided, especially not by means of empirical surveys.[9]

7.3 The role of empirical data within applied ethics

While the previous arguments in favor of empirical ethics pointed toward a methodological or theoretical impasse of the scientific prioritization debate, a second line of reasoning suggests that ethical theory is biased, incomplete, and too abstract. Therefore, involving the public on the level of theoretical reflections already is required in order to correct for the biases and to enhance the context-sensitivity of ethics by bringing in new ideas and perspectives. To give an example, Schicktanz (2009: 228) argues that due to cognitive, temporal, and spatial constraints, a person reflecting on a subject never comes up with all arguments and aspects relevant for the issue at stake.[10] This shortcoming of individual reasoning cannot be resolved by academic discussions either, because the scholars involved in these debates usually share a common background and a similar living situation, so that they cannot put themselves into the shoes of persons in totally different cultural or socio-economic circumstances. In effect, they become blind to certain arguments and considerations (see Düwell 2009: 206; Schicktanz 2009:

229). The problem is aggravated when it comes to questions of fairness because empirical research shows that individuals' opinions on justice are closely linked to their personal characteristics (see Gaertner/Schokkaert 2012: 10). That is to say, the typical male, white academic earning a mean income will have a very specific view on justice which is unlikely to coincide with the views held by other individuals with different personal traits. To this respect, it is argued that public participation has the potential of correcting biases by bringing in "new ideas and experiences" (Lengahan 1999: 47) and by offering new arguments, rationales, or solutions (see Bruni *et al.* 2008: 15; Gaertner/Schokkaert 2012: 11; Stumpf/Raspe 2012: 419; Frith *et al.* 2014: 18; Stumpf 2014a: 17f.). it is supposed to increase the "intellectual quality" (Schicktanz *et al.* 2012: 137) of ethical decisions and to counteract the creation of an expertocracy, in which a small circle of experts makes decisions on prioritization in a paternalistic fashion (see Stumpf/Raspe 2011: 316).

In a similar vein, some authors argue that ethical theory needs to be supplemented with empirical ethics since it is far too theoretical and out of touch with reality. Ethical theories, Richardson (2002: 637) objects, fail "to bridge the gap between theory and the requirements of practical action" and hence cannot provide concrete advice when it comes to the real-world issue of medical resource allocation.[11] Since professional ethics should not be divorced "from the world in which people are living and making ethical choices" (Levitt 2003: 24), investigating public preferences is required for improving the context-sensitivity of armchair-ethics (see Birnbacher 1999: 320f.; Musschenga 2005: 473ff.; Schicktanz 2009: 225; Schicktanz *et al.* 2012). According to this view, ethicists "should not limit themselves to formulating abstract and general principles" (Musschenga 2005: 473). Instead of restricting ethical inquiry to the theoretical investigation of a proposed ethical rule, ethicists have to "consider its practical feasibility, its psychological acceptability and its potential effectiveness in changing attitudes and behaviour in the desired direction" (Birnbacher 1999: 321). In order to make sure that the directives derived from ethical theory "connect with people's own feelings, attitudes and experiences" (Levitt 2003: 24) public preferences have to be accounted for on the level of normative-ethical reflections already.

While these arguments to some extent indeed provide a case for incorporating empirical data into ethical theory, they do not establish the need for empirical ethics as the term is understood here. With the purpose of illustrating this claim, two kinds of empirical data have to be distinguished.[12] Using the example of euthanasia it can be said that any thorough reflection of whether euthanasia is morally acceptable has to rely on empirical data, of course. It may, for instance, be relevant how many and which type of patients are uttering the wish to have their lives ended and for which reasons they are doing so. Furthermore, an in-depth theoretical debate on the subject should acknowledge the possibilities of palliative care and pain therapy. Such information may only be accessible by asking the patients concerned, their relatives, or the physicians dealing with fatally ill patients on a day-to-day basis. Socio-empirical research is thus indispensable in so far as it helps to integrate the specific knowledge and the particular experiences of the persons concerned into ethical theory (see Düwell 2009: 204f.). Beyond that, there are philosophical arguments inherently relying on empirical data, a good example being slippery-slope arguments.[13] These arguments reject certain practices not on the ground that they are regarded as morally objectionable per se, but because they are likely to trigger other actions with ethically obnoxious consequences. In the case of euthanasia, a slippery-slope argument could point out that although the practice as such is morally acceptable, it should not be allowed since, in the long run, it would erode the general prohibition to kill. The validity of the argument certainly hinges on the probability that the dreaded consequences will actually occur. When it comes to euthanasia, information about the practice and its consequences in countries where it is legally allowed can buttress or invalidate the slippery-slope argument. Again, this information gathering might imply asking the persons concerned. Generally speaking, empirical studies are of the utmost importance for ethics if an ethical evaluation of a certain practice requires knowledge only obtainable by asking the persons involved in that practice (see Düwell 2009: 204).[14] If empirical ethics is interpreted in this sense as empirically informed ethics, the term describes thoroughly conducted applied ethics and does not raise any controversy at all (see Goldenberg 2005: 4; Borry *et al.* 2005: 50).

The situation is entirely different when the empirical data in question are information on the moral judgments of the persons concerned, though. Using the example of euthanasia again, this kind of data would be gathered if the persons were asked whether they regarded euthanasia as morally acceptable or not (see Düwell 2009: 204). As the results of such surveys tell something about what the people think about the legitimacy of euthanasia, they fall into the realm of *descriptive ethics*, i.e., the branch of ethics aiming at describing the moral attitudes prevailing in a certain society or community. And yet, knowing what the people regard as just does not necessarily contribute to answering the question of what *is* just, that is, to the subject matter of *normative ethics*. Eliciting prioritization preferences, to be sure, is an endeavor in descriptive ethics, whereas allocating resources on the basis of these preferences assigns them a normative role. To quote Powers and Faden (2006: 185), equity weighting constitutes an attempt "to empiricize concerns about justice by turning these concerns into data about the public's distributive preferences." Recall, however, that some empirical studies on prioritization revealed discriminatory attitudes toward homosexuals and drug-users. Apparently, whether there are good moral arguments for a certain practice does not depend on what the majority regards as morally right (see Düwell 2009: 205f.). To put it pointedly, ethical questions can in no way be replaced by sociological questions (see Hausman 2000a: 38; Goldenberg 2005: 6).

Against the background of the distinction between these two fundamentally different types of empirical data, it becomes clear that the alleged lack of context-sensitivity of ethical theories does not provide an argument for empirical ethics. In fact, the dichotomy of context-sensitive empirical ethics on the one hand and armchair-ethics in the ivory tower on the other rests on a distorted image of (applied) ethics to begin with. The critics are actually "offering a 'straw man' account of applied ethics where absolutely no empirical considerations are included in the deductive process of ethical deliberation" (Goldenberg 2005: 3).

To repeat it, empirical information on the subject matter of ethical reflection is a *sine qua non* of applied ethics. Depending on the topic, this information can include knowledge on the living situation and the needs of, say, chronically ill persons with a particular socio-cultural background.

The question of whether applied ethics should include considerations of feasibility on the level of theoretical deliberation already is another issue yet.[15] Although discussing this issue at length is beyond the scope of this study, it should be noted that, for instance, the human rights or the animal ethics movement have enforced moral innovations against the then dominant *Zeitgeist* (see Birnbacher 2002: 104). To this effect, it can be argued with Unger (1996: 10ff.) that the task of moral theory is not to encompass people's views on justice, but to liberate people from their false convictions or misguided intuitions instead. That being said, as long as prioritization decisions are within the realm of the values of western liberal societies and are not conflicting "too flagrantly with the settled convictions," it is highly unlikely that they will be rejected by the public anyway (Hausman 2002: 645). As the subsequent section will show, respondents in citizen juries commonly refer to very broad ideals and values such as equality, human dignity, and solidarity. This is not surprising because, as pointed out above, most people probably have never thought about rationing decisions before so that they cannot be expected to have specific and strong opinions or even intuitions as to intricate issues of medical resource allocation. Therefore, the feasibility of a thoroughly developed and critically discussed rationing plan does not present a problem.

Finally, it remains to be emphasized that the term armchair-ethics invokes a seriously misleading image of a scholar sitting alone in his study day in, day out and thinking things through. If ethics, or any science for that matter, was conducted like this, the objection of epistemological skepticism would indeed be sound. And yet, both sciences and humanities are of a genuinely social character (see Goldenberg 2005). By taking part in conferences, engaging in research groups, and publishing results, each scholar participates in the professional and, at least to some extent, the broader public discourse. In doing so, he permanently makes his arguments and intuitions accessible to criticism. This is especially true for the realm of applied ethics, which *per se* requires interdisciplinary work and, thanks to its applied subject, is necessarily embedded in the socio-political discourse anyway (see Düwell 2000: 87; Düwell/Steigleder 2003: 31f.; Schicktanz 2009: 225). Nevertheless, due to the fact that this discourse is basically restricted to experts, the question indeed arises as to whether consulting the public on normative-ethical questions could enrich the academic debate on prioritization by bringing in new aspects, rationales, and perspectives. This query is tackled in the following section.

7.4 On ethical expertise

The hope that public deliberation exercises reveal new arguments, viewpoints, or criteria that did not come up in the academic discourse before is quite optimistic, to say the least. Consider the example of a citizens' conference conducted in

Lübeck, a small German town (see Stumpf/Raspe 2011, 2012).[16] In 2010, a group of nineteen citizens met for four weekends to discuss which criteria and principles should guide priority setting in health care.[17] In doing so, they were provided with information material on the subject matter and had the opportunity to consult experts on different aspects of health care resource allocation. In the end, the participants recorded the results of their deliberation process in a citizens' vote (*Bürgervotum*). The aims of the citizens' conference were basically threefold. Beside, first, a political interest in triggering the public debate and demonstrating that ordinary citizens are willing and able to engage in such intricate issues as prioritization, and, second, a scientific interest in the method of the citizen jury as such, Stumpf *et al.* (2014: 54), third, sought to discover new arguments and rationales.[18] Regarding the latter aim, the results are rather disappointing, though. As basic values, the participants enumerate "human dignity," "equality," "solidarity," and "efficiency," and the criteria which should govern resource allocation include "need," "the patient's will," "quality of life," and "cost-efficiency" (*Bürgervotum* 2014: 138, 140f.).[19] While it is certainly reassuring from a political point of view that citizens of a democratic state endorse these values and principles (see Stumpf/Raspe 2012: 423), the results are a far cry from providing new arguments or unexpected lines of reasoning. Hence, it is doubtable whether the conference actually established that citizens can make a "substantial contribution" to the prioritization debate, as Stumpf and Raspe (2011: 317) conclude.

The limited informational content for the academic debate of the *Bürgervotum* in particular and of any public participation exercise in general is not surprising, though, and the reasons for this finding point toward a serious shortcoming of these methods. Indeed, it is not very difficult to settle on such vague umbrella terms as equality or solidarity. The real controversies arise when it comes to the concrete interpretation of these concepts and when the different values or criteria conflict with each other. As to the clarification and operationalization of the notion of equality, Mullen (2008: 398) offers the following example:

> For instance it is possible to have agreement on the equal value of each person's life and hence the value of providing life saving [sic] treatment to any who need it, but to also have vehement disagreement on whether this should mean that priority is given to preventing as many deaths as possible, or to giving each person the same chance of receiving treatment if resources mean that not all can be treated.

Such considerations are lacking in the *Bürgervotum,* which is rather characterized by a pretty general style. To give an example, the participants state that each person has an equal claim to medical treatment, but at the same time postulate that resources should be allocated efficiently; yet, efficiency should be attributed less weight when medical need is high (see Stumpf/Raspe 2011: 317). Whether these considerations can be consistently connected with each other remains unreflected. The fact that the *Bürgervotum* does not offer such conceptual reflections is certainly not surprising given the fact that the authors are not trained in challenging conceptual work and thorough ethical reasoning. Considered against this background, the hope that the public might bring new ideas and arguments into the debate seems "to involve considerable optimism" (Mullen 2008: 407).

The previous reflections furthermore suggest that this hope seems to rely on a misapprehension of the special competence of philosophers in general and ethicists in particular (see Lübbe 2013: 255).[20] Although everyone is of course confronted with moral issues time and again, certain professional skills are essential when it comes to approaching more abstract and less quotidian normative questions. This is where ethical expertise comes in. Above all else, this expertise consists in the skills of analytical and critical thinking, the acquaintance with conceptual issues, and the ability of "the careful, critical evaluation of the soundness of arguments" (Brock 1995: 222).[21] Beyond that, a professional ethicist is usually familiar with different ethical theories and sensitive to the typical problems arising if one path of argumentation or the other is taken (see Birnbacher 2002: 100f.). Having spent much time on thinking about ethical theories and discussing different philosophical positions thus enables the ethicists to enter an ethical discourse with a map of possible paths the argument will take (see Rippe 2000: 159f.).[22] This is especially relevant in view of the fact that the academic discourse frequently precedes the public debate on a certain subject. Hence, when the ethicist moves in the public domain, he is already familiar with the major arguments and counter-arguments put forward in the academic sphere and has had the opportunity to carefully reflect on them (see ibid.). Furthermore, ethicists are used to raising disturbing questions and pointing out logical inconsistencies without necessarily being able to answer or solve them immediately. This requires a considerable amount of calmness and robustness, especially in the context of interdisciplinary debates (see Birnbacher 2002: 101). Against the background of these considerations, consulting the public can be seen as primarily serving an educational function, mirroring deliberation exercises in philosophy classes.[23]

Proclaiming that such an ethical expertise exists does not imply the assertion that ethicists also have a moral expertise and, hence, a privileged route to true moral knowledge, though.[24] In the present context, this means that the ethicist does not as a matter of principle know better than anyone else what a just resource allocation is. However, given his ethical expertise and due to the fact that he has much more time to think these things through than a lay person, he is more likely to do so. At least, although the professional ethicist cannot claim to provide the right arguments for the right conclusions, he is able to restrict the range of possible options by eliminating problematic arguments and conclusions (see Birnbacher 2002: 102; Gesang 2002b: 118). Crucially, the authority of the ethicists' moral advice solely derives from the authority, i.e., plausibility and coherence of their arguments (see Rippe 2000: 160f.; Düwell 2000: 106f.).

Beside the required skills in reasoning, the normative-ethical relevance of empirically elicited preferences is further challenged by the fact that dealing with prioritization decisions also requires a "quite particular empirical understanding" (Mullen 2008: 406).[25] Since the issue of health care resource allocation is characterized by considerable complexity and abstraction, well-considered, informative answers from lay persons cannot be expected (see Rippe 2000: 149). All in all, empirical ethics can be described with Hausman (2000a: 43) as a "counsel of despair": "Moral questions concerning health and health policy [...] are terribly difficult. [...] But if health administrators, economists, philosophers and theologians are all baffled, surely members of the target group who take the issue seriously must be baffled, too."

This emphasis of a special ethical expertise may aggravate the concern that decisions on priority setting are made by small and closed circles of experts or "philosopher kings." Yet, this fear is unsubstantiated. As pointed out already, ethicists cannot claim a special moral expertise *per se* so that the authority of their moral suggestions completely hinges on the quality of their arguments. Moreover, they certainly have no political authority to actually make the decisive decisions on priority setting. Rather, their task consists in the thorough reflection on the normative-ethical issues at stake, including in particular a detailed conceptual inquiry (see Lübbe 2015: 66). In order to avoid an undue influence of one particular person or theory, politicians and the public should be made aware of the differences in opinion that remain even after thorough discussion (see Gesang 2002b: 133). On this level, it is the ethicists' task to present their respective arguments in an intelligible way to the public so that the people gain the opportunity of evaluating them themselves.[26] After the proposals have passed the democratic decision process – during which deliberative exercises can certainly help informing the public, triggering a discourse etc. – the ultimate decisions on health policy are made by the sovereign, that is to say, the citizens anyway.[27] If, by contrast, normative-ethical reflections on priority setting supposed to inform the political decision making process relied on what the public think already, political consulting would be superfluous in the first place.

7.5 Respecting individual autonomy

Up to now, the arguments presented for involving the public in the debate on resource allocation focused on improving the prioritization decisions in one way or another. A different thread claims that in a liberal and democratic society, respecting individual autonomy requires public participation in order to legitimize prioritization decisions. Thereby, legitimization can be understood in two ways. First, it can be interpreted strategically, as Menzel's (1999: 262f.) following argument illustrates:

> the defense of a policy decision is more difficult if those who bear its primary effects have not had that notable input. The implications for the use of CEA are not hard to see [...] CEA's moral and political future will be brighter if it can note precisely where in its process influential values have been contributed by representatives of those who are affected by the final decision.

This rationale offered for the participation of stakeholders, i.e., the persons potentially affected by prioritization decisions (see Friedrich *et al.* 2012: 412), apparently refers to the political feasibility of CUA (see Walker/Siegel 2002: 268). Arguments along this line are common in the literature; public participation is endorsed in order to enhance both the public's "acceptance of priority-setting decisions," improve the people's "trust and confidence in the health care system" (Bruni *et al.* 2008: 15), and to "strengthen the relationship between citizens and decision makers" (Shah 2009: 82).[28] As stated at the outset of this chapter, such strategic functions of public participation are not of interest in the present context, though. Instead, the current concern is with the second meaning of legitimization, which refers to a profound moral legitimization of certain policy measures within a democracy (see Powers/Faden 2006: 179).

Such arguments for public participation rest on the assumption that, due to the basic value of autonomy, only the consent of the persons concerned can legitimize priority setting in health care: "If it is maintained that people should have control over the governance of their own lives and interests it seems plausible to suggest that they should have a say in deciding ethical frameworks" (Mullen 2008: 401).[29] This case meshes neatly with the economic emphasis on consumer sovereignty and anti-paternalism. Accordingly, it is reinforced by the claim that since the citizens finance the health care system, they should be the ones to decide about the distribution of its resources: because "health care is a public good [...] it makes sense to ask the public how it would choose to distribute the good" (Ubel/Loewenstein 1996: 234).[30] Taking these two arguments together leads to the claim that those "whose health is at stake and who are paying for the health care should be the ones to decide" (Hausman 2002: 643).

And yet, both the reference to individual autonomy and the alleged parallel between prioritization decisions and democratic decision making is mistaken. To begin with, autonomy, just as consumer sovereignty, concerns private decisions of the individual, the prime example being the choice of consumption goods (see Lübbe 2013: 254, 2015: 65f.). If individual liberty and autonomy are accepted as basic values, there is indeed "a strong moral argument to be made for letting competent adults make decisions about their own well-being" as long as the rights of others remain unharmed (Walker/Siegel 2002: 267). Issues of justice, by contrast, inherently involve considerations about the rights and the well-being of other persons. Referring to the individuals' autonomy when it comes to rationing decisions thus amounts to a category error. By the same token, the argument that those financing and potentially benefitting from the health care system should decide on the distribution of resources is erroneous, as Hausman (2002: 643) points out:

> If health and its protection raised no moral questions, there would be no question that health policies should depend on the wishes of those they serve. [...]. Funding cosmetic surgery rather than inoculations is not just a matter of social preferences. Age-weighting, discounting, and weighting of different health states all matter ethically, and no reason has yet been given why the evident interests of the target population should imply that their values govern.

The analogy between rationing decisions and democratic decisions, in turn, fails for two reasons. First and foremost, democracy obviously is not tantamount to the majority rule (see Price 2000: 276; Powers/Faden 2006: 180; Schicktanz 2009: 230). Instead, democratic processes are embedded in a constitutional framework guaranteeing fundamental rights and liberties, especially for minorities (see Sagoff 1986: 308; Hausman 2012: 97). To quote Dworkin (1978: 133f.), "*[d]e-mocracy* is justified because it enforces the right of each person to respect and concern as individual." Therefore, arrangements are required which make sure that democratic procedures do not undermine their own justification and this is the very rationale for a system of rights (see Dworkin 1978: 134).[31] Once rights and liberties are guaranteed, it is up to the individual to choose her preferred way of life as she sees fits, i.e., to lead an autonomous life according to her personal preferences (see Walker/Siegel 2002: 267). The debate on prioritization, however, is a dispute concerning the constitutional framework, so to speak, and not on the individual style of living. It is about the establishment of criteria for a just system of allocating medical resources, which needs to make sure that the rights to equal concern and respect are guaranteed.

The second discrepancy between democratic decision making and public participation in the rationing discourse consists of the kind of legitimization at stake. Involving certain samples from the public into the prioritization discourse can never virtually legitimize a collective decision the way a democratic vote does, of course. This is because in the former case, not everyone had the opportunity to participate in the respective survey or the deliberative group. Yet, it is precisely this "fundamental notion of equality" that provides democracy for its normative justification (Walker/Siegel 2002: 271). To this extent, even a statistically representative sample cannot represent the whole population in a morally relevant sense, for even if the elicited preference pattern was indeed identical with the preference pattern of the whole population, "the democratic procedural justification is lost" (ibid.).[32] As a result, "mimicking majorities" by means of empirical elicitation of prioritization preferences ultimately fails (Powers/Faden 2006: 184). To sum it up, quoting Hausman (2002: 644f.):

> Although moral questions concerning what is right and wrong are very different from most scientific questions, there is no stronger case for deciding moral decisions democratically than there is for deciding scientific questions democratically. [...] Those who support empirical ethics might complain that this disenfranchises the population. Of course it does. It disenfranchises everyone, because it maintains that the answers to evaluative questions, like the answers to factual questions, cannot be found in taking a vote. With respect to political decisions, on the other hand, there is, of course, no question of disenfranchising anyone.

Before concluding this chapter, a remark on a third possible line of argument for the empirical elicitation of prioritization preferences is required. It may be argued that the whole critique offered here is beside the point, since consulting the public is not connected with any normative intention at all, but merely amounts to descriptive, scientifically motivated research instead (see Friedrich *et al.* 2012: 415). A first reply to this argument was already given above. The endeavor of positively describing prioritization preferences apparently presumes the existence of something that can be described in the first place. As argued in the previous chapter, however, it is doubtable that subjects have certain prioritization preferences, just waiting to be elicited. By contrast, it is much more likely that they form their preferences during the elicitation task so that the elicitation methods gain pivotal normative importance. As shown by means of different deliberation exercises, respondents are also likely to change their normative framework during the task. Hence, the elicitation of prioritization preferences is a far cry from merely mirroring preference structures prevalent in the public. Beyond that, it should be noted that the discourse on resource allocation is not of mere academic interest, but is politically highly contested. Once published, the empirical data can, and most probably will be used to support or to reject certain policy measures (see Murray 1996: 2f.).[33] Also, they may enfold "the normative power of the factual," as Borry *et al.* (2005: 48) put it: "the publication of research data gives rise to standpoints and influences decisions which, in turn, can alter the normative structure of the reality of action." As to the current concern, this could mean that the more often empirical surveys show that the majority of subjects consider individual responsibility as the most important allocation criterion, the more this result becomes a fact itself. In the end, it seems all too easy to slide from mere descriptive data to normative conclusions (see Borry *et al.* 2005: 42f., Schicktanz 2009: 225ff.). Hence, claiming that the data elicited only serve a descriptive purpose is irresponsible.

In sum, the literature reviewed here does not offer any convincing arguments for the normative-ethical relevance of the public's prioritization preferences. The rationales focusing on the improvement of the prioritization discourse neglect the difference between empirically informed ethics on the one hand and empirical ethics on the other. In addition, it misconceives the competence of professional philosophers. The second group of arguments, in turn, basically relies on a consumer choice framework and disregards the difference between genuinely private choices on the one hand and moral judgments, concerning the rights and claims of other persons on the other. The parallel drawn between prioritization and democratic decision making is additionally flawed because the latter are characterized by provisions to protect individual rights and because including only a sample of the population in the prioritization discourse cannot confer democratic legitimacy on the results. Hence, even if the arguments put forward in this study were wrong, the weighting approach still would not offer an appropriate account of dealing with fairness problems. In conclusion, two important qualifications deserve to be repeated. First, none of this implies that ethical reasoning should be independent of empirical data. Quite to the contrary, as pointed out above, thoroughly conducted applied ethics certainly has to be empirically informed. Second, the previous considerations are not a plea for an expertocracy. When it comes to the implementation of health policy, the citizens have the last word anyway.

Notes

1 In view of this focus of interest, the questions of how or whom to ask can be neglected and the notion of "the public" will be used broadly. See on this concept Williams *et al.* (2012: 29) and Schicktanz *et al.* (2012: 134f.).
2 See also Marckmann/Siebert (2002b: 187), Gaertner/Schokkaert (2012: 14), and for a critique Lübbe (2015: 64).
3 See also Ubel *et al.* (2000b: 899).
4 In the same vein, Lengahan (1999: 47) states that "public involvement could resolve some of the dilemmas inherent in rationing decisions and lead to better decisions." See Richardson (2002: 627), Richardson/McKie (2005: 271), and Gaertner/Schokkaert (2012: 14).
5 See also Lomas (1997: 106) and Olsen *et al.* (2003).
6 See also Diederich/Schreier (2013: 280).
7 Olsen *et al.* (2003: 1171) observe a lack of "research to distinguish ethically based considerations from prejudices."
8 Italics added.
9 The same case is made by Hausman (2002: 644, 652), Walker/Siegel (2002: 267), Goldenberg (2005: 7), Powers/Faden (2006: 184, 190), Düwell (2009: 205), and Lübbe (2013: 254f, 2015: 67f.).
10 See also Schicktanz *et al.* (2012: 134).
11 See also Richardson/McKie (2005: 271).
12 For similar distinctions see Borry *et al.* (2004: 44ff.) and Düwell (2009: 204ff.).
13 The example of slippery-slope arguments is provided by Birnbacher (1999: 329), Musschenga (2005: 476), Düwell (2009: 205), and Schicktanz *et al.* (2012: 133).
14 The necessity of including empirical data into applied ethics is highlighted by Birnbacher (1999), Düwell (2000: 83), and Düwell/Steigleder (2003: 30ff.).
15 Note that there is no consensus about general questions as to the definition and, hence, the character and purpose of applied ethics. See Karminsky (2002: 37ff.).
16 See also the contributions in Stumpf/Raspe (2014).
17 On the concrete proceeding see Stumpf (2014b).
18 See also Stumpf/Raspe (2012: 419) and Stumpf (2014a: 17f.).
19 My translation.
20 For the sake of readability, I will refer to philosophers and ethicists in the following, but the same reasoning applies to anyone working in normative disciplines and having the required argumentative skills, such as law scholars (see ibid.). Note that both the nature and the very existence of a special ethical expertise are contested in the literature. See Düwell (2000), Rippe (2000), Birnbacher (2002), Gesang (2002b), Düwell/Steigleder (2003: 29), and Schicktanz *et al.* (2012).
21 See also Rippe (2000: 159), Düwell (2000: 107), Runtenberg/Ach (2002: 18f.), Kaminsky (2002: 36f.), Birnbacher (2002: 101), Goldenberg (2005: 5), Mullen (2008: 406), Schicktanz *et al.* (2012: 131), and Lübbe (2013: 255).
22 The image of a moral map is also invoked by Runtenberg/Ach (2002: 22f.) and Gesang (2002b: 133).
23 Daniels (1998: 41) states: "Anyone who has taught students or quizzed audiences at lectures on these types of cases knows that initial responses are modified once cases are given that probe the reasons for them."
24 The juxtaposition of ethical and moral expertise stems from Birnbacher (2002: 101). See Rippe (2000: 159), Düwell (2000: 106f.), and Gesang (2002b: 117ff.).
25 See also Goldenberg (2005: 5).
26 See Düwell (2000: 107) and Gesang (2002b: 132f.). This may constitute the pivotal difference between ethical experts and experts from other disciplines: when we seek technical advice, for instance, we usually trust the experts' statement and do not ask the technician how he came to his conclusion. The case is totally different when it

comes to moral questions, though. Here, it is crucial that the person seeking the advice understands and accepts the reasoning behind a certain conclusion. Developing and explicating this reasoning is thus the pivotal task of the ethical expert. See Düwell (2000: 107).

27 See also Price (2000: 276), Walker/Siegel (2002: 272), Bognar/Hirose (2014: 153), and Lübbe (2015: 66).

28 See also Friedrich *et al.* (2012: 412f.), Williams *et al.* (2012: 40ff.), Gaertner/Schokkaert (2012: 8f.), and Williamson (2014: 6).

29 See also Cookson/Dolan (1999: 64) and Schicktanz *et al.* (2012: 134).

30 See also Nord (1999a: 2), Bruni *et al.* (2008: 15), and Diederich/Schreier (2013: 265).

31 Hausman (2002: 644) states:

> Fundamental rights and liberties and a regime that secures the self-respect of citizens cannot be abrogated by majority vote. Permitting democracy to extend to such questions would lessen security and would place justice and equal moral status of adult citizen at risk.

32 See also Walker/Siegel (2002: 269) and Powers/Faden (2006: 187f.).

33 Murray *et al.* (2002a: 15) state:

> In examining the properties of various summary measures, it is important to bear in mind the ultimate goal of influencing the policy process [...]. Because of their potential influence on international and national resource allocation decisions, summary measures must be considered as normative measures.

8 Conclusion

The study scrutinized the attempts to solve CUA's fairness issue by attaching equity weights to QALYs. In order to reveal the underlying rationale and the implied assumptions of this endeavor, it offered an encompassing historical and conceptual analysis of the value-maximizing framework of economic evaluations. A leading motive running through the different chapters was the approaches' orientation toward the paradigm of consumer choice theory and the ideal of the market as allocation device. It became clear that both the methods of eliciting prioritization preferences and the tools and concepts used to describe the problem of health care resource allocation are rooted in consumer choice analysis. The effect of this unreflected transfer of concepts to the different area of distributional issues is twofold. For one thing, it causes considerable conceptual ambiguities, first and foremost as to the notion of social value. For another, the dead metaphors resulting from this transfer embody implicit assumptions that are totally inapt for an encompassing and satisfying consideration of fairness. In particular, the image of equity weights makes strong demands on the respondents' prioritization preferences in particular and on the way diverse reasons come together in moral decision making in general. As theoretical reflections and empirical evidence indicate, these assumptions are in all likelihood unwarranted so that the equity weights derived from the respondents' stated preferences constitute mere artefacts of the consequentialist framework presupposed by the surveys. Thus, equity weighting does not constitute a promising device to solve CUA's distributional problems.

To be sure, this study did not prove the general impossibility of representing non-consequentialist reasons within a value-oriented framework in terms of weighting factors. It is certainly imaginable that someday someone comes up with a complicated axiology which indeed embodies the actual reasons behind the respondents' choices and, hence, can be incorporated into a stable decision rule for resource allocation. Nevertheless, the study demonstrated that this endeavor is based on quite strong assumptions and touches on intricate philosophical issues, which still remain to be solved. Thus, anyone undertaking the task of establishing equity weights should be aware of the intricate conceptual and normative issues associated with this attempt and, hence, should be aware of the fact that he or she is likely to fail. Instead of investing ever more resources into research on "true" social values or the empirical elicitation of equity weights, it is much more worthwhile to work on a non-consequentialist theory of fairness in resource allocation and, thereby, develop alternatives to orthodox health economics.

Bibliography

Ackerman, F., Heinzerling, L. (2004) *Priceless: On Knowing the Price of Everything and the Value of Nothing.* New York/London, The New Press.

Alm, D. (2004) Atomism. *Australasian Journal of Philosophy* 82(2): 312–331.

Amadae, S. M. (2003) *Rationalizing Capitalist Democracy: The Cold War Origins of Rational Choice Liberalism.* Chicago/London, University of Chicago Press.

Amaya-Amaya, M., Gerard, K., Ryan, M. (2008) Discrete choice experiments in a nutshell. In: Amaya-Amaya, M., Gerard, K., Ryan, M. (eds.) *Using Discrete Choice Experiments to Value Health and Health Care.* Dordrecht: Springer, pp. 13–46.

Anand, P. (1987) Are the preference axioms really rational? *Theory and Decisions* 23: 189–214.

Anand, S., Hanson, K. (1997) Disability-adjusted life years: a critical review. *Journal of Health Economics* 16: 685–702.

——(1998) DALYs: efficiency versus equity. *World Development* 26(2): 307–310.

Arnesen, T., Nord, E. (1999) The value of DALY life: problems with ethics and validity of disability adjusted life years. *BMJ* 319: 1423–1425.

Arrow, K. J. (1963a/1966) *Social Choice and Individual Values*, 2nd edn. (1st edn. 1951). New York *et al.*, John Wiley & Sons.

——(1963b) Uncertainty and the economics of medical care. *American Economic Review* 53: 941–973.

——(1993) Contingent valuation of nonuse values: observations and questions. In: Hausman, J. A. (ed.) *Contingent Valuation: A Critical Assessment.* Amsterdam/New York *et al.*, North Holland, pp. 479–483.

Ashmore, M., Mulkay, M., Pinch, T. (1989) *Health and Efficiency: A Sociology of Health Economics.* Milton Keynes/Philadelphia, Open University Press.

Aslanbeigui, N. (1990) On the demise of Pigovian economics. *Southern Economic Journal* 56(3): 616–627.

Ayer, A. J. (1966) *Logical Positivism*. New York, The Free Press.

Backhouse, R. E. (ed.) (1994) *New Directions in Economic Methodology.* London/New York, Routledge.

——(1998a) The transformation of U.S. economics, 1920–1960, viewed through a survey of journal articles. In: Morgan/Rutherford (eds.) (1998a), pp. 85–107.

——(1998b) Rhetoric. In: Davis *et al.* (eds.) (1998), pp. 419–422.

——(2003) The stabilization of price theory, 1920–1955. In: Samuels *et al.* (eds.) (2003), pp. 308–324.

——(2004) *The Ordinary Business of Life: A History of Economics from the Ancient World to the Twenty-first Century.* Oxford *et al.*, Oxford University Press.

——(2005) The rise of free market economics: economists and the role of the state since 1970. *History of Political Economy* 37(5): 355–392.

——(2008a) Marginal revolution. In: Durlauf/Blume (eds.) (2008), http://www.dictionaryofeconomics.com/article?id=pde2008_M000392, December 13, 2011.

——(2008b) United States, economics in (1945 to present). In: Durlauf/Blume (eds.) (2008), http://www.dictionaryofeconomics.com/article?id=pde2008_U000076, December 9, 2012.

——(2009) Robbins and welfare economics. *Journal of the History of Economic Thought* 31(4): 474–484.

——(2010) *The Puzzle of Modern Economics: Science or Ideology?* Cambridge *et al.*, Cambridge University Press.

Backhouse, R. E., Medema, S. G. (2008) Economics, definition of. In: Durlauf/Blume (eds.) (2008), http://www.dictionaryofeconomics.com/article?id=pde2008_E000291, December 9, 2012.

——(2009a) Defining economics: the long road to acceptance of the Robbins definition. *Economica* 76: 805–820.

——(2009b) Robbins' essay and the axiomatization of economics. *Journal of the History of Economic Thought* 31(4): 485–499.

Baker, R., Bateman, I., Donaldson, C., Jones-Lee, M., Lancsar, E., Loomes, G., Mason, H., Odejar, M., Pinto-Prades, J. L., Robinson, A., Ryan, M., Shakley, P., Smith, R., Sugden, R., Wildman, J. (2010) Weighting and valuing quality-adjusted life-years using stated preference methods: preliminary results from the Social Value of a QALY Project. *Health Technology Assessment* 14(27).

Baker, R., Robinson, A. (2004) Responses to standard gambles: are preferences well-constructed? *Health Economics* 13: 37–48.

Barer, M. L., Getzen, T. E., Stoddart, G. L. (eds.) (1998) *Health, Health Care and Health Economics. Perspectives on Distribution*. Chichester, Wiley and Sons.

Baron, J. (1994) *Thinking and Deciding*, 2nd edn. Cambridge, Cambridge University Press.

——(1997) Biases in the quantitative measurement of values for public decisions. *Psychological Bulletin* 122(1): 72–88.

Baron, J., Ubel, P. A. (2002) Types of inconsistency in health-state utility judgements. *Organizational Behavior and Human Decision Processes* 89: 1100–1118.

Baron, J., Wu, Z., Brennan, D. J., Weeks, C., Ubel, P. A. (2001) Analog scale, magnitude estimation, and person trade-off as measures of health utility: biases and their correction. *Journal of Behavioral Decision Making* 14: 17–34.

Barry, B. (1965) *Political Argument.* London, Routledge & Kegan Paul.

Bekker-Grob, E. W. de, Ryan, M., Gerard, K. (2012) Discrete choice experiments in health economics: a review of the literature. *Health Economics* 21: 145–172.

Bennett, J., Blamey, R. (2001a) (eds.) *The Choice Modeling Approach to Environmental Valuation.* Cheltenham, Northampton, Edward Elgar.

Bennett, J., Blamey, R. (2001b) Introduction. In: Bennett/Blamey (eds.) (2001a), pp. 1–10.

Bentham, J. (1823/2007) *An Introduction to the Principles of Morals and Legislation,* reprint of a new edition, corrected by the author (1st edn. 1780). Mineola/New York, Dover.

Berg, M. (1999) Die innere Entwicklung: Vom Zweiten Weltkrieg bis zur Watergate-Krise 1974. In: Adams, W. P., Lösche, P. (eds.) *Länderbericht USA: Geschichte – Politik – Geographie – Wirtschaft – Gesellschaft – Kultur,* 3rd revised edn. Frankfurt a.M./New York, Campus, pp. 144–168.

Bicchieri, C. (1988) Should a scientist abstain from metaphor? In: Klamer *et al.* (eds.) (1988), pp. 100–114.

Birch, S., Donaldson, C. (2003) Valuing benefits and costs of health care programmes: where´s the 'extra' in extra-welfarism? *Social Science and Medicine* 56: 1121–1133.

Birnbacher, D. (1999) Ethics and social science: which kind of co-operation? *Ethical Theory and Moral Practice* 2: 319–336.

——(2002) Wofür ist der ‚Ethik-Experte' Experte? In: Gesang (ed.) (2002a), pp. 97–114.

Bjornstad, R. (1992) Misinformation helped sink plan. *The Register-Guard.* Eugene, Oregon. Tuesday, August 18, p. 1A, continued on p. 4A.

Black, C. (2008) Utility. In: Durlauf/Blume (eds.) (2008), http://www.dictionaryofeconomics.com/article?id=pde2008_U000047, November 26, 2013.

Blaug, M. (1980) *The Methodology of Economics or How Economists Explain.* Cambridge *et al.*, Cambridge University Press.

——(1997) *Economic Theory in Retrospect,* 5th edn. Cambridge *et al.*, Cambridge University Press.

——(2003) The formalist revolution of the 1950s. In: Samuels *et al.* (eds.) (2003), pp. 395–410.

——(2007) The fundamental theorems of modern welfare economics, historically contemplated. *History of Political Economy* 39(2) 185–207.

Bleichrodt, H., Diecidue, E., Quiggin, J. (2004) Equity weights in the allocation of health care: the rank-dependent QALY model. *Journal of Health Economics* 23: 157–171.

Blinder, A. S. (1987) *Hard Heads, Soft Hearts: Tough-Minded Economics for a Just Society.* Reading *et al.*, Addison-Wesley Publishing Company Inc.

Blume, L. E., Easley, D. (2008) Rationality. In: Durlauf/Blume (eds.) (2008), http://www.dictionaryofeconomics.com/article?id=pde2008_R000277, June 7, 2013.

Blumenschein, K., Johannesson, M. (1996) Economic evaluation in health care: a brief history and future directions. *Pharmacoeconomics* 10(2) 114–122.

Boadway, R. W., Bruce, N. (1984) *Welfare Economics.* Oxford/New York, Blackwell.

Bobinac, A., van Exel, J., Rutten, F. F.H., Brouwer, W. B.F. (2012) Inquiry into the relationship between equity weights and the value of the QALY. *Value in Health* 15: 1119–1126.

——(2013) Valuing QALY gains by applying a societal perspective. *Health Economics* 22: 1272–1281.

Bodenheimer, T. (1997) The Oregon Health Plan – lessons for the nation. *Health Policy Report* 337(9) 651–655.

Bognar, G., Hirose, I. (2014) *The Ethics of Health Care Rationing. An Introduction.* London/New York, Routledge.

Borry, P., Schotsman, P., Dierickx, K. (2004) What is the role of empirical research in bioethical reflection and decision making? An ethical analysis. *Medicine, Health Care, and Philosophy* 7: 41–53.

——(2005) The birth of the empirical turn in bioethics. *Bioethics* 19(1) 49–71.

Boulding, K. E. (1969) Economics as a moral science. *The American Economic Review* 59(1): 1–12.

Bowie, C., Richardson, A., Sykes, W. (1995) Consulting the public about health service priorities. *British Medical Journal* 311: 1155–1158.

Brazier, J. E., Deverill, M., Green, C., Harper, R., Booth, A. (1999) A review of the use of health status measures in economic evaluation. *Health Technology Assessment* 3(9).

Brennan, G., Buchanan, J. M. (1985) *The Reason of Rules: Constitutional Political Economy.* Cambridge *et al.*, Cambridge University Press.

Brock, D. W. (1995) Public moral discourse. In: Bulger, R. E., Meyer Bobby, E., Fineberg, H. V. (eds.) *Society's Choices: Social and Ethical Decision Making in Biomedicine.* Washington, National Academy Press, pp. 215–240.

——(2000) Health care resource prioritization and discrimination against persons with disabilities. In: Francis, L. P., Silver, A. (eds.) *Americans with Disabilities. Exploring Implications of the Law for Individuals and Institutions.* New York/London, Routledge, pp. 223–235.

——(2004) Ethical issues in the use of cost effectiveness analysis for the prioritisation of health care resources. In: Anand, S., Peter, F., Sen, A. (eds.) *Public Health, Ethics and Equity.* Oxford *et al.*, Oxford University Press, pp. 201–223.

——(2005) Priority to the worse off in health-care resource prioritization. In: Rauprich *et al.* (eds.) (2005), pp. 37–52.

——(2009) Cost-effectiveness and disability discrimination. *Economics and Philosophy* 25: 27–47.

Broome, J. (1978) Trying to value a life. *Journal of Public Economics* 9: 91–100.

——(1991a) *Weighing Goods: Equality, Uncertainty and Time.* Oxford *et al.*, Blackwell.

——(1991b) Utility. *Economics and Philosophy* 7: 1–12.

Brouwer, W. B. F., Culyer, A. J., van Exel, J., Rutten, F. F. H. (2008) Welfarism vs. extra-welfarism. *Journal of Health Economics* 27: 325–338.

Brouwer, W. B. F., Koopmanschap, M. A. (2000) On the economic foundations of CEA. Ladies and Gentlemen, take your positions! *Journal of Health Economics* 19: 439–459.

Brown, C. (2011) Consequentialize this. *Ethics* 121(4): 749–771.

Bruni, L., Guala, F. (2001) Vilfredo Pareto and the epistemological foundations of choice theory. *History of Political Economy* 33(1): 21–49.

Bruni, L., Sugden, R. (2007) The road not taken: how psychology was removed from economics, and how it might be brought back. *The Economic Journal* 117: 146–173.

Bruni, R., Laupacis, A., Douglas, M. K. (2008) Public engagement in setting priorities in health care. *Canadian Medical Association Journal* 179(1): 15–18.

Buchanan, J. M. (1964) What should economists do? *Southern Economic Journal* 30: 213–322.

——(1975) *The Limits of Liberty. Between Anarchy and Leviathan.* Chicago, University of Chicago Press.

Bürgervotum zur Prioritätensetzung in der Medizinischen Versorgung. In: Stumpf/Raspe (eds.) (2014), pp. 135–147.

Capron, A. (1992) Oregon's disability: principle or politics? *Hastings Center Report* 22(6) 18–20.

Clark, C. M. A. (1995) From natural value to social value. In: Clark, C. M.A. (ed.) *Institutional Economics and the Theory of Social Value: Essays in Honor of Marc R. Tool.* Boston, Kluwer Academic Publishers, pp. 29–42.

Clark, J., Friesen, L. (2008) The causes of order effects in contingent valuation surveys: An experimental investigation. *Journal of Environmental Economics and Management* 56: 195–206.

Coast, J. (2004) Is economic evaluation in touch with society's health values? *British Medical Journal* 329: 1233–1236.

Coast, J., Smith, R. D., Lorgelly, P. (2008) Welfarism, extra-welfarism and capability: the spread of ideas in health economics. *Social Science and Medicine* 67: 1190–1198.

Coats, A. W. (1976) Economics and psychology: the death and resurrection of a research programme. In: Latsis, S. J. (ed.) *Method and Appraisal in Economics.* Cambridge *et al.*, Cambridge University Press, pp. 43–64.

——(1989) Economic ideas and economists in government: accomplishments and frustrations. In: Colander, D. D., Coats, A. W. (eds.) *The Spread of Economic Ideas*. Cambridge *et al.*, Cambridge University Press, pp. 109–118.

Cohen, J. (1997) Putting a different spin on QALYs: beyond a sociological critique. In: Davis, J. B. (ed.) *New Economics and Its History*. Durham/London, Duke University Press, pp. 143–172.

Cohen, J., Ubel, P. A. (2001) Accounting for fairness and efficiency in health economics. In: Davis (ed.) (2001), pp. 94–109.

Colvin, P. (1985) *The Economic Ideal in British Government: Calculating Costs and Benefits in the 1970s*. Manchester/New Hampshire, Manchester University Press.

Cookson, R., Dolan, P. (1999) Public views on health care rationing: a group discussion study. *Health Policy* 49: 63–74.

Cookson, R., Drummond, M., Weatherly, H. (2009) Explicit incorporation of equity considerations into economic evaluation of public health interventions. *Health Economics, Policy, and Law* 4: 231–245.

Cookson, R., Griffin, S., Nord, E. (2014) Incorporating concerns for fairness in economic evaluation of health programs: overview. In: Culyer (ed.) (2014), pp. 27–34.

Coote, A., Mattinson, D. (1997) Twelve good neighbours: the citizen as a juror. Fabian Discussion Paper, Fabian Society, London.

Cooter, R., Rappoport, P. (1984) Were the ordinalists wrong about welfare economics? *Journal of Economic Literature* 22: 507–530.

Copp, D. (1985) Morality, reason, and management science: the rationale of cost-benefit analysis. In: P., E. F., Miller, F. D. Jr., P., J. (eds.) *Ethics and Economics*. Oxford *et al.*, Blackwell, pp. 128–151.

Corry, B. A. (2008) Robbins, Lionel Charles (1898–1984). In: Durlauf/Blume (eds.) (2008), http://www.dictionaryofeconomics.com/article?id=pde2008_R000161, November 26, 2013.

Cubbon, J. (1991) The principle of QALY maximization as the basis for allocating health care resources. *Journal of Medical Ethics* 17: 181–184.

Cudd, A. E. (1993) Game theory and the history of ideas about rationality: an introductory survey. *Economics and Philosophy* 9: 101–133.

Culyer, A. J. (1981) Health, economics, and health economics. In: Gaarg, J. v. d., Perlman, M. (eds.) *Health, Economics, and Health Economics*. Amsterdam/New York *et al.*, North-Holland, pp. 3–11.

——(1989) The normative economics of health care finance and provision. *Oxford Review of Economic Policy* 5(1): 34–58.

——(1990) Commodities, characteristics of commodities, characteristics of people, utilities, and the quality of life. In: Baldwin, S., Godfrey, C. (eds.) *The Quality of Life: Perspectives and Policies*. London/New York, Routledge, pp. 9–27.

——(1991) Conflicts between equity concepts and efficiency in health: a diagrammatic approach. *Osaka Economic Papers* 40(3–4): 141–154.

——(1997) Maximising the health of the whole community: the case for. In: New (ed.) (1997), pp. 95–100.

——(1998) How ought health economists to treat value judgements in their analyses? In: Barer *et al.* (eds.) (1998), pp. 362–371.

——(ed.) (2014) *Encyclopedia of Health Economics, Vol. 1*. San Diego, Elsevier.

Culyer, A. J., Newhouse, J. N. (eds.) (2000a) *Handbook of Health Economics*. Amsterdam *et al.*, Elsevier.

——(2000b) Introduction: the state and scope of health economics. In: Culyer/Newhouse (eds.) (2000a), pp. 1–8.

Cutler, D. M. (2007) Equality, efficiency, and market fundamentals: the dynamics of international medical-care reform. In: Culyer, A. (ed.) *Health Economics Vol. IV: Critical Perspectives on the World Economy*. London/New York, Routledge, pp. 385–419.

Dancy, J. (2004) *Ethics without Principles*. Oxford: Clarendon Press.

Daniels, N. (1991) Is the Oregon rationing health plan fair? *JAMA* 265(17): 2232–2235.

——(1993) Rationing fairly: programmatic considerations. *Bioethics* 7(2): 225–233.

——(1998) Symposium on the rationing of health care: 2. Rationing medical care – a philosopher's perspective on outcomes and processes. *Economics and Philosophy* 14: 27–50.

——(2008) *Just Health. Meeting Health Needs Fairly*. Cambridge *et al.*, Cambridge University Press.

Davis, J. B. (1990) Cooter and Rappoport on the normative. *Economics and Philosophy* 6: 139–146.

——(ed.) (2001) *The Social Economics of Health Care*. London/New York, Routledge.

——(2003) *The Theory of the Individual in Economics: Identity and Value*. London/New York, Routledge.

Davis, J. B., Hands, D. W., Mäki, U. (eds.) (1998) *The Handbook of Economic Methodology*. Cheltenham/Northampton, Edward Elgar.

Debreu, G. (1959) *Theory of Value: An Axiomatic Analysis of Economic Equilibrium*. New Haven/London, Yale University Press.

Diamond, P. A., Hausman, J. A. (1994) Contingent valuation: is some number better than no number? *Journal of Economic Perspectives* 8(4): 45–64.

Diederich, A., Schreier, M. (2013) Priorisierungskriterien in der gesundheitlichen Versorgung – Was meinen die Bürger? In: Schmitz-Luhn/Bohmeier (eds.) (2013), pp. 265–298.

Diekmann, A., Dippold, K., Dietrich, H. (2009) Compensatory versus noncompensatory models for predicting consumer preferences. *Judgment and Decision Making* 4(3): 200–213.

Dixon, J., Welch, H. G. (1991) Priority setting: lessons from Oregon. *The Lancet* 337: 891–894.

Dobb, M. (1973) *Theories of Value and Distribution since Adam Smith*. Cambridge *et al.*, Cambridge University Press.

Dolan, P. (1998) The measurement of individual utility and social welfare. *Journal of Health Economics* 17: 39–52.

——(1999) Drawing a veil over the measurement of social welfare – a reply to Johannesson. *Journal of Health Economics* 18: 387–390.

——(2001) Output measures and valuation in health. In: Drummond/McGuire (eds.) (2001), pp. 46–67.

Dolan, P., Cookson, R. (2000) A qualitative study of the extent to which health gain matters when choosing between groups of patients. *Health Policy* 51: 19–30.

Dolan, P., Edlin, R., Tsuchiya, A. (on behalf of the NICE Social QALY team) (2008) The relative societal value of health gains to different beneficiaries: a summary. Health Economics and Decision Science Discussion Paper Series 8/12, University of Sheffield, Birmingham, http://eprints.whiterose.ac.uk/10902/1/HEDS_DP_08-12.pdf, October 15, 2014.

Dolan, P., Green, C. (1998) Using the person trade-off approach to examine differences between individual and social utility. *Health Economics* 7: 307–312.

Dolan, P., Kahneman, D. (2008) Interpretations of health and their implications for the valuation of health. *The Economic Journal* 118: 215–234.

Dolan, P., Olsen, J. A. (2002) *Distributing Health Care: Economic and Ethical Issues.* Oxford *et al.*, Oxford University Press.

Dolan, P., Olsen, Jan A., Menzel, P., Richardson, Jeff (2003) An inquiry into the different perspectives that can be used when eliciting preferences in health. *Health Economics* 12: 545–551.

Dolan, P., Shaw, R., Tsuchiya, A., Williams, A. (2005) QALY maximisation and people's preferences: a methodological review of the literature. *Health Economics* 14: 197–208.

Dolan, P., Tsuchiya, A. (2003) The person trade-off method and the transitivity principle: an example from preferences over age weighting. *Health Economics* 12: 505–510.

——(2006) The elicitation of distributional judgements in the context of economic evaluation. In: Jones (ed.) (2006), pp. 382–391.

——(2009) The social welfare function and individual responsibility: some theoretical issues and empirical evidence. *Journal of Health Economics* 28: 210–220.

Donaldson, C., Baker, R., Mason, H. *et al.* (2011a) European Value of a Quality Adjusted Life Year. Final Publishable Report, http://research.ncl.ac.uk/eurovaq/EuroVaQ_Final_Publishable_Report_and_Appendices.pdf, May 12, 2012.

——(2011b) The social value of a QALY: raising the bar or barring the raise? *BMC Health Service Research* 11(8), http://www.biomedcentral.com/1472–6963/11/8, October, 22 2014.

Dreier, J. (1993) The structure of normative theories. *The Monist* 76(1): 22–40.

Drummond, M. F. (1989) Output measurement for resource allocation decisions in health care. *Oxford Review of Economic Policy* 5(1): 59–74.

Drummond, M. F., Brixner, D., Gold, M., Kind, P., McGuire, A., Nord, E. (2009) Toward a consensus on the QALY. *Value in Health 12,* supplement 1*:* S31-S35.

Drummond, M. F., McGuire, A. (eds.) (2001) *Economic Evaluation in Health Care: Merging Theory with Practice.* Oxford *et al.*, Oxford University Press.

Drummond, M. F., Sculpher, M. J., Torrance, G. W., O´Brien, B. J., Stoddart, G. L. (2005) *Methods for the Economic Evaluation of Health Care Programmes.* Oxford *et al.*, Oxford University Press.

Durlauf, S. N., Blume, L. E. (eds.) (2008) *The New Palgrave Dictionary of Economics*, 2nd edn. Basingstoke *et al.*, Palgrave Macmillan, http://www.dictionaryofeconomics.com/dictionary.

Düwell, M. (2000) Die Bedeutung ethischer Diskurse in einer wertepluralen Welt. In: Kettner (ed.) (2000), pp. 76–114.

——(2009) Wofür braucht die Medizinethik empirische Methoden? Eine normative-ethische Untersuchung. *Ethik in der Medizin* 21: 201–211.

Düwell, M., Steigleder, K. (2003) Bioethik – Zu Geschichte, Bedeutung und Aufgaben. In: Düwell, M., Steigleder, K. (eds.) *Bioethik: Eine Einführung.* Frankfurt a. M., Suhrkamp, pp. 12–37.

Dworkin, R. (1977/2013) *Taking Rights Seriously.* London *et al.*, Bloomsbury.

——(1978) Liberalism. In: Hampshire, S. (ed.) *Public and Private Morality.* Cambridge *et al.*, Cambridge University Press, pp. 113–143.

Earl, P., Kemp, S. (eds.) (1999) *The Elgar Companion to Consumer Research and Economic Methodology.* Cheltenham/Northampton, Edward Elgar.

Eddy, D. M. (1991) Oregon's methods: did cost-effectiveness analysis fail? *JAMA* 266(15): 2135–2141.

Edlin, R., Tsuchiya, A., Dolan, P. (2012) Public preferences for responsibility versus public preferences for reducing inequalities. *Health Economics* 21(12): 1416–1426.

Ellsberg, D. (1954) Classic and current notions of "measurable" utility. *Economic Journal* 64: 528–556.

Endres, A. M. (1999) Utility theory. In: Earl/Kemp (eds.) (1999), pp. 599–604.

Fehige, C. (2005) In the balance. Review of Jonathan Dancy, Ethics without principles. *The Times Literary Supplement*, 29 April 2005, pp. 12–13.

Fehige, C., Wessels, U. (1998) Preferences – an introduction. In: Fehige, C., Wessels, U. (eds.) *Preferences*. Berlin/New York, de Gruyter, pp. xx-xliii.

Fetter, F. A. (1920) Price economics versus welfare economics. *The American Economic Review* 10(3): 467–487.

Fischhoff, B. (1991) Value elicitation: is there anything there? *American Psychologist* 46(8): 835–847.

Fishburn, P. C. (1989) Retrospective on the utility theory of von Neumann and Morgenstern. *Journal of Risk and Uncertainty* 2: 127–158.

Fisher, I. (1918) Is 'utility' the most suitable term for the concept it is used to denote? *American Economic Review* 8(2) 335–337.

Foot, P. (1985) Morality, action and outcome. In: Honderich, T. (ed.) *Morality and Objectivity: A Tribute to J.L. Mackie*. London/New York *et al.*, Routledge and Kegan Paul, pp. 23–38.

——(1988) Utilitarianism and the virtues. In: Scheffler (ed.) (1988a) pp. 224–242.

Forget, E. L. (2004) Contested histories of an applied field: the case of health economics. *History of Political Economy* 36(3): 617–637.

Friedrich, D. R., Stumpf, S., Alber, K. (2012) Stakeholderpartizipation und Priorisierung – eine Betrachtung des normativen Status quantitativer und qualitativer Methoden. *Zeitschrift für Evidenz, Fortbildung und Qualität im Gesundheitswesen* 106: 412–417.

Frith, L., Young, B., Woolfall, K. (2014) Patient and public participation in health care: can we do better? *The American Journal of Bioethics* 14(6): 17–33.

Fuchs, V. R. (1987) Health economics. In: Eatwell, J., Milgate, M., Newman, P. (eds.) *The New Palgrave: A Dictionary of Economics*, Basingstoke *et al.*, Palgrave Macmillan, http://www.dictionaryofeconomics.com/article?id=pde1987_X001014, August 21, 2014.

Gaertner, W., Schokkaert, E. (2012) *Empirical Social Choice. Questionnaire-Experimental Studies on Distributive Justice*. Cambridge *et al.*, Cambridge University Press.

Garber, A. M., Weinstein, M. C., Torrance, G. W., Kamlet, M. S. (1996) Theoretical foundations of cost-effectiveness analysis. In: Gold *et al.* (eds.) (1996b), pp. 25–53.

George, D. (1996) The rhetoric of economics texts revisited. In: Alsanbeigui, Nahid, Naples, Michele I. (eds.) *Rethinking Economic Principles: Critical Essays on Introductory Textbooks*. Chicago *et al.*, Irwin, pp. 28–43.

German Ethics Council (2011) *Medical Benefits and Costs in Healthcare: The Normative Role of their Evaluation*. Opinion, Berlin.

Gesang, B. (ed.) (2002a) *Biomedizinische Ethik. Aufgaben, Methoden, Selbstverständnis*. Paderborn, Mentis.

——(2002b) Sind Ethiker Moralexperten? Überlegungen zu einer kritischen-rationalen Theorie des Überlegungsgleichgewichts. In: Gesang (ed.) (2002a), pp. 115–136.

Giocoli, N. (2003) *Modeling Rational Agents: From Interwar Economics to Early Modern Game Theory*. Cheltenham/Northampton, Edward Elgar.

Gold, M. R., Patrick, D. L., Torrance, G. W., Fryback, D. G., Hadorn, D. C., Kamlet, M. S., Daniels, N., Weinstein, M. C. (1996a) Identifying and valuing outcomes. In: Gold *et al.* (eds.) (1996b), pp. 82–134.

Gold, M. R., Siegel, J. E., Russell, L. B., Weinstein, M. C. (eds.) (1996b) *Cost-Effectiveness in Health and Medicine*. Oxford *et al.*, Oxford University Press.

Goldenberg, M. (2005) Evidence-based ethics? On evidence-based practice and the "empirical turn" from normative bioethics. *Medical Ethics* 6(11), http://www.biomedcentral.com/1472–6939/6/11, September 10, 2011.

Goodin, R. E. (1986) Laundering preferences. In: Elster, J., Hylland, A. (eds.) *Foundations of Social Choice Theory*. Cambridge *et al.*, Cambridge University Press, pp. 75–101.

Goodwin, C. D. W. (ed.) (1991) *Economics and National Security: A History of their Interaction*. Durham/London, Duke University Press.

——(2008) War and economics. In: Durlauf/Blume (eds.) (2008), http://www.dictionaryofeconomics.com/article?id=pde2008_W000136, April 24, 2014.

Green, C. (2001) On the societal value of health care: what do we know about the person trade-off technique? *Health Economics* 10: 233–243.

——(2007) *Justice, Fairness, and Equity in Health Care: Exploring the Social Value of Health Care Interventions*. Thesis (Ph.D), School of Medicine, University of Southampton.

Green, C., Brazier, J., Deverill, M. (2000) Valuing health-related quality of life: a review of health state valuation techniques. *Pharmacoeconomics* 17(2): 151–165.

Green, C., Gerard, K. (2009) Exploring the social value of health-care interventions: a stated preference discrete choice experiment. *Health Economics* 18: 951–976.

Greiner, W., Damm, O. (2012) Die Berechnung von Kosten und Nutzen. In: Schöffski/Schulenburg (eds.) (2012), pp. 23–42.

Griffin, J. (1986) *Well-being: Its Meaning, Measurement and Moral Importance*. Oxford, Clarendon Press.

——(1995) Consequentialism. In: Honderich, T. (ed.) *The Oxford Companion to Philosophy*. Oxford *et al.*: Oxford University Press, pp. 154–156.

Groenewegen, P. (2003) English marginalism: Jevons, Marshall, and Pigou. In: Samuels *et al.* (eds.) (2003), pp. 246–261.

Güth, W., Kliemt, H. (2013) Behaviorism, optimization and policy advice. Unpublished Manuscript of a Talk held at the Radein Workshop 2013.

Gyrd-Hansen, D. (2013) Using the stated preference technique for eliciting valuations: the role of the payment vehicle. *Pharmacoeconomics* 31: 853–861.

Gyrd-Hansen, D., Kjaer, T., Nielsen, J. S. (2012) Scope insensitivity in contingent valuation studies of health care services: should be ask twice? *Health Economics* 21: 101–112.

Hadorn, D. C. (1991) Setting health care priorities in Oregon: cost-effectiveness meets the rule of rescue. *JAMA* 265(17): 2218–2225.

——(1992) The problem of discrimination in health care priority setting. *JAMA* 268(11): 1454–1459.

Halévy, É. (1946/1965) *The Growth of Philosophic Radicalism,* reproduction of the corrected 2nd edn. (1st edn. 1928). New York, Augustus M. Kelley.

Hands, D. W. (2008) Philosophy and economics. In: Durlauf/Blume (eds.) (2008), http://www.dictionaryofeconomics.com/article?id=pde2008_P000084, July 6, 2012.

——(2010) Economics, psychology, and the history of consumer choice theory. *Cambridge Journal of Economics* 34(4): 633–648.

Haninger, K. M. (2006) *Valuing Health for Public Policy*. Ann Arbour, UMI.

Hansson, S. O. (2007) Philosophical problems in cost-benefit analysis. *Economics and Philosophy* 23: 163–183.

Hargreaves Heap, S. (1992) Rationality. In: Hargreaves Heap, S., Hollis, M., Lyons, B., Sugden, R., Weale, A. (eds.) *The Theory of Choice: A Critical Guide.* Oxford/Cambridge, Blackwell, pp. 3–25.

Harpham, E. J., Scotch, R. K. (1988) Economic discourse, policy analysis, and the problem of the political. In: Portis, E. B., Levy, M. B. (eds.) *Handbook of Political Theory and Policy Science.* New York *et al.*, Greenwood, pp. 216–230.

Harris, John (1985) *The Value of Life. An Introduction to Medical Ethics.* London/New York, Routledge.

——(1987) QALYfying the value of life. *Journal of Medical Ethics* 13: 117–123.

——(1997) The case against (what the principal objective of the NHS should really be). In: New (ed.) (1997), pp. 100–106.

Harris, Jose (1990) Economic knowledge and British social policy. In: Furner, M. O., Supple, B. (eds.) *The State and Economic Knowledge: The American and British Experiences.* Cambridge *et al.*, Woodrow Wilson International Center for Scholars and Cambridge University Press, pp. 379–400.

Harsanyi, J. C. (1953) Cardinal utility in welfare economics and in the theory of risk-taking. *Journal of Political Economy* 61: 434–435.

——(1955) Cardinal welfare, individualistic ethics, and interpersonal comparison of utility. *Journal of Political Economy* 63: 309–321.

Hasman, A. (2003) Eliciting reasons: empirical methods in priority setting. *Health Care Analysis* 11(1): 41–58.

Hausman, D. M. (2000a) Why not just ask? Preferences, 'empirical ethics' and the role of ethical reflection. Draft of 12 October 2000, forthcoming in a WHO volume edited by C. Murray and D. Wikler, http://philosophy.wisc.edu/hausman/papers/Hausman-why-not.pdf, October 14, 2014.

——(2000b) Review of Cost-Value Analysis in Health Care: Making Sense out of QALYs by Erik Nord. *Economics and Philosophy* 16(2) 333–378.

——(2002) The limits to empirical ethics. In: Murray *et al.* (eds.) (2002b), pp. 641–652.

——(ed.) (2008a) *The Philosophy of Economics: An Anthology,* 3rd edn. Cambridge *et al.*, Cambridge University Press.

——(2008b) Introduction. In: Hausman (ed.) (2008a), pp. 1–38.

——(2010) Valuing health: a new proposal. *Health Economics* 19(3): 280–296.

——(2011) Mistakes about preferences in the social sciences. *Philosophy of the Social Sciences* 41(1): 3–25.

——(2012) *Preference, Value, Choice, and Welfare.* Cambridge *et al.*, Cambridge University Press.

——(2013) A reply to Lehtinen, Teschl, and Pattanaik. *Journal of Economic Methodology* 10(2): 219–223.

Hausman, D. M., McPherson, M. S. (2006) *Economic Analysis, Moral Philosophy, and Public Policy,* 2nd edn. Cambridge *et al.*, Cambridge University Press.

——(2008) The philosophical foundations of mainstream normative economics. In: Hausman (ed.) (2008a), pp. 226–269.

——(2009) Preference satisfaction and welfare economics. *Economics and Philosophy* 25: 1–25.

Hausman, J. A. (2012) Contingent valuation: from dubious to hopeless. *Journal of Economic Perspectives* 26(4): 43–56.

Hawthorne, G., Richardson, J. (2001) Measuring the value of program outcomes: a review of multiattribute utility measure. *Expert Review of Pharmacoeconomics and Outcomes Research* 1(2): 215–228.

Heilbroner, R. L. (2000) *The Worldly Philosophers: The Lives, Times and Ideas of the Great Economic Thinkers,* revised 7th edn. London *et al.*, Penguin.

Henderson, W. (1994) Metaphor and economics. In: Backhouse (ed.) (1994), pp. 343–367.

——(1998) Metaphors. In: Davis *et al.* (eds.) (1998), pp. 289–294.

Hicks, John R. (1939) The foundations of welfare economics. *The Economic Journal* 49: 696–712.

——(1941) The rehabilitation of consumers' surplus. *The Review of Economic Studies* 8(2): 108–116.

——(1946) *Value and Capital: An Inquiry into some Fundamental Principles of Economic Theory,* 2nd edn. (1st edn. 1939). Oxford, Clarendon Press.

——(1959) *A Revision of Demand Theory.* Oxford, Clarendon Press.

Hicks, John R., Allen, Roy G.D. (1934) A reconsideration of the theory of value: part I. *Economica* 1: 52–76.

Howey, R. S. (1989) *The Rise of the Marginal Utility School 1870–1889.* New York/ Oxford, Columbia University Press.

Howson, S. (2004) The origins of Lionel Robbins's Essay on the Nature and Significance of Economic Science. *History of Political Economy* 36(3): 413–443.

Hurley, J. (1998) Welfarism, extra-welfarism and evaluative economic analysis in the health care sector. In: Barer *et al.* (eds.) (1998), pp. 373–395.

——(2000) An overview of the normative economics of the health sector. In: Culyer/ Newhouse (eds.) (2000a), pp. 55–118.

Huster, S. (2010) Knappheit und Verteilungsgerechtigkeit im Gesundheitswesen. *Deutsches Verwaltungsblatt* 17: 1069–1077.

——(2011) *Soziale Gesundheitsgerechtigkeit. Sparen, Umverteilen, Vorsorgen?* Berlin, Wagenbach.

Japenga, A. (1987) A transplant for Coby: Oregon's boy death over state decision not to pay for high-risk treatments. *Los Angeles Times,* December 28, 1987, http://articles.latimes.com/1987–12–28/news/vw-21384_1_marrow-transplant, October 18, 2014.

Jevons, W. S. (1911/2006) *The Theory of Political Economy,* reproduction of the 4th edn. (1st edn. 1871). London, Macmillan.

Johannesson, M. (1996) *Theory and Methods of Economic Evaluation of Health Care.* Dordrecht *et al.*, Kluwer.

——(1999) On aggregating QALYs: a comment on Dolan. *Journal of Health Economics* 18: 381–386.

——(2001) Should we aggregate relative or absolute changes in QALYs? *Health Economics* 10: 573–577.

Johannesson, M., Gerdtham, U. G. (1996) A note on the estimation of the equity-efficiency trade-off for QALYs. *Journal of Health Economics* 15: 359–368.

Johri, M., Damschroder, L. J., Zikmund-Fisher, B. J., Ubel, P. A. (2009) Can a moral reasoning exercise improve response quality to surveys of healthcare priorities? *Journal of Medical Ethics* 35: 57–64.

Jones, A. M. (ed.) (2006) *The Elgar Companion to Health Economics.* Cheltenham/ Northampton, Edward Elgar.

——(ed.) (2012) *The Elgar Companion to Health Economics,* 2nd edn. Cheltenham/ Northampton, Edward Elgar.

Jorgensen, B. S., Syme, G. J., Bishop, B. J., Nancarrow, B. E. (1999) Protest responses in contingent valuation. *Environmental and Resource Economics* 14: 131–150.

Kahneman, D. (1986) Comments on the contingent valuation method. In: Cummings, R. G., Brookshire, D. S., Schulze, W. D. (eds.) *Valuing Environmental Goods: An*

Assessment of the Contingent Valuation Method. Totowa/New Jersey, Rowman & Allanheld, pp. 185–194.

——(2011) *Thinking, Fast and Slow.* London/New York *et al.*, Penguin.

Kahneman, D., Knetsch, J. L. (1992) Valuing public goods: the purchase of moral satisfaction. *Journal of Environmental Economics and Management* 22: 57–70.

Kahneman, D., Ritov, I., Jacowitz, K. E., Grant, P. (1993) Stated willingness to pay for public goods: a psychological perspective. *Psychological Science* 4(5): 310–315.

Kaldor, N. (1939) Welfare propositions of economics and interpersonal comparisons of utility. *The Economic Journal* 49: 549–552.

——(1940/1968) A note on tariffs and the terms of trade. In: Page (1968) (ed.), pp. 384–387.

Kaminsky, C. (2002) Was ist angewandte Ethik? In: Gesang (ed.) (2002a), pp. 29–61.

Kaplan, R. M. (1992) A quality-of-life approach to health resource allocation. In: Strosberg, M. A., Wiener, J. M., Baker, R., Fein, A. (eds.) *Rationing America's Medical Care: The Oregon Plan and Beyond.* Washington D.C., The Brookings Institution, pp. 60–77.

Kaplan, R. M., Anderson, J. P. (1988) A general health policy model: update and applications. *Health Services Research* 23(2): 203–235.

Keaney, M. (2001) Proletarianizing the professionals: the populist assault on discretionary autonomy. In: Davis (ed.) (2001), pp. 141–171.

Kelleher, J. P. (2014) Efficiency and equity in health: philosophical considerations. In: Culyer (ed.) (2014), pp. 259–266.

Kelley, J. L. (1997) *Bringing the Market Back In: The Political Revitalization of Market Liberalism.* Basingstoke, Macmillan.

Kettner, M. (ed.) (2000) *Angewandte Ethik als Politikum.* Frankfurt a. M., Suhrkamp.

Keynes, J. M. (1923) *A Tract on Monetary Reform.* London, Macmillan.

——(1936/1964) *General Theory of Employment, Interest and Money.* London, Macmillan.

Klamer, A., McCloskey, D., Solow, R. (eds.) (1988) *The Consequences of Economic Rhetoric.* Cambridge *et al.*, Cambridge University Press.

Kliemt, H. (2009) *Philosophy and Economics I: Methods and Models.* München, Oldenbourg.

Kling, C. L., Phaneuf, D. J., Zhao, J. (2012) From Exxon to BP: has some number become better than no number? *Journal of Economic Perspectives* 26(4): 3–26.

Klonschinski, A. (2013) Das Kosten-Nutzen Verhältnis als Priorisierungskriterium? Eine philosophisch-dogmenhistorische Betrachtung des ökonomischen Paradigmas der Wertmaximierung. In: Schmitz-Luhn/Bohmeier (eds.) (2013), pp. 79–107.

——(2014) 'Economic imperialism' in health care resource allocation – how can equity considerations be incorporated in cost-utility analysis? *Journal of Economic Methodology* 21(2): 158–174.

Klonschinski, A., Lübbe, W. (2011) QALYs und Gerechtigkeit: Ansätze und Probleme einer gesundheitsökonomischen Lösung der Fairnessproblematik. *Das Gesundheitswesen* 73: 688–695.

Knetsch, J. L. (1994) Environmental evaluations: some problems of wrong questions and misleading answers. *Environmental Values* 3: 351–368.

Koslow, S. (1999) Conjoint analysis. In: Earl/Kemp (eds.) (1999), pp. 99–106.

Lagueux, M. (1999) Do metaphors affect economic theory? *Economics and Philosophy* 15: 1–22.

Lakoff, G., Johnson, M. (2003) *Metaphors we Live by.* Chicago/London, University of Chicago Press.

Lancaster, K. (1966) A new approach to consumer theory. *Journal of Political Economy* 74: 132–157.

Lancsar, E., Wildman, J., Donaldson, C., Ryan, M., Baker, R. (2011) Deriving distributional weights for QALYs through discrete choice experiments. *Journal of Health Economics* 30: 466–478.

Lancsar, E., Louviere, J. (2006) Deleting 'irrational' responses from discrete choice experiments: a case of investigating or imposing preferences? *Health Economics* 15: 797–811.

Le Grand, J. (1990) Equity versus efficiency: the elusive trade-off. *Ethics* 100: 554–568.

Lehtinen, A. (2013) Preferences as total subjective comparative evaluations. *Journal of Economic Methodology* 10(2): 206–210.

Lengahan, J. (1999) Involving the public in rationing decisions: the experience of citizen juries. *Health Policy* 49: 45–61.

Leonard, R. J. (1991) War as a "simple economic problem". In: Goodwin (ed.) (1991), pp. 261–283.

Levitt, M. (2003) Public consultation in bioethics. What's the point of asking the public if they have neither scientific nor ethical expertise? *Health Care Analysis* 11 (19): 15–25.

Little, I. M. D. (1957) *A Critique of Welfare Economics,* 2nd edn. Oxford, Clarendon Press.

Lloyd, A. J. (2003) Threats to the estimation of benefits: are preference elicitation methods accurate? *Health Economics* 12: 393–402.

Lomas, J. (1997) Reluctant rationers: public input to health care priorities. *Journal of Health Services Research and Policy* 2(2): 103–111.

Louise, J. (2004) Relativity of value and the consequentialist umbrella. *The Philosophical Quarterly* 54: 518–536.

Louviere, J. J. (2001) Choice experiments: an overview of concepts and issues. In: Bennett/Blamey (eds.) (2001a), pp. 13–36.

Lukes, S. (1996) On trade-offs between values. In: Farina, F., Hahn, F., Vannucci, S. (eds.) *Ethics, Rationality, and Economic Behaviour*. Oxford, Clarendon Press, pp. 36–49.

Lübbe, W. (2005) Wirtschaftlichkeit und Gerechtigkeit: Zwei ethische Gebote? Eine Grundlagenreflexion. *Das Gesundheitswesen* 67: 325–331.

——(2008) Taurek's no worse claim. *Philosophy and Public Affairs* 36(1): 69–85.

——(2009a) The aggregation argument in the numbers debate. In: Fehige, C., Lumer, C., Wessels, U. (eds.) *Handeln mit Bedeutung und Handeln mit Gewalt: Philosophische Aufsätze für Georg Meggle*. Paderborn, Mentis, pp. 406–421.

——(2009b) Aggregation in health resource allocation. Unpublished manuscript presented at the conference "Ethical issues in the prioritization of health resources", Harvard University, Boston, 24 April 2009, http://peh.harvard.edu/events/2009/priority_resources/day_2/weyma_lubbe_paper.pdf, October 10, 2014.

——(2009c) Postutilitarismus in der Priorisierungsdebatte. *Zeitschrift für Evidenz, Fortbildung und Qualität im Gesundheitswesen* 103: 99–103.

——(2009d) "Aus Ökonomischer Sicht . . . " – Was ist der normative Anspruch gesundheitsökonomischer Evaluationen? In: Baurmann, M., Lahno, B. (eds.) *Perspectives in Moral Science. Contributions from Philosophy, Economics, and Politics in Honour of Hartmut Kliemt*. Frankfurt a. M., Frankfurt School Verlag, pp. 451–463.

——(2010a) Sollte sich das IQWiG auf indikationsübergreifende Kosten-Nutzen-Bewertungen einlassen? (Should IQWiG revise its cost-effectiveness analysis in order to comply with more widely accepted health economical evaluation standards?) *Deutsche Medizinische Wochenschrift* 135: 582–585.

——(2010b) Medizinische Ressourcenallokation und die Produktivität der Volkswirtschaft. *Zeitschrift für Wirtschaftspolitik* 59(3): 275–283.

——(2010c) QALYs, Zahlungsbereitschaft und implizite Lebenswerturteile. In welchen Kategorien begreifen wir das Gesundheitswesen? *Zeitschrift für Evidenz, Fortbildung und Qualität im Gesundheitswesen* 104: 196–204.

——(2011) Dissenting opinion. In: German Ethics Council (2011), pp. 96–121.

——(2013) Kein empirischer Weg zu Priorisierungstabellen. Kritische Anmerkungen zur Idee, "Bewertungsdimensionen" im Rückgriff auf "Stakeholder-Präferenzen" zu gewichten. In: Schmitz-Luhn/Bohmeier (eds.) (2013), pp. 245–256.

——(2015) *Nonaggregationismus: Grundlagen der Allokationsethik*. Münster: Mentis.

Maas, H. (2005) *William Stanley Jevons and the Making of Modern Economics*. Cambridge *et al.*, Cambridge University Press.

Mandler, M. (1999) *Dilemmas in Economic Theory: Persisting Foundational Problems of Microeconomics*. Oxford *et al.*, Oxford University Press.

——(2001) A difficult choice in preference theory: rationality implies completeness or transitivity but not both. In: Milgram, E. (ed.) *Varieties in Practical Reasoning*. Cambridge/London, MIT Press, pp. 373–402.

Mankiw, N. G., Taylor, M. P. (2014) *Economics*. Andover, South-Western Cengage Learning.

Marckmann, G., Siebert, U. (2002a) Prioritäten in der Gesundheitsversorgung: Was können wir aus dem "Oregon Health Plan" lernen? *Deutsche Medizinische Wochenschrift* 127: 1601–1604.

——(2002b) Kosteneffektivität als Allokationskriterium in der Gesundheitsversorgung. *Zeitschrift für Medizinische Ethik* 48: 171–189.

Mas-Colell, A,, Whinston, M. D., Green, J. R. (1995) *Microeconomic Theory*. Oxford *et al.*, Oxford University Press.

McCloskey, Deirdre (1992) *If You're so Smart. The Narrative of Economic Expertise*. Chicago/London, University of Chicago Press.

——(1998) *The Rhetoric of Economics*, 2nd edn. Madison: University of Wisconsin Press.

McCloskey, Donald (1994) How to do a rhetorical analysis, and why. In: Backhouse (ed.) (1994), pp. 319–342.

McGregor, M., Cato, J. J. (2006) QALYs: are they helpful to decision makers? *Pharmacoeconomics* 24(10): 947–952.

McGuire, A. (2001) Theoretical concepts in the economic evaluation of health care. In: Drummond/McGuire (eds.) (2001), pp. 1–21.

McKie, J., Richardson, J. (2005a) Neglected equity issues in cost effectiveness analysis – part 1: severity of pre-treatment condition, realisation of potential for health, concentration and dispersion of health benefits and age related social preferences. Research Paper 7, Centre of Health Economics, Monash University, Melbourne, http://www.buseco.monash.edu.au/centres/che/pubs/rp7.pdf, October 15, 2014.

——(2005b) Neglected equity issues in cost effectiveness analysis – part 2: direct and indirect costs, the preservation of hope, the rule of rescue, patient adaption, and the ex ante/ex post distinction. Research Paper 8, Centre of Health Economics, Monash University, Melbourne, http://www.buseco.monash.edu.au/centres/che/pubs/rp8.pdf, October 15, 2014.

McKie, J., Shimpton, B., Richardson, J., Hurworth, R. (2011) The monetary value of a life year: evidence from a qualitative study of treatment costs. *Health Economics* 20: 945–957.

McMaster, R. (2001) The National Health Service, the 'internal market' and trust. In: Davis (ed.) (2001), pp. 113–140.

——(2007) On the need for heterodox health economics. *Post-Autistic Economics Review* 41: 9–22.

McPherson, C. B. (1987) *The Rise and Fall of Economic Justice.* Oxford *et al.*, Oxford University Press.

Menzel, P. (1990) *Strong Medicine: The Ethical Rationing of Health Care.* Oxford *et al.*, Oxford University Press.

——(1992) Oregon's denial: disabilities and the quality of life. *Hastings Center Report* 22(6): 21–25.

——(1999) How should what economists call "social values" be measured? *The Journal of Ethics* 3: 249–273.

Menzel, P., Gold, M. R., Nord, E., Pinto-Prades, J. L., Richardson, J., Ubel, P. A. (1999) Toward a broader view of values in cost-effectiveness analysis of health. *Hastings Center Report* 29(3): 7–15.

Mill, J. S. (1871a/1965) *Principles of Political Economy with some of their Applications to Social Philosophy,* reprint of the 7th edn. (1st edn. 1748). New York, Augustus M. Kelley.

——(1871b/2002) Utilitarianism, reprint of the 4th edn. (1st edn. 1863). In: *The Basic Writings of John Stuart Mull. On Liberty, the Subjection of Women, and Utilitarianism.* New York, The Modern Library.

Mirowski, P. (1988) Shall I compare thee to a Minkowski-Ricardo-Leontief-Metzler matrix of the Mosak-Hicks type? Or, rhetoric, mathematics, and the nature of neoclassical economic theory In: Klamer *et al.* (eds.) (1988), pp. 117–145.

——(1989) *More Heat than light. Economics as Social Physics, Physics as Nature's Economics.* Cambridge *et al.*, Cambridge University Press.

——(1991) When games grow deadly serious. In: Goodwin (ed.) (1991), pp. 227–255.

——(2006) Twelve theses concerning the history of postwar neoclassical price theory. In: Mirowski/Hands (eds.) (2006a), pp. 343–379.

Mirowski, P., Hands, D. W. (1998) A paradox of budgets: the postwar stabilization of American neoclassical demand theory. In: Morgan/Rutherford (eds.) (1998a), pp. 260–292.

——(eds.) (2006a) *Agreement on Demand: Consumer Theory in the Twentieth Century.* Durham/London, Duke University Press.

——(2006b) Introduction. In: Mirowski/Hands (eds.) (2006a), pp. 1–6.

Mishan, E. J. (1972) *Elements of Cost-Benefit Analysis.* London, Allen & Unwin.

——(1975) *Cost-Benefit Analysis: An Informal Introduction,* revised new edn. London, Allen & Unwin.

Mitchell, R. C., Carson, R. T. (1989) *Using Surveys to Value Public Goods: The Contingent Valuation Method.* Washington D.C., Resources for the Future.

Mitchell, W. C. (1918/1968) Bentham's felicific calculus. In: Page (ed.) (1968), pp. 30–48.

Mongin, P., D'Aspremont, C. (1999) Utility theory and ethics. In: Barbera, S., Hammond, P., Seidl, C. (eds.) *Handbook of Utility Theory Vol. 1.* Boston, Kluwer, pp. 371–481.

Mooney, G. (2009) *Challenging Health Economics.* Oxford *et al.*, Oxford University Press.

Moran, M., Rein, M., Goodin, R. E. (eds.) (2006) *Oxford Handbook of Public Policy.* Oxford *et al.*, Oxford University Press.

Morgan, M. S. (2003) Economics. In: Porter/Ross (eds.) (2003), pp. 275–305.

Morgan, M. S., Rutherford, M. (eds.) (1998a) *From Interwar Pluralism to Postwar Neoclassicism.* Durham/London, Duke University Press.

——(1998b) American economics: the character of the transformation. In: Morgan/Rutherford (eds.) (1998a), pp. 1–26.

Mortimer, D. (2005) On the relevance of personal characteristics in setting health priorities: a comment on Olsen, Richardson, Dolan, and Menzel (2003). *Social Science and Medicine* 60: 1661–1664.

Mullen, C. (2008) Representation or reason: consulting the public on the ethics of health policy. *Health Care Analysis* 16(4): 397–409.

Murphy, N. J. (2005) Citizen deliberation in setting health-care priorities. *Health Expectations* 8: 172–181.

Murray, C. J. L. (1994) Quantifying the burden of disease: the technical basis for disability-adjusted life years. *Bulletin of the World Health Organization* 72(3): 429–445.

——(1996) Rethinking DALYs. In: Murray, C. J. L., Lopez, A. D. (eds.) *The Global Burden of Disease. A Comprehensive Assessment of Mortality and Disability from Diseases, Injuries, and Risk Factors in 1990 and Projected to 2020.* Cambridge, Harvard University Press, pp. 1–89.

Murray, C. J. L., Acharya, A. K. (1997) Understanding DALYs. *Journal of Health Economics* 16: 703–730.

Murray, C. J. L., Ezzati, M., Flaxman, A. D., Lim, S., Lozano, R., Michaud, C., Naghavi, M., Salomon, J. A., Shibuya, K., Vos, T., Wikler, D., Lopez, A. D. (2012) GBD 2010: design, definitions, and metrics. *The Lancet* 380(9859): 2063–2066.

Murray, C. J. L., Salomon, J. A., Mathers, C. D. (2002a): A critical examination of summary measures of population health. In: Murray et al (eds.) (2002b), pp. 13–40.

Murray, C. J. L., Salomon, J. A., Mathers, C. D., Lopez, A. D. (eds.) (2002b) *Summary Measures of Population Health: Concepts, Ethics, Measurement, and Application.* Geneva, WHO.

Musschenga, A. W. (2005) Empirical ethics, context-sensitivity, and contextualism. *Journal of Medicine and Philosophy* 30: 467–490.

Nagel, T. (1979) *Mortal Questions.* Cambridge *et al.*, Cambridge University Press.

——(1986) *The View from Nowhere.* Oxford *et al.*, Oxford University Press.

Nelson, P. (1999) Multiattribute utility models. In: Earl/Kemp (eds.) (1999), pp. 392–400.

Neumann, P. J., Weinstein, M. C. (2010) Legislating against use of cost-effectiveness information. *The New England Journal of Medicine* 363(16): 1495–1497.

New, B. (ed.) (1997) *Rationing: Talk and Action in Health Care.* London, King's Fund.

NICE (2008) *Social Value Judgements. Principles for the Development of NICE Guidance,* 2nd edn, http://www.nice.org.uk/aboutnice/howwework/socialvaluejudgements/socialvaluejudgements.jsp, March 11, 2014.

Nord, E. (1991) The validity of a visual analogue scale in determining social utility weights for health care states. *International Journal of Health Planning and Management* 6: 234–242.

——(1993a) Unjustified use of the quality of well-being scale in priority setting in Oregon. *Health Policy* 24: 45–53.

——(1993b) The trade-off between severity of illness and treatment effect in cost-value analysis of health care. *Health Policy* 24: 227–238.

——(1993c) The relevance of health state after treatment in prioritising between different patients. *Journal of Medical Ethics* 19: 37–42.

——(1994) The QALY – a measure of social value rather than individual utility? *Health Economics* 3: 89–93.

——(1995) The person-trade-off approach to valuing health care programs. *Medical Decision Making* 15: 201–208.

——(1999a) *Cost-Value-Analysis in Health Care: Making Sense out of QALYS.* Cambridge *et al.*, Cambridge University Press.

——(1999b) My goodness – and yours: a history, and some possible futures, of DALY meanings and valuation procedures. Paper for WHO's Global Conference on Summary Measures of Population Health, Marrakech, 6–9 December 1999.

——(2001) The desirability of a condition versus the well being and the worth of a person. *Health Economics* 10: 579–581.

——(2005) Concerns for the worse off: fair innings versus severity. *Social Science and Medicine* 60: 257–263.

——(2014) Cost-value analysis. In: Culyer (ed.) (2014), pp. 139–142.

Nord, E., Daniels, N., Kamlet, M. (2009) QALYs: some challenges. *Value in Health* 1, supplement 1: S10-S15.

Nord, E., Menzel, P., Richardson, J. (2003) The value of life: individual preferences and social choice. A comment to Magnus Johannesson. *Health Economics* 12: 873–877.

Nord, E., Pinto-Prades, J. L., Richardson, J., Menzel, P., Ubel, P. A. (1999) Incorporating societal concerns for fairness in numerical valuations of health programmes. *Health Economics* 8: 25–39.

Nord, E., Richardson, J., Street, A., Kuhse, H., Singer, P. (1995a) Maximizing health benefits vs. egalitarianism: an Australian survey of health issues. *Social Science and Medicine* 41: 1429–1437.

——(1995b) Who cares about costs? Does economic analysis impose or reflect values? *Health Policy* 34: 79–94.

——(1996) The significance of age and duration of effect in social evaluation of health care. *Health Care Analysis* 4: 103–111.

Norman, R., Hall, J., Street, D., Viney, R. (2013) Efficiency and equity: a stated preference approach. *Health Economics* 22(5): 568–581.

Nygaard, E. (2000) Is it feasible or desirable to measure burdens of disease as a single number? *Reproductive Health Matters* 8(15): 117–125.

Oberlander, J., Marmor, T., Jacobs, L. (2001) Rationing medical care: rhetoric and reality in the Oregon Health Plan. *Canadian Medical Association Journal* 164(11): 1583–1587.

Okun, A. (1975) *Equality and Efficiency: The Big Trade-Off.* Washington D.C., Brookings Inst.

Oliver, A. (2004) Prioritizing health care: is "health" always an appropriate maximand? *Medical Decision Making* 24: 272–280.

Olsen, J. A. (1994) Persons vs years: two ways of eliciting implicit weights. *Health Economics* 3: 39–46.

——(1997a) Aiding priority-setting in health care: is there a role for the contingent valuation method? *Health Economics* 6: 603–612.

——(1997b) Theories of justice and their implications for priority setting in health care. *Journal of Health Economics* 16: 625–639.

——(2000) A note on eliciting distributive preferences for health. *Journal of Health Economics* 19: 541–550.

Olsen, J. A., Donaldson, C. (1998) Helicopters, hearts and hips: using willingness to pay to set priorities for public sector health care programmes. *Social Science and Medicine* 46(1): 1–12.

Olsen, J. A., Donaldson, C., Pereira, J. (2004) The insensitivity of 'willingness-to-pay' to the size of the good: new evidence for health care. *Journal of Economic Psychology* 25: 445–460.

Olsen, J. A., Richardson, J., Dolan, P., Menzel, P. (2003) The moral relevance of personal characteristics in setting health care priorities. *Social Science and Medicine* 57: 1163–1172.

Olsen, J. A., Smith, R. D. (2001) Theory versus practice: a review of 'willingness to pay' in health and health care. *Health Economics* 10: 39–52.

Orlans, H. (1986) Academic social scientists and the presidency: from Wilson to Nixon. *Minerva* 24: 172–204.

Osberg, L. (1995) The equity/efficiency trade-off in retrospect. Revised version of keynote address to the Conference on Economic Growth and Inequality, Laurentian University, Sudbury, Ontario, March 17, 1995, http://myweb.dal.ca/osberg/classification/articles/academic%20journals/EQUITYEFFICIENCY/EQUITY%20EFFICIENCY.pdf, October 23, 2014.

Page, A. N. (ed.) (1968) *Utility Theory: A Book of Readings.* New York/London *et al.*, John Wiley & Sons.

Pareto, V. (1927/1971) *Manual of Political Economy,* translation of the French edn. of 1927 (1st edn. 1906). London/Basingstoke, Macmillan.

Pattanaik, P. K. (2008) Social welfare function. In: Durlauf/Blume (eds.) (2008), http://www.dictionaryofeconomics.com/article?id=pde2008_S000172, February 19, 2014.

——(2013) The concepts of choice and preference in economics. *Journal of Economic Methodology* 10(2): 215–218.

Peart, S. (1996) *The Economics of W. S. Jevons.* London/New York, Routledge.

Pettit, P. (1991) Consequentialism. In: Singer, P. (ed.) *A Companion to Ethics.* Oxford *et al.*, Blackwell Reference, pp. 230–240.

Pigou, A. C. (1932/1962) *The Economics of Welfare,* reprint of the 4th edn. (1st edn. 1920). London, Macmillan.

Porter, T. M. (1992) Objectivity as standardization: the rhetoric of impersonality in measurement, statistics, and cost-benefit analysis. *Annals of Scholarship* 9: 19–59.

——(1996) *Trust in Numbers: The Pursuit of Objectivity in Science and Public Life.* Princeton, Princeton University Press.

Porter, T. M, Ross, D. (eds.) (2003) *The Cambridge History of Science. Vol. 7: The Modern Social Sciences.* Cambridge *et al.*, Cambridge University Press.

Portmore, D. (2007) Consequentializing moral theories. *Pacific Philosophical Quarterly* 88: 39–73.

Portney, P. R. (1994) The contingent valuation debate: why economists should care. *Journal of Economic Perspectives* 8(4): 3–17.

Powers, M., Faden, R. (2006) *Social Justice: The Moral Foundations of Public Health and Health Policy.* Oxford *et al.*, Oxford University Press.

Pressman, S. (2005) Income guarantees and the equity-efficiency tradeoff. *Journal of Socio-Economics* 34(1): 83–100.

Price, D. (2000) Choices without reasons: citizen's juries and policy evaluation. *Journal of Medical Ethics* 26: 272–276.

Quiggin, J. (1999) Utility. In: Earl/Kemp (eds.) (1999), pp. 590–594.

Rabin, M. (1998) Economics and psychology. *Journal of Economic Literature* 36: 11–46.

Rauprich, O., Marckmann, G., Vollmann, J. (eds.) (2005) *Gleichheit und Gerechtigkeit in der modernen Medizin.* Paderborn, Mentis.

Rawlins, M. D., Culyer, A. J. (2004) National Institute for Clinical Excellence and its value judgments. *BMJ* 329: 224–227.

Rawls, J. (1971/2005) *A Theory of Justice,* reprint of the original edn. Cambridge *et al.*, Harvard University Press.

Reinhardt, U. E. (1992) Reflections on the meaning of efficiency: can efficiency be separated from equity? *Yale Law and Policy Review* 10: 302–315.

——(1998) Abstracting from distributional effects, this policy is efficient. In: Barer *et al.* (eds.) (1998), pp. 1–47.

Richardson, J. (1994) Cost utility analysis: what should be measured? *Social Science and Medicine* 39(1): 7–21.

——(2002) The poverty of ethical analyses in economics and the unwarranted disregard of evidence. In: Murray *et al.* (eds.) (2002b), pp. 627–640.

——(2009) Is the incorporation of equity considerations into economic evaluation really so simple? A comment on Cookson, Drummond and Weatherly. *Health Economics, Policy and Law* 4: 247–254.

Richardson, J., Iezzi, A., Sinha, K., Khan, M. A., McKie, J. (2014) An instrument for measuring the social willingness to pay for health state improvement. *Health Economics* 23: 792–805.

Richardson, J., McKie, J. (2005) Empiricism, ethics and orthodox economic theory: what is the appropriate basis for decision-making in the health sector? *Social Science and Medicine* 60: 265–275.

——(2007) Economic evaluation in the context of a national health scheme: the case for an equity-based framework. *Journal of Health Economics* 26(4): 785–799.

Richardson, J., McKie, J., Olsen, J. A. (2005) Welfarism or non-welfarism? Public preferences for willingness to pay versus health maximisation. Research Paper 10, Centre for Health Economics, Monash University, Melbourne, http://www.buseco.monash.edu.au/centres/che/pubs/rp10.pdf, October 14, 2014.

Richardson, J., McKie, J., Peacock, S. J., Iezzi, A. (2011) Severity as an independent determinant of the social value of a health service. *European Journal of Health Economics* 12: 163–174.

Richardson, J., Sinsha, K., Iezzi, A. (2010) Measuring the importance of efficiency in the equity-efficiency trade-off. Research Paper 65, Centre for Health Economics, Monash University, Melbourne, http://www.buseco.monash.edu.au/centres/che/pubs/researchpaper65.pdf, October 14, 2014.

Riley, J. (2008) Utilitarianism and economic theory. In: Durlauf/Blume (eds.) (2008), http://www.dictionaryofeconomics.com/article?id=pde2008_U000073, October 8, 2012.

Rippe, K. P. (2000) Ethikkommissionen in der deliberativen Demokratie. In: Kettner (ed.) (2000), pp.140–164.

Robbins, L. (1934) Remarks on the relationship between economics and psychology. *The Manchester School* 5(2): 89–101.

——(1935) *Essay on the Nature and Significance of Economic Science,* 2nd edn. London: Macmillan.

——(1938a) Interpersonal comparisons of utility: a comment. *The Economic Journal* 48(192): 635–641.

——(1938b) Live and dead issues in the methodology of economics. *Economica* 5(18): 342–352.

——(1952) *The Theory of Economic Policy in English Classical Political Economy.* London: Macmillan.

Robertson, D. H. (1954) *Utility and All That.* In: Robertson, D. H. *Utility and All That and Other Essays.* New York, Augustus M. Kelley, pp. 13–41.

Robinson, S. (2011) Test-retest reliability of health state valuation techniques: the time trade off and person trade off. *Health Economics* 20: 1379–1391.

Robinson, S., Bryan, S. (2013) Does the process of deliberation change individuals' health state valuations? An exploratory study using the person trade-off technique. *Value in Health* 16: 806–813.

Runtenberg, C., Ach, J. S. (2002) Bioethik zwischen Disziplin und Diskurs. In: Gesang (ed.) (2002a), pp. 15–28.

Russell, L. B., Siegel, J. E., Daniels, N., Gold, M. R., Luce, B. R., Mandelblatt, J. S. (1996) Cost-effectiveness analysis as a guide to resource allocation in health: roles and limitations. In: Gold *et al.* (eds.) (1996b), pp. 3–24.

Ryan, M., Bate, A. (2001) Testing the assumptions of rationality, continuity and symmetry when applying discrete choice experiments in health care. *Applied Economic Letters* 8: 59–63.

Ryan, M., Gerard, K. (2003) Using discrete choice experiments to value health care programs: current practice and future research reflections. *Applied Health Economics and Health Policy* 2(1): 55–64.

Ryan, M., Gerard, K., Currie, G. (2006) Using discrete choice experiments in health economics. In: Jones (ed.) (2006), pp. 405–414.

Sagoff, M. (1986) Values and Preferences. *Ethics* 96(2): 301–316.

——(1988) Some problems with environmental economics. *Environmental Ethics* 10: 55–74.

——(2004) *Price, Principle, and the Environment.* Cambridge *et al.*, Cambridge University Press.

Salomon, J. A., Vos, T., Hogan, D. R. *et al.* (2012) Common values in assessing health outcomes from disease and injury: disability weights measurement study for the Global Burden of Disease Study 2010. *The Lancet* 380(9859): 2129–2143.

Samuels, W. J., Biddle, J. E., Davis, J. B. (eds.) (2003) *A Companion to the History of Economic Thought.* Malden/Oxford *et al.*, Blackwell.

Samuelson, P. A. (1938) A note on the pure theory of consumer's behaviour. *Economica* 5(17): 61–71.

——(1947) *Foundations of Economic Analysis.* Cambridge, Harvard University Press.

——(1948/1968) Consumption theory in terms of revealed preferences. In: Page (ed.) (1968), pp. 149–157.

Sassi, F., Archard, L., Le Grand, J. (2001) Equity and the economic evaluation of health care. *Health Technology Assessment* 5(3).

Satz, D. (2010) *Why Some Things should not be for Sale: The Moral Limits of the Market.* Oxford *et al.*, Oxford University Press.

Scanlon, Thomas M. (1982) Contractualism and utilitarianism. In: Sen/Williams (eds.) (1982a), pp. 103–128.

——(1988) Rights, goals and fairness. In: Scheffler (ed.) (1988a), pp. 74–92.

——(1998) *What We Owe to Each Other.* Cambridge/London, Belknap Harvard.

——(2000) The aims and authority of moral theory. *Oxford Journal of Legal Studies* 12(1): 1–23.

——(2001) Symposium on Amartya Sen's philosophy: 3. Sen and consequentialism. *Economics and Philosophy* 17: 39–50.

Scarantino, A. (2009) On the role of values in economic science: Robbins and his critics. *Journal of the History of Economic Thought* 31(4): 449–473.

Schabas, M. (1990) *A World Ruled by Number: William Stanley Jevons and the Rise of Mathematical Economics.* Oxford *et al.*, Princeton University Press.

——(1998) William Stanley Jevons. In: Davis *et al.* (eds.) (1998), pp. 260–261.

——(2003a) From political economy to positive economics. In: Baldwin, T. (ed.) *The Cambridge History of Philosophy* 1870–1945. Cambridge *et al.*, Cambridge University Press, pp. 235–244.

——(2003b) British economic theory from Locke to Marshall. In: Porter/Ross (eds.) (2003), pp. 171–182.

——(2007) *The Natural Origins of Economics.* Chicago/London: University of Chicago Press.

Schefczyk, M., Priddat, B. P. (2000) Effizienz und Gerechtigkeit. Eine Verhältnisbestimmung in sozialpolitischer Absicht. In: Kersting, W. (ed.) *Politische Philosophie des Sozialstaats.* Weilerwist, Velbrück, pp. 428–466.

Scheffler, S. (ed.) (1988a) *Consequentialism and its Critics.* Oxford *et al.*, Oxford University Press.

——(1988b) Introduction. In: Scheffler (ed.) (1988a), pp. 1–13.

——(1988c) Agent-centered restrictions, rationality and the virtues. In: Scheffler (ed.) (1988a), pp. 243–260.

Schicktanz, S. (2009) Zum Stellenwert von Betroffenheit, Öffentlichkeit und Deliberation im Empirical Turn der Medizinethik. *Ethik in der Medizin* 21: 223–234.

Schicktanz, S., Schweda, M. (2009) "One man's trash is another man's treasure": exploring economic and moral subtexts of the "organ shortage" problem in public views on organ donation. *Journal of Medical Ethics* 35: 473–478.

Schicktanz, S., Schweda, M., Wynne, B. (2012) The ethics of 'public understanding of ethics' – why and how bioethics expertise should include public and patients' voices. *Medicine, Health Care and Philosophy* 15: 129–139.

Schkade, D. A., Payne, J. W. (1994) How people respond to contingent valuation questions: a verbal protocol analysis of willingness to pay for an environmental regulation. *Journal of Environmental Economics and Management* 26: 88–109.

Schlander, M. (2005) Kosteneffektivität und Ressourcenallokation: gibt es einen normativen Anspruch der Gesundheitsökonomie? In: Kick, Hermes Andreas, Taupitz, J. (eds.) *Gesundheitswesen zwischen Wirtschaftlichkeit und Menschlichkeit.* Münster, LIT-Verlag, pp. 37–11.

——(2007) The use of cost-effectiveness by the National Institute for Health and Clinical Excellence (NICE) No(t yet an) exemplar of a deliberative process. *Journal of Medical Ethics* 34: 534–539.

——(2009) Gesundheitsökonomie: der Effizienz auf der Spur. *Zeitschrift für Evidenz, Fortbildung und Qualität im Gesundheitswesen* 103: 117–125.

Schmidt, V. (1994) Some equity-efficiency trade-offs in the provision of scarce goods: the case of lifesaving medical resources. *The Journal of Political Philosophy* 2(1): 44–66.

Schmitz-Luhn, B., Bohmeier, A. (eds.) (2013) *Priorisierung in der Medizin: Kriterien im Dialog.* Berlin/Heidelberg, Springer.

Schoemaker, P. J. H. (1982) The expected utility model: its variants, purposes, evidence and limitations. *Journal of Economic Literature* 20(2): 529–563.

Schofield, P. (2008) Jeremy Bentham. In: Durlauf/Blume (eds.) (2008), http://www.dictionaryofeconomics.com/article?id=pde2008_B000109, September 19, 2012.

Schöffski, O. (2012a) Introduction. In: Schöffski/Schulenburg (eds.) (2012), pp. 3–12.

——(2012b) Grundformen Gesundheitsökonomischer Evaluationen. In: Schöffski/Schulenburg (eds.) (2012), pp. 43–70.

——(2012c) Nutzentheoretische Lebensqualitätsmessung. In: Schöffski/Schulenburg (eds.) (2012a), pp. 341–392.

Schöffski, O., Greiner, W. (2012) Das QALY-Konzept als prominentester Vertreter der Kosten-Nutzenwert-Analyse. In: Schöffski/Schulenburg (eds.) (2012), pp. 71–110.

Schöffski, O., Schulenburg, J.-M. Graf v. d. (eds.) (2012) *Gesundheitsökonomische Evaluationen,* 4th revised edn. Berlin/Heidelberg, Springer.

Schroeder, M. (2007) Teleology, agent-relative value, and 'good'. *Ethics* 117: 265–295.

Schroth, J. (2008) Distributive justice and welfarism in utilitarianism. *Inquiry* 51(2): 123–146.

Schulenburg, J.-M. Graf v. d. (2012) Die Entwicklung der Gesundheitsökonomie und ihre methodischen Ansätze. In: Schöffski/Schulenburg (eds.) (2012), pp. 13–21.

Schulenburg, J.-M. Graf v. d., Greiner, W., Jost, F., Klusen, N., Leidl, R., Mittendorf, T., Rebscher, H., Schöffski, O., Vauth, C., Volmer, T., Wahler, S., Wasem, J., Weber, C., and members of the 'Hannoveraner Konsens' (2007) Deutsche Empfehlungen zur gesundheitsökonomischen Evalaution – Dritte und Aktualisierte Fassung des Hannoveraner Konsens (German recommendations on health economic evaluation – third and updated version of the Hanover consensus. *Gesundheitsökonomie und Qualitätsmanagement* 12(5): 285–290.

Schwappach, D. L. B. (2002) Resource allocation, social values and the QALY: a review of the debate and empirical evidence. *Health Expectations* 5: 210–222.

Schwarzinger, M., Lanoe, J.-L., Nord, E., Durand-Zaleski, I. (2004) Lack of multiplicative transitivity in person trade-off responses. *Health Economics* 13: 171–181.

Sculpher, M. (2001) The role and estimation of productivity costs in economic evaluation. In: Drummond/McGuire (eds.) (2001), pp. 94–112.

Sculpher, M., Claxton, K., Akehurst, R. (2005) It's just evaluation for decision-making: recent developments in, and challenges for, cost-effectiveness research. In: Smith *et al.* (eds.) (2005), pp. 8–33.

Sen, A. (1979) Utilitarianism and welfarism. *The Journal of Philosophy* 76(9): 463–489.

——(1988) Rights and agency. In: Scheffler (ed.) (1988a) pp. 187–223.

——(2002) Why health equity? *Health Economics* 11: 659–666.

Sen, A., Williams, B. (eds.) (1982a) *Utilitarianism and Beyond.* Cambridge *et al.*, Cambridge University Press,

——(1982b) Introduction: utilitarianism and beyond. In: Sen/Williams (eds.) (1982a), pp. 1–21.

Shah, K. K. (2009) Severity of illness and priority setting in health care: a review of the literature. *Health Policy* 93: 77–84.

Shaver, R. (2004) The appeal of utilitarianism. *Utilitas* 16(3): 235–585.

Sigot, N. (2002) Jevons's debt to Bentham: mathematical economy, morals and psychology. *The Manchester School* 70(2): 262–278.

Sinnott-Armstrong, W. (2011) Consequentialism. In: *Stanford Encyclopedia of Philosophy*, http://plato.stanford.edu/entries/consequentialism, October 14, 2014.

Smith, K. (2006) Economic techniques. In: Moran *et al.* (eds.) (2006), pp. 729–743.

Smith, P. C., Ginelly, L., Sculpher, M. (eds.) (2005) *Health Policy and Health Economics: Opportunities and Challenges.* Berkshire/New York, Open University Press.

Smith, R. D., Richardson, J. (2005) Can we estimate the 'social' value of a QALY? Four core issues to resolve. *Health Policy* 74: 77–84.

Spash, C. L. (1997) Ethics and environmental attitudes with implications for economic valuation. *Journal of Environmental Management* 50: 403–416.

——(1999) Contingent valuation. In: Earl/Kemp (eds.) (1999), pp. 128–135.

——(2000) Ethical motives and charitable contributions in contingent valuation: empirical evidence from social psychology and economics. *Environmental Values* 9: 453–479.

——(2002) Empirical signs of ethical concern in economic valuation of the environment. In: Bromely/Paavola (eds.) *Economics, Ethics, and Environmental Policy: Contested Choices.* Oxford, Blackwell, pp. 205–221.

Stigler, G. (1950a) The development of utility theory I. *Journal of Political Economy* 58(4): 307–327.

——(1950b) The development of utility theory II. *Journal of Political Economy* 58(5): 373–396.

Stumpf, S. (2014a) Bürgerbeteiligung in der Priorisierungsdebatte: Hintergründe und bisherige Erfahrungen. In: Stumpf/Raspe (eds.) (2014), pp. 13–41.

——(2014b) Vorbereitung und Ablauf der Bürgerkonferenz. In: Stumpf/Raspe (eds.) (2014), pp. 79–96.

Stumpf, S., Meyer, T., Raspe, He. (2014) Vorgeschichte, Rahmenbedingungen und Ziele der Lübecker Bürgerkonferenz. In: Stumpf/Raspe (eds.) (2014), pp. 43–57.

Stumpf, S., Raspe, H. (2011) Über Priorisierung sprechen – insbesondere mit den Betroffenen. *Deutsches Ärzteblatt* 108(7): 316–317.

——(2012) Deliberative Bürgerbeteiligung in der Priorisierungsdebatte: Welchen Beitrag können Bürger leisten? *Zeitschrift für Evidenz, Fortbildung und Qualität im Gesundheitswesen* 106: 418–425.

——(eds.) (2014) *Die Lübecker Bürgerkonferenz zur Priorisierung in der medizinischen Versorgung. "Was ist uns wichtig – und wie können wir darüber entscheiden?"* Lage, Jacobs Verlag.

Sugden, R. (1991) Rational choice: a survey of contributions from economics and philosophy. *The Economic Journal* 101: 751–785.

Sugden, R., Williams, A. (1978) *The Principles of Practical Cost-Benefit Analysis.* Oxford *et al.*, Oxford University Press.

Sumner, L. W. (1989) *The Moral Foundation of Rights.* Oxford, Clarendon Press.

——(1996) *Welfare, Happiness, and Ethics.* Oxford, Clarendon Press.

Taurek, J. (1977) Should the numbers count? *Philosophy and Public Affairs* 6: 293–316.

Tay, R. S. (1999) Discrete choice models. In: Earl/Kemp (eds.) (1999), pp. 156–164.

Tengs, T. O., Meyer, G., Siegel, J. E., Pliskin, J., Graham, J., Weinstein, M. C. (1996) Oregon's Medicaid ranking and cost-effectiveness: is there any relationship? *Medical Decision Making* 16: 99–107.

Teschl, M. (2013) Asymmetrical paternalism for economists. *Journal of Economic Methodology* 10(2): 211–214.

Thompson, G. L. (2008) von Neumann, John (1903–1957). In: Durlauf/Blume (eds.) (2008), http://www.dictionaryofeconomics.com/article?id=pde2008_V000043, December 3, 2013.

Thurow, L. C. (1973) Toward a definition of economic justice. *Public Interest* 31: 56–80.

Torrance, G. W. (1986) Measurement of health state utilities for economic appraisal. *Journal of Health Economics* 5: 1–30.

Tsuchiya, A. (1999) Age-related preferences and age weighting health benefits. *Social Science & Medicine* 48: 267–276.

——(2012) Distributional judgements in the context of economic evaluation. In: Jones (ed.) (2012), pp. 406–414.

Tsuchiya, A., Dolan, P. (2005) The QALY model and individual preferences for health states and health profiles over time: a systematic review of the literature. *Medical Decision Making* 25: 460–467.

——(2009) Equality of what in health? Distinguishing between outcome egalitarianism and gain egalitarianism. *Health Economics* 18: 147–159.

Tsuchiya, A., Williams, A. (2001) Welfare economics and economic evaluation. In: Drummond/McGuire (eds.) (2001), pp. 22–45.

Tullock, G. (2008) Public choice. In: Durlauf/Blume (eds.) (2008), http://www.dictionaryofeconomics.com/article?id=pde2008_P000240, October 11, 2012.

Ubel, P. A. (1999) How stable are people's preferences for giving priority to severely ill patients? *Social Science and Medicine* 49: 895–903.

——(2001) *Pricing Life. Why it's Time for Health Care Rationing*. Cambridge/London, MIT Press.

Ubel, P. A., Baron, J., Asch, D. A. (1999a) Social responsibility, personal responsibility, and prognosis in public judgments about transplant allocation. *Bioethics* 13(1): 57–68.

Ubel, P. A., Baron, J., Asch, D. A. (2001) Preference for equity as a framing effect. *Medical Decision Making* 21: 180–189.

Ubel, P. A., Baron, J., Nash, B., Asch, D. A. (2000a) Are preferences for equity over efficiency in health care allocation 'all or nothing'? *Medical Care* 38(4): 366–373.

Ubel, P. A., DeKay, M. L., Baron, J., Asch, D. A. (1996a) Cost-effectiveness analysis in a setting of budget constraints: Is it equitable? *The New England Journal of Medicine* 334: 1174–1177.

Ubel, P. A., Loewenstein, G. (1995) The efficacy and equity of retransplantation: an experimental survey of the public. *Health Policy* 34: 145–151.

——(1996) Public perceptions of the importance of prognosis in allocating transplantable livers to children. *Medical Decision Making* 16: 234–241.

Ubel, P. A., Loewenstein, G., Jepson, C. (2003) Whose quality of life? A commentary on exploring discrepancies between health state evaluations of patients and the general public. *Quality of Life Research* 12: 599–607.

Ubel, P. A., Loewenstein, G., Scanlon, D., Kamlet, M. (1996b) Individual utilities are inconsistent with rationing choices: a partial explanation of why Oregon's cost-effectiveness list failed. *Medical Decision Making* 16: 108–116.

Ubel, P. A., Nord, E., Gold, M. R., Menzel, P., Pinto-Prades, J. L., Richardson, J. (2000b) Improving value measurement in cost-effectiveness analysis. *Medical Care* 28(9): 892–901.

Ubel, P. A., Richardson, J., Baron, J. (2002) Exploring the role of order-effects in person trade-off elicitation. *Health Policy* 61: 189–199.

Ubel, P. A., Richardson, J., Menzel, P. (2000c) Societal value, the person trade-off, and the dilemma of whose values to measure for cost-effectiveness analysis. *Health Economics* 9: 127–136.

Ubel, P. A., Richardson, J., Pinto-Prades, Jose L. (1999b) Life-saving treatments and disabilities: are all QALYs created equal? *International Journal of Technology Assessment in Health Care* 15(4): 738–748.

Unger, P. (1996) *Living High and Letting Die: Our Illusion of Innocence*. Oxford *et al.*, Oxford University Press.

Vanberg, V. (1986) Individual choice and institutional constraints: the normative element in classical and contractarian liberalism. *Analyse und Kritik* 8: 113–149.

Vilks, A. (1998) Axiomatization. In: Davis *et al.* (eds.) (1998), pp. 28–32.

Viner, J. (1925/1968) The utility concept in value theory and its critics. In: Page (ed.) (1968), pp. 123–138.

——(1949) Bentham and J. S. Mill: the utilitarian background. *The American Economic Review* 39(2): 360–382.

Viney, R., Lancsar, E., Louviere, J. (2002) Discrete choice experiments to measure consumer preferences for health and health care. *Expert Review of Pharmacoeconomics & Outcomes Research* 2(4): 319–326.

Von Neumann, J., Morgenstern, O. (1953) *Theory of Games and Economic Behavior*, 3rd edn. (1st edn. 1944). Princeton: Princeton University Press.

Wagstaff, A. (1991) QALYs and the equity-efficiency trade-off. *Journal of Health Economics* 10: 21–41.

Wailoo, A., Tsuchiya, A., McCabe, C. (2009) Waiting must wait. Incorporating equity concerns into cost-effectiveness analysis may take longer than expected. *Pharmacoeconomics* 27(12): 983–989,

Walker, R. L., Siegel, A. W. (2002) Morality and the limits of societal values in health care allocation. *Health Economics* 11: 265–273.

Warke, T. (2000a) Mathematical fitness in the evolution of the utility concept from Bentham to Jevons to Marshall. *Journal of the History of Economic Thought* 22(19): 5–27.

——(2000b) Multi-dimensional utility and the index number problem: Jeremy Bentham, J.S. Mill, and qualitative hedonism. *Utilitas* 12(2): 176–203.

Weinstein, M. C., Manning, W. G. Jr. (1997) Theoretical issues in cost-effectiveness analysis. *Journal of Health Economics* 16: 121–128.

Weinstein, M. C, Stason, W. B. (1977) Foundations of cost-effectiveness analysis for health and medical practices. *The New England Journal of Medicine* 296: 716–721.

Weinstein, M. C., Torrance, G., McGuire, A. (2009) QALYs: The basics. *Value in Health* 12, supplement 1: S5-S9.

Weintraub, E. R. (2002) *How Economics became a Mathematical Science.* Durham/London, Duke University Press.

Weintraub, E. R., Mirowski, P. (1994) The pure and the applied: Bourbakism comes to mathematical economics. *Science in Context* 7(2): 245–272.

Welch, H. G., Larson, E. B. (1988) Sounding board: dealing with limited resources: the Oregon decision to curtail funding for organ transplantation. *JAMA* 319(3): 171–173.

White, M. V. (2004) In the lobby of the energy hotel: Jevons's formulation of the postclassical "economic problem". *History of Political Economy* 36(2): 227–271.

Whynes, D. K., Sach, T. H. (2007) WTP and WTA: Do people think differently? *Social Science & Medicine* 65: 946–957.

Williams, A. (1985a) Economics of coronary artery bypass grafting. *British Medical Journal* 291: 326–329.

——(1985b) The value of QALYs. *Health and Social Service Journal,* July 18: 3–5.

——(1988) Ethics and efficiency in the provision of health care. In: Bell, J. M., Mendus, S. (eds.) *Philosophy and Medical Welfare.* Cambridge *et al.*, Cambridge University Press, pp. 111–126.

——(1991) Some methodological issues in the use of cost-benefit analysis in health care. *Osaka Economic Papers* 40(3–4): 63–69.

——(1995) Health economics and health care priorities. *Health Care Analysis* 3: 221–234.

——(1997) Intergenerational equity: an exploration of the "fair innings" argument. *Health Economics* 6: 117–132.

——(2000) Review of Cost-Value Analysis in Health Care: Making Sense out of QALYs by Erik Nord. *Health Economics* 9: 739–742.

——(2001a) How economics could extend the scope of ethical discourse. *Journal of Medical Ethics* 27: 251–255.

——(2001b) The 'fair innings argument' deserves a fairer hearing! Comments by Alan Williams on Nord and Johannesson. *Health Economics* 10: 583–585.

Williams, A., Cookson, R. (2000) Equity in health. In: Culyer/Newhouse (eds.) (2000a), pp. 1863–1908.

——(2006) Equity-efficiency trade-offs in health technology assessment. *International Journal of Technology Assessment in Health Care* 22(1): 1–9.

Williams, A., Tsuchiya, A., Dolan, P. (2005) Eliciting equity-efficiency trade-offs in health. In: Smith *et al.* (eds.) (2005), pp. 64–83.

Williams, B. (1972) *Morality: An Introduction to Ethics.* Cambridge *et al.*, Cambridge University Press.

——(1988) Consequentialism and integrity. In: Scheffler (ed.) (1988a), pp. 20–50.

Williams, I., Robinson, S., Dickinson, H. (2012) *Rationing in Health Care: The Theory and Practice of Priority Setting.* Bristol, Policy Press.

Williamson, L. (2014) Patient and citizen participation in health: The need for improved ethical support. *The American Journal of Bioethics* 14(6): 4–16.

Wolfe, B. (2008) Health economics. In: Durlauf/Blume (eds.) (2008), http://www.dictionaryofeconomics.com/article?id=pde2008_H000031, July 5, 2012.

Wolff, J., Haubrich, D. (2006) Economism and its limits. In: Moran *et al.* (eds.) (2006), pp. 746–770.

Wong, S. (1973) The "f-twist" and the methodology of Paul Samuelson. *American Economic Review* 63(3): 312–325.

Index

Acharya, A. K. 171
Ackermann, F. 77, 79, 165
action: as opposed to outcome 161, 169; right 106, 109, 132f., 140
age 99, 134, 137f., 142, 175f.
ageism 134
age-related preferences 134
aggregation 97, 106, 108, 122, 124, 168; additive 101, 109; problem 97
Allen, R. G. D. 9, 33–6, 39, 42
allocation rule 96, 108, 133, 151, 182
alternatives: individual definition of 48–51, 134, 151; ordering of 19, 28, 135; relative values of 4, 117, 131; values of attributes 135, 137, 139, 154, 167
altruism 125f.
Amadae, S. M. 43, 64
Americans with Disability Act 96
analog scale (AS) 89, 152, 158
anchoring 161, 163
anti-paternalism 198
applied ethics *see* ethics
armchair-ethics 192–4
Arnesen, T. 172
Arrow, K. 123, 125
articulated value perspective 158, 164f.
Ashmore, M. 69
atomism 4,135, 139, 146
attitude change 169
authority: of economic evaluation 3, 61, 75; of economists 64, 67; of ethicists 196f.; of mathematics 67; of science 27
autonomy 4, 186, 197–9
axiological consistency 177f.
axiological modification 4, 117, 174
axiology 88, 99, 107, 110, 182, 203; atomistic 151; multidimensional 141
axiomatization: of economics 39, 41, 45; of mathematics 40f., 43; of utility theory 39, 43–5, 47
axioms: DCEs 137; ordinal utility theory 47f., 50, 135; VNM 44f., 47, 90

Backhouse, R. E. 29, 39, 40, 45
Bain, A. 13
Baker, S. 137, 164, 166
balancing of feelings 16, 22
Baron, J. 154, 158, 161, 164
Barry, B. 129–31
basic value perspective 159, 163–5, 170
behaviorism 28, 33, 36f., 44f.; informal 38, 76, 158
behaviorist account *see* behaviorism
behaviorist reading of Pareto 32–4
Bentham, J. 15–19, 22, 107
Bergson, A. 122
Bergson-Samuelson SWF 122f.
bias 151, 158, 163, 167, 186; of the academic discourse 191f.; payment-vehicle 166
Blaug, M. 36, 41, 46
blindness 89f., 154, 181
Boadway, R. W. 123
Bobinac, A. 102, 157, 160
bone marrow transplant 94f., 169
Borry, P. 200
Bourbaki group 40f., 43
Bourbaki, N. 40
Bourbakism *see* Bourbaki group
Bowie, C. 170
Britain 11, 69
Broome, J. 20
Bruce, N. 123
Bürgervotum 195
Bush, G. 96, 112

calculus: differential 9, 20, 22; efficiency 99; of pleasure and pain 12, 22; *see also* felicific calculus
cardinal measurability 32, 36
cardinal representation theorem 44, 47
cardinal scale 31
cardinal utility 23, 25, 30, 33f., 39, 42, 44, 90
cardinal utility function 32, 44
cardinality 32
Carson, R. T. 157
category error 5, 127, 131, 198
CBA *see* cost-benefit analysis
CEA *see* cost-effectiveness analysis
certainty 15, 18
choice 8, 29; observable 125, 151; and preferences 37–39, 48–50; reasons behind 151, 171f.; as trade-offs 4, 29, 117–19, 140f.; *see also* consumer choice, consumer choice framework, rational choice
choice determination 49, 125
citizen jury 169, 194f.
citizens' conference 194f.
citizens' vote 195; *see also Bürgervotum*
classical economics 9, 10, 25, 62
Cold War 39–41, 43f., 65
colon cancer 162, 171
commodity bundles 36, 38, 123
commodity price 12, 14f., 20, 48
compensation 74, 76, 130, 181
compensatory decision making 137, 166
complete information 72
complete preferences *see* completeness
completeness 19, 37, 41–3, 48, 50, 137, 159
consequentialism 105f., 109f., 132f., 138; aggregative 138, 140, 151; applied 88, 105, 109; foundational 106f., 132, 140, 151; representational 131–3, 140, 151
consequentializing 132
consistency 41, 48, 158, 171–74; of arguments 5, 7; axioms 50, 135, 161; checks 158, 165, 171; in decision making 103
constitutional framework 199
consumer 35, 38, 44, 46, 48, 73f., 96, 130, 136; behavior 8, 12, 15, 36, 52; sovereignty 71f., 78, 198
consumer choice 117, 129f., 137, 155; framework 119, 131, 159, 173, 200, 203; theory 8, 23, 26–47, 52, 117, 121, 130, 136, 146, 155–7, 165, 203
consumption goods 14, 129, 155f., 198
Consumption Theory in Terms of Revealed Preferences 37
context-independence 139, 159
context-sensitivity of ethics 191–3
contingent valuation (CV) 76f., 135, 155–60, 165
contingent valuation method (CVM) 76f., 155, 168
continuity 43, 137, 167
Cookson, R. 99, 102f., 134, 146, 164
Corn Laws 74
cost-benefit analysis (CBA) 3, 52, 61, 64, 66f., 70–81; and CUA 92f., 105
cost-effectiveness 94–6, 180, 190f.
cost-effectiveness analysis (CEA) 80, 188, 197
cost-efficiency 145, 195
cost-utility analysis (CUA) 81, 88–93; fairness issue 93–9
cost-value analysis (CVA) 101
Council of Economic Advisers 65
Cowles Commission 41
Cowles, A. 41
Culyer, A. 69f., 93, 99, 103, 142

Damm, O. 80
Dancy, J. 135
Daniels, N. 190
DCE 135, 137f., 166–8
deafness 181
Debreu, G. 41–3, 45
decision analysis *see* decision theory
decision rule 102f., 108f., 134, 182, 203
decision theory 44, 47, 69, 110
decision-maker approach (DMA) 101f.
degree of utility *see* utility
deliberation 168, 170, 186, 190f., 194–6, 200
deliberative approach 170, 197
deliberative groups 170, 191, 199
deliberative methods 165, 168f.
deliberative studies 168, 190
demand theory 8, 21f., 28, 31–4, 36–9, 42, 46–8, 136
demarcation problem 24
democracy 168, 198f.; deliberative 168, 186
deontological rules 161
deregulation 66, 69
descriptive research 199f.
desires: vs. preferences 49f., 159; vs. values 123

Desvouges, W. H. 156
Diamond, P. A. 161
differential calculus *see* calculus
dignity 164, 169, 194f.
diminishing marginal utility 9, 21f., 26, 35, 46
disability 4, 92, 175, 177f., 181; discrimination 151f., 173–80; weights 171f.
disability-adjusted life year (DALY) 171f.
discrete choice experiment *see* DCE
discrimination 5, 99, 146; disability *see* disability; homosexuals and drug-user 193; potential to benefit and live-saving treatment 97, 173
distributional preferences 101; *see also* social preferences
distributive justice 3, 94, 146, 188
distributive neutrality 97
Dolan, P. 7, 109, 125f., 164
Donaldson, C. 7
Drummond, M. 104
duties 13, 107, 133, 139f., 164
Dworkin, R. 144, 199

ECHOUTCOME 114
economic advice 25, 27, 37, 62, 66, 69
economic agent 14, 21–3, 35, 38, 42, 46, 123
economic evaluation: applied 80; as applied consequentialism 105, 109f.; increasing popularity 69; normative status of results 101f.; purpose 73; and representational consequentialism 131; and transferability of values 133; welfare economic framework 75
economic growth 64, 68
economic imperialism 46, 60, 63
The Economics of Welfare 25
economists: as opinion leader 70; authority and prestige of 61–8; and the war 39f., 63
economization 1, 70
Eddy, D. M. 97f.
Edgeworth, Y. 30, 53
education 65f., 80, 93, 104f., 121, 196
efficiency 70f., 101, 118, 126; allocative 71, 94; ideal of 61, 65f.; normative status 142–6; persuasive notion 66, 68, 72; technical 71, 94; overall 78–81, 93; *see also:* calculus, equity-efficiency trade-off, Pareto efficiency
egalitarianism 142
Ellsberg, D. 44f.
embedding effect 155–7
emotivism 24
empirical data within ethics 192–4
empirical ethics 187, 189–93, 197, 199f.
environmental economics 77, 151, 156
environmental issues 159f.
equal chances 139
equal respect 139, 144f., 152, 199
equal value of life approach (EVL) 173–82
equality 134, 164, 178, 194f., 199; and efficiency 65, 128–30; and utilitarianism 142, 144
equilibrium 15, 21f., 30, 41, 71–3; as metaphor 119
equimarginal principle 21f.
equity weights: as artefacts 117, 139f., 173; as corrective device 99; definition 99, 119; elicitation 105, 167; as explanatory variables 133f.; Johannesson's 176; metaphor 121, 135, 141, 146; and the relevance of reasons 134f., 138; Williams' 176
equity-efficiency trade-off: danger of 145f.; in health care resource allocation 2, 101, 118, 127–9, 163; metaphor 129, 141–5; origin of cliché 65
An Essay on the Significance of Economic Science 23, 25, 28f.
ethical expertise 194, 196
ethical theory 108, 188, 191f.
ethics: applied 7, 193f., 200; descriptive 193; normative 193
euthanasia 192
existence value 77, 155
expected utility 44, 51, 90
expected utility theory 44
“Experience Requirement” 51
extra-welfarism 93, 101
expertocracy 192, 200
Exxon 76f.
Exxon Valdezz 76

Faden, R. 78, 80, 104, 193
fair innings 176f., 180–2
fairness intuitions 1, 105, 140, 189
feasibility and applied ethics 194
fecundity 18
Fehige, C. 135
felicific calculus 15–18; modification of 19f.
Fischhoff, B. 171
Foot, P. 109
formalist revolution 32, 41

foundational consequentialism *see* consequentialism
fundamental theorems of welfare economics 72f.

game theory 43, 47
Garber, A. M. 78
GDP 65, 68, 93
gender 166, 175, 180
general equilibrium theory 41
Giocoli, N. 31f., 35, 38
goodness of states of affairs 77, 106, 108f., 126f., 129
Great Depression 40, 61f.
Greiner, W. 80
guaranteed income 65
Gyrd-Hanson, D. 157

Hadorn, D. C. 143
Hands, W. 37
Haninger, K. 137
Hansson, S. O. 138f.
happiness 17, 20, 46, 98, 107f., 143
Harris, John 176
Harris, Jose 25
Harsanyi, J. 124f.
Haubrich, D. 92
Hausman, D. 47, 50, 72, 99, 197f.
Hausman, J. 161
health care system 69, 73, 93, 179, 198
health economics as discipline 60f., 63, 66–70
health insurance 60, 63, 73, 190
health maximization 93, 104, 128, 134, 142–4
health possibility frontier 127f.
health state classification system 95
health-related preferences 92
health-related quality of life (HrQOL) 1, 88, 92f. 173–5, 177, 180f.
health-related social welfare function (HrSWF) 127f.
heart attack 156
hedonic concepts 8, 31f., 130f., 136, 160
hedonism 14, 24f., 32, 34, 39, 46, 108, 138; *see also* utilitarianism, utility
Heinzerling, L. 77, 79, 165
Henderson, W. 121
heuristic 117, 167
Hicks, K. 9, 29, 33–39, 42–4, 46, 48, 74f., 129
Hilbert, D. 43
historical consciousness 3, 9
holism 138f., 182
Howard, C. 95
HrQOL *see* health-related quality of life
HrSWF *see* health-related social welfare function
human capital 79; as metaphor 121
human capital approach 79f.
human mind as a balance 13, 15, 21
humanities 194
Hurley, J. 68

impersonal point of view 109, 124f.
incommensurable principles 129
incremental cost-effectiveness ratio 95
indifference 8, 28, 36f., 48, 90, 131f., 181
indifference curves 30f., 35f., 42, 44, 47, 129f.
indifference map 38, 130
inequality aversion 126f.
informational asymmetries 73
insatiable wants 35
intensity: desire 33; feeling 32, 44; pleasure 15f., 18; preference 36, 45
interpersonal comparison of utility *see* utility
interpersonal comparisons of pleasure *see* pleasure
interval scale 91f., 134
introspection 10, 24, 28, 36, 45–7

Jennings, R. 20
Jevons, W. S. 8–24, 28, 46
Johannesson, M. 125, 175–8, 180–2
Johnson, L. B. 64f.
Joint Ways and Means Committee 94f.
justice 142, 146, 189, 191f.; concern for 135, 193f.; demands of 5, 145; issue of 125, 131, 169, 198; public view of 187, 192, 194; *see also* distributive justice

Kahneman, D. 155, 159
Kaldor, N. 73–5
Kaldor-Hicks criterion 70, 74f.
Kennedy, J. F. 64
Keynes, J. M. 62
Keynesianism 62, 66
kitchen-scale model 135
knee damage 152f.
Knetsch, J. L. 152f., 156, 159, 161

labor theory of value 12, 22
Lancaster, K. 51, 136, 154
Lancsar, E. 167
laundering of preferences 188f.
law of exchange 21

law of the variation of utility 20
lay persons 67, 71, 104, 196f.
league table *see* QALY
leaky bucket 65
Lengahan, J. 170
levels of resource allocation 93f.
liberal society 186, 194, 197
liberty 144, 198
life-saving treatment 96–8, 166, 172–5, 180; *see also* discrimination
Little, I. M. D. 36, 130
Lloyd, A. J. 158
logical positivism 23f.
Lübbe, W. 2, 61, 124, 139–42, 145, 179
Lübeck 195
Lukes, S. 130, 141

Maas, H. 10f., 22
Mandler, M. 32, 34, 42
Manual of Political Economy 30
Marckmann, G. 93
marginal rate of substitution (MRS) 34–6, 117, 127, 130
marginal revolution 8f., 20, 23, 25
marginal utility 13, 20f., 24, 26f.; *see also* diminishing marginal utility
marginalists 10, 12, 25, 44, 46, 50
market 34, 62, 66, 72f., 76, 158; exchange 21, 72, 155, 158; failure 62f., 66, 73, 76; ideal of 3, 52, 60f., 66, 70, 73, 81, 203; mechanism 22, 61, 63, 65, 69–73, 123; metaphor 120; perfect 73
Marshall's demand theory 33
mathematics: authority 67; formal 39–43; language 40; and marginal revolution 10–14, 18, 22
maximand 18, 93, 99, 101, 127, 132; modification 2, 5, 98f.
maximization *see* social value maximization, pleasure maximization, utility maximization, QALY maximization
McCarthy era 40
McCloskey, D. 119
McKie, J. 79f., 89, 145
McNamara, R. S. 64
McPherson, M. S. 72
meaningless responses 159, 170–2
measurability 31–33; of pleasure 14, 16, 19
measurement scale 31; *see also* cardinal scale, interval scale, ordinal scale, ration scale
mechanistic metaphors 119
Medema, S. G. 29, 45
Medicaid 64, 94–6, 162
medical need 145, 195
Medicare 64
meningioma 152f.
mental states 11, 35, 51
Menzel, P. 7, 98, 188
merit good 73
metaphors 117, 119–21; dead 120f., 146, 203; mechanical 10, 21, 119; *see also* equity weights, equity-efficiency trade-off
Mexico 190
microeconomics 14, 23, 36, 38, 71, 73
Mill, J. S. 10, 143
Mishan, E. J. 75
Mitchell, R. C. 157
moral expertise 196f.
moral judgments 17, 131, 139, 182, 193, 200
moral philosophy 2, 88, 105, 139
Morgan, M. S. 63
Morgenstern, O. 43
Mortimer, D. 189
motives: higher and lower 13f.; underlying 51, 134
MRS *see* marginal rate of substitution
Mullen, D. 195
multiplicative connection of weights 101
multiplicative intransitivity 151–3, 155, 164, 168
multiplicative transitivity 152–4, 165
Murphy, N. J. 170
Murray, C. J. L. 80, 171

National Commission on Guaranteed Income 64
National Health Service (NHS) 63, 142
National Oceanic and Atmospheric Administration 77
Natural Elements of Political Economy 20
natural price 12
natural sciences 10f., 22, 24, 39
neoclassical economics 9, 13, 21, 23, 25, 51, 73
neoclassical welfare economics 26, 61, 73, 78
New Deal 62, 64
New Zealand 96
Newhouse, J. N. 69f.
Newton, I. 17
Nixon, R. 64
non-consequentialist categories 139, 152, 165, 179

non-consequentialist reasons *see* reasons
non-consequentialist theories 132, 110, 203
non-consequentialists 109, 133, 168
non-discrimination 4, 152, 180, 182
non-traders 165, 167f., 170
Nord, E. 92, 97f., 100–4, 130, 133f., 172–80
Norman, R. 166f.
normative ethics 193
normative framework 61, 70, 146, 200
normative individualism 122
A Note on the Pure Theory of Consumer's Behavior 37

objectivity 13, 67
Okun, A. 65
Oliver, A. 89f., 180–2
Olsen, J. A. 65, 156f.
ophelimity 30f., 123
opportunity costs 29, 70f., 103, 118f., 140, 167, 170
opportunity set 50, 127, 161
ordering effect 163
ordinal interpretation of Pareto 32f.
ordinal representation theorem 43
ordinal revolution 8, 23, 30, 39, 71
ordinal scale 31, 191
ordinal utility: concept 9, 31; function 48; theory 37f., 42–7
ordinalism 33, 36, 46f.
ordinality 32
Oregon Basic Health Service Act 95
Oregon experiment 93f., 96f.
Oregon Health Service Commission 95
Oregon Plan 97
organ donation 121
organ transplantation 140, 145, 189
outcome measure 88, 93, 105

"priorities problem" 97
paraplegia 173–5, 177, 181
Paretian welfare economics *see* welfare economics
Pareto efficiency 71–3, 123
Pareto improvement 71, 73f.
Pareto optimum *see* Pareto efficiency
Pareto principle 72, 74, 122f.
Pareto, V. 29–34, 39, 44, 123
parts of alternatives 135, 138f., 154, 167
partworth utilities 136f.
payment vehicle-bias 166
Payne, J. W. 160
perfect competition 21, 72f.
person trade-off (PTO) 100, 125f., 134f., 151–5, 158, 161, 164–7, 171–4
philosopher kings 188, 197
philosophical radicals 71
physics 10f., 24, 39
Pigou, A. C. 25–8
Planning-Programming-Budgeting System 64
pleasure: Bentham's concept 15–17, 107; interpersonal comparison 25, 27; Jevons' concept 13–15, 18–23, 44, 46f.; maximization 21–23, 46; measurability 14; and ophelimity 31f.; as preference satisfaction 106; value of 107, 129, 145
pluralism 139, 187f.
Political Argument 129
political deliberation 168
political economy 9f., 14
political process 73, 101, 168, 186
politicians 63, 65, 104, 197
positive economics 24, 27, 30, 47, 75
positivism *see* logical positivism
positivist image: of economics 23, 74, 187; of science 25, 37
potential Pareto improvement *see* Kaldor-Hicks principle
potential to benefit 97, 100f., 127
Powers, M. 78, 80, 104, 193
preference: actual 125, 170, 172; all things considered 49, 92; altruistic 125f.; as total comparative evaluations 49; "ethical" 124; health-related 92; impartial 125; individual 47, 91f., 98, 101, 123–5, 129, 177–80; lexicographic 166f.; rational 44; "self-regarding" and "other-regarding" 126; stated 105, 159, 173, 203; "subjective" 124; true 151, 158f., 162; underlying 37, 158f.; weak 48; *see also* revealed preferences, social preferences
preference anomalies *see* preference inconsistencies
preference elicitation methods 89, 92, 156, 158, 172f.; deliberative 168, 186; revealed 76; social 48, 167; stated 135, 151, 155, 158f.; *see also* rating scale, standard gamble, time trade-off
preference inconsistencies 4, 48, 105, 146, 151f., 157–9, 161, 171, 173
preference ordering 22f, 28, 30–2, 34, 43, 47–52. 135f., 154, 175; of social states 121–7
preference ranking *see* preference ordering
preference satisfaction 71f., 101, 106, 125

pressure on respondents 159, 165, 170–3
price mechanism 119f.
price *see* commodity price, natural price
Price, D. 169
priming 161–63
Prince William Sound 76f.
principle of diminishing marginal utility *see* diminishing marginal utility
prioritization 67, 94, 100, 174, 180, 186, 195; criterion 145; debate 4, 121, 186f., 191, 194f., 199f.; decisions 4, 117–19, 137–40, 170, 180, 186, 192–200; preference 4, 49, 51, 99f., 105, 131, 139, 151, 162–4, 173, 186–90, 193, 199f., 203; problem 119; question 159, 163–65, 181; studies 152, 193
priority-view 108
productivity 65, 74, 80, 92, 134
professional ethicists 5, 192, 196, 200
propinquity/remoteness 15, 18
protest responses 4, 165f., 168, 173
psychological assumptions 8, 28, 32–4, 36f.
psychology 11, 13f., 21, 24, 28
psychophysics 11, 13–14, 20f., 24, 45, 91
psychophysiology 11, 22
PTO *see* person trade-off
public goods 73, 76f.
public participation 4, 94, 186f., 192, 195–9
public policy 5, 60, 103, 131; and CBA, 3, 52, 61–66, 70, 75; and rhetoric 1, 66f., 70
public spending 66
purchase model 154f., 158f.
purity 15, 18

qualitative studies 4, 139, 160, 164, 173, 181
QALY: concept 88f., 92f.; league table 95; trap 175–77; upper-end compression of scale 100f.; weighted 99, 101, 103, 117, 127, 134, 142, 167, 174
QALY maximization 1, 89, 96f., 99, 102–32, 167, 173
quality of well-being scale 95
quality-adjusted life expectancy (QALE) 176
quantification of concerns for fairness 103f.

RAND 43, 64
random utility 136
Raspe, H. 195
rating scale (RS) 89, 91, 95, 98
ratio scale 92
rational choice 110, 125, 130
rational choice theory 8, 45–8, 64, 66, 135, 152, 154, 161
rationality 23, 43, 110, 137
rationing 63, 94–6, 170; debate 94, 141, 199; decisions 119, 153, 166, 190, 194, 198f.; judgments 166; plan 194; preferences 152; procedures 174
Rawls, J. 110
Reagan, R. 66
Reagonomics 66
reasons: actual 4, 131, 139f., 203; atomistic *see* atomism; behind choices 125f., 134f., 141, 151, 160–5, 172, 181; irrelevance of 28, 47, 110; non-consequentialist 139, 161, 182, 203
A Reconsideration of the Theory of Value 33
redistribution of income 26, 65, 73
Reinhardt, U. 68
relative value *see* value
responsibility: delegation 68; of the government 168; for outcomes 160f.
revealed preference theory 32, 36–8
rhetoric 61, 66f., 70, 102, 119f.
The Rhetoric of Economics 119
Richardson, J. 79f., 89, 102, 145, 188, 192
rights 139, 141, 165, 198–200; framework of 131, 179–81; and value-maximization 109, 144f.
risk 44f., 76, 156f., 162
Robbins, L. 23–9, 39, 45f., 60, 71, 74, 117f.
Roosevelt, F. D. 62, 64
rule of rescue 167
Rutherford, M. 63

sacrifice 8, 65, 90, 118f., 127, 130
Sagoff, M. 50, 141, 160
Samuelson, P. 29, 36–9, 44, 46f., 122
satisfaction *see* preference satisfaction
Scanlon, T. 106f., 132f.
Scarantino, A. 27
scarcity definition of economics 23, 28f., 45, 60
Schabas, M. 13
Schicktanz, S. 121
Schkade, D. A. 160
Schmidt, V. 2
Schroth, J. 108
Schwappach, D. L. B. 7
Schwarzinger, M. 165

Schweda, M. 121
scope effect 151, 155f.
scope sensitivity *see* scope effect
Seguro Popular 190
self-interest 8f., 49, 51, 72, 126
Sen, A. 77, 105f., 108, 180
sensations 15f., 18, 20, 32
Servicemen's Readjustment Act 40
severity of illness 2, 97, 99–101
Should the Numbers Count? 143
Siebert, U. 93
Siegel, A. W. 189
slavery 72
slippery-slope arguments 193
smoking cessation 78
Social Choice and Individual Values 123
social choice theory 47, 124
social preferences 2, 7f., 98, 117, 121–7, 141, 167, 177f. 189; measurement 100f., 135; studies 48, 117, 139, 151
social sciences 1, 10, 24, 40, 67
social value 2–4, 7f., 88f., 98f., 101–3, 121, 126, 131–5, 141, 154, 167, 177, 182, 203
social value maximization 102, 117, 131, 154
social welfare 25, 71, 74, 93, 122f., 128, 169
social welfare function 122–3, 125, 127f.; *see also* Bergson-Samuelson SWF, Utilitarian SWF
societal perspective 78, 80, 165, 170
solidarity 164, 194f.
Soviet Union 40
Spash, C. L. 168
Sputnik-shock 40
stability 48, 137
stagflation 65
stakeholder 197
standard gamble (SG) 89–91, 152, 164, 181
Stason, W. B. 89
statistics 14
strategic behavior 157
Stumpf, S. 195
subjective theory of value 12, 19, 39
suffering 107, 180
Sumner, L. 108
sum-ranking 106–8
Sweden 96
systems analysis 64

tastes: versus preferences 49; versus values 123f., 131
Taurek, J. 144
Tay, R. S. 51
telephone survey 77, 95, 156
terminology of economics 66f., 70, 92
Theory of Games and Economic Behavior 43f.
Theory of Political Economy 10, 12–14, 23
Theory of Value 42f.
time trade-off (TTO) 89–91, 152
trade-off: choices as 4, 29, 117–19, 140f.; metaphor 129–31; in terms of production 127; in terms of value 128–30; unrestricted 137; *see also* equity-efficiency trade-off
transaction costs 21, 72
transferability of values 138
transitivity 19, 42f., 48f.; *see also* multiplicative transitivity
transparency 103f.
Tsuchiya, A. 7, 109

Ubel, P. 90f., 98, 100, 139, 152f., 157, 162–66, 172–77, 188–90
uncertainty 15, 44
Unger, P. 194
United Kingdom (UK) 63, 68, 169
United States of America 41, 43, 62, 64, 68, 76, 96
unwillingness to trade 167
use-value 77
Utilitarian SWF 122
utilitarianism 1, 34, 106–10, 142–45; Bentham's 16f., 22; classical 3f., 117, 138; and equality 142, 144; hedonic 88, 105f., 138; Mill's proof of 143
utility: axiomatic 47; Bentham on 17–19, 22; cardinal 23, 25; concept 3f., 8; curve 21; degree of 20f.; formal 3, 8f., 125; hedonic 8f., 23, 32, 51, 126; Hicks and Allen on 33–6; index 31, 51; Jevons' on 9f., 12f., 18–23; Pareto on 30f.; Samuelson on 36–39; *see also* cardinal utility, expected utility theory, marginal utility, ordinal utility, utility maximization, VNM utilities
utility function 18, 21, 27, 30–2, 42–4, 47f.; individual 49, 124f., 136; random 136
utility maximization 8, 10, 22f., 46f., 117, 121, 142

validity 117, 158, 167
Value and Capital 33
value: and preferences 127, 131; economic 155, 159, 160; monetary 76, 78, 160,

166; relative 4, 100, 118, 135, 154; theory of 88, 106, 132, 151; to society 79f., 134; true 158; units of 81, 100, 108f., 110, 132, 142; in the vernacular 140; *see also* social value
value judgements 73, 92, 141; in economics 23f., 71f.; in welfare economics 27, 71f., 122; economists' reluctance to introduce 100, 187
value maximization 88, 119, 131
value-maximizing choices 119, 131, 140, 146
value-maximizing framework 97, 139, 172, 186; of CUA 2, 142, 182; of economic evaluations 5, 8, 93, 119, 146, 167, 203; of surveys 152
verbal arguments 103
verbal tradition of political economy 12
Victorian Britain 11
Vienna circle 24
Viner, J. 19
VNM utilities 44, 47
voluntary exchange 73, 123
voluntary unemployment 62
Von Neumann, J. 43

wage-risk trade-off 76
Wagstaff, A. 127f.
Wailoo, A. 105
Walker, R. L. 188f.
Walras, L. 9
War on Poverty 64f.
Warke, T. 16
warm glow hypothesis 159
wealth 17, 25f., 62, 73, 142
Weber, M. 25
Weinstein, M. C. 89
Weintraub, R. 42
welfare 25f., 72, 74, 107f., 121, 126; overall 71, 79; *see also* social welfare
welfare economics 61, 71–5, 78, 81, 121–5, 131; new 23, 29, 75; Paretian 93, 122; Pigou's 26f.
Welfare Proposition of Economics and Interpersonal Comparisons of Utility 74
welfare state 63, 65
welfarism 77, 93, 105–8, 125
well-being 25, 142, 178f.; and health 92; of others 126, 164, 198; overall 25; preference satisfaction view of 71; society's 7, 127
wheelchair 179
Williams, A. 99, 103, 118, 128, 134, 142, 170, 175–80, 187
willingness to accept (WTA) 76
willingness to pay (WTP) 75, 77, 80f., 137, 142, 155–7, 160–6; *see also* CV, scope effect
Wolff, J. 92
World Health Organization (WHO) 171
World War I 62
World War II 24, 39f., 43, 62f., 67
worth of persons 178f.

zero responses 165f.